Thank You

Second Edition

I0004437

The story of how IBM helped today's technology millionaires and billionaires gain vast fortunes.

IBM is the oldest commercial computer company in the world. Its roots spring from the merger of The International Time Recording Company Computing Scale Company, and the Tabulating Machine Company in the 19th century. The merged company became known as International Business Machines Corporation (IBM) in 1924.

IBM has coined many terms such as word processing, teleprocessing, and eBusiness over its 100 years of operation. The company has also done the background work for many computer sub-industries, such as disk, tape, data communications, personal computer, relational database, RISC processing, microchips, mainframes, and of course the IBM PC & others.

IBM continues to be the leader in mainframe computers and cloud computing, though at one time it dominated all areas of computing. Over the years, IBM's concentration on mainframes permitted billionaires to be created in sub- industries, in which IBM unwittingly chose not to compete. For example, Bill Gates, who supplied just two software products for IBM's 1981 PC is now the richest man in the world. IBM could have been a much more successful company if it had paid attention to its many different businesses. Since IBM did not pay attention, there are tens of thousands of extra millionaires & billionaires in the computer field, who one day should stop and thank IBM for their success. That's what this book is about! Just say:
Thank You IBM!

BY

Brian W. Kelly

Copyright © March 2016, Brian W. Kelly   Editor: Brian P. Kelly
Thank You IBM! Second Edition   Author Brian W. Kelly

Published by: LETS GO PUBLISH!
Editor in Chief   Brian P. Kelly
Email: Iinfo@letsgopublish.com
Web site   www.letsgopublish.com

Library of Congress Copyright Information Pending
Book Cover Design by Michele Thomas,
Editor—Brian P. Kelly

ISBN Information: The International Standard Book Number (ISBN) is a unique machine-readable identification number, which marks any book unmistakably. The ISBN is the clear standard in the book industry.159 countries & territories are officially ISBN members. Official ISBN For this book: **978-0-9962454-4-9**

The price for this work is:					**$ 25.50 USD**				
10	9	8	7	6	5	4	3	2	1

Release Date: May 2016

Dedication

This book is dedicated to my immediate family.
My wife Pat makes everything work
My son, Brian has the gifts of goodness and magic
My son, Michael has the gifts of love and humor and decisiveness
My daughter, Kathleen has the gift of sweetness and she shares her gift in song for all to enjoy

My family is always supportive of my efforts in everything. Thank you.

You are the most precious people in life.

Acknowledgments:

I appreciate all the help that I have received in putting this book together as well as all of the other 61 books from the past.

My printed acknowledgments had been so large that book readers "complained" about going through too many pages to get to page one of the text.

And, so to permit me more flexibility, I put my acknowledgment list online, and it continues to grow. Believe it or not, it costs about a dollar less to print each book.

Thank you and God bless you all for your help.

Please check out www.letsgopublish.com to read the latest version of my heartfelt acknowledgments updated for this book. Click the bottom of the Main menu!

Thank you all!

Preface:

Since the 1950's, IBM has been synonymous with innovation, cutting-edge technology, and major league research and development. IBM pushed the boundaries of what computers were capable of doing with technology. As of the last several years, that storied legacy may be ending as IBM is sorting out its future as a company in the IT industry. IBM thinks its future, as clear as they can see it; is quite cloudy!

It would take a crowd of people to come up with the right number of fingers to match the number of marketing opportunities that your author saw the IBM Company turn over to its competitors over the years. It is inexplicable and as a stockholder, I feel it is unforgivable. Yet, IBM still turns a profit.

At a worldwide level, if IBM were ever again to become the leader in a given IT industry sub-segment, based on its track record, we could all predict with 100% accuracy the final outcome. First, after bleeding cash from the entity, Big Blue would claim that profits were not up to the company's expectations. Then, IBM would make a quick exit to conserve the company's cash reserve. The company would then bail and sell out the entire sub-industry business to whomever it could as quickly as it could. They would then express shock as the business they shed became a leader in the industry.

In 2014, IBM again executed this formula for failure. It first sold its PC x86 powerful server business to Lenovo for $2.1 billion. This is the typical IBM modus operandi. But, then Big Blue pulled a surprise in what goes down as an industry first in enabling a purchase. IBM "*sold*" its highly advanced Power Chip foundries for a negative $1.5 billion payable over three years.

Yes, that is correct and confirmed by IBM. You read that correctly. IBM is *paying* GlobalFoundries $1.5 billion in cash to take the "loss-making" unit off its hands. In the deal, IBM promises to buy its chips exclusively from GlobalFoundries and the foundry promises to make the chips for IBM's needs for the next ten years.

Who knows what the cost will be if IBM decides to leave the mainframe business; sells it off; and exits hardware completely?

Right now, TSMC, GlobalFoundries, Intel, and Samsung are the only companies in the chip industry with cutting-edge deployments. Once again, in an industry that IBM created, the IBM Company could not compete, and others will definitely prosper.

Is it not fascinating how one company can thrive off the product line leavings that another throws away. There are always companies that can run profitably what others cannot. One can legitimately ask if IBM just recently has become the *company that can't* or perhaps Big Blue really has been this way for a long time. Perhaps all the easy cash sources have just now dried up?

Even when the company was tops in innovation and product excellence, IBM could not hold on to major subindustries—those that it created and even those acquired such as Rolm and Satellite Business System. The IBM Company inevitably lost money in these industries, and had to sell off divisions and companies. I have concluded that IBM does everything right except for one thing: *It simply does not know how to run a business in which there is both opportunity and competition.*

If IBM had no mainframe product line, its staple for revenue over the years, there would not have been enough profits to sustain the company through 2015? With CEO Rometty having placed a big X (target) on hardware for dissolution within IBM, industry analysts are not sure how long even the mainframe will last. Why trust Rometty? Who knows if mainframes will even be a part of the IT landscape in another ten years? Then what for IBM?

In its formative years, IBM owned whatever IT sub marketplaces in which it chose to compete. Things were literally too good as it was so easy, IBM forgot how to compete. The magnitude of IBM's financial opportunity loss in many such instances has been staggering.

When IBM ignored obvious high potential sub-marketplaces such as the PC area, for its own reasons, more often than not, the revenues ballooned. But, the revenue was collected by other companies such as Microsoft, Intel, Phoenix Technologies, and Dell. The combined revenues of these newly formed companies became several times larger than the IBM Corporation itself.

Just looking at Intel and Microsoft for the last year—just two of many companies in the huge PC industry, the total is a staggering $150 billion and growing rapidly. Compare this with IBM's declining revenue now slipping downwards from $92.7 billion. Apple tops the charts at over $200 Billion.

Without Intel, Microsoft alone pulled ahead of IBM in 2015 with about $94 billion, up from $77 billion in 2013. Somebody is making money—lots of money—but it is not IBM. Intel pulled in about $54 billion up slightly from 2013.

For IBM, nothing seems right. Sales are down for the 13th quarter in a row. Big Blue brought in $6 billion less in 2014 than in 2013 and the company was down $14 billion from 2012. Thankfully for stockholders, IBM's bottom line is not yet in the red. But marketing tricks cannot promise anything sustainable for IBM's future.

The PC industry sub-segment is the one area that most industry-watchers understand. It became IBM's worst loss ever from bad management decisions and neglect.

Many programmers are fully aware that in 1980, IBM took a pile of bugs, and rewrote the Microsoft DOS PC operating system that Gates tried to say was ready to go. IBM cleaned up 300 bugs before giving it back to Bill Gates for no charge whatsoever. Gates is now the richest man in the world. Meanwhile IBM is selling off once profitable segments faster than the industry is creating new opportunities. IBM's stockholders have been shortchanged for a long time.

IBM also got snookered by Intel. Big Blue could have tied Intel up with an exclusive contract on its 8088 microprocessor for the IBM PC but again IBM executives chose to permit Intel to call the shots. Intel would not have been so greedy if IBM controlled the marketplace. Instead, they would have literally done anything to maintain the IBM contract.

IBM asked for nothing. Unbelievable! Worse than that, Big Blue gave Intel the tacit OK to sell the 8088 to all comers with no restrictions knowing IBM's PC would be the direct competitors of the newly established clone PCs. Clone company entrepreneurs were carrying loads of "IBM" cash to their banks.

The clone makers of course owed IBM nothing and soon learned how to out-IBM, IBM. The leader in the IT Industry had forgotten how to protect its intellectual property, its assets, and its future profits. IBM forgot how to sell; or it chose not to sell. Either way, IBM lost one major product line sales opportunity after another.

During this time, clearly IBM was not paying attention to the needs of its stockholders as its biggest sin was not protecting future stockholder opportunity for profits. Ironically, IBM showed more respect for Microsoft and Intel than for its own investors and employees.

IBM wrote many other operating systems between 1964 and 1980 and it could have written the 4,000 lines of assembler code turned over by Microsoft, in its sleep. IBM's OS/360 operating system built in 1964 checked in initially with 1 million lines of code and before it was replaced, it had grown to 10 million lines. IBM knows operating system.

Big Blue chose to ignore the prospects for substantial revenue from operating systems by making it so easy for Microsoft to win the day. The net loss for IBM for not knowing how to run its PC business, is over a trillion dollars. Think about that for a while. Let it set in.

That is what this book is all about. Think of what IBM could have been. Think of how successful IBM made IT industry technology pioneers. The stories are phenomenal because they are real and truthfully told. You won't believe how rich everybody else in subindustry after sub-industry has become, and I am not highlighting just the $1trillion PC area. There are many others.

From RISC computers to telecommunications, to disk drives and tape drives, to networking, to microprocessors, to minicomputers, to storage systems, to Unix, to relational database, to clones and to BIOS vendors and to various sized PCs and x86 PC servers, and on and on, IBM stockholders seem to have been the only losers while others became billionaires.

When I began to write this book over twenty years ago, I knew that I wanted to tell the true story about how IBM made a lot of brand new IT companies successful by choosing not to compete against them in the PC arena and other marketplaces. I knew there was a lot more than just the PC industry that IBM's style precluded the company from dominating. I saw it when I was an employee.

I began to write about those stories twenty years ago. But until this past summer, I had not closed them all out. The stories were easy to find and easy to finish. I had written the facts down from the 1990's and then in the summer of 2015, I proved or disproved my suppositions and ideas through research at many levels. This book came together quickly.

Nobody can deny that the PC marketplace continues to be a $1 trillion loss to IBM's annual revenue—each and every year. It is IBM's biggest blunder but few know that it is just one of many. In industry sub-segment after sub-segment over the years, IBM failed miserably and sold-out. Ironically, IBM did so well in managing its earnings that it rarely came close to hurting itself for all of its bad decisions.

In this second edition, I added software opportunities to the list of IBM's squandering's. IBM owned the application software industry when the computer industry was in its infancy. It had little foresight into what application software would become. The prognosis for IBM by industry analysts is not promising. Without a major revenue improvement from its current $7 billion level in cloud computing revenue, the new IBM future is not going to carry the day. IBM gave up on application software years ago and does not even have a small share of this $200 Billion market. We discuss this in the new Section V in this book.

When IBM almost died at the time that John Akers was selling off plants and businesses, Lou Gerstner immediately realized the way IBM ran its hardware business was not the answer. He arrived at IBM after multi-billion dollar annual losses. Gerstner was very smart. He cleverly picked software and was able to move the company forward while reducing expenses by 60,000 employee cuts.

Gerstner saw the obvious. However, he picked middleware and expensive services, not customer application software such as IUPs, SAP, or the packages acquired by Microsoft and Oracle. Gerstner's IBM did not think that it needed to engage in the application software business at all. In fact, in his biggest mistake, Gerstner pulled the plug on a revived application software business, the linchpin of cloud computing. This huge mistake is now coming home to roost big time as companies in the cloud do not need middleware.

That's why this book has a lot of great stories to tell you and why there is lots of interesting stuff that you can learn. Who made out the best? Who has the money? Who does not and who does owe IBM a big *thank you* for Big Blue's misgivings about being too successful.

IBM executives over the years from the CEO on down were all paid very well; but they seemed to understand just one aspect of IBM—its mainframe business. So they lost in just about all other marketplaces. They simply handed very crafty "entrepreneurs," the whole game. In Microsoft internal meetings, they openly mocked IBM and laughed about how gullible IBM was as a company.

In many cases, IBM executives simply gave it all away because they thought they were giving away nothing. They did not understand the opportunities, which they completely controlled. So, they held nothing back for IBM and its stockholders. IBM got no requisite share of its own successful innovations in tons of industry sub-segments. Instead, the Company unwittingly created many industry tycoons by not properly watching its assets.

The tycoons went on to become multimillionaires or billionaires. Microsoft alone has four documented billionaires on its list which is topped by Bill Gates, the richest man in the world at $79 billion. Additionally, there are over 12,000 other Microsoft employees who became millionaires. IBM paid for all of these millionaires' good fortunes out of what would have been stockholder dividends.

Considering that IBM's relationship with Microsoft started by IBM accepting a dirty OS that Microsoft had not even written itself, and then IBM rewrote this operating system to remove over 300 bugs for Bill Gates and Big Blue took nothing in return, one can see what a major disservice IBM executives of this era did for the company's future and the stockholders share value.

In Chapter 1, your author presents the list of most of the billionaires and millionaires who benefitted from IBM's lack of prudence. It is a very long list. I wonder if any of these folks have ever called up the IBM Company just to say thank you.

Is IBM a Poorly Run Company?

The biggest story is about Microsoft and IBM and the PC. But there are many other stories. There are so many that IBM should be embarrassed. Your author tells the essence of the full Microsoft / IBM story along with many other stories of IBM squandering real opportunities. You will enjoy the intrigue in these stories and the stories themselves. It may even cross your mind that no company executives could have consistently made such poor decisions without being part of a conspiracy to defraud the IBM Company. Could this have been? I do not think so. But it would make a good movie.

Industry analysts, however, who have never loved IBM, and have never been employed by IBM are making noises to suggest that perhaps IBM is simply a poorly run company, and that makes the analysis very simple. This surely shines a negative light on IBM's current management and past management back to the Watson era.

In January, 2015 a group known as 24/7 Wall Street declared IBM as the worst run company in America. This is the criteria they used. You make the call:

"In order to be considered truly poorly run, a company must have a track record of missed opportunities, mismanaged risks, poor operational decisions or executive malfeasance. In short, a company must demonstrate a pattern of decision-making that calls into question the ability of its management and directors to adequately provide returns to shareholders."

What would 24/7 Wall Street think about a company whose shareholders benefitted very little while the employees of its competitors—as many as 15,000, became millionaires and multimillionaires—and the executives of its competitors—as many as 90—became billionaires and multibillionaires.

These lucky people gained their fortunes as a direct result of IBM's poor executive decision making in dealing with non-mainframe sub-industries.

If IBM were not so poorly run over the past thirty-five years with the exception of the Gerstner years, one might even accuse executives at Big Blue of malfeasance. How else can we explain stockholders being shortchanged a trillion dollars a year in lost PC sub-industry revenue?

But, to be fair, nobody has ever suggested IBMers on the front line or at the top desks ever took bribes from Microsoft or Intel or Compaq or Phoenix Technologies or anybody. There are no reports of IBM executives shortchanging the company for their own enrichment. The simple truth appears to be that IBM just blew it.

You'll love this book.

Where we have taken the reader in this Preface is more of a primer than a peek, I hope that we have proven that you are going to love this book. It is designed by an IBM insider and told with respect for IBM and with the truth that all of these great stories deserve. You will not want to put this book down.

Brian W. Kelly, my dad, not only gives the facts about how these billionaire entrepreneurs made their fortunes; he shows which IBM executives gave way the store. Kelly lived through these days and saw it unfold at IBM and in the industry. He knows what he is talking about. Kelly also provides a rich history lesson about the entire computer industry that will capture your imagination.

The book begins with the introduction of the first computer and it takes you on a ride through all of the major events that occurred during each IBM CEO's tenure. The story thus begins with Thomas Watson Sr, as CEO and continues with son, Thomas Jr. as CEO. The book then progresses section by section and chapter by chapter to the state of the computer industry today. Kelly does it all in 57 easy-to-read, highly enjoyable chapters.

Few books are a must-read but <u>ThankYou,IBM.</u> will quickly be at the top of your list and America's most read list.

Who is Brian W. Kelly?

Brian Kelly is one of the leading authors in America with this his 62nd published book. He continues to be an outspoken and eloquent expert on IT topics. Of his 62 books, Kelly has written over thirty books and several hundred articles on IT topics that either teach technology or they tell a story about technology.

Brian has been writing books and articles for more than thirty years and he has many great books to his credit.

He also writes patriotic books and some of these include: *Saving America*; *Taxation without Representation*; *Jobs! Jobs! Jobs!*; *The Constitution 4 Dummmies!*; *America 4 Dummmies!* -- as well as many others. Kelly's books are highlighted at many web site sales sites including <u>www.letsgopublish.com</u>. They are also for sale at <u>www.bookhawkers.com</u>

Enjoy and please tell others about your enjoyment!

The best!

Sincerely,

Brian P. Kelly, Editor in Chief

Table of Contents

About the Author

Brian W. Kelly retired as an Assistant Professor in the Business Information Technology (BIT) program at Marywood University, where he also served as the IBM i and Midrange Systems Technical Advisor to the IT Faculty. Kelly designed, developed, and taught many college and professional courses. He continues as a contributing technical editor to a number of IT industry magazines, including "The Four Hundred" and "Four Hundred Guru," published by IT Jungle.

Kelly is a former IBM Senior Systems Engineer and IBM Mid Atlantic Area Specialist. His specialty was designing applications for customers as well as implementing advanced IBM operating systems and software facilities on their machines.

He has an active information technology consultancy. He is the author of 62 books and numerous technical articles. Kelly has been a frequent speaker at COMMON, IBM conferences, and other technical conferences.

Brian was a candidate for US Congress from Pennsylvania in 2010

Section I

Introduction to the Book & Section I

This is the first of six separate and distinct sections in this book. In the chapters within this section, we discuss IBM's lost opportunities throughout its corporate life. We also introduce the fact that IBM's performance pleased its stockholders. There were very few complaints about how IBM management steered the Big Ship IBM. Yet, history as scribed in detail in this book is not kind to IBM. It shows that when IBM lost an industry, somebody with no IBM affiliation often stepped in, succeeded, and within just a few years, became a millionaire or billionaire. Meanwhile IBM received no compensation for the hard work and innovations that enabled so many other entrepreneurs.

IBM mainframes always made lots of money for the Company and because of this, IBM stockholders never saw the true value of the non-mainframe parts of the business, which IBM executives frittered away. The opportunity loss can be measured in $trillions. Look at the value of Apple, Microsoft, Intel, Oracle, and others and their billionaire founders to see just how much IBM stockholders lost by IBM's poor management of the non-mainframe parts of the Company.

In this section, following Chapter 1, which sets the stage for IBM's lost chances, we take you right to the present time to see where the IBM Company is right now. We also ask some important questions to get us all thinking about the essence of this book. We then look at a number of the opportunities that IBM missed by examining the companies that took those opportunities and ran with them.

Moving right along, we look at the IBM Company and its groundbreaking products. IBM may have squandered its opportunities along the way but the Company created all of those opportunities for itself. Nobody gave IBM anything. Finally we take a look at the future of IBM.

IBM really knows how to make great computer systems and the accoutrements that differentiate their great products. If only

IBM's marketing and its corporate management were as good as its research, development, and product support.

Get ready for an interesting and eventful ride. The five chapters in Section I are as follows:

1. IBM's many opportunities and many disappointments
2. Fast forward to today. Has IBM improved? Will IBM succeed?
3. Can a company pass on opportunities and survive
4. The IBM story continues
5. IBM was destined for fortune.

Following Section 1, we move into the five other sections of the book. Each of these sections coincides with products and or events that occurred during a particular IBM CEO's time at the helm: The five sections of the book are as follows:

Section I: Introduction to the Book and Section I

Section II: The Watson years

Section III: T. Vincent Learson and Frank T. Cary move IBM past the Watsons

Section IV: CEOs John J. Opel & John Akers together almost sunk IBM

Section V: Application Software: From Watson to Rometty

Section VI: Lou Gerstner, Sam Palmisano, & Ginni Rometty bring us to today

Chapter 1

IBM's Many Opportunities & Many Disappointments

IBM's failings made a lot of one-time little guys very rich

This book is the story of the many opportunities which have been presented to IBM over the years and how the Company managed to fritter away a disproportionate share of those opportunities. In addition to bungling phenomenally big chances over the years, there were other times in which IBM actually won; but the odds of winning were so poor, and the risks were so great, that most other companies would not have taken the gamble.

In some instances, such as the $5 Billion gamble with the System/360, no perfectly sane person would have ever put so much on the line for any size potential chance of success. That IBM achieved success in such instances may be attributed to fate or manifest destiny as much as to excellent planning and execution. IBM defined computing in the early days when just about everything worked the way IBM dictated.

There is no question that IBM's mark on the world has been its major computing innovations and its original ability to sell such solutions to the business masses. We discuss these aspects of IBM in this book.

However, in a pop-culture world, IBM's modern legacy may very well be that it lent more than a helping hand to create so many technology billionaires and multi-millionaires—

starting with the richest man in the world, Bill Gates. The list is enormous and in this book we tell the story behind each name on the list.

Thank You IBM!

Before we move on with the stories, let's take a look at a list of most of the billionaires and multi-millionaires that IBM helped create over the years. By not capitalizing on its own innovations, IBM turned over a large share of IBM stockholder wealth to anybody that cared to take it.

Besides IBM's founders and other CEOs, which are not on the list, only one person on this list, the late Ted Codd hails from IBM. Codd invented relational database while an employee at IBM. Yet, he made his money as do all entrepreneurs, by creating his own Company and working hard after his IBM career.

The major players on this list are from companies you will recognize, and you will also recognize many of the names. Some of their pictures are on the book's cover. They are on this list because of their own motivation for sure. However, their chances for success were multiplied as IBM was paying attention to other matters, and was not concerned with minding its core business. IBM forgot about making money the old fashioned way—by accepting new challenges and winning new opportunities.

This list is not 100% complete but it is close. IN subsequent book revisions, we'll make it better. It contains the names of prominent people and their companies in the IT industry. The names on this list benefitted most from IBM's belief that it was a mainframe-only company and everything else was secondary.

If you are unfamiliar with IBM as you go through the stories in this book, you will be amazed that the Corporation's board of directors waited so long to take action against the many top executives in IBM that compromised the stockholders' good fortune. The companies behind the billionaires took what would have been IBM earnings for IBM stockholders and profited in industries in which IBM somehow once led in many cases and then somehow could not compete. IBM created more millionaires than most would ever believe.

IBM after the Watsons had a basic unwillingness to protect its business assets, its inventions, and its many opportunities. The Watsons who first managed IBM did very well in this regard, but when they were gone. IBM managers focused on the low-lying fruit and short-changed stockholders by their shortsightedness. They ignored huge industries in which Big IBM had the upper hand in controlling and realizing substantial profits. This book is about all of that.

To whet your appetite for the stories behind the list, I present the list of the many billionaires, multimillionaires and plain old millionaires below. All of these entrepreneurs owe IBM a huge thank you in one way or another for making them so successful:

Please note that this list is in sequence of net worth. This list is more current than text notions of net worth. This list was updated right before printing whereas text notions remained as they were. As most already know at the very top of the list is Microsoft's former Chairman, Bill Gates with a net worth of $84 Billion even after having given over $30 Billion to charity over the years. As of 2016, Gates had been at the top for 17 of the last 22 years. More than anybody else on the list, Mr. Gates owes his great fortune to IBM for IBM's gullibility at a time that it should have been very watchful and cautious in picking its partners and friends.

Technology Billionaires & Millionaires – Thank you IBM!

Company	Person	Position	Amount
Microsoft	Bill Gates	Founder	84 Billion
Amazon	Jeff Bezos	Founder	58.2 Billion
Facebook	Mark Zuckerberg	Founder	46.1 Billion
Google	Larry Page	Founder	38.9 Billion
Oracle	Larry Ellison	Founder	38.8 Billion
Google	Sergey Brin	Founder	38.2 Billion
Microsoft	Steve Ballmer	Founder	23.5 Billion
Microsoft	Paul Allen	Founder	18 Billion
Dell	Michael Dell	Founder	17.7 Billion
Facebook	Alisher Usmanov	Invester	12.3 Billion
Apple	Steven Jobs (D)	Founder	11 Billion
SAP	Hasso Plattner	Founder	10.5 Billion
Google	Eric Schmidt	Chair	10.2 Billion
SAS	James Goodnight	Founder	10.1 Billion
HP	William Hewlett (D)	Founder	9 Billion
Facebook	Dustin Moskovitz	Founder	8.6 Billion
SAP	Dietmar Hopp	Founder	7.2 Billion
SAP	Klaus Tschira D)	Founder	7.2 Billion
EBAY	Pierre Omidyar	Founder	6.9 Billion
Intel	Gordon Moore	Founder	6.3 Billion
PeopleSoft	David Duffield	Founder	5.8 Billion
Sun	A. Bechtolsheim	Founder	4.8 Billion
SAS	John Sall	Founder	4.4 Billion
Intel	Robert Noyce (D)	Founder	4 Billion
Facebook	Sean Parker	1st President	2.8 Billion
Facebook	Peter Thiel	Invester	2.7 Billion
Facebook	Eduardo Saverin	Founder	2.7 Billion
Epic Systems	Judy Faulkner	Founder	2.4 Billion
GoDaddy	Bob Parsons	Founder	2.2 Billion
HP	Meg Whitman	CEO	2.2 Billion
SAP	Hans-Werner Hector	Founder	1.8 Billion
Sun	Vinod Khosia	Founder	1.69 Billion
SAP	Claus Wellenreuther	Founder	1.6 Billion
Silicon Graphics	James H Clark	Founder	1.51 Billion
HP	David Packard (D)	Founder	1.5 Billion

Sun	Bill Joy	Founder	1.5 Billion
Microsoft	Charles Simonyi	Office	1.5 Billion
EMC	Richard J. Egan (D)	Founder	1.3 Billion
Facebook	Mark Pincus	Patents	1.3 Billion
EMC	Roger Marino	Founder	1.2 Billion
Apple	Mike Markkula	Chair	1.2 Billion
Computer Assoc.	Chrales B. Wang	Founder	1.2 Billion
Facebook	Yuri Milner	Invester	1.1 Billion
Cisco	John Morgridge	ChrEmir	1.04 billion
Bell Labs	Ken Thompson	Engineer	1 Billion
Motorola	Paul Galvin	Founder	1 Billion
Cisco	John Chambers	CEO	1 Billion
Sun	Scott McNealy	Founder	1 Billion
Gateway	Ted Waitt	Founder	1 Billion
Novell	Ray Noorda	Founder	1 Billion
Facebook	Sheryl Sandberg	COO	1 Billion
SPSS	Norman Nie	Founder	1 Billion
Facebook	Chris Hughes	Founder	935 Million
Oracle	Bob Miner	Founder	600 million
Linux	Linus Torvalds	Founder	150 million
Apple	Stephen Wozniak	Founder	100 million
Yahoo	Carol Bartz	CEO	100 Million
Computer Assoc.	Russel M. Artzt	Founder	100 million
DEC	Ken Olsen	Founder	Multimillionaire
DEC	Harlan Anderson	Founder	Multimillionaire
HP	Carlton Fiorina	CEO	Multimillionaire
HP	Michael Capellas	CEO	Multimillionaire
DG	Edson deCastro	Founder	Multimillionaire
TI	Jack Kilby	Engineer	Multimillionaire
Shockley	William Shockley	Founder	Multimillionaire
Intel	Andy Grove	1st Empl	Multimillionaire
Zilog	Federico Faggin	Founder	Multimillionaire
AMD	Jerry Sanders	Founder	Multimillionaire
MOS Tech	Chuck Peddle	Engineer	Multimillionaire
Commodore	Jack Tramiel	CEO	Multimillionaire
Radio Shack	Charles Tandy	Founder	Multimillionaire
Radio Shack	John Roach	CEO	Multimillionaire

Oracle	Ed Oates	Founder	Multimillionaire
Ethernet	Robert Metcalfe	Ethernet	Multimillionaire
Cisco	Leonard Bosack	Founder	Multimillionaire
Cisco	Sandy Lerner	Founder	Multimillionaire
Cisco	Kirk Loughheed	Founder	Multimillionaire
Cisco	Greg Satz	Founder	Multimillionaire
Cisco	Richard Troiano	Founder	Multimillionaire
Compaq	Rod Canion	Founder	Multimillionaire
Compaq	Jim Harris	Founder	Multimillionaire
Compaq	Bill Murto	Founder	Multimillionaire
Gateway	Norm Waitt Jr.	Founder	Multimillionaire
Gateway	Mike Hammond	Empl #1	Multimillionaire
Novel	Drew Major	Founder	Multimillionaire
DR CP/M	Dr. Gary Kildall (D)	CP/M Inventor	Multimillionaire
SMS	Big Jim McAleer (D)	Founder	Multimillionaire
SMS	Dr. Clyde Hyde	Founder	Multimillionaire
SMS	Harvey Wilson	Founder	Multimillionaire
Bell Labs	Dennis Ritchie (D)	Engineer	Millionaire
Bell Labs	Brian Kernighan	Engineer	Millionaire
IBM-RDBMS	Tedd Codd (D)	Inventor	Millionaire
APPCON	Garry Reinhard	Founder	Millionaire
Harkins Audit	Paul Harkins	Founder	Millionaire
Xperia	Gene Bonett	Founder	Millionaire
Webclients	G. Scott Piotroski	CEO	Millionaire
Microsoft	12000 Employees	Employees	Millionaire
Cisco	2500 Employees	Employees	Millionaire
Google	1000 Employees	Employees	Millionaire

IBM's Thomas Watson, Sr.

In many ways Thomas Watson Sr., IBM's founder, was blessed in the same fashion as Apple's founder—the late Steven Jobs. Everything the senior Watson touched was successful. His only real historical faux pas was that he chose to resist computers until it was almost too late. But, again fortune came his way, as his son Thomas Jr. was able to put a team together quickly in the 1950's, to gain back the lost ground in the computer industry.

Watson Sr. gave IBM a proud legacy and a loyal constituency. Watson Sr. created an environment for employees that encouraged their best, and best efforts were always rewarded. The Company was family first and for this, Watson Sr. received the full loyalty of all of his employees. The Company had been profitable for over forty years when Tom Sr. turned the reins over to Tom Jr. Tom Sr. had accumulated lots of cash. I mean lots of cash. He was an astute businessman.

IBM has been well known through most of its recent history as one of the world's largest computer companies and systems integrators. The Company has well over 400,000 employees worldwide. At one time, I was included within the ranks.

Big Blue has always been one of the largest and most profitable information technology employers in the world. IBM has a history of inventing things—even things that it could not sell as completed products. And so the Company today brings in a lot of revenue selling the rights to its many patents.

Big Blue holds more patents than any other U.S. based technology company. It has eleven research laboratories worldwide. Each and every year IBM files more patents than any other corporation by a wide margin.

Patents are something IBM pursues and a major area in which it excels. One can argue that IBM today continues to be the most innovative corporation in existence—even compared to Apple. in IBM's case, it takes a very long-term view of the value of innovation. This book in many ways reflects the big difference about how very innovative they are; versus how poor they are at actually bringing their

innovations to market and making a big splash with them.
IBM has struck out so many times in the latter, I was
compelled to write this book.

Besides production workers, IBM employs knowledge
workers and marketers. The Company has many scientists,
engineers, consultants, and sales professionals working in
over 170 countries. IBM is recognized as a great
technological company as its employees have earned five
Nobel Prizes, four Turing Awards, five National Medals of
Technology, and five National Medals of Science. And,
folks, IBM even today still spends tons of money on pure
research and development. It pays off.

For example, on January 12, 2015, IBM announced that it
had received a record 7,534 patents in 2014 -- marking the
22nd consecutive year that the Company topped the annual
list of U.S. patent recipients. No US company has ever
received more than 7,000 patents in one year.
Congratulations, IBM.

IBM has deep roots

IBM's roots go back even further than Thomas J. Watson,
Sr. but the IBM that most of us know began when Watson
Sr. took the helm. You have to go back to the 1880s, long
before electronic computers to find the first "IBM"
employee.

The IBM structure which we see today was formed long ago
by the merger of three companies: (1) The Tabulating
Machine Company of Washington, D.C., a firm which
began in the 1880's; (2) The International Time Recording
Company, a 1900 era company founded in Endicott, and (3)
The Computing Scale Company, which began in 1901 in
Dayton, Ohio.

Going back to a 1911 stock prospectus states, we can see that actually four companies were consolidated to form IBM--the three described by IBM and another known as the Bundy Manufacturing Company, which was begun in 1889. Reading this history tells us that the reports of a merger were not true either as the IBM predecessor Company that emerged—the Computing-Tabulating-Recording Company (CTR), was in fact a holding company.

In other words, the individual separate companies continued to operate using their particular names until the holding company itself was brought to an end in 1933. CTR had been incorporated on June 16, 1911 in Endicott, New York, U.S.A.

Tom Watson Sr. was hired to run IBM

The man who had engineered the merger and the creation of the Computing-Tabulating-Recording Company (CTR) was Charles Ranlett Flint. Mr. Flint was not as good at managing companies as he was at putting deals together. So, he naturally found it difficult keeping the operation going. He looked to the NCR Corporation and specifically to one of their best and brightest—Thomas J. Watson Sr. Flint hired Watson to manage the new company.

T. J. Watson, Sr. became general manager of C-T-R on May 1, 1914 when the Company had just about 1300 employees. Eleven months later as the tale goes, Watson became president of CTR and four years after that, this superior businessman doubled its revenues to $9 million. Watson ran C-T-R like it was his own company and in fact, in many ways, it was. The Watsons made billions at IBM.

IBM stock at one time was increasing at a blistering pace. In discussing Watson Sr. and IBM's stock prowess in 1982, the NY Times recorded the following:

"It would have cost $2,750 to buy 100 shares of the Company's stock in 1914, the year Mr. Watson took over. Anyone exercising rights accruing to those shares through 1925 would have increased his cash investment to $6,364 for 153 shares.

"Such a person would now (1982) hold 3,990 shares, and would have obtained a value of $2,164,000 based on market prices this year and cash dividends of $209,000 paid thus far.

In 1924, Watson, Sr. renamed the Company International Business Machines Corporation (IBM). Considering that the *On to Europe* campaign had not yet started, it was a brash move including the word *International* in the Company name. Watson made IBM into the Company he viewed with the name change.

IBM as run by Watson, was such a dominant company in whatever areas it touched that the federal government filed a civil antitrust suit against it in 1952. IBM was king of business data processing at the time, even before many of its fine computers had ever seen the light of day from its research laboratories.

IBM owned and rented to its customers more than 90 percent of all of the heavy electromechanical tabulating machines in the United States at the time. When Watson died in 1956, IBM was still making a killing every year on gear that had been recycled many times, and each time the customer found benefits.

Figure 1-1 Early Hollerith Tabulator

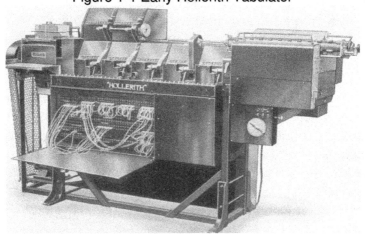

IBM's annual revenues were $897 million, and the Company had grown from 1300 to 72,500 employees. Thomas Watson Sr. was personally responsible for this success. He knew success and he demanded success from all his employees. IBMers delivered success in all areas for Watson Sr.

Thomas Watson Sr. had this thing about renting machines from which businesses could continually gain value. He justified machines based on the salaries of a number of future bookkeeping employees a given company could save by not having to hire them in the first place. He also sold the companies on being able to process more orders in the future with fewer people. Their salaries were "justification" for the data processing machines.

If Watson had sold instead of rented the machines, he would have to sell something new and better every five years but by renting them, he could merely increase the rental every now and then and sell more customers on the idea of getting more efficient.

And, so in Watson's C-T-R, and then Watson's IBM, not only was there lots of money continually streaming in from long-term rentals of tired old equipment, written off many times, Mr. Watson also inspired a crackerjack field sales force to keep selling more and more and even more stuff.

Spare parts fix broken machines

Much of what IBM sold and rented cost companies a good penny per month but the companies saved even more in expenses by deploying Watson's data processing technology. Ironically, if it had not been for a business model that put old machines back in inventory for long periods of time until they were rented again, TJ Watson Sr.'s rental business would have had no value at all.

IBM built more than enough spare parts for its aging rental electromechanical behemoths and the machines often lasted more than thirty years before reaching their discard point.

IBM's year to year financial sustenance and growth was always assured through its rentals. Even if nobody sold anything new for a long, long time, with Tom Sr.'s cherished rentals, there would still be a big wad of cash coming into the Company's coffers. But, of course that was not the objective. Watson played the game of business to grow IBM's revenue each and every year.

IBM loved to get new accounts

Watson loved to win new business, and so he kept hiring the best and the sharpest sales personnel. His son, Thomas Jr. used the same model. In later years, the sales personnel Marketing Representatives to differentiate IBM's talented few from the run of the mill pitch men.

The Watson objective was always to make a buck... but not at all costs. Both Watson Sr. & Watson Jr. believed that "If you take care of the people (the employees in the business), the people will take care of the business." The Company thrived on new sales.

The IBM which Watson Sr. passed on to Watson Jr., was so well blessed with momentum and assets, it could literally afford to make lots of mistakes, though not necessarily the huge mistake that could have come about from Thomas Watson, Jr. overplaying his $5 billion hand in IBM's biggest marketing gamble.

Thomas Watson Sr. Dies at 82 Years of Age

On June 20, 1956, one day after his death, the NY Times praised Watson Sr. in an obituary that had all the markings of a printed eulogy. Watson was exceptional and his style created an exceptional company with exceptional employees. This is an excerpt from the Times article:

> "Mr. Watson was of that breed of capitalists to whom the accumulation of huge personal fortune and the building of a vast business empire became opportunities for the spreading of huge personal benefactions and the accomplishment of widespread public service.
>
> To a great extent, the International Business Machines Corporation is a reflection of the character of the man who led it to a position of eminence among the business machine manufacturers of the world.
>
> From the slogans that adorn its walls in eighty nations and the expenditures made from its treasury for good works, to the methods by which it introduces recruits to what may be called the I.B.M. way of life, the company is the creature of the man who commanded it for forty-two years."

TJ Watson Jr, a great leader succeeds his father as chairman

Like his Dad, Thomas Jr. did not make many big mistakes. However, he was much more inclined to take a gamble than his ultra conservative father. On Tom Jr.'s watch, IBM achieved its first $billion year, and the Company was closing in on $10 billion per year in revenue when TJ Jr. passed the reins to the first non-Watson, a gentleman by the name of T. Vincent Learson.

The caretakers to whom Watson and Learson passed the Company, however, were not as vigilant with the Company's assets and options as were the Watsons and Learson. They brought nothing close to the business acumen both Watsons brought the company. My suspicion is that if Learson put in more than the two years he was permitted, he would have made a better CEO than all of the non-Watson CEOs with perhaps the exception of Lou Gerstner.

Having graduated to success through selling big iron (mainframe computers) to big companies and big government, the latter day IBM CEOs always had a difficult time figuring out how to be successful with any other product line than the largest of large mainframes. In other words, they were blinded by the existing success of IBM and so they did not see opportunities that were not as obvious to them as mainframes and supercomputers.

This mainframe predisposition of IBM, which could easily be described as "mainframe über alles," and mainframe myopia, cost the Company big time over the years. Those of us working on the IBM team during this period, watching from the playing field, never saw any recognition from the mother ship of this huge mistake. We saw it but IBM did not often ask its minions about its big decisions.

Big egos like those in IBM in the 1970s through the 1980's, *made no mistakes*. Big Egos at IBM as Big Egos in many organizations provide negative energy. They simply destroy things. Their biggest affirmation of successful management, even though they were neglecting major opportunities was the principle of "non-neglect." Nobody could say they were losing when profits were so good.

Even if it had nothing to do with their principles and plans, it was OK regardless of the marketplace and their participation. IBM's huge profits always came in as anticipated and that is all that mattered even if the business were being run poorly. IBM was so well-endowed with opportunities, for years it simply could not possibly fail financially. Nobody questioned whether the captains were steering the ship properly. Stockholders were happy and employees were paid well.

Even if profits were based on the work of prior IBM leaders, the current leader always got to take the full credit. Credit, not reality, was what success was all about for CEOs post Watson.

In other words, IBM thought that it was doing fine as a company because its bottom line was always well above low water. And so ignoring opportunities was simply part of its game. IBM executives joked about leaving 90% of the great ideas from R&D in R&D—never to see the light of day. I often wondered what it would have been like if IBM did not care as much about which division brought in the most revenue.

The culture of the day favored the mainframe and IBM felt it held a grip on those American and international corporations that required huge mainframes to run their huge enterprises. Nobody could compete with IBM in this arena. For business analysts doing an autopsy on a failed IBM, there is a lot of material to support this view.

A cursory analysis shows that were many more dollars left on the cutting room floor than those that found their way into the IBM coffers. After the Watsons, and I include Learson in this, IBM management seemingly never had the guts of Thomas Watson Jr. to dream up and then capitalize on risky ventures. In fact, latter day IBM managers often did not take the time to peek around the corner just to see what was there.

IBM stockholders should be upset at its cost to them. Yet, somehow even Warren Buffet remains hopeful that IBM is a good stock market bet. As an IBM stockholder, I hope he is right, but with a duet of Palmisano and Rometty at the top, I do not see from where the necessary leadership will come.

Stockholders need to begin asking IBM's top executives tough questions. In this book, we demonstrate so many lost opportunities, it is amazing how easy the owners of this one-time great company have been on management. In a natural business life, surely some opportunities would have been missed. IBM failed so frequently in areas of endeavor in which less skilled teams would win that it is highly problematic.

How big was the cost of missing all the opportunities portrayed in this book? The answer I give is truthful and the facts about IBM giving up its dominance in so many industries is legendary. I won't add it up completely for you, but you will have what you need to form your own conclusions. In the PC area alone, IBM's opportunity loss approaches $1trillion per year in revenue that other companies now claim as theirs. That trillion dollars' worth of IBM leftovers provides a lot of non-IBM stockholders a growing fortune.

Overnight it seemed that before the end of 1982, with the IBM PC having been announced just sixteen months earlier, IBM quickly had lost over 90% of the PC market that the Company had just created. Industry bloodhounds smelled the money and IBM ignored the scent. This is a huge loss for IBM stockholders.

When we consider that today IBM has no share at all of the most lucrative technical marketplace in the world, we must ask whether it was malfeasance or incompetence. How could such a real loss of business have happened to any company that had in fact invented that marketplaces that survived and now thrive?

IBM did not bet the farm but the Company lost the whole farm several times over nonetheless by not even being willing to intelligently conduct business. You will learn in this book that IBM's # 1 goal through the 1980's was to be a $100 billion dollar company before 1990? Unfortunately for stockholders, Big Blue did not even come close. The Company finally got above $100 billion in 2011 with a year-busting revenue of $107 billion.

Is it appropriate to ask "why IBM could not sustain that revenue amount?" Another appropriate question is "why has yearly revenue fallen from that $107 billion to $92.7 billion as of 2014?" Something still seems to be very wrong inside IBM and there may not be enough cash on hand to save the Company from bad management this time.

Will IBM recover? Facetiously, I might suggest that perhaps IBM does not have to recover if it could simply drive all expenses from the Company and not worry about maintaining or increasing its sales. That's what it seems to be proposing but the logic is non sequitur.

Here we go again! Before Lou Gerstner, John Akers tried the same thing. Gerstner, much more astute than the average CEO of any company, realized that if the Akers approach were deployed continuously, eventually, there would be no IBM products to sell and thus, no IBM.

As noted twenty-one years past due, IBM did make it to the $100 billion mark. Ironically, the value of just IBM's 1981 PC business, one small segment of IBM at the time, is now worth a staggering in the neighborhood of $1 trillion per year. It really is too bad for all IBM stockholders that IBM no longer lives in that neighborhood.

Should IBM stockholders feel aggrieved that none of this huge revenue stream has ever come back to IBM, the Company that created the PC? Yes, stockholders should be very upset unless they are not in it for the money!

Thinking that it is a mainframe company rather than an information technology computer company hurt IBM more than analysts and IBM managers seem willing to ever admit. In many ways it is like the analogy of those in the railroad industry not believing that they were really in the transportation industry.

IBM has never been in the mainframe industry. It was and is in fact in the general computer industry—aka the information technology industry. IBM competes against all shapes, sizes, and models of information technology hardware and software. Management after Watson just liked the mainframe business more than all other sources of revenue.

The impact of this mistake has been monumental and would be in the morning news if IBM somehow over the years had not been able to make a huge profit each year despite its stumbling. Even as IBM loses revenue today, its profits magically are increasing. After so many divestitures shall we ask how much of IBM can be left for the future?

IBM is not even a player in this opportunity-rich marketplace—the market in which most profits occur today—the PC market. It is hard to believe and bears repeating that IBM invented and owned the PC marketplace but lost it through poor management decisions. The Company has demonstrated many times that it does not understand long term opportunity assets. Otherwise the Company would still be renting machines to somebody.

The Big Blue Company was not suffering for revenue until the 1990's and theoretically, it was not looking for more success than it already enjoyed. Yet, with its market ignorance and poor management practices, IBM left hundreds of billions of dollars for other companies to enjoy. Yes, for a while, IBM stockholders got rich on the easy pickings—the low lying fruit. If IBM had played its cards to win, many IBM employees would be millionaires.

Eventually when a corporation does not take its future product mix seriously, and it plays only to its cash cows, the milk ultimately dries up. Moreover, other companies looking to make it big choose to take those chances seriously that companies like IBM consistently leave on the table.

In this light, the IT world seemed surprised that on May 3, 2002, Hewlett Packard (HP), a company that was not even a PC pioneer when IBM introduced its life changing unit, bought Compaq, the premier non-IBM PC Company in the industry. The industry was even more surprised three years later when HP under Carly Fiorina surpassed IBM as the largest technology company in the world—bigger than IBM itself. Ms. Fiorina, a candidate for President in 2015, was CEO at HP during this period. She took IBM on; punched it black and blue; and she won.

There is not much more one can say to excuse IBM from its mismanagement in losing the PC marketplace. Among other things, the Company had clearly miscalculated which industry players were friends and worthy of partnership and which ones were cutthroat foes with no concern at all for trusting relationships.

In many ways the Company did not consider the industry competition as competition as it went about its business. With 13 years of antitrust action weakening the combative resolve of IBM executives, during this time period, the IBM team began to believe that their worst enemy had become the US government, and not industry competition. Microsoft had no such fear and so, it kicked IBM down the street and buried it.

Fearing the government is not a good enough excuse for IBM as it mocks the reality of the day. The government decided to drop its Anti-Trust Case less than six months after IBM released its original PC. An IBM that had chosen to take the business wherever it could get it, could have immediately prospered in all of its many businesses. But, it did not. It did not recalculate its enemies list and it did not recalculate its opportunities list. It simply capitulated in all areas that were not mainframe.

IBM and Wintel: trust but verify

When the Reagan administration withdrew its antitrust actions against IBM in 1982, the Company remarkably took no immediate action to claim back the PC territory it had given to others. Intel and Microsoft had gained the most and should have had the most to fear. In 1982 both were very vulnerable and IBM had the upper hand. But, IBM played its hand like it was the lesser and the Wintel group was the greater.

Their affiliation with IBM took both Wintel companies from little more than also-rans in a big industry to multi-billion dollar behemoths in an industry both eventually dominated. It got so bad that IBM was no longer even considered a worthwhile competitor. None of its "friends" offered IBM a helping hand as Big Blue had given them when it made them billionaires.

Bill Gates played IBM as a fine tuned instrument while Intel gained from IBM's indifference to not having "IBM inside." History proves that IBM's loss of preeminence in the computer field was caused more by a poor choice of friends and partners than their perceived enemy, Uncle Sam.

Both IBM's fear of government intervention, and its belief that it was a mainframe company, were major contributing factors to the Company getting off-track in the microcomputer / PC market. But, it was clearly the myopic mainframe vision which did the Company in.

For years, IBM sat idly by, as an entire industry of PC competitors (the compatibles vendors) came into being and were permitted to prosper and thrive. It was minicomputers all over again. Against microcomputer vendors, IBM fared even poorer. At least IBM today continues as a major player in the minicomputer aka small business computer marketplace but Wintel is even closing in on that.

IBM aided and abetted its own demise. The emerging PC leaders helped take the edge from Big Blue by using IBM's own intellectual capital and original ideas. Some of the takers were partners while others were just good entrepreneurs. There were lots of takers.

It was not long before this burgeoning industry seceded from the IBM mother-ship, and became self-sustaining as the "clones." The PC marketplace no longer was defined by IBM. Even then IBM still chose not to fight back like it cared and acknowledge the real fight that was happening in this IBM-created industry. IBM simply laid down and died.

As we will see in this book, quite a bit of time passed after the PC business was released from the IBM barn. Eventually, the IBM Company reacted as if it had finally realized what it had lost. When it finally comprehended that it had to close the door, however, it was too little... but more importantly, it was too late.

The best technology loses to the best marketing plan.

IBM always had a major touch of arrogance to back its one-time industry leadership. Sometimes in the Watson years, even when its technology did not win the day, its arrogance and cunning would win and keep the ship afloat. While its PC customers wanted to buy IBM compatible units for the least cost, IBM chose to win back the PC marketplace with earth-shattering improvements in PC technology. Big Mainframe IBM must have made that decision because the word small systems never was a frightening term to big system IBM.

The Company planned to use its OS/2 and PS/2 "earth rattling" announcements in 1987 to "reclaim" the industry it had created and lost. After losing the keys to the kingdom, IBM at least began to show an interest in knowing how it could find its keys.

Unfortunately, IBM's mainframe arrogance resurfaced. Big Blue believed that just being IBM would be more than enough to win back corporate America and all those individuals who had not been able to afford IBM PC products in the past. Unfortunately for IBM, many of the same people making the decisions in corporate America had already been successfully using Compaq and Apple PCs in their personal lives for years.

Therefore many of the same people had primarily selected Compaq as the company to save their organizations from having to pay the huge IBM PC price tag. Apple was not as well-known and their wares were a bit more pricy than IBM, but the Apple zealots clearly hated IBM, Microsoft and Intel for sure. IBM had few regular people rooting for it.

Why? IBM seemed like a company selling bread and milk that noticed the river banks had just gone over and so they raised the prices ten-fold to capitalize on the newness of the issue. IBM was many more times more expensive than the clones.

IBM seemed to have no knowledge of the concept of price sensitivity. And, of course there were many IBM large and small clients alike, who had no forgotten the snubbing of having to go to the PC stores and not their IBM sales representative in order to buy one PC or thousands of PCs.

When it was too late; it was too late

With the PS/2, IBM thought that it had made all other compatible clones, incompatible. Instead, IBM had made itself incompatible to the PC industry standards, which were developed without IBM's assistance.

Though IBM was clearly ready to bully the marketplace; the marketplace actually began to bully IBM. The big-time PC partners, which IBM had created from dust, Microsoft and Intel, were not ready to give up their new opportunities to help IBM in any way in its attempted leadership resurgence.

With Microsoft's Operating Systems and Intel's chips well in their camp, PC clone manufacturers, such as Compaq and Hewlett Packard and Dell and Gateway were emboldened and began to ignore IBM as a leader in the industry. They had no regard for the fact that the IBM Company had created the PC.

Even Intel, but more especially Microsoft, surprised IBM with their independence and lack of sensitivity to IBM's plight. And. so, despite its massive PS/2 investment, IBM failed again. It had created a phenomenally new type of PC but nobody wanted it. IBM's marketing efforts were outgunned by the new PC industry that had formed—the one that felt it did not need IBM.

Mainframe- cause of success & cause of failure

Even today, the failure point of IBM throughout the years, the mainframe, still dominates the IBM corporate culture. It has provided the bulk of the revenue for years so nobody was complaining during those years. Nobody is brave enough to complain even today. IBM continues to protect its mainframe business above everything else. Today, IBM's largest computers provide 25% of the Company's revenue.

IBM has been, continues to be, and seems like it is always going to be in the mainframe business, even if that business is renamed to "Cloud Computing." The Company executes precisely in the mainframe business. IBM is acclaimed as best of breed as a supplier of huge computers. Everything else in IBM has always been and continues to be a sideshow to the big mainframe event. IBM needs another Lou Gerstner, not a couple half-baked Gerstner clones that he thought might do OK!

Big IBM has found that it is very difficult to believe that it is in the information technology business. It cannot accept that mainframes are just a segment in the major IT industry. Thus, in most of its other business areas (non-mainframe), IBM continues to prove that it is easy pickings. Its new breed of competitors are better schooled in marketing in the modern era than Big Blue.

Let's now fast forward to today to get a feel for how this predisposition to mainframes has panned out for the IBM Company. We have much more to discuss about particulars and details in later chapters. We'll be back to a chronological look at IBM through its various CEOs in later sections after we take you to today and back. We'll be back in the past before you know it.

Figure 1-2 IBM's Newest Mainframe—the Z13

Chapter 2

Fast Forward to Today... Has IBM improved? Will IBM Succeed?

Will IBM continue to be a hardware vendor?

In her annual letter to shareholders in 2014, Virginia Rometty, IBM CEO, admitted that the IBM Company, under her direction had failed to meet its own expectations in 2013. She vowed a 2014 turnaround to the Company's troubled hardware business and she claimed that divesting the IBM Company of its hardware business was not in her plans.

Rometty's letter was included in the annual report. In the note to stockholders she declared that "2013 was a year of transformation." She said her 2014 plans were to position the Company so its customers could mine data, move to cloud computing, and engage more with its customers. She said she saw hardware as a big earnings problem with its 2013 half billion dollar pretax loss and she suggested Big Blue will be shifting the hardware business for new realities and opportunities.

To me a CEO who is making profit numbers by reducing expenses, who sees hardware as a $½ billion dollar distraction will cut its losses quickly. The more somebody denies something, the more likely it is true. And, so, many analysts in 2014 saw this letter as the beginning of the end for IBM as a mainstream hardware vendor.

Rometty noted that its mainframe business, once the mainstay of the corporation, was already migrating from proprietary operating systems to the open Linux system. Another way of saying this is that IBM is going to change its mainframe strategy to use non-IBM operating system software. She noted this would be the model for IBM's other hardware businesses but in this letter, she did not explain how or which other areas of IBM's hardware portfolio were under consideration.

Some of us who know the AS/400 heritage product line would love to see IBM sell this particular hardware line to a company that appreciates a great product. Instead, IBM looks at this leading edge technology as politically incorrect v its mainframe lines. IBM has not yet learned that it is in the IT business, not the railroad business.

Rometty thinks she can accelerate the move of its hardware product set, especially its shrinking Power Chip and storage businesses, to Linux and other "growth opportunities." The way she explained it, it made little sense to me, a long time tech guy. She did not do a good job of telling customers and analysts alike how the Company can be successful with its transformation in place. So far, her results are very poor and with this strategy I would expect less not more from IBM.

Watch what she does; not what she says. She has begun. IBM kicked off 2014 by selling its low-end server business to Lenovo, but Rometty indicated this would not happen with the rest of the hardware line. Sure Virginia, and IBM wants us to believe there really is a Santa Claus!

Rometty said it this way: "Let me be clear, we are not exiting hardware... IBM will remain a leader in high-performance and high-end systems, storage and cognitive computing, and we will continue to invest in R&D for advanced semiconductor technology." Aha!

She did not say in this letter that Big Blue would continue to power the Power Chip. So, there was much speculation that in like spirit to everything else that IBM has been doing to make up for bad management at the top, the chances that Big Blue would soon be offloading its chip manufacturing looked like it would happen.

It was definitely on the table. In February, 2014 even the Wall Street Journal had reported that IBM was taking a look at selling its chip manufacturing operations.

I keep thinking first PCs, then servers, now chips. All of these and more are about to be thrown overboard. Analysts see IBM going through its biggest shakeup in years, as it attempts to pivot from hardware to the cloud. Of course, the cloud must be retrofitted for IBM mainframes for the deal to work for IBM...unless IBM ditched the mainframe?

So, now we are well into 2015, with 2014 in the books. How does the new scenario look? After a year of mulling over its woes in hardware, IBM began to take stock in what would be left of the Company if it divested hardware entirely.

It found that its software business was the Company's second-largest income source with almost $26 billion in revenue in 2014. IBM clearly wants to be a software and services company. Big Blue has always had a problem managing anything that involved hardware items that produced less revenue than a mainframe.

In 2014, IBM's overall hardware revenue fell again by 26%. And, so, Rometty's IBM decided to go for the sky, well, the clouds anyway. The cloud computing business is clearly soaring, while IBM's management of its hardware business has put it in the toilet with gobs of Charmin Ultra Strength preventing a quick escape.

Many analysts blame IBM's recent demise on Sam Palmisano, the CEO before Rometty, in the same way those IBMers employed in the Akers' years blame the many John Akers' failings on John Opel. One thing is for sure—IBM knows how to lose and has almost eaten the farm on occasion. Steve Denning, writing for Forbes does not see huge hope for Big Blue in his May 2014 article titled: *Why IBM Is in Decline!*

Sam Palmisano's plan for managing investors was to manage earnings and the share price even if it killed the underlying health of the business itself. He called his vision "Roadmap 2015." Ginny Rometty, when she took over in 2012, embraced Palmisano's Roadmap and has steered the big blue ship into a lot of troubled water. Steve Denning nets it out pretty good below:

"Roadmap 2015 is precisely what is killing IBM. According to BW [Business Week] , 'IBM's soaring earnings per share and its share price are built on a foundation of declining revenues, capability-crippling offshoring, fading technical competence, sagging staff morale, debt-financed share buybacks, non-standard accounting practices, tax-reduction gadgets, a debt-equity ratio of around 174 percent, a broken business model and a flawed forward strategy.'

"According to BW, IBM's Roadmap 2015, if adhered to, virtually guarantees that its woes will worsen." It would be hard enough for Rometty to bring IBM into the cloud era,' analyst Bill Fleckenstein is quoted by BW. 'Doing so while yoked to her predecessor's $20-per-share earnings promise is almost impossible.' Even if IBM does somehow manage to make its earnings-per share targets, what will be left of this once-great firm?"

IBM has been unsuccessful in lots of businesses over the years because of selfish managers who could not see well into the future. IBM's does not have a positive legacy in many ways. It makes me wonder if the few shares of stock I have left should be sold while they still have some value. By the way, I just sold half of my IBM shares. I am not suggesting you do so, but I was not willing to wait until IBM ends its share price slide.

Many tech companies would love to have had IBM's many business opportunities. However, none would accept IBM's dismal losing record in trying to make a profit on those opportunities. Think about the short list of IBM failures. Getting rid of old product lines and blaming circumstances beyond their control is not a new strategy for IBM management.

Over the years, Big Blue failed in typewriters, copiers, printers, laser discs, satellite communications, telephone switches, networking services, network hardware, hard disk drives, PCs, PC servers, PC Operating Systems, database software, RISC technology; Internet facility, etc. etc. etc. It seems to me that IBM is now about to fail again—this time in high powered system chips. Despite its denials, IBM dumped its Power Chip business overboard. IBM is very proficient at losing.

IBM never waits for full failure before it acts and it rarely tries to rejuvenate product lines that management deems as done. Instead, as an anonymous columnist for the Financial Times has determined: "When IBM sees profit draining away, it sells..."

This columnist and I differ on his close. He continues with the quote: "...and its timing is usually good." I disagree. When IBM leaves an industry segment, there is always a company or two left that buy or are bequeathed IBM's leavings and continue to be successful. Many have become multi-millionaires and or billionaires. Thank You, IBM. IBM not being able to make a killing in that industry, IMHO, is that it has lost its desire to fight for business that is not about to fall into its E-Z basket. I think IBM should be ashamed of its record in running so many lucrative businesses into the ground.

A number of analysts have examined IBM's role in the semiconductor (chip) business and most agree that it was not the Company's favorite business. Mainframes are Big Blue's favorite business to a fault. However, IBM had been smart enough to realize that in order to have the fastest super-computers and business computers such as mainframes and IBM Power Systems capable of huge processing workloads for its largest customers, the Company had to have a bona fide semiconductor business. Well, we'll see what not having its own foundry business does to the products that depend on the best of Power technology. I don't bet against IBM but I do not smell success in its future.

Chip foundries have become ubiquitous. So, IBM thinks that now all it needs to do is design a chip and other people's foundries (OPF) will build the chips perfectly. I hope so, but I would not be optimistic enough to bet *my* business on it.

For years, from System/360 onward, IBM believed that it needed to be in the chip business to be in the mainframe business and to create the fastest business machines imaginable. This is true! I do admit that at the time with System/360, when IBM got into the chip business, there wasn't much of a foundry industry. What there was of it, was not very advanced. Yet, it was IBM's own and it set the company up to win or to lose.

IBM built its own foundries and designed its own chips, and it did a great job of doing so—even though management was unable to see the many opportunities for its innovations. IBM had to make significant technology advances over the years to stay competitive.

In the recent past, Big Blue has had a close relationship with a company called Global Foundries, a chipmaker spun off by IBM friend AMD (Once known as Advanced Micro Devices). AMD and IBM have been long-time very friendly partners in the fabrication of x86 chips to compete directly against Intel.

IBM exits semiconductor business

IBM says it is quite confident that Global can meet its foundry chip needs, and so it sold its semiconductor business, including foundries to Global Foundries near the end of 2014. The irony is that it sold its business for sure but to get the deal it had to agree to fork over about $500 million per year so that Global Foundries will build IBM's newly designed Power chips for the next ten years. Was IBM's chip business in that bad shape? Who knows?

Industry analysts think this is a good move for IBM. To me it just looks like a typical bail out when profits are not as expected. They say that there is no reason for IBM to build its chips at great expense when it can simply rent the capacity it needs. Well, if IBM stopped making hardware systems completely, maybe it could save even more bottom line dollars? Maybe that too would not be a good idea! Maybe IBM can rent mainframes from somebody! Now, there is a company-saving thought!

We must remember that there was a time in which IBM had 100% of the PC business. The Company is counting on Cloud Computing, a relatively new notion, to bolster its earnings back to the $100 billion level and beyond. IBM's cloud business right now is # 1 in the world—by far. From 2014 on, Rometty's dream of resting on the cloud perhaps has begun to come true. But, will it happen? And if not, then what?

IBM's sales in this brand new arena grew by 60% in 2014 and analysts expect even more huge increases thus driving sales revenue up in 2015 and beyond. IBM operates cloud services today on every continent, and I do admit that the Company is attacking this segment as if it has mainframe potential. And, so, IBM may finally win a marketplace. If so, it will be the first since the Watsons.

Timothy Prickett-Morgan writing for theplatform.net offered his brilliant perspective on IBM's system business after Big Blue turned in its thirteenth operating loss in a row in the second quarter 2015. Prickett-Morgan is a bit more optimistic on IBM's strategy than I as he can see it achieving long-term success. I just keep thinking that IBM at one time had 90% of the overall computer business in the world and when it announced the IBM PC, it held a 100% market share. Now it has no share of the PC market and a dwindling share of the overall computer market—cloud computing or not!

I would ask you not to get upset with me as I make no predictions about IBM's future. I still hold half of my IBM stock and so that says something. Our intention in this book is not to analyze IBM's future but instead to comment on its blunders over the past fifty or so years and how its blunders made others not have to work as hard to become multi-millionaires and billionaires. I do wish IBM success and hopefully the new formula will do it for Big Blue. Please enjoy a piece of Timothy Prickett Morgan's analysis as presented below:

"It is ironic that IBM is talking up a cloud that is based on X86 servers while trying to convince the world that Power-based systems are better than X86 iron for lots of workloads; IBM doesn't have to push the System z mainframe so much as keep it on a Moore's Law curve of its own and keep the price/performance improving to keep those customers in the mainframe fold. We hesitate to say to keep those customers happy, considering how expensive mainframes and their software is relative to other platforms.

But the fact remains that with well over $1 trillion in software investments on mainframes, the 6,000 or so enterprises that use IBM mainframes are the die-hards who will not move off the platform because of the cost and disruption this would cause to their businesses. IBM can count on a certain level of money from the System z line that it just cannot with the Power Systems line. [Power Systems include former AS/400 machines and IBM proprietary Unix and Linux boxes using the Power Technology.]

"Over time, as Power-based systems get commoditized by IBM's partners in the OpenPower Foundation and more of the Linux stack moves over to Power-based iron, we can expect for IBM to eventually deploy lots of Power server nodes in its SoftLayer cloud. The idea is to make Power machines look as much like X86 iron as possible, as Rackspace Hosting is doing with its Power8-based "Barreleye" server and as Google is examining doing with its own search and advertising workloads.

IBM wants to sell raw capacity for customers to run their own applications and also has a set of its own applications – including Watson cognitive computing services – which it wants to deploy on its cloud, allowing it to carve out a profitable niche against Amazon Web Services, Microsoft Azure, and Google Cloud Platform. But it is important to remember that IBM is still a systems company, one that sells top-to-bottom platforms that enterprises, government agencies, and other organizations rely on to run themselves."
http://www.theplatform.net/2015/07/21/inside-ibms-real-systems-business/

Read more of author Timothy Prickett Morgan's great
articles on IBM technology, mostly for free at
http://www.theplatform.net/author/tpmn/

In Chapter 3, we go back again to the past.

Chapter 3

Can IBM Continue to Say "No" to Opportunities and Still Survive?

Has IBM lost its will to fight?

Like a big docile fish in a sea of Oscars and piranha, the big IBM has been attacked and severely beaten, conquered, and mostly digested by just about every little company that chose to take it on. From Univac to Digital Equipment Corporation (DEC) to Cray, to Intel, to Oracle, to Microsoft, to TI, to Sun, the Big Blue IBM mainframe company has been clobbered and has barely survived the vicious attacks on its periphery.

With each attack, IBM has been left with less. But just like the railroad companies could not admit they were in the transportation business before they failed, IBM chooses to continue to believe it is not in the IT Business. It thinks it is in the Mainframe Business just as in the good ole days.

Over the years, the docile IBM Company, good guys for sure to their loyal mainframe customers, saw other companies, such as Microsoft, who were far bolder than they. Companies such as Microsoft were successful enough to aim right for the Company's heart. After playing IBM for a patsy, Microsoft's eventual goal was to deliver a death blow in IBM's prime business area, servers... even mainframe servers.

PC manufacturers created the term servers, which is a euphemism for the term of the day—mainframes. For IBM to compete in the PC created server business, it actually had to beg the argument that mainframes were intrinsically servers.

IBM had survived for a long time from a direct Microsoft attack on the heart of its business, because, as some would say: "Microsoft would have a hard time recognizing a heart if it stumbled on one."

But, many of us in the industry, while Microsoft was conquering IBM at every turn, were just not sure whether IBM had the mettle or the inclination to persevere and survive in a battle with the crafty and agile Bill Gates.

There is symbolic irony for those who have watched Mr. Gates win victory after victory over his competitive foes. As an entrepreneur, Mr. Gates never operated without a locked and loaded monopolistic penchant to wipe out every competitor by hook or by crook. IBM happened to be one of those competitors but IBM thought that Bill Gates was a buddy, not a foe.

Is IBM unarmed today?

The answer to that question is that IBM might as well be unarmed since its great arsenal of potential weapons are not permitted to be deployed with the typical vim and vigor of an IBM marketing campaign.

Many, including IBM itself, do not realize that the Company still has a secret weapon, just waiting for its chance to be deployed. It is the machine created by the best IBM scientists in the world. They were brought together to design the most advanced computer architecture of all time to replace the System/360 architecture. IBM canceled this future system project for mainframes as being too expensive, but permitted it to be used for its midrange System, which at the time was known as the IBM System/38.

Later the System/38 became the AS/400. Any industry analyst worth her salt, who would examine the "innards" of the AS/400 would conclude that in the second decade of the twenty-first century, there still is no machine that can compare to it.

This integrated hardware / software machine was a unique, all-IBM computer system, introduced and marketed by a rogue division within the Company at a time when IBM was looking for a great system for the other IBM to sell. At the time, the one and only IBM Company was preparing to be split by the government.

This system, with its advanced architecture would be well know today, and well marketed, if it were a traditional mainframe. More precisely, if IBM had not given this system the kiss of death due to its superiority when compared to IBM's vaunted mainframe systems. This magical system is so good that for years and years, Microsoft used it to run its business... until they were discovered while trying to sell Microsoft Servers to their customers.

One time IBM Executives permitted the AS/400 to win in the marketplace. History credits this secret IBM weapon with bringing down the once mighty Digital Equipment Corporation (DEC). It was thus nicknamed as the Digital "VAX" killer, until all of the Vax's were dead. IBM chose not to unleash this unit on Microsoft. Perhaps it was because Microsoft was using tons of AS/400 machines to run its own business at the time. Perhaps it is because if a machine is not a mainframe, IBM does not want it to succeed?

Thus, there is one big problem with deploying IBM's secret weapon. IBM as a company has always rejected it for they feared that it was actually superior to the home brew mainframe that IBM executives respected. The IBM Company's team of top executives never believed in the Company's own unique design.

This unit is not a mainframe. Ironically, it was created by the finest mainframe IBM scientists who had ever lived. It is the only IBM system ever built as a result of the IBM Future Systems Project. Chairman and CEO at the time Frank Cary commissioned its creation to be the weapon the other IBM Corporation would use against the real IBM if the Justice Department were ever to split Big Blue into two separate companies.

Because IBM does not highlight this unit, computer experts are mostly unaware of its unique attributes. In its initial release in 1980, the AS/400 was and still is, a better computer system than the mainframe. More importantly, in the early PC wars, in smaller sizes, its unique architecture could have been the weapon IBM used against Microsoft and Intel to win the day as it had with DEC.

IBM did not believe in winning against small server competitors if it made the profitable mainframe look bad in any way. Consequently, corporate IBM ordered its own divisions to stand down, rather than market a machine that would outclass an IBM mainframe. IBM management lied to themselves to save their mainframe investments, which were and continue to be very lucrative for the bottom-line. After all, IBM is a business.

About ten years ago, I wrote a book about this all-everything machine that IBM had not fully unleashed. The book is still selling and it is called The All-Everything Machine. See Fig. 3-1. It is in its second edition refreshed for 2016, available on bookhawkers.com, amazon.com, and Kindle.

IBM's foreign operation was the biggest customer for my book. Big Blue in IBM Italy ordered five-hundred copies as a gift to its loyal AS/400 customers at a huge sales rally in Murano, Italy. They did not invite me but I would have given them a speech that would have gotten and would have kept their attention.

Figure 3-1 All-Everything Machine

Apple and IBM Chips

At one time not too long ago, IBM sold to Apple's Manufacturing Divisions a stripped down version of the AS/400's Power-chip engine, which is the underpinning of this secret weapon. For many years Apple successfully deployed IBM PowerPC chips in its Power Mac. Then, because IBM and Apple were snubbing each other, IBM no longer cared about keeping Apple happy, and Steven Jobs was ready for a break-away from IBM.

Intel, however, who learned to lie almost as well as Microsoft, was happy to get the Apple business. Steven Jobs signed up with Intel to power Apples with Intel after IBM had the business for years. Surely, no chicanery was deployed in any way!

How much of a marketing edge did IBM lose by Steven Jobs thumbing his nose at the IBM Company and going with Intel? I think a lot! This was not a marketing savvy move on IBM's part even if it saved some headaches.

Every now and then a wise person in IBM arrives but not often enough. Here we are in the second half of the second decade of the second millennium and Apple is reengaging with IBM for the latest incarnation of the Power Chip known as the Power 8, the lowest power consuming, highest performance chip in the industry. It will be the new iPhone processor. This time, while this deal is going on, IBM is in the process of getting out of the chip business. I hope that is not a deal spoiler.

How do you think that is going to work out? Oh, I should tell you all that Apple is now a $200 billion dollar company while IBM is still struggling to get back to the $100 billion mark.

Nothing fully explains IBM's continual failure in the hardware and OS software battles. IBM executives who should have retired early after all their mainframe-bias induced failings, continually choose not to upset the still powerful mainframe contingent within the IBM Company.

Having multiple product lines, a blessing for most real companies, has been an apparent big burden for mainframe IBM. As a result, the Company continues to minimize the power and uniqueness of its one shining star product. IBM has masked and homogenized the AS/400 heritage systems into something much less obvious than the best technology in the universe. It is as if IBM did not like it simply because the mainframe boys in Poughkeepsie, their better friends, had not invented it.

Rather than highlight this wonderful unit, IBM's "marketing" group took all of the Company's server lines at the turn of the millennium, and tried to morph them into servers that all looked and performed the same. I did not buy into the morph. Customers did not buy it either. An apple; an orange; a mango, and plum, even with a nice IBM e-server logo, were not and never could be the same fruit. But the IBM namers and product consolidators were not convinced.

A Tom Watson Sr. or Tom Watson Jr. could not be found among the many IBM executives who failed the Company during this period. Rather than have the PC competitors crave to be accepted as mainframe-viable and be denied, IBM acquiesced and chose to call its mainframes and all other IBM systems as eServers. Server is a term invented by the small PC aficionados. Mainframe means power. IBM capitulated though it could have changed its own destiny.

Mainframe was and continues to be a term meaning the most powerful computer of the day. Microsoft and Intel know nothing about how to make their systems mainframes. They also do not know how to add the advanced architecture to their units at the hardware chip and operating system level and so the Wintel duo continue to produce inferior machines to those that IBM could release if the new units would not embarrass the mainframe part of IBM and the mainframe-loving IBM executives.

Even in terminology in modern days, the Company that coined eternal terms such as word processing, eBusiness, and teleprocessing, again got beaten to the marketing punch. IBM's computing families were a lot more than just PC servers, aka eServers. Why IBM Execs could not see that puzzled many of us who worked for IBM or who had retired. IBM had set itself up to lose and few former IBMers needed an explanation as to why in subindustry after subindustry, IBM failed even when it had created the subindustry.

In other words, when no IBM product was selling well against the one time PC vendors, the IBM brain-trust chose a model of selling that said "our products are all the same but different enough to earn your business." I was with IBM during much of this period and that is what I heard and that is what my customers heard. Nonetheless, it was a deceitful message.

Of course, we all know that with homogenization, there is no cream left in the brew that can rise to the top. With IBM wanting to be the same rather than different (better) than the competition, IBM's opponents won the game and Big Blue kept losing entire industry sub-segments and market share in the full IT industry.

IBM decision makers never took the blame. Management blamed marketing circumstance when its labs produced the best of the best and the IBM management team could not find a positive marketing message in all those achievements.

IBM in effect had merely put the same lipstick on all of its systems. This did not make them the same. They gave products new clothes and an umbrella. The emperor would be proud of IBM's accomplishments at the time but IBM clients were not looking to buy homogenized computer systems, whose strengths could not be differentiated, even by IBM decree. If everything is the same, why have four different server sub-families in the eServer family? Nobody in IBM could answer that question.

IBM stockholders were buffaloed into thinking this was OK but they lost share price because of such poor decisions. History will show this as another big gift to the enemies of IBM. It is worthy of a big thank you to IBM from all of the industry competitors at the time. Many of these folks became millionaires and billionaires because IBM did not know what it was doing. Thank you, IBM.

The eServer market competition had a fun time differentiating their products from the indistinguishable wares of the emperor. The emperor IBM claimed all of its different products were the same. The competition's reward for winning was to increase its market share. IBM continued to flounder.

When I wrote this paragraph originally many years ago, it looked like there would be nothing new in the future for the IBM story. It looked like it would be all about the same old botching and floundering as in the past. But with the cash reserves dwindling along with the opportunities, even before I left the Company, IBM had a new worry - survival.

Relying solely on the mainframe as its version of the IT marketplace was not going to help IBM survive. The industry was changing rapidly and simply being the same as everybody else turned out not to be a very positive marketing mantra. IBM was declining even while its bottom line inched upwards. This phenomenon has gone on for about three years in a row. Sales and revenue are down and profits are up! How long can that go on before there is no division left to sell?

Chapter 4

The IBM Story Continues

Can books get better by aging?

I began writing this book more than twenty years ago but after about 900 plus 8.5 X 11 pages, and an English teacher who could not stand my writing style, I put the book down. I never intended to pick it up again. I had never written a book before in my life. My neighbor, a great Literature Teacher had returned this book after struggling to edit just ¼ of its content. I always wanted to finish it but even when I looked at it, I felt that Carolyn Langan, my wonderful literary neighbor was right.

I am pleased that after all these years, with 61 books in the published column, I was able to pick up this book again. I reread this book and decided keep the stuff that was well done and relevant and redo the stuff that I wrote so poorly in the past that my neighbor returned not fully edited. Dear book reader—thank you for reading this book that is partly about historical things from twenty years ago along with a lot of new material that makes the content current. In fact, in this second edition, I added about 100 pages mostly about IBM's failings in application software. See Section V.

IBM has been and continues to be the biggest story of all time in the computer industry so the material, poorly written as it may have been twenty years ago, is really timeless in its history. In this book, we made it all better. I am a better writer for sure and stories initiated in the 1990's are now completed.

I tell a good part of a great story in this book. Not only do I tell you about IBM, but in order to tell the full IBM story in the best way possible, I take a look at just about every computer company (hardware or software), which has come along to challenge Big Blue's dominance in any particular sub-industry area... not just PCs.

It is surprising how successful many of these startup companies have become. It is equally surprising that IBM has survived with these piranha companies continuing to attack. They are some of the biggest threats to IBM's continual existence.

In this book, we tell you who the IBM challengers were and are; who founded these companies; what they started with; how they came to claim IBM's business; and how well they did—mostly quite well. When we get you that far, like whipped cream on a deliciously tantalizing cake, we top the discussion off by pointing out IBM's role in their success. It may be tough to believe but there were times that IBM insisted that these competitors simply take the money.

Finally we look at how IBM came to lose one competitive game after another. This was the typical outcome during the 1980's and early 1990's until Louis V. Gerstner took the reins of IBM on April-Fool's Day, 1993. Mr. Gerstner really knew what he was doing. IBM stockholders could use another Lou Gerstner to come along to help the Big Blue Company again right now.

So, yes, we can say this is a history book for it certainly is. It is about many computer companies in mostly all aspects of computing. It is reported from the perspective of their impact on the IBM Company and the industry in general. It chronicles IBM's weak response to the real threats to its core businesses that came its way from companies that it should have dominated and eliminated.

As you read this book you will be taken back at how IBM was able to get life support, when it was resuscitated so effectively by Lou Gerstner after his IBM-bred predecessors had allowed many formerly toy-sized companies to just about suck the living breath and the blood from the IBM Company.

When I first wrote chapters of this book in the 1990's as an IBM employee and IBM stockholder and later as an IBM retiree, I was hoping that I could slip this book into the reading lists of the IBM leaders at the time. I was hoping to effect some change in IBM before it was too late. It got too big and I was unable to bring it to completion. I have written more than sixty books since I tried to make this one my first. Fifty-nine of these have already been published and so that makes this # 60. Not too shabby for a guy from Wilkes-Barre Pennsylvania.

I wanted to help IBM executives see clearly what they were doing to the IBM Company. I have learned that executives do not want to be reached and so I find consolation in knowing that even if I completed the book and did it well, and all my stories were perfectly correct, I could not have found a secretary in IBM who would have permitted my message to come through—even if I agreed to pay my own way to Armonk, NY to tell the story in person. No IBM executive would have OK's my trip!

The fact is that when I began the book, I really could not write very well. So, I left about 800 pages of this book unfinished and I went on to write another 59 other books before I came back to this book in summer 2015 to finish it off positively.

My original wish was that while I loved the IBM of yesterday, I hoped to give enough evidence of malfeasance from IBM managers of the period that the IBM Corporation would never again leave the corporation's assets unprotected as gifts to competitors for the taking. Too many multi-millionaires and billionaires enjoyed the lack of attention of IBM's top management team as a major part for their success.

Thankfully, IBM hired Lou Gerstner at a time when John Akers, the existing CEO was befuddled. IBM was heading south at the speed of a bullet. Akers had no idea how to solve IBM's problem du jour. Lou Gerstner did not care about IBM per se. He was not a guy would had come up in the IBM ranks.

So, Mr. Gerstner did not have the "rah-rah" loyalty of many long-term IBMers. Instead, he cared about IBM as a guy whose job it was to save the Company. He chose to preserve IBM and its parts rather than continuing to dismantle it. The dismantling process had begun under John Akers' watch. Yes, in futility, it had already begun when Gerstner arrived.

The fact is that Akers was burdened by a John Opel who had come before him and had destroyed most of IBM. Akers could not accept that Opel was wrong as IBM had done so well while Opel was destroying the company. With Akers not acknowledging IBM's desperate times, thinking Opel was Superman, only a real Superman could take such a desperate company and make it OK again.

Yes, only a company in which a super human being, such as Lou Gerstner were charged with managing the company after the Opel damage, could IBM become IBM again. In a normal IBM, Akers may have done fine.

However, Akers' own personal arrogance and his sharp tongue, which he unabashedly used to lash out against regular hard working IBM employees left little endearment for this, the most notable failing IBM chairman of all time. Nobody who I knew cared a hoot about Akers, and in fact, many hated him for ruining IBM. While I was with the Company, we the employees returned Akers' nastiness via emails against us with an often-discussed desire for him to be gone. Akers was permitted to stay too long. Almost every IBM employee wanted him o-u-t.

How fruitful for IBM that Thomas Watson Jr. picked up Louis V. Gerstner Jr. at the airport on his trip to IBM for his first day of work. Watson told Gerstner to save IBM. Period.

Before you move ahead with the next chapter, to have some fun, consider taking an old Dion record from your archives, or from your parent's archives, and get ready for the music of Dion's most popular song brought to some new lyrics remastered as "They Call Me the Squanderer." Go to www.letsgopublish.com to see the new lyrics.

Chapter 5.

IBM Was Destined for Fortune.

IBM was once the dominant computer industry force

Once the many industry watchers have chronicled the behavior of IBM as a company presented with many chances over the years, they will conclude that IBM should have owned the entire computer industry. For its own reasons, IBM's management did not capitalize on what was presented and so neither IBM nor its stockholders gained the benefits that should have been theirs.

Before I had amassed, through extensive research, all of the history for this book, I did not have any idea that there were so many losing incidents in which IBM had control. IBM is a very lucky company to have survived its own self destruction attempt.

As I was unearthing these IBM stories, I began to see the pattern. I began to expect the inevitable, and I was rarely wrong in my expectations. Many obvious opportunities would knock on the Company's door. But, more than the potential to have the best product in a given area or to dominate a major sub-segment of the IT industry, it seemed that the potential impact of any new venture on the mainframe business was always given paramount consideration.

The Company would sometimes ignore the knock of success at its door and other times it would respond to such fortuity half-heartedly. Its competition for the prize would then aggressively pursue the chance as a real moment for them. They would snatch it all away from IBM sometimes even before Big Blue even realized what it was losing. Thank You, IBM.

From the time Thomas Watson Jr. and T. Vincent Learson turned the reins over to Frank T. Cary in January, 1973, IBM missed out on one good fortune after another. The opportunities all had IBM's name written on them, but IBM management after Learson were too conservative. After just a bit more than twenty years with no Watson blood in the Company, the Board of Directors finally had enough with IBM-bred top management to fire somebody who had messed up the Company.

It was no wonder IBM's Board had to look outside of the Company for the first time in history for a CEO who had a track record for doing the job. IBM analysts suggest that John Opel had already destroyed the Company and John Akers had no chance to resuscitate it. During the John Akers years, IBM was at its obvious worst, suffering from a malaise that made all IBM-loving IBMers sick.

Akers commissioned the sale of precious assets--even venerated divisions—just to keep his version of the IBM ship afloat. Lou Gerstner, Akers' successor, is credited with saving IBM from itself. Akers would have destroyed IBM. Gerstner's lack of a long term connection with IBM helped him save IBM.

If you happen to be a tried and true IBM lover or a closet fan of IBM, then like me, you may have a difficult time when IBM does not do the right thing, especially when the obvious right moves are not considered. Therefore, I must caution you that your confidence in IBM may be further eroded as you proceed in this book.

I wish it were not so as like you, I sure could handle a doubling of IBM stock returns in the short term. Yet, the facts bear this out that given potential good fortune, in the 20 + years from the last Watson to Gerstner and now post-Gerstner, the Company has been hapless and has made one bad decision after another.

For now, let's take a positive historical look at the IBM that was highly successful throughout most of its history. We'll begin with an examination of the Company's founding and its many successful product lines. There were many real good business days in the Watson years.

Section II

The Watson Years

During the Watson years, IBM as a corporation came into being and it was very successful. Chairman Thomas J. Watson Sr., who came on board in 1914, was always searching for excellence and he would not settle for less. He was a model for the rest of the Company and IBM sales were literally out of this world.

IBM lived and thrived during the Great Depression and Watson Sr.'s company did the right thing for the country and for its employees during World War II.

IBM was not in the computer business early on. In fact, until the 1950's, there was no computer business anywhere in the world. IBM was happily in the TAB Equipment data processing business. In other words IBM sold huge electromechanical devices such as accounting machines, sorters, keypunches, collators, and calculators. It rented these machines to its customers for well over fifty years.

Thomas Watson Jr. assumed the IBM Presidency and the Chair in 1956 and he ushered in IBM's first mass-produced computer system. The machine used first generation (tube) technology. This is the time when the IBM mainframe era officially began. Soon IBM was making smaller footprint computers (second generation--transistors). These were much faster than the tube models.

In the mid 1960's Watson Jr. took a $5 billion gamble with the design and introduction of the third generation (integrated circuits - chips) of computing with the IBM System/360 family of computers. Each machine in the line was upgradable to any higher model without scrapping the prior machine. It was an industry first.

At the same time IBM came out with the notion of full function operating systems (OS). It soon developed an OS for larger mainframes and another one for smaller mainframes. Following the System/360, in 1970, IBM introduced the System/370 and later in the mainframe line right before the millennium, IBM brought out the System/390 models. These were the forerunners to today's modern day z-Series of mainframes. Along with System/360, at the time, IBM also used third generation technology for its inexpensive 1130 Scientific Computing system.

During T.J. Watson Jr.'s tenure as CEO, IBM also introduced System/3, System/38 and a host of other small business minicomputers. At the time, the competition for these new units consisted of vendors grouped together under a heading called minicomputers.

In 1988 IBM replaced its advanced System/38 with the AS/400 which today is known as the IBM Power System with IBM I (operating system)

In the early 2000's, IBM merged its RS/6000 line of scientific RISC machines with the AS/400 line and together they are now called IBM Power Systems.

In 1971, Thomas Watson Jr. stepped down as Chairman and CEO, leaving IBM for the first time in care of non-Watsons.

My recommendation for those who followed T. Vincent Learson in IBM would have been for the new CEOs to read, reread, and read again the story of both IBM Watsons who served as corporate CEO's. Unfortunately, post Watson / Learson, the caretakers of the IBM Corporation were not good thinkers.

Please enjoy Section II of this book

Chapter 6

IBM's Thomas Watson Sr.: In Search of Continuous Excellence

IBM roots go way back

To the third millennium and beyond, IBM continues to be a great company with great products and great opportunities. The Company traces its "computing" roots back to Dr. Herman Hollerith and his invention of the 80 column punched card.

It was Herman Hollerith's inventions which led to the processing of the 1890 census in 2.5 years using electro-mechanical machines, the forerunners of today's massive computer systems. Without Hollerith's invention, the ten-year 1890 census was not expected to have been completed until 1905.

The census had been taking 10 years to complete before this improvement and it was estimated as the population grew that the time required to process the census data would soon be longer than the ten year interval between censuses.

Hollerith, a statistician for the Census Bureau, and an entrepreneur looking for success, formed the Tabulating Machine Company, which was later combined with the Computing Scale Company of America and the International Time Recording Co. to form the C-T-R company.

Yes, Virginia, IBM was once into meat scales and time clocks. Hollerith's role in all of this action is always magnified. His invention of the Hollerith code and the Hollerith punch card are of major historical significance.

Thomas Watson Sr. takes the "IBM" reins

In his twenties, Thomas Watson Sr. an entrepreneur and a master salesman by nature, opened a butcher shop. One of his major assets was an NCR Cash Register. Watson learned that not everything he touched turned to gold real early as his Butcher Shop business failed.

Yet, somehow, that NCR Cash Register that he owned made an impression on him. It prompted him through grit and determination to succeed. Watson decided he wanted to work for NCR, and he would use his best sales skills to get the job.

When he visited the NCR Sales Branch Office in Buffalo, NY to discuss the disposition of his old butcher business cash register, he had the good fortune to meet John J. Range, the Buffalo NCR Sales Office Branch Manager. Watson had no qualms about asking Range for a job on the spot. He did not get the job the first time he asked but he was determined nonetheless.

He knew he would be back. Watson repeatedly called on Range to get a job with the NCR Company. Eventually, after a number of unsuccessful attempts, he finally was hired in November 1896, as sales apprentice to Range. That was a very big deal for a young "whippersnapper."

Though encouraged and happy to have the job, Watson Sr. was no smashing success as a sales trainee. In his first assignment, after ten days on the road, he did not sell a single machine. He returned home dejected and had a heart to heart with his sales supervisor. Instead of a reprimand

and a caution. Watson got a pep talk that included homilies such as the kind that football coaches use between the halves.

This one-on-one conference was a game changer for Watson's attitude. He was encouraged to succeed despite the apparent odds. From this day, Mr. Watson was always a champion of the idea that one of the chief duties of a supervisor is the encouragement of those below him. He never forgot the lesson. Watson quickly became a crackerjack salesman and he moved quickly up the ranks of the NCR Corporation.

In 1914, Thomas Watson Sr. at age 40, was fired from his job as general sales manager of the National Cash Register Co. (NCR), after a dispute with the president, John H. Patterson. Watson wasted no time finding a new top level position. He joined C-T-R as its general manager. He had almost become an adopted son of the NCR President. John Patterson had taken him under his wing, and guided him at the Company. The senior Watson paid great attention to the handiwork of the master, Patterson.

He adopted a number of Patterson's more effective business tactics to help move the combined C-T-R business forward. These included: generous sales incentives, an insistence on well groomed, dark suited salesmen and an evangelical fervor for instilling company pride and loyalty in every worker. He preached a positive outlook, and his favorite slogan, "THINK," became the marching orders for C T R's employees.

Watson also stressed the importance of the customer. He well understood that the success of the customer translated into the success of the company. He treated employees with the highest regard, and in return, he received their full loyalty and hard work. .

Figure 6-1 Watson Sr.'s Five Points for IBM Progress

He became President of C-T-R within 11 months of joining
the Company. In 1917 in Canada, and 1924 in the U.S.,
Watson changed C-T-R's name to the International
Business Machines Company (IBM) to better reflect his
business expansion goals for the Company.

Thomas Watson, Sr. saw big success coming in Europe and the rest of the IBM globe he announced IBM as the new name of the C-T-R Corporation in 1924. C-T-R had begun operations in Germany in 1910 and by 1924, the company was ready to win Europe for IBM. The international global business objective was quickly achieved.

The picture below shows President Watson's five point program for expediting IBM success. Watson was also determined to be successful in Europe. You can see "On to Europe," neatly printed on this flip chart paper along with IBM's earlier globe-shaped logo depicted in this famous picture, which I display in my Sunroom. It is shown in Figure 6-1

IBM did right thing with Great Depression

During the Great Depression of the 1930s, Watson kept IBM workers employed by building new machines even though the demand was slack. Meanwhile, of course, the rest of the economy was floundering. Undaunted by the hard economic times, Watson continued to take care of his employees.

Watson's IBM was recognized as being a real pioneer in providing benefits to his loyal employees. IBM was always an employee-first company under Watson and it always took pride in being a leader in providing its workers with a secure employment position with an accent on the importance of the family.

For example, in the mid 1930's the Company was a leader in providing life insurance, survivor's benefits, and even paid vacations. And, until I left the Company in the 1990's and even since, unions have not been able to crack the moral code of the Company.

IBM's altruism to its employees during the depression not only paid off in employee morale but also prepared IBM for what was to come. The Social Security Act of 1935 brought with it the requirement for substantial data processing. Watson grabbed a landmark contract with the government to maintain the employment records for 26 million US workers.

IBM was able to fulfill the contract with the inventory of machines that the Company had built during the lean years. The lean years were over. Orders from other U.S. Government departments and major worldwide businesses continued to make the IBM Company a success.

Chapter 7

The Early IBM Product Line of Electromechanical Devices

IBM TAB gear lasted a long time

IBM's product line at the time consisted of big, bulky electromechanical 80 column tabulating (TAB) card machines. The names of these machines reflected their purpose. There were keypunches, sorters, collators, reproducers, interpreters, calculators, and accounting machines. All of these machines operated on a punch card similar to that designed by Dr. Hollerith for the 1890 Census.

IBM survived and in fact thrived on heavy office equipment that today can only be found in museums. Since punch card processing is not understood at all by most millennials, let's discuss the purposes of some of these machines.

Keypunches were used to put holes in cards. They looked like overgrown typewriters but when they operated, and the operator said "release," by pressing the REL button, out came a card punched with rectangular holes. The holes punched in the card represented what the operator had keyed. Funny as it may sound, the holes represented the data. The lack of a piece of card in a given spot meant data was present.

Using a Sorter machine, the cards were able to be sorted (arranged) in a designated sequence, such as by customer #. Using a Collator machine, two different stacks of cards, already in sequence, could be merged or matched with each other, often to prepare them for printing on an Accounting Machine, or for specific filing in metal card files.

When companies did their billing, for example, they would take the master records representing their customers, and they would place them in one Collator input hopper and they would take the transactions (invoice records keypunched in card form) and place them in a second Collator hopper. The resulting merged file deck of cards would be stored in huge file drawers and eventually carried over to the Accounting Machine for printing statements and for analysis reporting.

Because local IT Managers, called Data Processing Managers back in those days were concerned about cards falling on the floor or somebody placing cards in the wrong sequence in the deck, they took precautions. When they completed much of the processing mission with the cards, they duplicated the deck to assure no shenanigans or perpetrations could occur.

Reproducers were the machines they used to punch duplicate cards just as copiers are used to produce duplicate sheets of paper today. When a copy of the cards was necessary, the unit would read the holes in one deck of cards and create another new identical deck from it. The new deck however, would not have printing on the top of each card column. Another machine would perform that function. The card printing machines were known as Interpreters. Their sole mission was to read the holes in the card, interpret their meaning print the contents from the holes, A, B, C, 1, 2, and 3, on top of each card.

After the cards were arranged in the sequence desired for printing, if multiplication or division or addition or subtraction were required, they would be taken from their 3000 card capacity file drawer to a machine known as a

Calculator. This machine would read sets of card columns, such as pay rate and hours, and would calculate results, such as gross pay. The calculator would then punch the holes representing gross pay into these same cards or produce new cards in preparation for further processing / paper printing in an Accounting Machine.

All of these large and bulky machines were "programmed" with wires. For example a wire might connect the card column 3 with the print position 50. The accounting machine would dutifully advance the forms one line and print the contents of a card read from column 3 into printer position 50 each time the machine automatically read a new punched card. Accounting machines were very sophisticated and were often used to print on special forms such as invoice paper or pay checks or on regular green bar computer paper.

IBM made a ton of money renting these types of electromechanical machines. The first customers were the largest businesses in the world. Then, as newer and better machines were created, some with computer capability, the IBM Company took back the old machines and resold them to new customers.

They refurbished the old machines and then they rented the same machines, long after the accountants had written them off the IBM books. Since they were already paid off, IBM reduced the prices when necessary and rented the older machines to small and medium sized customers. They were doing this well into the 1970s when smaller, highly capable but inexpensive computers were introduced. IBM got decades of service and payback from the same machines. The rental price gave IBM profits and it paid to maintain the equipment in top running order.

Many years of service rental from the same machine was extremely profitable. Much of the equipment had been in

service for ten to forty or more years and had paid for itself
many times over. Each additional day was found money for
IBM. Tom Watson Sr. believed renting machines was the
big secret to continued financial success. Those were surely
the good old days for IBM.

IBM worked hard for US in WWII

When World War II began, Watson volunteered all IBM
facilities for the use of the U.S. government. IBM plants
were used to make bombsights, rifles, engine parts and
several dozen other hardware items necessary for the war
effort. The same Thomas Watson Senior, who pioneered
IBM's favorable employee benefits plan, used the same
sense of kindness and grace to establish a fund for widows
and orphans of IBM war casualties, using the nominal one
percent profit on those war products as a means to finance
this benevolence. IBM was a patriotic participant in the US
War efforts.

Chapter 8

IBM's Early Efforts with Real Computers

ASCC (aka—the Harvard Mark I)

During the war years in the late thirties and early 1940's, IBM still was able to engage in lots of research and development activity (R&D). The work of Harvard's Howard Aiken, working with IBM during this period produced a one of a kind computer prototype called the IBM Automatic Sequence Controlled Calculator, (ASCC), which was also called the Harvard Mark I. It was completed in 1944 after six years of development with Harvard University. Aiken's work is considered to be the first digital computer, though its architecture differs significantly from modern machines.

The Harvard Mark I, also simply called the Mark I, was comprised of many electro-mechanical calculators, each of which, worked on parts of the same problem. All of the calculators were guided by a single control unit. Though there was no memory per se, the Mark I's instructions were read using paper tape. Data upon which the instructions were to operate was provided via punched cards, and then read through IBM developed 80-column card readers. Since there was no memory, there could be no logic unit as exists today in modern computers. Thus, operations could be performed only in the sequence in which they were received... thus the IBM chosen name, the Automatic Sequence Controlled Calculator was most appropriate. Harvard preferred the name Mark I.

The Mark I was truly a positive major IBM research accomplishment. It was constructed out of many of the devices which were already being used in IBM's Tab line of gear. It used switches, relays, rotating shafts, and clutches, and at the time, it was thought that the cacophony of the machine in operation resembled a "roomful of ladies knitting."

The Mark I was very substantial. It was certainly not a light undertaking. It contained more than 750,000 components. It was 50 feet long, and 8 feet tall, and it weighed approximately 35 tons! How about that?

Figure 8-1 the Harvard Mark I

This mega machine was built in the IBM laboratories in Endicott, New York. Aiken, a Harvard professor, was helped by three IBM engineers in this endeavor. Working with the IBM engineers, Aiken developed the ASCC, which was completed in 1943. It was later moved to Harvard in 1944, where it was "programmed" by one of the world's first programmers, the well acclaimed to-be Admiral Grace Hopper.

IBM was originally not committed to computer technology. Thomas Watson Sr. loved renting machines until they would no longer run. IBM brought in a lot of cash with this business model. Thomas Watson Jr., born the year his dad took over the reins of IBM, believed that computer technology was the future. The elder Watson saw the entire marketplace for computer systems at five units in total. The son saw computers eclipsing and replacing the big iron electromechanical devices of the day.

It was well known that Watson reportedly expressed his disfavor of investing heavily in computers with his alleged 1943 statement, "I think there is a world market for maybe five computers." Nobody has verified that Watson actually made that statement but it does capture his sentiment towards investing heavily in the unknown.

Eventually Thomas Watson Jr. convinced his father that the Company should invest heavily in computer technology, though Watson Senior insisted that the new machines become a part of IBM's huge rental business. And, so Thomas Watson Jr. is responsible along with many other things for pushing the development of the IBM 701 and the IBM System/360 machines which revolutionized computing and gave IBM a preeminent leadership position. These two units were major landmark developments in the history of the computer.

IBM was not the only organization developing new technology. There are many reasons why John Von Neumann is known as the "Father of the Modern Computer." Back in 1945, von Neumann conceived of a new way to execute computer instructions. He wrote a draft of a report for a machine to be known as the EDVAC.

This machine was a planned successor machine to the ENIAC, one of the first American computers. In this draft, von Neumann proposed a notion, which he called the stored program concept. Instead of being read in on paper tape or being wired into circuit boards, programs would be stored in some type of computer memory and the instructions telling the machine to add or subtract or compare values and branch to specific memory locations would be executed within the central processor of the machine.

There were a number of efforts underway in companies other than IBM to create a computer using the Von Neumann concept of stored programs. The most notable projects of this type were the ENIAC and EDVAC efforts of John Mauchly and J. Presper Eckert. These two scientists later brought their skills to Remington Rand, which was IBM's biggest competitor at the time. Despite the movement forward by other companies, IBM did not immediately pick up the torch for computers. But, IBM's time was getting close.

Chapter 9

Thomas Watson Jr. Assumes the IBM Presidency and the Chair

IBM's computer age was just beginning

Because of Watson Sr.'s negative perception of their business potential, IBM's proclivity for computers could not really be found until Thomas Watson Jr. became the President of the IBM Corporation in 1952. Watson Jr. was expected to become chairman and he eventually assumed the CEO spot in 1956 after his father's death.

Thus, the early 1950's were Remington Rand's to win since IBM was not really committed to the computer business. Remington Rand, not IBM introduced the first commercially viable computer system built to be sold and resold. It was known as the Univac I. It was the hit of early TV B/W programs offered in the 1950's.

Throughout the 1950's and the 1960's IBM's competition as a group was known as the BUNCH. The BUNCH included Burroughs, Univac (Remington Rand), NCR, Control Data, and Honeywell. These were the top five who competed directly with IBM in the mainframe arena. This group was reasonably successful but nobody outcompeted IBM at the time.

For a while when IBM put out its System/360 product line, RCA and GE also got into the mix. Both had offerings modeled after the IBM System/360 in the 1960's. When

RCA and GE were included, instead of the BUNCH, the group was euphemistically known as "IBM and the seven dwarfs." RCA and GE did not last long in the business.

In the 1970's Amdahl, a company founded by Gene Amdahl, the IBM engineer who built System/360 for IBM had its own models to compete against IBM. The Company created plug compatible powerful machines that could be used with the same hardware and software as IBM offerings, but the Amdahl units were substantially less expensive to purchase.

IBM's first mass-produced computer

In 1952, IBM introduced its IBM 701 unit, its first large computer. It was based on the vacuum tube technology of the day. The mainframe era was just getting started. This machine used much smaller tubes and was much more nimble than IBM's Harvard Mark I. But the machine that took the industry by storm and became the most popular computer of its day was the IBM 650.

Whether we like it or not, electricity travels a constant 186,000 miles per second and so the only conceivable way to make computers perform their work any faster is to reduce the distance between circuits. That is why miniaturization in hardware technology is so important. Nobody has ever discovered how to get an audience with God to plead for an increase in the speed of light / electricity and so it seems electricity / light speed will be the ultimate determinant of computer speeds for some time to come.

Knowing the speed of light and its limitations has helped computer designers create new computer components with reduced size. Their knowledge of physics trained them that the smaller they made their new components, the faster the new machines would perform.

Today, some circuits are not more than several atoms apart and so the scientists are working on doing more things at the same time using multiple processors operating in parallel. The IBM 650 was well ahead for its time but its electronic circuit paths were substantially longer than today's.

The IBM 650 was much smaller and much more agile than IBM's breakthrough 701. It was introduced in December, 1953. By hook or by crook, Watson Jr. was getting computer products developed and out the door. By 1956 over five-hundred IBM 650's had been produced. This clearly established it as the computer industry sales leader. This was huge news. Prior to this, for the most part, machines were one-of a kind with major differences in design. Being able to build 500 of any one particular machine type was a breakthrough.

Thirty years later in 1986, more than five-hundred computers were sold every hour. But, in 1956, five hundred was a huge number of units for any company to have produced in a year or even a few years. The success of the IBM 650 signaled to the world that the computer revolution had begun.

While I am writing this particular paragraph on June 24, 2015 at midnight (4200 hours into the year 2015), over 121,780,450 computers have already been sold in 2015. At 4200 hours into the year, that means that just about 30,000 computers have been sold in each hour of 2015. That's 60 times more units than were sold per hour in 1986.

It is safe to say that the computer industry is very successful today and that computers and computer devices are everywhere.

The June 24 data comes from http://www.worldometers.info/computers/. When you have a moment take a run out to this site and watch the number change as sales increase. Go ahead and do it now if you have the time.

If we count all computers that are more than mere chips, including smartphones and iPhones etc., the Gartner group has the total approaching 3 billion units to be sold for the whole year 2015. That of course makes over 340,000 computer devices per hour sold in 2015. For those of us paying attention that is about 700 times the number sold in 1986. The IBM Company has played a major pioneering role in these notable technological achievements. Apple, with its "I" series of products, of course, is now the world's leader in sales and revenue.

Business expansion overseas

Arthur K. Watson, Thomas Jr.'s younger brother was given the mission by his father to build the Company's sales business overseas. Thomas Watson Sr. believed in "World Peace through World Trade." Watson Sr. had aggressively worked IBM into the international marketplace to achieve the most sales of computers possible.

Thomas Watson Sr. started the IBM World Trade Corporation and he trusted his offspring so much that he gave his second son Arthur, who was just twenty-two years old and fresh out of college, major control of this new IBM division. After a short while Watson Sr. gave Arthur K. command of the whole overseas business.

The IBM World Trade Corporation handled all of the IBM Company's foreign operations. Though not as well-known as his older brother, Arthur K. Watson's achievements catapulted IBM into a dominant position in Europe. For example, in the 1960's IBM installed over 90% of all computers in Europe.

In spite of the young Arthur Watson's inexperience, he thrived in the position—making investments in manufacturing and sales that paid off as Europe roared back to life economically in the 1950s and 1960s. To put Arthur Watson's accomplishments in perspective, foreign sales were less than $50 million a year in 1949. When Arthur Watson resigned in 1970 to become US Ambassador to France, foreign sales had grown to more than $2.5 billion, and the Company had operations in 108 countries. IBM was well on its way.

Unbundling changed IBM during Watson era

On June 23, 1969, Brian Kelly, your humble scribe came to work for the IBM Corporation at 1423 Genesee Street, Utica New York. It was his first day on the job. On this day, IBM chose to ignore celebrating Kelly's first day of work and instead concentrated on its major announcement of the year called "Unbundling."

For the IBM Company, this was one of the most significant announcements ever. In essence IBM no longer provided 100% support for each machine sold. IBM services and IBM software were no longer bundled with the purchase of a new unit from IBM. Kelly observed that the IBM donuts and coffee were especially good that day as the Company provided lots of discussion time about how to proceed after the announcement.

Ironically in many ways, as one of the services IBM had always given away with computer sales, IBM Systems Engineering Services, the team that Kelly joined, were hereafter required to bill IBM customers for all such work after a grace period of six months. Twenty-two dollars per hour was the lowest rate and in 1969, that was a hefty fee. IBM gave its customers six months to complete projects mutually undertaken before they were charged for expended

IBM services and software. In other words IBM customers once got free service and on the day I started working for the Company, IBM announced that practice was to be discontinued by the end of 1969.

From then on customers had to pay for Systems Engineers (SEs), such as Brian Kelly to arrive for any onsite work. It was tough for all of IBM to transition to this model. It was tough even for young Kelly to absorb the new environment. It had once been easy to get on-the-job-training since services were free, but customers balked at paying for technicians with minimal technical experience.

Customers also had other issues with the new IBM. For all the "goodies" IBM took away from its rental customers on June 23, 1969, it gave its customers a paltry 3% rental discount. IBM set its business back years with this announcement in my opinion. From then on, as Tom Watson Jr. was getting ready to retire, it was one bad decision after another.

Chapter 10

The Mainframe Era Begins!

The IBM Mark I and then others

Though it can be argued that all early computers were mainframes, a better argument is that very powerful mainframes did not come into being until the transistor was invented. Regardless of which camp you choose, since machines such as IBM's Harvard Mark I, and those tube models of 1950 vintage were so big (room sized) that only the biggest companies could afford the next iteration using tubes. Therefore both IBM and many historians suggest that the Mark I, a first generation computer (used vacuum tubes) from 1944 was in fact a mainframe.

However, during the second generation of computing, which was brought on by the miniaturization of vacuum tube functions using transistor technology, both large and small computer systems were able to be built. The largest of them were clearly mainframes. The smaller ones ultimately were called minicomputers.

Transistor technology

Moving back just a bit in technology time from when I joined IBM in 1969, those of us who were around just before then, may remember the tiny radios in the late 1950s. Most of these radios seemed to have been imported from Japan. Japan had not yet earned its respect in the technology industry. Some may recall that these miniature units were called "transistor" radios. They were the rage for sure and in their early incarnations, they brought in as much static as music from the airwaves. They were cheap enough, however, that a kid with a paper route could easily afford one.

People were thrilled to have one. They bought them in droves for you could take these battery powered guys anywhere to hear your favorite tunes. I think you could get a 2.5 inch by 5 inch by 1.25 inch transistor radio in the late 1950's for less than five bucks, which is more than $40.00 in today's dollars. Over time, Japanese technology improved significantly.

IBM adapts computers to transistors

In 1959, IBM began to take advantage of this transistor technology in computers. Instead of choosing to use the bulkier, less reliable and more costly vacuum tubes of the day, IBM figured out how to use these smaller, faster, and more capable switching circuits to enhance the speed of computer logic hardware. Transistors thus brought about what is known as the second generation of computers. Tube machines were the first generation.

Transistors were able to perform the same logic switching functions as tubes, but they were substantially smaller and required much less power. Since smaller size means faster processing, they also permitted processing at far greater speeds. In 1959 the IBM Company introduced its 7000 series of mainframes which were the Company's first transistorized machines, and they were blazing fast for the day.

The most powerful of the 7000 series was the 7030 which was also known as the "Stretch." Some of the other notable IBM units of this transistor era were the 1401 business computer and the 1620 scientific computer, which I trained on at King's College. The 1401 became the most popular business mainframe computer of the day, and the 1620 took off in the scientific realm.

IBM did not seem to have a problem differentiating its products back then. In those days, the lower numbered models were typically far less expensive and fairly powerful, but much less powerful than those machines designated with the higher numbers as names. Eventually, as expected, IBM ran out of four digit numbers.

Too difficult to migrate to new computers???

The technology advances had some drawbacks, however. Each generation of computer hardware required a totally new set of programs (software) to get the same job done, though in less time. To move from the IBM 650 (very popular vacuum tube model), for example, to the transistor-built IBM1401, all programs had to be re-coded by a human-being programmer in a 1401 high level language, such as AutoCoder.

Then, the program had to be correctly retranslated into the 1401's machine language, and then, before being deployed, it had to be tested with reality-based test data to make sure it did the job in the same fashion as on the IBM 650.

Another problem was that machines that used expensive hardware to optimize business applications could not perform scientific / mathematical operations very well. To add business facility to scientific machines would add cost. To add scientific technology to business computers would also add cost. And, so in this early stage of computing, IBM opted to have two separate lines—business and scientific, each with the power to solve the mission for which the specific machine was intended.

According to Doug Spicer who is the chief content officer for the Computer History Museum: "IBM in a sense was collapsing under the weight of having to support these multiple incompatible product lines." To solve this huge logistical problem, Thomas Watson Jr. set IBM's scientists, engineers, and programmers, on a path to design and build a family of computers. This family was designed that when it was fully implemented, it would be able to perform both scientific operations and business operations equally well.

Thomas J. Watson Jr. spearheaded this effort, with great help from his compadre, T. Vincent Learson. Historians call this IBM's $5 billion dollar gamble. Besides handling business and scientific processing equally well, the new machines were also to accomplish another design goal. When a new model in the new line family were introduced, it would not require its customers to reprogram anything.

Operating Systems right around the corner

In addition to the hardware in each of the models having to be compatible, IBM recognized that it could also mask hardware differences by offering operating systems to supervise the operations on compatible computer lines. And, so IBM prepared to introduce two operating systems with its new line of computers. DOS was the name of the operating system for small mainframes and OS (some called it the BIG OS) was for the larger, more powerful, more expensive models. There were a few other operating systems of less historical systems brought out at the same time, namely BOS (Basic Operating System with a 4 K supervisor) and TOS (Tape Operating System). These were designed for IBM's smallest sized potential customers.

IBM announces the System/360

T J Watson Jr. loved the promise of computers for the IBM Company over the years in which he had influence. As noted, he moved the corporation in that direction from his first day as CEO. He spent lots of the Company's cash reserves assuring that IBM would produce the most innovative computer architecture ever conceived and that the IBM Company would make a big buck from it.

Watson discounted the competition's potential retaliatory efforts as he knew IBM's $5 billion design would make competing against Big Blue next to impossible. Meanwhile, the US government was watching closely for monopoly violations

The major dollars in research that Thomas J. Watson Jr. invested in computer technology paid off on April 7, 1964, just over fifty years ago, when the IBM Company was able to introduce the IBM System/360. IBM executives knew this was big and so the marketing department rented a train from New York City to bring technology reporters to Poughkeepsie, where most of the new IBM System/360 was developed.

IBM had become a world class computer company and so the event in Poughkeepsie had a lot of attendees. There were simultaneous IBM announcements in 165 other US cities, and 14 other countries. The total audience was well over 100,000 IBM customers and rubber-neckers. This was big-time worldwide news.

Thomas Watson Jr, at the Poughkeepsie conference said that the System/360 was a "sharp departure" from previous computing concepts. He noted that "the result will be more computer productivity at lower cost than ever before. This is the beginning of a new generation - not only of computers - but of their application in business, science and government." He was not kidding.

This family of computers running at different speeds and purchasable at prices within the power scale, represented the first large "family" of IBM mainframe computers to use interchangeable software and peripheral equipment.

Peripheral equipment at the time was defined as those hardware pieces not part of the central computer complex but necessary for it to function. The devices included paper tape readers and punches, tape drives, disk drives, card readers, card punches, printers, and terminals.

The word system was selected because the whole System/360 product line was devised as a system of similar computer units. A system as we know from science class is a group of interrelated parts working together as a whole. All models and all parts of this particular new System/360 were interrelated and most were interchangeable.

After IBM had considered System/500 as the machine family's name, 360 became the number, representing each degree on the compass. This was to indicate the new processors were useful for any job, any size. Additionally of course, there were also 360 degrees in a circle. No matter where a client might be in need of a solution, the System/360 family could provide that solution.

The system thus had an all-encompassing objective. All applications, even those with diverse purposes, such as those with a business and/or scientific aspect, were to be accomplishable using this new adaptable IBM System/360.

Third generation computing by IBM

With the first generation of computers using vacuum tube technology, and the second using miniaturized transistors, the hallmark of the third generation (1964-1971) was integrated circuits. The development of the integrated circuit (IC) by Texas Instrument's Jack Kilby, was the hallmark of the third generation of computers. IC is a single component containing a number of transistors.

The transistors were miniaturized and placed on silicon chips, called semiconductors, which drastically increased the speed and efficiency of computers. IBM used a notion called *solid logic technology* in its 1st third generation computer family, the IBM System/360. Big Blue is most often cited as the company to first deploy third generation technology in commercially available computer systems.

For those who like to read ahead, you will be pleased to learn that the fourth generation of computing has been going on since 1971 and it is characterized by the microprocessor, which is in essence a whole computer on a chip.

We have yet to reach the fifth generation but it is expected to move technology to the artificial intelligence realm. Perhaps one day we will see a HAL 9000, the protagonist star of the movie 2001: A Space Odyssey, operating as if it were "almost" human. If so, we will know that we have entered the fifth generation of computer technology. IBM's Watson Supercomputer has such characteristics.

System/360 made upgrading computer hardware and software a non-issue

Besides providing substantial growth without reprogramming when moving throughout the family, System/360 designers accommodated the notion of IBM customers upgrading computers to better models, rather than being forced to scrap their current computers 100% in order to purchase and use the newest technology. As a benefit to IBM, the Company could upgrade a customer rental computer without having to ship a new unit from the plant and ship the old one back for refurbishing and reselling. It was win-win.

With System/360, IBM customers could simply upgrade parts of their hardware to add speed or capacity. IBM, at the time, the best computer marketing organization in the world, knew how to bill its clients for specific upgrades so that Big Blue lost no profits in the transitions.

Moreover, the Company developed microprogramming based emulation facilities on System/360 to enable older IBM programs from machines such as the IBM 1401 to be able to perform well in the new hardware architecture. This may be computer speak at its worst. It simply means that the phenomenal IBM System/360 could pretend to be an IBM 1401 and it could run the same programs that had once run on a 1401 without changing a line of programming code.

The IBM System/360 was very capable and could do almost anything. It could pretend to be an IBM 1401 but it could not pretend to be President Kennedy, President Johnson, or President Nixon, who were US Presidents around that time, no matter how hard the designers tried to include such advanced capabilities. Despite this one deficiency, it seemed that the IBM System/360 could do everything else imaginable for a business / scientific computer family of systems.

The System/360 was so all encompassing that IBM almost did not get it finished and out the door. Announcing a system and delivering the first one on-time are two different notions. The next time this happened to IBM was in 1978, with the corporate announcement of the IBM System/38, a minicomputer by the standards of the day. With the complex and innovative System/38, the first shipment was delayed ten months

Fortune magazine dubbed Watson Jr's System/360 project as: "IBM's $5 billion gamble." It was a gamble, however, which fortunately paid off in a big way. IBM had great engineers dedicated to the cause. Failure at IBM was never an option.

S/360 launched IBM into a pre-eminent position in mainframe computing. Nobody could touch IBM's new advanced architecture and its new capability of helping its customers move their programs painlessly, without a zillion dollar conversion effort, from older technology to the new. It was a show-stopper for the competition that none could match.

Unfortunately, and I do hate to offer a negative as we examine such a triumphant introduction of technology, IBM without Tom Watson Jr.'s technical and moral compass, lost its way over the years leading to today. IBM's top managers began to believe their decisions were good—simply because they were the IBM leaders who had made them.

After 360 comes 370!

IBM leveraged its 1964 System/360 gamble even further in 1970, one year after then trainee Brian Kelly (me) had joined the Company in Utica NY. At a major event in Utica, NY and in similar events across the world, IBM introduced the System/370 mainframe family of computers.

The following is the beginning of the text of an IBM Data Processing Division (Mainframe Sales) press release distributed on June 30, 1970. I read it first as an IBM employee. I had joined IBM just a year earlier.

"A new computer system - - the IBM System/370 - - was announced worldwide today by International Business Machines Corporation. Its two models use advanced design techniques previously available only in IBM's ultra-high-performance computers."

"Introducing the new system at a press conference here, Thomas J. Watson, Jr., IBM chairman of the board, said:"

"We are confident that the performance of System/370, its compatibility, its engineering and its programming will make it stand out as the landmark for the 1970s that System/360 was for the Sixties."

"System/370 Models 155 and 165 can provide computer users with dramatically higher performance and information storage capacity for their data processing dollars than ever before available from IBM in medium- and large-scale systems."

The Company continually enhanced this mainframe line of computers, upgrading and reintroducing an enhanced family every five to seven years. Along the way, after success with the terms System/360, and System/370, IBM temporarily abandoned the word System in front of its mainframe models. Instead, IBM went back to a four digit nomenclature similar to its early computer models.

For example, it used numeric terms such as 3090, as product family names rather system names as in System/370. However, as time changed, though it skipped System/380, IBM ultimately came back to its 1964 nomenclature when it called its next line of computers, introduced in 990's—the System/390.

More succinctly, in 1990, IBM announced a newer, more powerful set of computers, which it called the System/390 (S/390). The System/390s were pegged as IBM's mainframes for the millennium.

System/390

In addition to changing system family names, IBM was continually fine tuning the names for its manufacturing and marketing divisions with the Company's expanding size and influence. Thomas Watson Jr. had long retired and other chairmen, who were not part of the Watson family guided IBM in the 1970's and 1980's and into the 1990's and beyond.

The following is the beginning text of an IBM U.S.
Marketing & Services press release distributed on September
5, 1990.

*"In its most comprehensive announcement of products, features
and functions in more than a quarter century [System / 360], IBM
today introduced System / 390 -- the industry's most advanced
integration of system architecture, design, technology and function.*

*System / 390 -- with its broad array of product options -- is designed
to satisfy computing needs for the Nineties as defined by IBM's
customers who want to manage their information system resources
better and integrate them with strategic business processes for
competitive advantage.*

*In addition to a new, enriched family of Enterprise Systems
Architecture / 390 operating systems, a new connection architecture
and many functional enhancements, System / 390 introduces the
IBM Enterprise System / 9000 family of 18 new processors - -
including the most powerful the Company has ever offered.*

*The new processor family provides significant price-performance
gains and flexible growth options spanning a 100-fold performance
range increase from the smallest model to the most powerful.*

*New hardware and software functions focus on almost every aspect
of enterprise-wide computing, extending the customer's ability to
interconnect systems of varying types and allowing end users to
access data wherever it may reside in an enterprise," said IBM
Senior Vice President George H. Conrades, head of the Company's
U.S. Marketing and Services organization.*

*System / 390 offers customers more flexibility, greater ability to
manage global networks, and unprecedented levels of security,
while protecting their investments in current systems. And that
means a new world of computing usefulness and economy."*

*The new ESA / 390 architecture and new MVS / ESA, VM / ESA
and VSE / ESA operating systems, along with new technologies,
facilitate the function and computing power of System / 390."*

Sounds pretty sophisticated, doesn't it? It was and still is. It really takes an awful lot of words to describe how powerful computers are today. When we consider this announcement was from 1990, more than 25 years ago—knowing technology does not stand still, words simply will not be able to describe the full function of the huge, powerful mainframes of the future.

One thing we know for sure is that mainframes cost a ton of dollars and a lot of years to perfect. All of IBM's competitors from long ago, including the whole BUNCH, and the full seven-company team from IBM and the Seven Dwarfs, are long gone. IBM is the only mainframe company in existence in the second decade of the newest millennium.

Chapter 11

Modern Mainframes

"z" in IBM means most powerful

Once the year 2000 had come, IBM went back again to the name game but this time the Company chose to use the word system with a letter notion. And so, the mainframe names changed as well as all the names of all mainframe computer servers.

On October 3, 2000, the Company introduced the z-Series of computers, as a rebranding of its entire System/390 product line. Perhaps that meant that the S/390 was not the mainframe for the millennium as IBM had promised in 1990, or it simply showed that IBM management had a penchant for renaming things that did not need renaming as opposed to making good management decisions for the business.

When was the first time you heard the word *Windows? How about Windows 10?* Simplicity works! Ask Bill Gates why he has never introduced *The Microsoft –e-Business Windows— Windows Ten Full-Window Server with Agitator Technology for the Millennium.* If IBM's namers got a hold of that name folks, somehow, it would be too tough for Big Blue to resist placing it on a product—even if its customers had no idea what it meant. Moving on...

IBM chose the name IBM System z, though officially the computer line is known as "IBM z Systems." This family name has been used by IBM for all of its mainframe computers from the last days of the System/390 in 2000 to modern times.

It was an expected announcement at the beginning of the millennium. IBM renamed the existing IBM System/390 line to become the IBM eServer zSeries with the e displayed in IBM's new red trademarked symbol. No specific machine names were changed for System/390, and so older System/390 models that were not replaced actually existed early on as zSeries family computers.

IBM's intention in its naming scenarios is always difficult to understand but one thing for sure happened in 2000— novices could no longer understand IBM's mainframe product line as easily as in the past. In my focus area of midrange computers, my clients were uncomfortable with what the IBM namers had done to their special IBM product line.

Technicians from IBM midrange and PC systems had a tough time knowing what was going on in the mainframe area, They did not get the definitive explanations about what IBM's mainframe message had become and what it meant. IBM for its own reasons had chosen not to simplify the rationale behind its product names.

There were official names, common-use names, internal names, and pseudonyms, all of which confused IBM marketing rather than helping it. I had been out of IBM about seven years at this time and even today I still cannot fully comprehend the meanings and the relationships of all the names. I ask IBM if they think it helps to sell computers when potential buyers do not relate to the name of the systems. Technical people like the higher number notion as it tells us what system is more powerful than what other system. IBM clearly did not think this had value.

I am glad this is not a technical book since I do not have to learn about this stuff in order to communicate it. It is all blabbermouth to me. Most of us in the industry who do not follow every IBM move feel the same.

One example of IBM doublespeak is that the term zSeries in common use in early 2000 referred only to the z900 and z990 generations of mainframes. What is a z900 and z990 generation of mainframes? Your guess is as good as mine. And, if we knew what they were, what would that really mean in human speak. Which generation is more desirable? IBM lost its ability to describe its offerings in intuitive language.

To simplify the scenario, ahem, in April 2006, IBM came out with another generation of mainframe power level products. The official family name was changed to IBM System z, which included both older IBM eServer zSeries, the IBM System z9 models, the IBM System z10 models, and the newer IBM zEnterprise. Well, that sure made it better.

The zSeries, System z and zEnterprise families were named for their availability — z stands for zero downtime. The systems were manufactured with two sets of many parts. These "spare" components gave the units capability for hot failovers to ensure continuous operations. The capabilities are great but the names stink.

When the system detected a failing part, it was smart enough using duplicate circuitry to switch immediately or as soon as possible to the backup component or part. Maybe there were a few better ways to explain such facilities in system names but they eluded Big Blue.

The System z family in addition to having its own bells and whistles, preserved the IBM notion of no conversions for upgrading software. And so, in other words, it therefore maintained full backward compatibility. In effect, current systems are the direct, lineal descendants of System/360,

announced in 1964, and the System/370 from the 1970s.
Many applications written for these systems continue to run
unmodified on the newest System z over five decades later.
Who knows how well they will do when forced to move to
the cloud?

In the mainframe hardware and software world, IBM has
been, is, and should continue to be by far the champion. Its
recent (though long ago) competition was with Hitachi and
Amdahl (Fujitsu). In early 2000, due to strong technical
innovations and major price reductions, Hitachi chose to
give up. Hitachi was unable to compete with IBM in the
mainframe space, and they discontinued their complete
mainframe clone line of computers.

IBM's only mainframe competition for years was Amdahl,
which was taken over by Fujitsu. However, Big Blue's clear
dominance in this market and its newly found competitive
spirit in mainframe hardware forced even Fujitsu to pack up
its Amdahl bags and head for the same hills as Hitachi.

"IBM knows mainframes." And so, we can readily say that
by the late 1990s, and into 2000, all of the other mainframe
makers decided to abandon "plug compatible mainframe
technology," because it was too expensive to keep up with
IBM's custom chips and software.

In 2009, there were no real mainframe competitors per se.
However, Sun Microsystems, Hewlett Packard, and
Microsoft, for years have been eying the huge IBM
mainframe customer base and they have attempted to devise
ways to sell their "little" products to displace mainframes.
These efforts have been mostly unsuccessful even though the
companies were able to develop products that handled
similar tasks but ran on smaller server technology.

There is definitely a multi-billion dollar mainframe bogey
for other technology companies to attempt to crack into.

The allure may attract other technology companies but IBM got here after fifty years of continual enhancements.

My opinion is that IBM mainframe technology is untouchable in hardware and OS software. When IBM competitors figure out how to convert IBM mainframe customer software to run on their 100% different hardware solutions than an IBM mainframe, IBM in the mainframe space may need to worry again. But that day will be long time coming! Moreover, when it comes, IBM will have already made another technology leap in hardware and/or operating systems.

Despite no competition per se in this huge niche marketplace, IBM is still at it. In mid-January, 2015, for example, Big Blue announced another even more powerful z-model mainframe computer.

When IBM launched the new z13 machine, it was not just to say it had beefed up capacity and increased performance. Instead, it billed the Z13 as the first mainframe specifically designed to accommodate the booming mobile app economy.

IBM's mainframe customers love these behemoth sized machines because they run their software flawlessly and they are the fastest machines on the planet. Yes, they are all pre-PC architecture computers and yet IBM customers in government, corporations, and huge independent laboratories love their mainframes to pieces.

As we noted in this book, IBM's first mainframe was introduced almost sixty-five years ago in 1952. Along the way, many have traced IBM's reinventions of the IBM mainframe to become a provider of business services and cloud computing on more and more powerful machines.

Lou Gerstner, from 1993 on until his retirement changed IBM into a major services company, not just a company that manufactures hardware. Yet, the old mainframe standby is still around and it is delivering huge profits today for the IBM Company. Whether IBM permits such hardware to continue over time, is up to new CEO Virginia Rometty.

IBM loves to brag about the resilience of its mainframe line of computers. It has a real right to do so as nothing is as good anywhere on the planet. On a website touting IBM's success with mainframe technology for example, the Company once used a Mark Twain-like quote to put the mainframe's unprecedented success in perspective:

> *"Reports of the death of the mainframe were premature Source: IBM Annual Report 2001" Here are two more quotes: (1) "I predict that the last mainframe will be unplugged on March 15, 1996." – Stewart Alsop, March 1991.*

> *(2) "It's clear that corporate customers still like to have centrally controlled, very predictable, reliable computing systems – exactly the kind of systems that IBM specializes in." – Stewart Alsop, February 2002.*

These two quotes show that long time computer gurus and prognosticators, (Alsop) are not always perfect.

Powerful operating systems for mainframes

IBM's simple operating systems of the 1960's became increasingly larger and more sophisticated as time went on. IBM never started over. It just modified and added to the existing OS code base.

With the major announcements of virtual storage in the early 1970s, data base and data communications subsystems, and the various evolutionary architecture extensions, which were made to accommodate advances in hardware technology, client based computing and cloud computing, IBM's mainframe operating systems had to be substantially reworked over the years.

During this time, IBM's early operating systems evolved with more and more capabilities. The IBM Namers could not resist making their names seemingly more attractive and marketable. The products came from such simple names as S/360 DOS and S/360 OS into the 1990s version called Operating System / 390 or OS/390. But, since then, the names have gone wild.

Along with the many name changes in the hardware lines, IBM has kept pace by tweaking its standard fare operating systems and today they all have names that include IBM's new favorite letter, "z." And, so, just like the IBM System/360 and the IBM System/370 from the 60's and 70's, the IBM z Systems servers support multiple operating systems. Today's names—similar but different. Sample list includes z/OS, z/VSE, z/TPF, Linux on z Systems and the z/VM hypervisor. Glad I got that cleared up!

Blades, Blade Servers; Systems; Centers

Instead of standalone huge computer systems with several main processors, the computer industry with IBM among the leaders, decided to put complete computers on a card that would plug into a reasonably dumb computer case with a powerful bus. The computer itself was called a blade and it came to life when it was inserted into a *blade server* case.

Ironically, a blade has also been labeled as a blade server. It is a thin, modular electronic circuit board containing one, two, or more microprocessors and memory, that are/is intended for a single, dedicated application (such as serving Web pages). The blade card can easily be inserted into a space-saving rack (Blade System or Blade Center) with many similar servers.

So far, we have briefly examined the fact that In the last ten years, new hardware technology has arrived in which multiple systems can be built in a small form factor known as a blade and as many as fifteen or so blades can be packaged in one enclosure known by HP as a Blade System and known by IBM as a Blade Center.

The blades are connected to an internal bus and the enclosure rack has all of the power, heating, and cooling facilities required to operate the blades. Often the blade centers support Storage Area Networks (SANS) which are independent storage systems, comprised of disk drives that may be under the control of more than just one computer system.

SAN units can be shared by many systems connected via the blade housing technology. To keep this all working in harmony, special operating system extensions to support multiple systems running within one or more blade centers or servers are needed.

IBM's mainframe offering which is really an IBM Operating System extension known as *zBladeCenter Extension (zBX)* hybrid computing capabilities. With this blade software, IBM has expanded the number of workloads that can run on z Systems with operating system support for AIX (Unix) on Power, Microsoft Windows® and Linux on System x blade servers. The notion of interconnected blades has added the opportunity to mix and match different processors, and different operating systems in one enclosure. It is a notion not for the faint of heart.

Chapter 12

IBM Small Business Computers

Computers were once reasonably "easy" to understand

The computer industry is huge and nobody can understand it all. Back in the 1950's through 1980's the notion of computing was understandable and explainable to regular human beings using small paragraphs. These days, understanding what's going on internally with systems has changed. I repeat that it is not for the faint of heart. Let's enjoy going back to those simple times for a while. I think I can explain this stuff without anybody getting sick on a tech overload.

Along with its System/360 announcement, in 1964, IBM introduced a system at the very bottom of the System/360 product line. It was known as the System/360 model 20 and it fit in well with small businesses that were doing well and could afford computers with monthly rental price tags from just less than $2000 to as high as $10,000 or more.

Most companies that could afford System/360 model 20's were already paying IBM for a host of huge electromechanical units in the form of Tab systems. Most Model 20s that were sold by IBM were at the bottom of the S/360 power spectrum and did not have disk drives.

However, the system architecture permitted them to upgrade to larger capacities with faster card readers and printers, and later bigger disk drives. They could also upgrade their model to a model 30, 40, or 50 if business needs warranted. IBM would take back the rental Model 20 and ship in a model 30 or whatever size was needed and the client's monthly rental bill was increased accordingly.

The Model 20 was the smallest member of the IBM System/360 family announced in November 1964. It supported only a subset of the full System/360 instruction set, with binary numbers limited to 16 bits and no floating point (scientific facilities). Model 20 software could be recompiled to run on faster S/360 models but larger S/360 model software was not compatible if anybody attempted to run it on a model 20.

In later years as companies including IBM introduced even cheaper machines, the model 20 would be re-classified as a 16-bit minicomputer rather than a mainframe. However, in 1964, there was no term such as "minicomputer" when IBM introduced this machine. Regardless, IBM's marketing intentions were to emphasize the compatibility of the Model 20 with the rest of the System/360 rather than highlight its differences.

Showing that IBM was an international manufacturing and development computer; this machine was developed by IBM in Böblingen, Germany. It was intended for data processing as all computers but, as noted, it was specifically designed and built as an affordable replacement for TAB gear (the big iron electromechanical devices Watson Sr. liked to rent or lease).

IBM 1130 – A third generation machine for the scientific community.

Another machine, which used similar components but which was incompatible with System/360 was introduced the following year (1965) as the IBM 1130. It was designed for scientific and engineering computing. A System/360 model 20 card-only (no disks) system would rent for as little as $2,000 per month—the cost of several office personnel at the time. The IBM 1130 System rented for as little as $695 per month. Consequently, though IBM built this machine for scientific processing, it was so inexpensive that many companies and universities, including Marywood University, where I once served as a professor, used this machine to run its business operations. When I was with IBM, as an Account Systems Engineer, Marywood was my client.

The IBM 1130 Computing System was announced in February 1965 as the "lowest-priced stored program computer ever marketed by IBM." Capable of performing 120,000 additions a second, the system was offered for lease for as little as $695 a month and for sale at $32,280. The 1130 used microelectronic circuits employing IBM's Solid Logic Technology similar to those used by the IBM System/360. It was manufactured in San Jose, Calif., and Greenock, Scotland.

Based on number of System/360 model 20 systems sold, the smallest member of the line was the most successful model of System/360. IBM wrote that the number of Model 20 processors installed by the end of 1970 in the United States exceeded 7,400. Other System/360 models with higher price tags, faster processors, and more capacity brought in far greater revenue per unit.

The 1130 also sold very well and it had many uses. The estimated production run for IBM 1130 systems is 10,000. I would have suspected that it was over 20,000. When I worked for IBM in my first years, 1130's seemed to be everywhere. The machine was aimed at price-sensitive, computing-intensive technical markets like education and engineering. It succeeded the transistor based second generation IBM 1620 in that market segment. By the way, to remind the readers, the 1620 was the machine on which I learned Data Processing at King's College in Wilkes-Barre, PA.

An enhanced process control real-time variant of the 1130 was marketed as the IBM 1800. This machine was intended for scientific purposes as well as real time processing and sensor based applications. In other words, the 1800 could control robot pickers in a warehouse as easily as it could control the traffic lights in a major city.

Chapter 13

IBM System/3 Starts a New Age

General Systems Division was an innovator

In 1969, IBM formed the General Systems Division (GSD) which many believe the Company created to compete against the big IBM Company in the event of a government break-up of the Big IBM. The division was formed as a company in itself. It had its own manufacturing plants; its own marketing force; and its own customer engineering (CE) team. The CEs fixed the GSD machines in customer premises when they would break (not too often).

So the new division had its own minicomputer-like flagship computer line, but no units in this class of computers were ever permitted to be called minicomputers. They were known as small business machines.

In 1969, IBM's General Systems Division (GSD) announced a new batch processing computer, which used a funny little 96-column card. They called it the IBM System/3. This machine was intended for small businesses. It was substantially less powerful than IBM's large scale computers and offered no threat to IBM's mainframe sales. It replaced the IBM System/360 model 20 and the 1401, and it also replaced IBM Tab gear systems.

The first model of System/3 (model 10) had no disk drives or tape drives. Instead, it had a multi-function card unit (MFCU) which had two 96-colomn card input hoppers and four output card stackers. The machine could read and/or punch cards simultaneously from both input hoppers and it could direct cards read as well as cards punched to any of the four stackers. When a card sorting program was run on the System/3, the machine could use the four stackers and two hoppers to create one sorted deck. Thus, smaller IBM customers did not need a card sorter.

Figure 13-1 96 column card– three tiers. 5496 was a keypunch

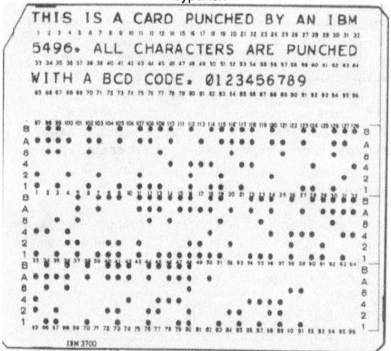

The first S/3 models also came with an IBM 5203 printer that was attached to the frame of the machine. The IBM 5203 chain line printer could print at 100 to 200 lines per minute.

All System/3 derivatives (follow-on machines) including the IBM System/38 were low powered, low capacity compared to the IBM mainframe offerings. The IBM System/3, which as noted was introduced in 1969, was discontinued in 1985. It had lasted sixteen years.

System/3 was thus a low-end third generation small business computer aimed at new customers and organizations that still used IBM 1400 series computers (second generation) or unit record (TAB) equipment. IBM sales personnel sold (typically as a rental) the machine to many first time clients, which the Company's marketing force referred to as new accounts.

Figure 13-2 IBM System/3 Model 10

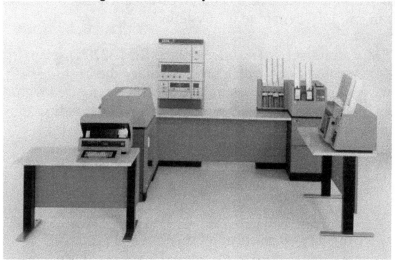

As the businesses using System/3 grew in size, they demanded that IBM make the System/3 bigger to help them upgrade for their business needs in a non-disruptive fashion. IBM had always been very accommodating with upgrades when its customers were willing to spend their money on IBM gear.

As noted, the Company introduced its first model System/3 with no disk and tape (model 10) and followed it up with models 4, 6, 8, 12, 15, and 15d. The 15D was the largest and most powerful System/3 with 512k of memory, up to 447 megabytes of IBM 3340 disk drives; up to four IBM 3410 tape drives, locally attached terminals, and a number of high speed printers such as IBM's classic 1100 line per minute 1403.

The 1403 printer had its life extended from its days as the fast line printer on the IBM 1401 second generation business computer. IBM was great at mechanical engineering and could keep its well-built mechanical devices alive forever as its rental plans permitted boxes to be redeployed years later. The 1403 served the System/3 larger customers quite well. IBM also retrofitted its 80-coumn card readers and punches from the 1401 system to the System/3.

IBM mainframes at the time used the IBM 3270 Display System as terminals with a program called the Customer Information Control System (CICS). GSD contracted with big IBM to have these tubes (display terminals) made usable on the System/3. GSD's lab in Rochester then created a program called the Communication Control Program (CCP), which was a mini CICS. Eventually all models of the System/3 could run CCP. Therefore, all S/3 models could support terminal oriented online processing.

Along the way, to create a lower entry level price point for business computers IBM announced a System/3 Model 6 which had a built in keyboard and a slow printer, and a small disk capacity. It could not attach tape or large disks or large printers and it could not run CCP so it could not attach 3270 terminals.

As the Model 6 was aging and memory prices declined, IBM added a lot of memory to the former model 6 and re-introduced it as a CCP enabled machine that could support up to eight directly attached terminals. The new model name was the Model 4.

All System 3 models were equipped with a Report Program Generator II (RPG II) compiler (a business language), and they all used a simple job control language called Operator

Control Language (OCL). OCL was functionally similar to IBM's famous Job Control Language from its mainframes, but it was substantially easier to learn and use.

To control the multi-programming and terminal environment on model 15D units, IBM's most powerful System/3's, the Company developed a set of operator control commands known as OCC. Over the years, IBM also introduced FORTRAN and COBOL compilers for its System/3 models.

The System/3 and successor GSD systems (System/32, System/34, System/36, System/38, and then the IBM AS/400, iSeries, System i and Power System with IBM I, have generally been referred to as minicomputers or in IBM terminology "midrange systems."

This is in contrast to IBM's more traditional large mainframes. At some point the S/3X offerings from IBM became known as midrange systems, which was a change in focus from the days when they were simply known as small business systems.

After System/3 became very successful, there was demand by IBM marketers for an even smaller and less expensive computer to address the needs of even smaller businesses, who could not afford a machine with the price tag of a System/3 (about $1000 per month rental).

The IBM System/32

In 1975, IBM introduced the desk-sized (not desktop) IBM System/32 which was a single station unit with a keyboard and an attached printer. It was like the System/3 model 6 but substantially smaller. It used a different, simpler operating system than the System/3 but it was similar enough that System/3 programmers caught on quickly.

IBM added commands to this model's RPG Programming Language to address the keyboard and a small System/32 display. This computer system became very successful as it was easy to program and easy to use and manage for IBM customers.

Figure 13-3, IBM System/32

IBM System/32

The IBM System/34

Using the highly easy to use System/32 operating system and RPG II as its basis, in 1977, IBM stole some hardware from its not-yet-announced IBM System/38 and it created a larger, but somewhat more expensive multi-user version of its System/32.

IBM called this box—The IBM System/34. For its day, System/34 offered revolutionary capability to painlessly support a multi-user terminal environment. You could not help like the System/34. There was no complexity.

I can still recall a fellow IBM Systems Engineer, and good friend, George Mohanco, sitting next to me the first day that we were briefed on the System/34. George looked at me mid-way through the presentation and said: "Kell, Phew! It's getting out of hand." He and I knew how difficult it had been with a System/3 to do simple things like light up a 3270 terminal screen with CCP. On the System/34, Interactive programming was a breeze.

The IBM System/36

In 1983, IBM upgraded the System/34 to become the System/36, and added a small amount of well needed memory, disk capacity and additional software facilities such as a full office and word processing software package. Many believe that it was the S/36 that legitimized IBM's presence in the midrange marketplace and paved the way for the 1988 introduction of the AS/400.

As I recall the numbers, at the time that the AS/400 was announced, IBM had sold about 20,000 S/38's in the US and an equal number throughout the rest of the world. In contrast, over 200,000 S/36's had been sold worldwide. That level of customer acceptance on the part of the S/36 provided fertile ground for the early marketing efforts for the AS/400. AS/400 ran both System/36 and System/38 programs virtually unchanged.

Chapter 14

The IBM System/38—the Most Advanced Computing System Ever

Future systems project in a small package

In June 1978, IBM announced the System/38 as the successor system for its small business customers who had been using IBM's largest System/3 units. The new System/38 had been developed over eight years by IBM's laboratory in Rochester, Minnesota.

Figure 14-1 IBM System/38 & attached terminals in office

Using the advanced criteria from a canceled "future systems" project as a function guideline, it took substantially longer than IBM had anticipated for the product to be able to be ready to ship to real customers. In August, 1979, IBM was forced to delay its first customer ship date by nine months because it could not get the machine stable in time.

In early 1980, along with other US Systems Engineers, your humble scribe was invited to Rochester Minnesota to serve a two-week internship to help make the System/38 ready for shipment. Many IBM programmers and technicians from across the globe were in Rochester at the same time to help stabilize the machine and help with the completion of promised capabilities. Many of those on the full resuscitation team were in Rochester for substantially longer projects than the one in which I was engaged.

New versions of the new System/38 Control Program Facility Operating System (CPF) were being released almost every day during my time working in Rochester. Each new release meant that number of crashes per day were reduced. IBM called System/38 operating system crashes "function checks." For the time I spent in Rochester, as much time was spent re-booting the system from function checks as in making productive changes to code. I learned to smile and take it.

Eventually IBM got it right. It was the most complicated mission ever undertaken by any IBM division ever, and without extra funding and extra people to make it acceptable, when it was already supposed to be ready, it would have died without ever having lived. In fact, it was the most complicated system ever developed by any computer company, including IBM, ever—to this day. The bottom line is that for what System/360 was in hardware innovation, the IBM System/38 was *even more so* in operating system software innovation.

Only IBM could have brought this splendid machine to life. In fact, as promised, IBM began shipments in the second half of 1980. In late summer, 1980, the corporation shipped a System/38 to our local IBM Branch Office in Scranton. It was several months before our local customers needed it for final testing of their migrated S/3 programming code. It ran lots cleaner than the test system that I had worked with in the Rochester Labs.

The Scranton Times and Marywood University in Scranton, PA, and St. Joseph's Hospital in Hazleton were to receive the first System/38 shipments from our local Scranton office. I got pretty good as a System/38 expert after my Rochester Minnesota internship.

I also had the good fortune of attending lots of formal classes in Philadelphia including those taught by Don Wickham and Skip Marchesani. Then, to add the graduate level course, there was the substantial time that I was permitted to spend to set up the IBM branch office system and the local customer environments for testing. Later as the customers came in to convert from S/3 to S/38, it was indeed a rarity to behold.

I was privileged to work with the new system as our office prepared local overstretched System/3 Model D customers for their movement to the new IBM System/38. They had been waiting since October 1978 for their new systems, and they were all just about out of "gas." These three Scranton branch office customers received their own systems before the end of 1980 and all three went live with their converted business applications shortly thereafter. It worked and the customers loved it.

The System/38 was like nothing that had come before it. Its architecture and functionality were years ahead of the mainframes at the time. It just happened to be slow compared to the mainframes of the day but it was substantially faster than the System/3 in all of its models. In terms of architecture, just looking at the machine, it was easy to tell that it represented all IBM knew about computers. It was every bit as advanced as the IBM System/360 was advanced for its day.

To protect IBM's mainframe business the IBM Company delivered the System/38 with minimal memory and storage, as well as a slow CPU engine. But, the architecture was futuristic. It was an IBM first, well worthy of supporting IBM's fastest mainframes. It was an industry first. No machine today has yet to catch up with the advanced capabilities of IBM's System/38 from 1978. I am not kidding.

Several years ago I wrote two books about the AS/400, the follow-on IBM product to the System/38. One book was called The All-Everything Machine! The other was called The All-Everything Operating system. Both sold very well. In fact IBM in Italy bought five hundred books the day the first book was made available.

For technology starters, the System/38 used 48-bit hardware instead of the 24 bit processors prevalent in the System/360 and S/370 line of mainframes at the time. Internally, however, through software microcode, the system used a 128-bit addressing scheme, which is still unheard of today.

To make this super addressing work, every System/38 program was compiled into a quasi-machine language state and each program carried around a 128-bit address for each "machine" instruction. Besides the 128-bit address space, what was special about the System/38 was its unprecedented level of integration between the hardware and software.

This integration supported the most advanced computing concepts of the day. In fact, as noted but worth repeating, most of the facilities built into the 1980 System/38 have not yet appeared in IBM's mainframe line and none are in any competitor's machines.

The fact that IBM chose not to highlight this machine gave its competitors an undeserved advantage. That is another of the major reasons why I wrote this book Thank You, IBM. Many billionaires and multi-millionaires out there in tech-land today owe IBM a big thank-you. IBM withheld its best computer system from being its competition-destroyer.

I will repeat this later but to show how powerful the System/38 was in terms of its productivity facilities and advanced architecture, IBM competitors, Apple and Microsoft both used System/38 technology to run their businesses. They both owned a lot more than one IBM System/38. Repeat! They did not use IBM's most powerful systems—the mainframes; they used IBM's most advanced system as it enabled them the flexibility to create the applications needed to drive their businesses.

The IBM System/38, introduced in 1978, took many of IBM's most advanced mainframe notions that it had been saving for its largest systems. IBM Rochester implemented them in a much smaller hardware box as dictated by mother IBM.

The computer industry recognizes System/38 as a direct descendant of the abandoned IBM Future Systems Project, which had been designed as the replacement for the System/360 and System/370 mainframe architectures. Gutless IBM chose never to bring such technology even to its mainframe customers.

As a perspective, the System/z, today's mainframe still does not include the advanced technology notions of the System/38. But, IBM chooses to tell its largest mainframe customers nothing about this very special machine/OS combination now known as the IBM Power System with IBM i. If IBM customers knew about another IBM system being the best, would they run their companies on any other technology?

At a time in which relational database was an unproven concept, the IBM System/38 boasted an integrated (built-in) relational database and a full lunch pail of other high tech goodies, which made it appear as a machine for which to kill. IBM purposely limited its hardware power and capacity as it did not want to "eat its own children," by displacing mainframe units.

Some other advanced notions supported by the System/38 included integrated security through capability based addressing, object-based processing, a high-level machine interface, and single level storage. You may thank me for not explaining these concepts when we meet at a book-signing someplace in the future. However, I do explain these notions in both of my "All-Everything" books.

IBM's S/38 is the best technology and IBM is the best technology company in the universe, because it built the System/38. Too bad IBM cannot get behind its own innovations and bring them to market.

Chapter 15

The AS/400 Comes Invited to the System/38 Party

Three machines in one

In 1988, with the introduction of the AS/400, IBM began to permit the advanced concepts from the IBM System/38 to grow using much faster and more capable hardware. Some think the AS/400 was merely a faster and bigger System/38. In many ways it was. It supported all of System/38 code but it could also run System/36 programs and something called Native AS/400 code. It was three machines in one. Most remember the AS/400 as a more perfect IBM System/38 with the governor removed.

In addition to more capability and facility, as noted, the new AS/400's also ran System/36 programs, basically unchanged. This provided an even broader marketplace for the units. Just now, well into the second decade of the new millennium, are we beginning to see some of the thirty-eight year-old technology firsts introduced in October, 1978, with the System/38.

I would not say they are becoming the rage but they are slowly being explored and then introduced into other products from IBM and IBM's competitors. Still nothing is close to the original capabilities of the first IBM System/38.

IBM continues to enhance the AS/400 heritage product line today on a regular basis but just like the mainframe, the

Company has been changing the name of the AS/400 for quite a number of years.

Specifically, on June 21, 1988 IBM introduced the Application System/400 (dubbed as the AS/400). It was billed as a new family of easy-to-use computers designed for small and intermediate-sized companies. IBM did not tell the world that this machine was more powerful than many of the mainframe boxes being pumped out of the IBM Endicott Plant.

Figure 15-1 IBM AS/400 Line on Announcement Day June 1988

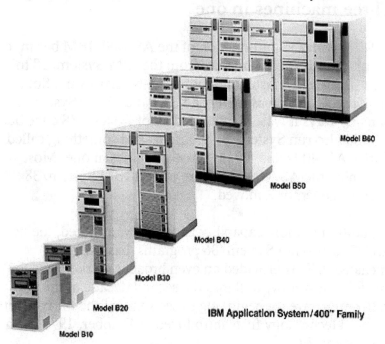

As part of the worldwide introduction of this fantastic machine, as the follow-on to the IBM System/36 and the IBM System/38 lines, IBM and IBM Business Partners worldwide rolled out more than 1,000 software packages in the biggest simultaneous applications announcement in computer history.

The system family consisted of small foot print hardware models as well a large rack configurations with huge power, memory, and storage. So, just like the System/360 announcement 24 years earlier, there were varying sizes and configurations available in the initial offering to suit the expected marketplace.

The AS/400 family line quickly became one of the world's most popular business computing systems. Many suggest that this one time that IBM let the machine loose in the marketplace, it decimated the DEC minicomputer offerings and basically put DEC out of business.

Unfortunately, after the destruction of DEC, IBM began to pull its punches with this phenomenal system. IBM permitted its competition to fight another day when IBM could have delivered a knock-out punch to them all. I must repeat that the companies left in the minicomputer world such as HP, owe IBM a big Thank You. However, IBM stockholders are far less rich because of how IBM managed its technology treasures.

By 1997, IBM had shipped nearly a half-million AS/400s. The 400,000th AS/400 was presented on October 9, 1996, in Rochester, Minnesota to Greg LeMond, the three-time winner of the Tour de France bicycle race. Lemond was also a small business entrepreneur who enjoyed IBM technology solutions.

The AS/400 family was succeeded in 2000 by the IBM eServer iSeries. All follow-on AS/400 products incorporated the one-of-a-kind System/38 exclusives as well as all the enhancements of the AS/400 and follow-on units. iSeries machines were a series of high-performance, integrated business servers for mid-market companies. During the last sixteen plus years the system (AS/400, iSeries, etc.) has continually evolved.

Even before this, IBM was revving up its processor chip technology and the AS/400 team in IBM Rochester, Minnesota chose to use the best of IBM's newest processor chips for its "AS/400 line." And, so the IBM Company made the move to RISC (Reduced Instruction Set Computing) from CISC (Complex Instruction Set Computing) for its "AS/400 type hardware units."

The internal hardware address space was expanded at the same time in 1995 when IBM chose to use the RISC PowerPC RS64 chip, a 64-bit processor. This replaced the System/38 and AS/400 systems' 48-bit CISC processor.

IBM 64-bits and no buts.

The mainframe was still more powerful from a CPU power perspective at the time; but the Company was on a trajectory to create an extremely powerful "AS/400" line of RISC processors that would rival mainframes in power and overall processing capability. IBM always left a few items out of the equation so that mainframe customers would not be motivated to wholesale abandon their systems.

At the time of initial implementation, no other vendor and no other system besides IBM and its RISC based AS/400 system was using 64-bits. IBM had set its lab programmers on a mission to make the operating system transition from CISC to RISC using object oriented coding—the most advanced programming methodology of the day.

Figure 15-2 1996 Computerworld Ad -- AS/400 64-bits. No buts.

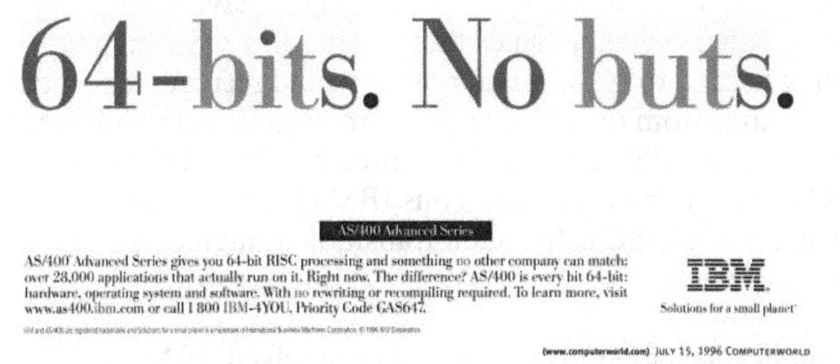

And, so IBM made the transition by rewriting the internal licensed code of the CISC AS/400 using object oriented coding and then deploying the new code as the microcode of the new RISC models. Leaving all of the links in place by design, the operating system was always intended to be able to link to any licensed internal code by using the same high level interfaces built into the operating system from way back in the System/38 days.

IBM proved the concept worked by completely rewriting the lowest level of the OS—that part which spoke to the processor and the machine's disk devices and all other hardware devices and attachment cards. It was like rewriting the BIOS. IBM called this portion licensed internal code whereas technology would label it microcode or firmware or BIOS as on a PC.

IBM did not have to rewrite the other part of the OS known to its compilers and thus to its customer's programmers. Since the high level OS, which gave the machine its personality was already written at the 128-bit level with a high level machine interface, IBM's job was to rewrite the lower level code (microcode) with OO programming facilities and then superimpose the existing AS/400 external OS on top of the resultant machine level microcode.

It simply worked. IBM customers did not have to recompile their source code but since there were some OS changes, they needed to run a program that would recreate the object programs from the existing program objects and relink them to the new RISC OS. IBM had already relinked the new RISC OS to the firmware. Thus IBM clients moving to RISC from CISC called their transition a migration and not a conversion.

Application programmers were not involved. IBM customers did not have to locate their source code. Source code was not involved. Systems programmers made the weekend transition whereas application programmers got a few nights off.

It was nothing like the old source code conversions of the 1950's, 60's, and 70's. And, so, programs written in 1980 for System/38 worked unchanged with the new 1996 RISC-based 64-bit version processors of IBM's newest AS/400 style systems. Microsoft never was able to achieve anything close to that.

IBM's AS/400 customers did prepare themselves for the migration. My role as an AS/400 consultant, at the time, was to make sure their preparations were complete and then I would assure that the migration steps were executed properly and the transition went cleanly as scheduled. The customers merely had to find all of their already compiled code that was running every day. Again, source code was not necessary as the program objects included enough of the source to make the transition.

To move to the new RISC based operating system from the CISC based system, the object code had to be located on the same disk drives that once served the CISC processor. Since the object code held a high level image of the program, not machine specific code, the IBM migration program automatically would locate the object, modify the object, compile it under the covers without concern for its original source language, and then relink it to the new RISC OS.

No other vendor could do that. Yet, IBM was never written up for its advanced migration facilities nor for its advanced architecture that would enable such a transition. It surely was 64-bits and no buts. What once ran on 48-bits—after migration two days later; ran on 64-bits. What ran on a CISC processor—after migration two days later ran on a RISC processor based system. Nobody but IBM could have achieved this technological marvel.

To say this in a different way, to effect the move from CISC to RISC processors, all of the programs ever written by customers had to be migrated via a special IBM supplied program. They would be untouched by human hands; reworked by IBM internal code, and then attached to the RISC processor OS without a rewrite. Amazing? You bet!

Yes, it was quite an achievement but IBM rarely receives the credit it is due from the technology press. IBM's ad at the time said: "64-bits, No Buts!" I know what I have written is somewhat repetitive. It is intentional because this process could never have been accomplished on any other machine.

That's all there was but it took over ten more years from 1995 for any hardware vendor or software vendor to achieve 64-bit technology in an operational, saleable unit. That includes Intel and Bill Gates' Microsoft Windows in all its incarnations on whatever platforms he chose to reinvent Windows.

By the way, it helps to remember that the IBM AS/400 Operating System from System/38 onward was written to emulate 128-bit hardware, which still is not readily available in the marketplace on any system through any operating system. In other words, AS/400 programs carry around a big 128-bit address, which is unbelievable even for big time tech gurus to fathom.

Microsoft code would not survive a migration from Windows 3.11 to Windows 95 or to NT or to any other version. It always needed a full source rewrite.

The big reason behind the development of the IBM PowerPC chips was not the AS/400. In fact there was a time when IBM was selling a derivative of this chip to "power" Apple systems before their deal with Intel. IBM also sold versions of the RISC based power chips for other equipment manufacturers (OEMs) to use in many different applications such as automobiles, trains, planes, and phones. IBM itself used the chip in its Unix based systems.

Since this material about the RISC and Power Systems began in this section (Section II), we continue rather than moving this to Section IV (John Opel) in which most of it was implemented. Why? Because the RISC AS/400 could always run Unix but not as good as Unix systems that used the Power chip. For now, let's move on to Chapter 16 to take a deeper look at IBM's Power Chip and Unix along with some "goodies" that were definitely out there even during the Learson/Cary years.

Chapter 16

IBM merges System i and System p computer lines (AS/400 & RS/6000)

Short history of IBM homemade systems that could run Unix

In 1986, IBM decided it should have a PC that could run Unix, The Pick Operating System, and even something called the Academic Operating System, or AOS. IBM engineers developed great hardware and the labs developed great OS software but marketing in IBM did not understand the Unix-type environment.

The first IBM RISC system was introduced in 1986 as the RT/PC (RISC Technology Personal Computer) and ran AIX 1.x and 2.x, the Academic Operating System (AOS), and the Pick operating system.

Undaunted by its lack of knowledge of the Unix Industry, Big Blue announced a Unix box, dubbed as RT/PC. The box used a first-generation RISC processor that was unique but already too old to be faster than the competition. I went to an IBM Education Center in Texas to learn about AIX and the RT/PC. Because it was not very powerful; the RT/PC was not well received. It was not a big IBM success.

Yet, it was a fine machine other than that it used an older era RISC processor and could not cut it compared to the competition from SUN. It did however give the world a message that IBM was thinking RISC and it was thinking Unix.

Moving along, in February 1990, IBM recognized that the RT/PC was not going to do it for the Company in the RISC / Unix space, and so IBM brought to market the end result of a lot of chip design and system design. IBM announced nine new RISC based workstations called the RS/6000 system family that were at the time, the fastest Unix processors in the industry.

The IBM RS/6000 was very successful with non-traditional IBM customers because it was a superior performer and it ran Unix—their OS of choice. Because it was an IBM developed system with an IBM perfected version of Unix known as IBM's Advanced Interactive Executive, it ran Unix in a bullet-proof, crash-proof fashion. IBM had overnight become the leading Unix vendor both with the RS/6000 and the clean Unix that came from IBM's labs.

The chip designs for the RS/6000 formed the basis for the PowerPC chips and by 1995, the PowerPC chip technology as already discussed reached the AS/400 with its RISC models. So, for a number of years from 1995 on, both the AS/400 and the RS/6000, IBM's two cash-cow midrange systems used the same processor technology.

IBM had this unwritten goal of having the systems that used the same disks, tapes, memory, and processors to be manufactured in the same plant and be able to run each other's OS interchangeably. I do not recall IBM's customers wanting this but IBM was determined to have Power Systems built from these chips all built in the same plant.

IBM chose not to market its midrange systems as the best during this period. The Company concentrated on simply merging the technology. IBM customers did not care about the merge. Whatever IBM saved in hardware costs, it lost in customer loyalty to the systems. RS/6000 machines and AS/400 machines were a world apart despite what IBM planners believed.

Eventually IBM directed Rochester Minnesota to manufacture both systems in the same plant where once just the AS/400 was manufactured. Over time the notion of a consolidation of the hardware product lines was seen as the penultimate for IBM.
Again, let me say that IBM customers cared nothing about this secret IBM goal. Nonetheless RS/6000 hardware was reintroduced as System p, and AS/400 hardware became known as System I, and that was only the first phase of the merge.

Along the way to today, IBM, the premiere chip designer in the industry at the time, and to this day, created what it dubbed the PowerPC Chip, also called the Power Chip. There were variations in the circuits and different software deployed on various versions of this RISC-based IBM designed, developed, and manufactured chip.

Before we move fully on to the facts about the merge, let's get a recap of the AS/400 renaming over the years. From the 1988 machines known simply as AS/400, IBM moved the product name over time to AS/400e, eServer iSeries, eServer i5 running i5/OS, System i5, and finally System i.

The System i was the last hardware box ever produced within the AS/400 line of computers. Today the hardware on what was once the AS/400 model set is called The IBM Power System and the operating system is known simply as IBM i. I never saw any of that name joggling as an advantage to IBM customers.

IBM also merged its RS/6000 (Unix) computers, which in 2008 became known as System p with the System i (AS/400). By the time of the merge, both product lines were already using almost identical hardware. For years both had been using IBM special Power Chip Technology.

By 2008, all of the instructions to support Unix via IBM's Advanced Interactive Executive (AIX), a bona fide 100% Unix OS—both 32-bit and 64-bit versions—were built into the Power Chip. Additionally, IBM packed instructions for i5/0S (OS/400) and some IBM AS/400 business applications into the chip. The chip was a phenomenon itself with plenty of room for personality-altering OS instructions.

There was lots more built into each chip including enabling microcode for advanced functions such as DB2/400, the native free-of-charge AS/400 database. It was indeed an extremely powerful multi-purpose chip. AS/400 heritage customers were not impressed that the chip that powered AS/400 facilities also powered Unix. I suspect Unix aficionados had a similar reaction to the merge. The merge was for IBM and not for IBM's customers.

The AS/400 OS from 2003 was able to support logical partitioning with up to ten guest operating systems even before the merge. IBM's AS/400 heritage line eventually with just one processor could run as an AS/400 in the main partition while running Linux and/or AIX (IBM Unix) in the other partitions.

Thus, in many ways, the IBM desired merge was not really required. However, it certainly took the notion of integrated hardware from the AS/400 line and it confused Unix aficionados. Yet, IBM viewed the merge as a "mission from God." It certainly did not specifically help the AS/400 or the RS/6000 customer base. I keep saying that because it was another IBM blunder that did nothing to sell more systems or promote IBM products. Its impact in fact was the opposite.

IBM formally announces the merged system

In early April 2008, at the COMMON midrange user group conference in Nashville, Tennessee, IBM chose to announce the formal merging of the System i (AS/400) and System p (RS/6000) brands.

Instead of two separate systems the Company created a single IBM Power Systems product line with two models initially for sale. They were known as the Power 520 and Power 550 servers, and were hardware only. By the way Willie Nelson showed up unexpectedly at the Grand Ole Opry while I was at the Conference and sang three of his classic tunes. It was the Conference night that my cohorts Dennis Grimes and Joe McDonald and I went to the Opry.

IBM also announced an operating system for the former AS/400 line and it called it i 6.1 (formerly known as i5/OS V6R1). More than being innovative for a product line known for simplicity, IBM seemed to be making things more complex than necessary with its weird naming ideas. Additionally, IBM seemed to be challenging its AS/400 legacy clients to get on board to the merge history or be declared dumb. This was not an effective marketing strategy for any company. IBM found much more value in this merge than the customers who just lost a product that once had a recognizable name.

IBM over time became more cryptic in naming products and its customers became less forgiving as they could not figure out the function of the product from the product name. That's how it is still shaking out. In addition to the initial models of the non-AS/400 specific Power models, IBM also delivered the top-end 64-core (64-computers in one machine) Power 595 server. It would have been an AS/400 but only those really tuned in would know.

Then, according to top AS/400 and Unix industry analyst Timothy Prickett-Morgan, IBM also did a little product cleanup by merging the formerly distinct System i and System p versions of the System I model 570. Today IBM has simplified its AS/400 heritage operating system. It is known simply as IBM i. In so doing, the Company left a lot of small customers in the dust. They simply were not interested in IBM's naming complexities.

IBM iterations are admittedly hard to follow. I am giving just a sketchy story because this is not supposed to be a hardware or software tech book. The key point in all of this information just discussed is that both the operating systems from the legacy AS/400 and the legacy RS/6000 now run on the same hardware, which is known today as The IBM Power System.

From 2008 on, the System I and the System p no longer exist. In other words, today there is no AS/400 hardware and there is no RS/6000 hardware but their functionality lives on when IBM customers use the IBM Power System with IBM I or AIX / Linux.

If you have had enough of this tech stuff, this is the end for a while. If you want just a bit more, I have a snippet of a piece written at the time in 2008 by my friend Timothy Prickett-Morgan, a great computer industry analyst. This is followed by a small piece that I wrote when all of this was happening to the AS/400 and I did not like it one bit.

The first piece is from a Timothy Prickett-Morgan Report. For novices, in technology, this may be too heavy and not readable right now. If so, skip it and come back someday and read it if you feel inclined. Here is Tim's "snapshot:"

"So now, the entire Power Systems product line has been consolidated down to only a handful of machines. On the commercial processing front, the line includes the Power

520 (up to four cores), the Power 550 (up to eight cores), the Power 570 (up to 16 cores), and the Power 595 (up to 64 cores) in rack or tower configurations; the product line also includes the dual-core JS12 blade server and the quad-core JS22 blade server. All use variants of the Power6 processor, and all of machines support i5/OS V5R4 or i 6.1, AIX 5.3 or 6.1, and Linux 2.6 from Red Hat and Novell.

"On the technical computing front, customers can use any of those above-mentioned servers, but they also can deploy QS21 Cell-based blade servers (which support Linux), Blue Gene/L massively parallel machines (which also run Linux, too), and the 32-core Power 575 behemoth (which was launched last week as well and which supports AIX and Linux)..."

Goodbye, AS/400, Old Friend by Brian Kelly

I wrote a piece for IT Jungle about my reaction to no longer having an easily identifiable IBM midrange product with which to work. When all this was happening, my emotions got the best of me as I am a long term AS/400 aficionado, and I happen to love the legacy and the capabilities of the AS/400. Just like my recommendation for Tim's technical summary, I would recommend the same for my nostalgic look back at the AS/400 when it was also a hardware box.

If you like the technology, you should like my short analysis below. If you are a non-IT guy, please skip this little ditty. I originally wrote this piece for IT Jungle and it was published on April 7, 2008 at the time of the merge. You may like it. Tim is the editor of IT Jungle and he keeps the whole library of articles alive so if you want to read the whole article (it is long) put the title in your browser and you can read the entire piece.

Goodbye, AS/400, Old Friend
http://www.itjungle.com/tfh/tfh040708-story05.html
Published: April 7, 2008

By Brian Kelly

"The AS/400 is dead. Long live the AS/400. This phrase as associated with my favorite "midrange system" has changed over the years to meet the many successor systems that IBM has put forth to replace our good ole AS/400. In fact, even before the litany of replacement systems, the AS/400 itself was involved in a replacement act of its own when it was brought forth to succeed both the System/38 and the System/36. As we in this "AS/400 community" well know, nothing was and nothing will ever be as revolutionary to the world of computing as the System/38 in its day, even if we choose to call it an AS/400 or something else.

The System i, also known as our beloved AS/400, today [2008] is nothing more than an operating system. IBM would like us to see the new physical incarnation of the AS/400 in its new IBM Power System line. But, it isn't there. The System p has been able to run the i5/OS operating system for quite some time. It still can, but now with no holds barred.

There is no new System i. IBM this week chose to remove the identity of the AS/400. It no longer exists under any name. Get used to it. Our old friend is gone. Besides AIX and Linux, these new Power 520, 550, and 570 servers also run a proprietary operating system known as IBM i.

This fact enables it to run your workloads, almost as if your workloads are being re-hosted on a non-AS/400. Well, at least emotionally.

All of this is unsettling for me and for those of us who think a combination of box and identity removal is not the best way to highlight our favorite machine. Overall, it is a good time for IBM since its 25-year homogenization goal is all but accomplished. While I continue to digest the implications of last week's news, I thought I would sit down and put together a little piece of documentation about the good friend I remember so well. Goodbye, AS/400, old friend."

Now, don't say anything or I'll get emotional. That is all there is on this article in this book. To read more, take the link above in the title. For now, this is the end...

The place where great ideas once were permitted to grow

The IBM Plant in Rochester, Minnesota, first opened its doors in 1956 and later it shipped its first product, the IBM 077 numeric collator. By 1957, the plant began pounding out other electro-mechanical units, such as the IBM 514 Reproducing Punch and the IBM 523 Gang Summary Punch. You see, in the 1950s, there were no Rochester Labs creating the most sophisticated operating system software in the world. There was the beginnings of a plant complex that was designed to build huge electromechanical units, each of which existed on a diet of lots more than 100 boxes of 80-column punch cards every day. In 2016, the Plant is for sale.

IBM's mainframe bias kept the Company from staying number one!

FYI, HP is now number one in the non-phone, non-pad technology business but this changes from time to time. Apple of course is the leading producer of computer-driven electronics as it now exceeds $200 billion in revenue per year. IBM checks in at $92.7 billion and its revenue is sliding downwards.

In this book, my mission is to discuss those who have benefitted by IBM's choosing not to play its best systems' hands for all they are worth. This is IBM's legacy: marketing programs that eliminate its own best products and focus on low-lying fruit and cash cow opportunities.

Those who look at the inner strengths of the AS/400 system as a simple example, especially its unprecedented elegance and functionality cannot believe that IBM let Microsoft, Intel, HP, Sun, Oracle, and many others kick its pants in areas in which the AS/400 would have saved the day one way or another. As previously noted, within a short while

after announcement, IBM destroyed DEC with the AS/400;
then IBM went to sleep again.

Without getting technical at all, I can explain why IBM lost
and continues to lose. In the AS/400 arena, as a technical
corporation, IBM, dominated by politically correct
mainframe executives at the corporate level dislikes its very
own AS/400 product line. Why? It is simply because the
AS/400 was not invented by IBM elites in Endicott or
Poughkeepsie.

Yet, these same elites did not descend on Apple or
Microsoft to sell them a mainframe computer to run their
business. Instead, they permitted GSD sales personnel,
without mainframe technology in their sales kit, to offer the
System/38 and then the AS/400 to both Apple and
Microsoft so they could more effectively run their complete
businesses.

When Bill Gates decided that his Windows servers should
be able to take on AS/400s in the marketplace, IBM reacted
like duds as usual and did not refute Gates' claims. After all,
Gates' company was running on IBM AS/400 technology.
How about that? Politically correct IBM would not even
speak up for itself.

Yet, Bill Gates, when he decided to crush IBM in the small
business marketplace had forgotten that he was not using his
own server technology for his own business needs. IBM
chose not to remind him or anybody else in the industry
even though it would have helped IBM sales v Windows
solutions. Why was Bill Gates predestined to win? Answer:
After the Watsons, IBM was always ready to back down
from a fight

It took years for Microsoft to make the transition of their
business software to Windows Servers from the AS/400
line. Along the way, it was often reported that Microsoft

opted to use a secret service bureau running AS/400s rather than continue with their own AS/400 in-house processing to get their work done. So, they hired others to run their business software and take over their daily operations.

Microsoft never denied that the systems used by the secret service bureau were AS/400s. So, why could IBM not have made a killing on an IBM system that Bill Gates and Steven Jobs both used to run their companies? After all, both would have liked all businesses across the globe to buy their systems rather than anything from IBM?

Why could IBM not have ruled the entire computer industry with a computer that could scale from a desktop to a mainframe and make life easier for all businesses across the globe? From my eyes, it is part of a mainframe myopia that IBM still seems to have even today when software and services provide the bulk of the revenue. It is manifested by the Company divesting its product lines because they do not bring in enough profits? What will IBM do when all divisions are sold and nothing is on the shelf?

Chapter 17

Thomas Watson Jr. Steps Down as Chairman and CEO

Learson was CEO for about two years

In 1971, just two years after the introduction of the System/3, and two years after I joined the Company, Thomas J. Watson Jr. suffered a heart attack and subsequently stepped down as Chairman and CEO. He was succeeded by T. Vincent Learson, a long-time Watson supporter and extremely loyal IBM executive.

At this time, IBM informally began the tradition of CEOs leaving the chairmanship at age 60. Learson, who was 58 at the time of his leadership assumption, dutifully turned the reins over to Frank T. Cary when he turned sixty in 1973.

Tom Watson Jr. continued his public and business life after IBM retirement. He was appointed U.S. ambassador to the Soviet Union. He served there from 1979 to 1981. He remained a member of IBM's board of directors until he resigned from the post in1984. Thomas Watson, Jr. died on December 31, 1993, shortly before his 80th birthday

When Lou Gerstner took over for John Akers in 1993, Tom Watson Jr. picked him up at the airport for his first day of work. Watson wanted Gerstner to know how precious IBM was to so many people. Many of us who were once on the IBM active team are so glad that Louis V. Gerstner Jr. got

that pep talk. He worked hard to pull IBM out of the gutter
in which the Company had been placed by the John Opel
and John Akers duo. Thanks Lou! I know many IBMers
appreciate your good work.

Re: Thomas Watson, Jr. from IBM's Archives:

*Immediately after Tom Watson, Jr.'s death on December 31,
1993, the IBM employee publication Think published a final
remembrance of the man entitled "Corporate Legend, True Human
Being," written by Ames Nelson, in its January-February 1994
issue. The following is the text of that article.*

*Called the "most successful capitalist who ever lived" by Fortune
magazine and named one of the 25 people "who changed the
world" by Computerworld, Thomas J. Watson, Jr., transformed
IBM into the model of the modern multinational corporation.
Commented Le Monde in Paris, "He made the Company into a
formidable technological and especially commercial engine, and
gave IBM its international dimension."*

*He was born the year his father became president of a small firm
that later would become International Business Machines
Corporation, and he died December 31, 1993, shortly before his
80th birthday.*

*As IBM's chief executive between 1956 and 1971, Watson had the
insight to recognize the profound change electronics could bring to
industry and then champion the change needed to make his own
company the leader in the computer industry it spawned. "I knew
in my gut," he later said, "we had to get into computers even
though they seemed like another kind of animal." In the mid-'50s
it was not at all clear IBM would succeed in its transition from
typewriters and punched-card tabulators to transistors and
integrated circuits. But Watson boosted the Company's R&D
budget, hired thousands of engineers, and embarked on projects
that tested the limits of computing know-how.*

*He was best known for his landmark decision to develop the
System/360 "the most influential computer system the world has
known, until the personal computer," according to The Economist*

of London. The all-purpose family of computers made existing machines (IBM's included) obsolete almost overnight when introduced in 1964.

A Leading Innovator
Even before that, Watson was acknowledged as a leading innovator in American enterprise. In a 1963 cover story, Business Week described IBM as "a vastly different company in product mix, in production technology, in management structure" since he had taken over.

If Watson was visionary about the potential of technology, he was equally in the vanguard concerning social issues. He abolished the hourly wage in IBM, introduced tuition loans and pioneered matching grants for charities. As an industry spokesman and public servant in various posts for several U.S. presidents, he advocated federal aid for the impoverished, better national health care and nuclear disarmament.

A fiercely competitive business leader, Watson also carried his taste for challenge into private life. He was a seasoned yachtsman, a superb skier and a passionate pilot of all manner of machines from biplanes and gliders to helicopters and private jets.

At a memorial service shortly after his death, friends and colleagues remembered Watson with admiration and affection. Former U.S. Secretary of State Cyrus Vance praised Watson's belief in the "social and humanitarian responsibility business must carry." and cited Watson's "gift to brush aside the irrelevant and get to the core" of an issue.

"He was a critical lover and loving critic" of his alma mater, remembered Brown University President Vartan Gregorian, as he vividly recalled an "extraordinary man -- passionate, humorous, hot-tempered, curious, generous ... and a ruthless competitor who valued integrity and perseverance.

Said retired broadcaster Walter Cronkite, "Tom was a sailor -- he was a great sailor." His passion for adventure and the unknown was an "expression of the man [and] the enthusiasm he brought to everything he touched." And, in a fond recollection of the man he knew as "Skipper." grandson T. William Watson said: "He always tried to get to places he wasn't supposed to go. "

[Think Magazine continued] --- What Legends Are Made Of

Watson's character and convictions left indelible impressions on thousands of IBM employees, as well, from the board room to the branch office. Said former IBM Chairman Frank Cary: "He urged everyone to bring their ideas forward to improve the business, and his instincts always favored the regular employee. "

Bonnie Greer, operations support manager for the Connecticut Central Trading Area, would agree: "I went to New Managers' School last March and Mr. Watson paid us a surprise visit. I don't ever remember being star-struck at the sight of someone ... [but] his presence was captivating.

"He spoke to us with a down-to-earth quality as if he were one among us. His wisdom was simple and humorous, and I thought how easily he drew the room into realizing an immense leader is also a true human being. "He was what corporate legends are made of ... and remembered for. "

On January 5, 1994, IBM memorialized Watson Jr. with a full page advertisement in the Wall Street Journal (Figures 17-1 & 17-2). My good friend John Anstett, who lives across the street knows my devotion to the good parts of IBM, which include the Watson legacy. He brought over the Wall Street Journal page when he read it, and I framed it and I have it hanging in my Sunroom, where it still stands today. The text of this ad, under a distinguished picture of the former IBM Chairman, captures the essence of the man:

Figure 17-1 Wall Street Journal Watson Tribute Text Jan 5, 1984

Thomas Watson Jr.

1914 - 1993

For all his achievements—
as visionary, entrepreneur, corporate leader,
and distinguished statesman—
we will remember Thomas J. Watson Jr. most
for his adventurous spirit,
his innate sense of fair play, and the vigor of his friendship.
We mourn his passing, but
we will forever be grateful that he lived.

This picture hangs in my Sun Room to this day. I am honored to have the Chairman in my favorite room.

Figure 17-2 Wall Street Journal Tribute to Thomas Watson, Jr.

When Tom Watson Jr. stepped down from all IBM duties in 1984, the era of Watson leadership and Watson guidance had come to an end for IBM. There are many former IBMers and many others who believe that IBM's best chances of returning to its former greatness as a company may very well be a return to the Watson instilled beliefs which inspired this posthumous tribute. From Watson's perspective, everybody was important, from customers to employees, to the families of employees. I know I felt a difference within IBM, from the day Thomas J. Watson Jr. retired.

Section III

T. Vincent Learson and Frank T. Cary Move IBM Past the Watsons

CEO Learson was not around too long but in his time, he honored the Watson tradition. Frank Cary succeeded Learson and he was the CEO whose mission it was to handle mainframe competition from the BUNCH and the competition from a group of independents known as minicomputer vendors.

Frank Cary was also the CEO who saw all the micros including the Altair, Radio Shack TRS-80, Apple II, and a host of chip makers such as Motorola, TI, Intel and others grow up in the midst of IBM's mainframe orientation. In Cary's later years as CEO, these would form the basis for the PC revolution. Thus in Frank Cary's day job, he worked tirelessly to defeat IBM mainframe competition; and then he struggled against the upstart minicomputer vendors that had become real competition. Meanwhile microcomputers were coming of age and getting more capable and more powerful each year. Frank Cary was there for it all.

Cary noticed when Digital Equipment Corporation (DEC) invented the minicomputer that IBM's small system competition began to make itself well known. These vendors were confident that IBM would not retaliate as the Company was worried more about the government than the new minicomputer industry. DEC quickly became the leading minicomputer vendor of the day. Despite their prominence in the marketplace, it took many years for IBM to even acknowledge the existence of minicomputers, and years after that to create a real minicomputer itself.

DEC got its start in Maynard Massachusetts with the Programmed Data Processor 1 (PDP 1). Then, it built the first "Minicomputer" - The DEC PDP-8. Eventually DEC got very sophisticated with its Alpha and of course its VAX's and its Unix derivative, VMS

William Hewlett and David Packard found too many opportunities for Hewlett-Packard to not take its computer expertise into the minicomputer arena. Along the way, HP became the unquestioned leader in inkjet and laser printers for small computers. Then, when CEO Carly Fiorina thought that it was the right time, HP merged with Compaq, then a PC clone leader.

Data General came along as a minicomputer-only company with its DG Nova, and ultimately its sophisticated NUMA architecture. Soon after DG was successful, EMC, who had been beating IBM to a pulp in the disk business, used its excess cash to buy DG and by default, EMC had entered the minicomputer marketplace. IBM and EMC were hard-nosed competitors but EMC had the hardest nose as it beat IBM in the disk technology game even though IBM had created the game with its 305 RAMAC in the 1950's. EMC and IBM were storage nemeses but eventually EMC prevailed as did most competitors who took on IBM after the Watsons.

Recognizing the existence of minicomputers a bit late, IBM introduced its Series/1 as a minicomputer but forgot a few things such as an operating system and necessary software.

During the microcomputer revolution, Texas Instruments became a micro technology pioneer and they were eternal Innovators. Their guy, Jack Kilby, invented the integrated circuit along with Robert Noyce from Intel to enable a host of creative developments from the microcomputer world.

Shockley Semiconductor, a pioneering company, hired many of the industries bests for its new semiconductor company but could not keep them interested. So, a number went to Fairchild Semiconductor. Shockley was really upset and called them *the traitorous eight.*

Motorola had been around for a while doing great things for the armed services and making sure those motor radios (Motorola) were quality units. The 1950 generation automobiles played sweet, sweet, music. Motorola eventually made a chip that Apple loved for its Apple I and Apple II PCs but MOS Technologies could make the same thing a lot cheaper so the Woz and Jobs went with MOS for its Apple I and Apple II units.

Some of the traitorous eight founded Intel and created the Intel 4004, the world's first microprocessor. Of course nobody really knows what IBM had in its research labs. IBM simply did not tell anybody but it always had a lot of groundbreaking technology that it never released. In retrospect, this was a definite flaw in IBM strategy.

Zilog became another microcomputer pioneer. MOS technologies got acquired by Commodore and for the longest time supplied chips to Apple.

Chips alone do not make microcomputers spin in people's homes. Before the IBM PC, Radio Shack had put out the world's first personal computer. Of course Jobs' & Wozniak's Apple piqued the home computerist in us all.

Apple was founded by a couple of regular guys, who just happened to be geniuses. Woz (Steve Wozniak) was an electronics "nut." Jobs' MO was to surface, go under, resurface; then go back under, and then resurface. The Apple I, is a product of iterative design that was sold to the money people by Jobs and built by the "Woz." The Seeds of the Apple organization began with the Home Brew

Computer Club and the rest is history. Apple now brings in more revenue than any other technology company.

Meanwhile technology was erupting all over the place, not just in the microcomputer arena. For example, IBM invented hierarchical databases and made lots of money on them.

While taking money to the bank from its hierarchical database products, IBM's Ted Codd invented Relational Database Management Systems (RDBMS). Unfortunately, IBM did not want to sell Codd's invention because its hierarchical style database products were still selling very well. Big Blue would risk losing tons of dollars of revenue from its customers if it were forced to cancel its huge stable of hierarchical DB software licenses. So, for many years IBM sat on relational technology while Ted Codd the IBM inventor got more and more frustrated.

Larry Ellison and a few other gurus read Ted Codd's thesis on RDBMS and knew they could make it work while IBM was still sitting on its hands. Oracle did it and had great success with IBM's relational database ideas. Ellison is now the world's # 3 richest person. How much did IBM lose on that bungle?

Oracle beat IBM to market in relational database. Oracle V2 became the first commercial relational database. When it finally woke up, IBM began working overtime to surpass Oracle in RDMS technology after not caring.

Let me say it one more time. Larry Ellison, Oracle's major founder and company sustainer is # 3 on the richest man in the world list at $54 billion net worth. This was all IBM's if it had only listened to Ted Codd. IBM has nobody on the rich list.

IBM, the Company that coined the term teleprocessing forgot that it owned this industry. Big Blue did not even see it as an industry. The Data Communications industry was also all IBM's. In the early days, IBM invented all parts of the solution. Big Blue had the technology but it had little marketing vision.

IBM cared more about mainframes communicating with mainframes and though it was the leader in data communications since it was the next logical step after card readers and printers, IBM lost. Big Blue gave up its edge in modems and LANS, routers, switches, hubs, and whatever its customers wanted—including TCP/IP, the protocol of the Internet. Then there was a company named CISCO that cared about all of the things IBM had forgotten to pay attention to in the data communications / networking area. And. so in teleprocessing, IBM's term for all forms of networking, IBM had the crying towel handed to it by Cisco. Stockholders should be weeping.

Chapter 18

Starting with Learson

Learson loved the Watsons and IBM

T. Vincent Learson's facial characteristics still remind me of
Vincent Price the melodramatic actor who died in 1993 at
the age of 82. Learson, a Harvard mathematics major, was
the first chairman who was not a Watson. He was more
than not a Watson. He was a path maker in IBM and his
work helped the success of the Company's gamble on a new
generation of computers in the early 1960's. It was a $5
billon dollar gamble and as a major proponent and
implementer of the project, Learson helped insure IBM's
prosperity for two decades.

Like the successful people at IBM, Learson had a "blue
ticket," and as such he rose through the ranks in sales,
marketing and management jobs. Unlike most blue ticket
holders in IBM, Learson, the ultimate student in the
executive resources program took it all the way to becoming
chairman and chief executive officer for two years starting in
1971, when Watson Jr. retired.

In two years, Learson did not gain much of a CEO legacy at
IBM but IBM maintained its leadership during his short
tenure. More importantly, T.V. had already had his day
before this, helping Thomas Watson Jr. as a trusted aide to
make the right decisions. Learson is well known for pushing

for the development of the IBM 360 mainframe computer.
What a legacy!

Watson, with Learson at his side, according to Fortune
Magazine, moved forward on a project that was "the most
crucial and portentous—as well as perhaps the riskiest—
business judgment of recent times." Watson was not short of
praise for Learson and his ascension to the top spot in the
Company is proof of that. If you have read Watson's
autobiography, "Father, Son & Co.," published in 1990 by
Bantam, you can see Mr. Watson's admiration as he
described T. Vincent Learson as "the father of our new line."

Learson's physical characteristics were very imposing. He
was a tall man at six feet, six inches tall. Vincent Price was
six feet four inches tall so there is that resemblance again.
Unlike the smooth talking Price, Learson is said, by those
who knew him best to have been very blunt.

In a final NY Times column on his life, the writer quoted
Thomas Watson Jr.'s take on how Learson was a very
imposing man: "He was 6 feet 6 inches tall, and his mere
presence in a room was enough to get people's attention."
Surely T.J. Watson, Jr. enjoyed writing that about his friend
in his autobiography as he liked and respected the first
chairman after a Watson.

And, so, in summary, it was not Learson's superior
achievements as IBM Chairman that has become his legacy.
Instead, it is the work he did to deserve the chair from
Watson's eyes. By the time TVL assumed the IBM Chair in
1971, he presided over a vast, immensely profitable
enterprise. It was his decisions that would keep IBM the
same, make it less, or make it more. Learson was well aware
of his possibilities. Like his major mentor, T.J. Watson, Jr.,
he ran the Company with an open-door management style.
He recognized IBM's size advantage and he is not known to

have pushed for a bigger IBM. Learson knew that simply being a big company did not make IBM a great company.

He was a true IBMer and he wanted the best for IBM. He loved IBM and he loved being part of IBM for all of his career as most IBMers once did. He was around for such a short time as CEO that either Watson or Cary received credit in the history books for the major achievements of the era in which he presided. It would not matter to Learson as long as IBM got credit. Nobody can say that T. Vincent Learson did not provide a fine transition from Watson management to non-Watson management. He was a good guy!

Chapter 19

Frank Cary, the Mainframe, Mini, and Micro CEO

Frank Cary was successful at IBM

As I look back upon my own career with IBM and I think about who ran the Company during those times, I would suggest that based on how he reacted to IBM challenges in a very challenging time, Frank Cary would go down in IBM history as having the most successful career of all IBM CEOs after Watson. Cary managed well and kept IBM financially stable while enabling the Company to go after many new marketplaces regardless of the pressure of US government interference. The next two CEOs were 100 pound weaklings compared with Cary

Mr. Cary took over as I.B.M.'s chief executive spot on Jan. 1, 1973, three months after T. Vincent Learson, his 60-year-old predecessor, tendered his resignation as Chair.

I.B.M. had clearly flourished under the control of Thomas J. Watson and his son, Thomas J. Watson Jr. At a minimum, during his tenure, Mr. Learson kept the Company intact and ready for another non-Watson CEO without giving them a burden to carry. The job of moving IBM forward was left largely to Mr. Cary. He set the agenda in the post-Watson era.

Litigation, especially antitrust lawsuits, was a constant threat to IBM during Mr. Cary's tenure. IBM's board had a tough time thinking about opportunities with the government threatening the Company's very existence. Yet, the job of the CEO, though surely to recognize and minimize risk, is mostly known for recognizing and maximizing opportunity.

History shows that a government antitrust action of the 1970's was aimed to split IBM into many companies. This action began in 1969, when I joined the Company and it dragged on until the Justice Department abruptly dropped their complaint in 1982. IBM was a great competitor but was ordered to not compete by the US government. This is the only excuse for IBM's bad behavior in a number of its marketing opportunities.

We all know that Bill Gates basically ran roughshod over the Justice Department's case v Microsoft. Ironically, having watched Microsoft as a player in the industry, the government's case against Bill Gates was actually much more timid than Microsoft's downright nasty actions against its competitors.

IBM was almost always more concerned about its survival after a successful government action than it was about competing against those who hoped to take away all of its customers. In many ways if the government nailed IBM, its customers would win but if IBM's customers won because IBM chose to be inept, IBM would win its case against the government. Neither option was good but IBM, unlike Microsoft, decided to let it all happen. IBM lost its chutzpah and ultimately it lost its stake in many markets that it had started and owned. IBM had to work very hard to give up so many opportunities.

In the 1970's the government threatened the very being of IBM. In essence it threatened IBM with extinction or worse as Cary feared the government would break the Company into many small parts. Many private patent and antitrust cases also plagued the IBM Company at this time. Frank Cary felt strongly that IBM was a just and fair competitor and he knew the Company needed to fight in court to maintain its freedom to compete effectively. As an IBM employee, I know all employees were always counseled about competing fairly.

"He endured hundreds of days of depositions," noted John R. Opel, who succeeded Mr. Cary in 1981 as its chief executive and in 1983 as IBM's chairman. Opel was amazed as are most human beings that IBM was inhibited from competing merely by the imposition of court actions. Cary carried a huge burden to be successful as a chairman, and to fight for the Company to not be adversely affected by a nasty business-hating government. Does this sound familiar to the current situation with government? Few can objectively suggest that government is a friend of business today.

Mr. Cary used IBM's precious capital reserves to fight competitors and to fight a government that wanted to dissolve the Company. The Japanese were whacking the American car industry, TV and radio industries, and anything else where they saw a weakness. When the government of the US was trying to inhibit its US companies from competing, the Japanese and others took the advantage. IBM knew the government was not its friend but at this time hundreds of great US companies were forced by government policies to do less than fully compete against the foreign company "invasion."

Cary could not ignore the government but he could also not ignore what was best for IBM and best for America. This Chairman presided over heavy investments to help make IBM an even more efficient manufacturer in response to Japanese imports and the rise of manufacturers like Amdahl. This competitor, founded by the very same Gene Amdahl who had "invented" the System/360 for IBM in 1964, sold IBM-compatible mainframe computers at cheaper prices.

To help win against the mainframe competition, coincidental with its huge mainframe line, manufactured in Poughkeepsie, IBM also developed a highly successful range of midsize mainframe computers known as the 4300 series in the mid-1970's. These were more costly and more powerful than the Rochester built System/3 family of machines. They were designed with mainframe architectures and used mainframe operating systems to attract companies that were predisposed to mainframe processing and / or mainframe applications. The 4300 series was manufactured in Endicott, NY.

Mr. Cary also pursued a number of ventures that failed to prosper, including I.B.M.'s effort to overtake Xerox in copiers. He also focused major investments in satellite communications—aka Satellite Business Systems (SBS.) Both of these ventures were unsuccessful.

One time in early 1980, I interviewed with SBS in Reston Virginia while I was employed at IBM. From what I saw, SBS had a solid game plan, but the market was so far into the future that IBM could not collect any revenue until the market came forth. Sometimes waiting for revenue is the proper approach. IBM instead sold SBS to MCI and others made the profits destined for IBM's coffers without feeling the need to say Thank You, IBM.

IBM's first personal computer, a project initiated by Frank Cary, which took market leadership away from Apple Computer at the time, reached retail stores in August 1981, the year that Mr. Opel took over. But the product's popularity did not turn it into a long-term moneymaker for IBM as Big Blue never managed this business to gain its ultimate potential.

Through the 1970's until the end of Frank Cary's watch, when he stepped down in 1981, I.B.M. had doubled its revenue and profit, yet, despite this superlative performance IBM's stock had lost its reputation for high growth. Some think it was the looming government anti-trust suit that kept stock prices depressed. I think it was poor execution by IBM's top management.

Chapter 20

Digital Equipment Corporation Invents the Minicomputer

IBM's competition made itself known

As noted in previous chapters, T. Vincent Learson was not around for very long to be noticed by the history of computing. However, Frank Cary's tenure was filled with adventure. IBM found itself in a number of new marketplaces, and there was no shortage of excellent ideas and projects within IBM. New competitors seemed to continually emerge from the shadows, and Frank Cary's IBM dealt with them as they should be dealt—as competitors.

In the very late 1960s and early 1970's, a number of startup companies had emerged as competitors of IBM, but in a completely different way. This period predated the home computer revolution. The companies called the computers they made minicomputers, but for little machines, they were capable of doing quite a bit of work.

Unlike the original BUNCH (Burroughs, Univac, NCR, Control Data, and Honeywell), GE and RCA, who competed directly with IBM in the mainframe arena, this group did not have large computers in their bag of tricks. Thus, they typically marketed to small companies and departments of large companies. To make their sales, they used the same successful techniques which PC vendors, ten years later, would use to get around the MIS hierarchy in their customer accounts.

These companies included Data General (DG), Digital Equipment (DEC), Hewlett Packard, Prime, and Wang. They built strong product lines and became formidable IBM foes. Though minicomputers operated best in a scientific environment, and real time, such as in the control of traffic signals, they were morphed enough to become reasonably capable business machines. During this time, Bell Labs perfected the original Unix Operating System (OS), and eventually most of the minicomputer vendors began to offer their systems with a Unix OS option.

DEC was the leading minicomputer vendor

Let's take a look at Digital Equipment Corporation (DEC and later DIGITAL), one-time American manufacturer of high technology products. DEC had heretofore created a new line of low-cost computers, known as minicomputers. These units were especially useful for laboratories and research institutions but were so inexpensive for the 1950's that they soon were adapted for general business data processing purposes.

The DEC Company had been founded in 1957 by Kenneth Olsen and Harlan Anderson. Both were electronics engineers at the Massachusetts Institute of Technology (MIT). The Company employed more than 140,000 people worldwide at its peak in 1990 and it had earned more than $14 billion in revenue. It was bought out by Compaq Computer Corporation in 1998.

Both Olsen and Anderson became multimillionaires, and though they clearly did their own thing with no IBM help, they both owe a big thank you to IBM because Big Blue let them alone to be successful, when it could have simply crushed them.

IBM already had better technology for small computers but did not release it because it feared the notion of "eating one's own children" might eat away IBM's vaunted mainframes. Moreover, because of the anti-trust action, IBM was concerned about dominating all computing sub-markets.

Each time IBM felt this way, I surmise that if they had spun off a new company instead of becoming soldiers without weapons, IBM today would be pulling in sales of about $500 billion per year instead of trying to reach $100 billion again. Despite what might have been, IBM has dipped far below the $100 billion line which they had been seeking for over thirty years.

Olsen, a multi-millionaire in an era where there were far fewer such wealthy entrepreneurs than there are today, was known to drive a modest car around town and do his own grocery shopping. He also had a plain office for a man who controlled so much possibilities. In February, 2011, Ken Olson passed away at 84 years of age.

When Harlan Anderson, Olsen's co-founder, turned 80, he wrote some memoirs. As noted, with Ken Olsen in the drivers' seat, Anderson and Olsen founded Digital Equipment Corp. With Harvard and MIT on opposite ends of the city and a lively Square in between, lots of great things happen in Cambridge Massachusetts every day. DEC was one of these circumstances.

There was this notion of a Route 128 era in Massachusetts at the time, and DEC became one of the pillars of this era. At one point, the Company could honestly claim being the second-biggest technology company in the world.

DEC gets its start in Maynard Massachusetts

As the DEC story goes, back in August, 1957, the Company got its start in an old woolen mill in Maynard, Massachusetts. While IBM was busy selling its innovative 650 line of mainframe computers, improving its RAMAC ground-breaking disk technology, and preparing for its transistorized computer lines, the seeds of a new computer world were being planted by Ken Olsen and Harlan Anderson as they founded the Digital Equipment Corporation and set up shop.

IBM would actually be able to decommission its 650, the RAMAC, and the whole transistorized product lines, - 1400, 1620, and 7000 series, and be well immersed into the System/360 before Big Blue actually chose to pay any attention to Olsen and company. In hindsight, they should have looked over their shoulder a lot sooner.

IBM was surely the last thing on Ken Olsen's mind, as he and Anderson were able to ship their first products—laboratory modules. By February, 1958, they were shipping systems modules which were used for computers, memory testers and other complex systems of logic. In July, by the end of the Company's first fiscal year, they had sold almost $100,000 worth of modules and beefed up the Company's workforce to 60 employees. Though they were not selling computers, they were certainly in the "computer" business.

The Programmed Data Processor 1 (PDP 1)

By August, 1959, just two years after the Company began operations, they hired a bright, young hardware engineer named Ben Gurley to design their first computer, the Programmed Data Processor 1 (PDP 1). Unlike the six years it took to build the Mark I, within three and a half months, the prototype Programmed Data Processor 1 (PDP 1) was complete and was demoed at a conference in Boston which was being held in proximity of the "old mill."

Olsen's Digital, never stopped at tubes along the way to building their first, solid state, general purpose computer. The PDP-1, as the precursor to the minicomputer was built with transistors, and was instantly as technologically advanced as the IBM units of the day. A reasonably large machine, somewhat more like a mainframe than a mini, DEC was able to build and ship about 50 of them.

The PDP-1 sold for $120,000 and it came with a cathode ray tube display. The PDP-1 was one of the first machines to operate at room temperature - no air conditioning required. Another unique attribute of this new system compared to mainframes was that the unit needed just one operator.

More and more models

DEC seemed to like the computer business. They kept building new and different machines. They had a major penchant for making the boxes smaller, and more affordable. Meanwhile over in the IBM labs, the big decisions were whether to use water or air to cool the big monsters, which were on the drawing boards. IBM had blocked the notion of small computers from their revenue planning charts. All planning charts at the time seemed to originate in Poughkeepsie New York, home of IBM's largest mainframes. DEC benefitted immensely from IBM's mainframe myopia.

In July, 1961, Gordon Bell, another famous Digital engineer, who was in Microsoft Research Labs until his death in 2007, designed the PDP-4, Digital's second 18-bit computer. The unit began shipping in July, 1962. Bell was at it again before the end of the year when he began the design work on the architecture of the PDP-5, DEC's first 12-bit computer. This was announced in 1963. Gordon Bell worked very hard to attain millionaire status by the time of his death. Thank you, IBM.

In 1964, just four months after IBM had introduced its System/360 family of mainframes, Digital again introduced a new machine - the PDP-6. This was their first 36-bit computer. In December they introduced another 18-bit computer - their third. This was known as the PDP-7. IBM was not paying attention and did not seem to notice the existence of DEC in the marketplace.

The first "minicomputer" - the DEC PDP-8

In April, 1965, just one year after IBM introduced the family notion (360) as well as third generation hardware in mainframes, DEC raised the notch again with even smaller systems. This new unit, called the PDP-8, gets credit for being the world's first mass-produced, commercially successful minicomputer system.

Figure 20-1 DEC PDP-8 the First Minicomputer

The PDP-8 cost about $18,000, which was substantially less than the just-under six figure price of a small System/360 mainframe. Because of the affordable price, and the small size and low environmental needs of the PDP-8, manufacturing plants, small businesses, and scientific laboratories brought them in by the thousands. DEC was off and running, and would continue to be a major thorn in IBM's side until the 1988 introduction of the "DEC-Killer" machine, IBM's always unsung soldier, the AS/400.

Thus, DEC is credited with establishing the "minicomputer" industry, a term coined by Digital, though some suggest the name came about as the miniskirt was becoming very popular. The term "mini" computer seemed to fit the times. The PDP-8 positioned DEC at the top of the pack in this new minicomputer industry. It was technologically sound, and capitalized on the existing solid state "not-yet chip" technology.

Though it took some time to achieve all of the features which minicomputers are historically credited to possess, as time went on, these machines became very feature rich. In addition to the ahead-of-its-day time sharing environment which permitted multiple users with typewriter like terminals and later ASCII terminals to share the resources of the system, these boxes had some other capabilities, such as analog and digital ports for real-time control of foreign devices.

Thus, in one product line, DEC could offer real-time, and scientific math/number crunching, as well as commercial applications. This is the part that IBM never got. It took the mainframe short-sighted IBM fifteen years to respond with its own minicomputer, but even when it did, the Company did not combine scientific and commercial capabilities into the same box. Thus, while minicomputers were the rage, DEC never lost its edge.

Unlike IBM, DEC had no mainframe or rental business to protect, so they kept driving computing prices way down. Eventually, this forced IBM to lower its mainframe prices in order to compete, Though IBM had more than five years from the PDP-1 (50 units sold), to the PDP-8 (thousands of units sold) to observe what was happening at DEC, Big Blue was unprepared for the impact this small computer company was going to have on its large computer business.

IBM squandered its opportunity to introduce its own minicomputer in a timely way. This would have sent DEC packing in the same fashion as the System/360 did for GE and RCA in the mainframe arena. IBM feared taking on the competition at the time.

An enigma: why did IBM not engage?

One might think that IBM, once recognizing the reality of this frontal attack, would do something to protect itself and launch a counter-attack. After all, it was only the best of comebacks which allowed IBM's 701 and 650 to win the day from Remington Rand's Univac I.

But, with a combination of arrogance and perhaps a bit of unexpected ineptness, and with a singularity of purpose to promote and protect only its mainframe business, IBM failed the challenge and missed this opportunity to make a comeback. They were beaten to the mini market... and they stayed beat for a long time. One would have to conclude that IBM was operating according to its strategic plan—its own interpretation of what was best for IBM. In this stodgy IBM world, the word minicomputer more than likely did not exist.

OEM's: everybody was selling DEC

DEC was not constrained by IBM traditions and legacies. For example, it did not have any issue with other industry players, who became known as original equipment manufacturers (OEM), taking the PDP-8 and embedding it into their product, and reselling it under a different name. For example if a software company developed a program to service public libraries, and they called their software "BESTLIB/1", they were given the right to repackage the PDP-8 (and subsequent DEC brands) and sell the software and hardware as one. In this case, the name "BESTLIB/1" would represent both the software and the DEC hardware included in the package.

What a great deal for DEC. Though its customers were looking for a different marketing model, IBM would doggedly hang on to the notion that IBM would sell the hardware, and an independent software company would sell the customer the software, and IBM would not choose to broker the deal. (See Section V for the details of how IBM failed in the applications software industry.) Neither IBM nor the application software company could sell both. It was against IBM's rules. Since DEC did not have to follow IBM's rules, DEC consistently beat IBM where it counts— in the marketplace.

DEC, in essence began to bundle solutions, giving third parties more control of their boxes. The third party did the work. The third party sold the solution. The solution required a DEC box with a third party name. It was OK! DEC became very successful.

DEC got the hardware business. A simple notion! This drove IBM nuts. Always trying to maintain customer account control, IBM had a real problem recognizing that there are different types of prospects for computers, and totally missed this part of the computer industry. Meanwhile the DEC spawned OEM business, arranged with DEC for the rights to repackage their units under many names. Then, the OEMs went out and sold hardware for DEC but never IBM as IBM said: NO! This was a great deal for both DEC, the software supplier, and for the customer.

Lower and lower prices

In marketing, we learn that each time the price of a product is reduced, it becomes affordable by a substantially larger audience. By driving down computer prices, DEC brought hundreds of thousands more viable computer prospects into the show. IBM did not even have the names of these potential customers in its prospect list.

IBM saw these new computer customers coming out of the woodwork to buy tons of computers. Despite that reality, the IBM Company could not make up its mind about whether to sell to these new folks. After all, the new customers might not be able to afford a mainframe.

IBM was concerned, that it would not make enough money on each unit, selling "onesies." They were concerned about the relationship of profit margin and the cost to sell just one box. They were also concerned that their high-earning sales force might not even engage the new market, because of the low commission probability. Additionally, they were concerned that if they did engage, by being "bugged" by these small businesses, the IBM reps would miss the bigger opportunities at the bigger accounts. I was in the marketing offices when this was all happening. I saw it happen.

The biggest shock for IBM was that, as the minicomputer industry matured, the IBM Company would ultimately be sucked in. IBM would have no choice but to participate or it would lose its existing customers to the newer, better, smaller, less expensive minicomputer models. Very large companies began to buy very small computers. Some bought hundreds and some bought thousands.

All of a sudden a company's paper work did not have to be mailed to central processing sites for batch operations on big mainframes. The work for multi-site businesses could be done at the regional offices or even the local branch offices. IBM had no coherent solution for this decentralized model as it became a reality, and IBM, again was not prepared to be defeated by companies that earned their living this way.

IBM did not understand the new way and showed a remarkable disinterest in learning.

The small customers which IBM willed away, kept DEC and other minicomputer manufacturers in business while they were selling multiple systems (not onesies) to the former IBM-only accounts. In trying to ignore reality, IBM was in effect denying its customers the right to choose their own form of IBM computing - centralized or decentralized.

When they chose decentralized or even partially decentralized approaches, since IBM had no solid all-in-one solution, they had no choice but to abandon IBM computing. Companies like DEC, Hewlett Packard, and Data General, and even Wang, were happy to sell their minicomputer systems in this new environment. More than anything, they seemed to love beating IBM. Unlike the BUNCH, they hurt IBM, but Big Blue really was not watching! It did not feel the pain as its other businesses were bringing home a lot of bacon.

Did DEC make the first PC?

As a point of note, even IBM killers have their faults. There were versions of the PDP-8 that were very small. DEC salesmen would transport the units in the trunks of their cars. Looking back from the year 2000, one might suggest that, with a few size alterations to the PDP-8, DEC could have brought the first personal computer to market 15 years before the IBM PC.

In this book, we would readily conclude that DEC most certainly squandered this particular opportunity. "There is no reason anyone would want a computer in their home." This quote from none other than Ken Olson, chairman, CEO, president and co-founder of Digital Equipment

Corporation (DEC) in 1967 shows that even DEC did not always get it right.

However, if DEC were to have put a mini under the covers of a PC way back then, we must ask what this would have done to IBM's chances of introducing the first IBM commercially successful PC? Would this not have been an even greater squander than DEC ... for IBM to have missed both the minicomputer and the personal computer revolution?

Perhaps this would have been IBM's greatest sin of all... the ultimate squander. It may have even taken the Company down. But it did not happen. And for this, IBM can thank Ken Olsen, who absolutely had no interest in going in that direction. Frank Cary is responsible during this period for putting IBM on its path to building the IBM PC.

The PDP-8 was not only the embodiment of inexpensive computing in its day, but it served as the model for the micro revolution. Without the PDP-8, the micros would not have come until even later. As Ken Huff designed Intel's first microprocessor, he was more than inspired by the PDP-8 as a full working system.

More and better DEC PDPs

DEC continued enhancing its PDP line. In April, 1970 the PDPs went from 8 to 16-bits. The new models became the PDP-11 line. The first of these was the model 20. DEC also introduced their UNIBUS architecture with the PDP-11. The PDP 11 was a family very much like the System/360. It would soon become the world's most successful minicomputer family.

In 1971, DEC introduced a major operating system for its PDP-11 line. Called RSTS 11, its claim to fame was that it was the first general purpose small computer operating system with generalized device handling. RSTS 11 was particularly well suited to commercial applications because of its sophisticated file handling and protection capabilities. This machine family was fully prepared to take on the task of tackling the small business community.

IBM's 1969-released System/3 did provide much resistance to DEC winning the small business marketplace.

Yet, DEC continued to introduce the PDP-11 family throughout the early 1970-s. Models included the 11/45, and the 11/70. In mid-1975, it began to work on a new hardware architecture which would move the platform to 32-bits. DEC also moved into the video terminal business with their VT52 offering. Later in 1975, they announced the PDP-11/34 which became their most successful machine in terms of volume, and it was the smallest PDP ever.

Here come the VAX-s and VMS

In October, 1977, Digital announced their VAX architecture. It was designed to alleviate the PDP 11's most severe limitation: an address space that was too small for many applications. The Virtual Address eXtension (VAX) increased the address space from 16 to 32 bits. The number of general registers also doubled from 8 to 16. It was a mini that was ready for a maxi job.

In February, 1978 their new VMS (Virtual Memory System) operating system was ready for shipment. It had been developed in parallel with the VAX, to allow for better integration of hardware and software. The overall aim during development was to achieve compatibility between systems so that information and programs could be shared.

VMS pushed memory to a 64 megabyte limit, provided an event driven priority scheduler, a process swapper, and a number of other goodies which had been missing from prior DEC operating systems. This was the system and operating system, which would be taking on the new midrange business entry from IBM, the System/38.

At a time when many other software vendors were also trying to relieve themselves of paying Unix royalties to AT&T, DEC also brought out its own version of Unix called ULTRIX 32. It was an interactive, timesharing operating system derived from VM/Unix Version 4.2 BSD developed at the University of California at Berkeley. ULTRIX 32 combined all the features of 4.2 BSD with enhancements for serviceability, documentation and the ability to tailor the kernel without needing source code.

Minis with mainframe power

In January, 1987 DEC was at it again with the introduction of the VAX 8978 and VAX 8974, which again were DIGITAL's most powerful systems to date, offering up to 50 times the power of the original VAX 11/780. Their development had really pushed the top end of the product line into the mainframe power arena.

In 1989, DEC decided to go even one step further into mainframe territory with its VAX 9000. This machine was their best to date, and it held nothing back. As a point of note, this mini driven company was about to switch to microprocessor technology in its hardware lines. The 9000 was Digital's last system to use their traditional minicomputer based processor engines.

OpenVMS—the new standard

In 1990, not quite ready to give up on VMS, but tuning in to
the reality of Unix based systems and applications, DEC
announced OpenVMS. This brought VMS, DEC's
proprietary operating system, into compliance with the
widely accepted POSIX (Unix) standards of the IEEE
(Institute of Electrical and Electronics Engineers).

Additionally, OpenVMS passed the X/Open (nonprofit
consortium of the world's many information system
suppliers) standard and thus was able to use the Unix brand.
For many DEC software engineers, this OS was too much
of a departure from VMS and this hastened their departure
from the Company. As we will see later, Microsoft met
many of the departing DEC engineers with open arms and
plane tickets to Redmond, Washington for employment.

In 1992 DEC built a super microprocessor called the Alpha.
It was really something to behold. It used a new, open, 64-
bit RISC (reduced instruction set computing) architecture
designed to increase performance by a factor of 1000 over its
anticipated 25 year life. Though these numbers may at first
seem unbelievable, if we move past the year 2000, eight to
10 years later, Alpha chips continued to be blazing fast, and
continued to be improving, but once COMPAQ bought
DEC, that was the end of Alpha.

Bye bye VMS

In 1993, as perhaps the last nail in the VMS coffin, DEC
announced DEC OSF/1 Unix for Alpha. It was designed to
take advantage of the speed of Alpha, and to support
emerging applications such as multimedia, real-time
manufacturing resource planning (MRP) and multi-year
simulations.

With DEC's survival as a computer entity in question, even before this time, DEC's leading VMS developer and a number of other team members would make the trip to Redmond Washington and they would stay to develop VMS for Bill Gates...on an Intel platform... but it would be called Windows NT.

OSF/1 Unix was really the end of VMS for DEC. DEC's loyal customers would have to switch to Unix or OpenVMS, or keep running the old stuff on old machines. Unfortunately for DEC aficionados, the Real VMS never made it to the Alpha. VMS was a fine operating system from every review I have read.

In 1995 DEC was hurting big time. Trying on some survival strategies, the Company even began to schmooze Microsoft with offers of alliances and support for each other in the marketplace. Ostensibly, this was because Microsoft ruled the desktop part of client/server, and DEC believed it had a lead role in Enterprise systems.

In 1995, if anybody knew Microsoft was interested in the same server business in which DEC was interested it should have been DEC, since it was the VMS crew out in Redmond doing the work for "trust-me-let's-be-partners" Gates.

In 1996, DEC began to market Intel servers and Alpha servers, each running you-guessed-it, VMS... only kidding. They were running Windows NT, from Microsoft... Digital's new buddy. Of course, Windows NT had been built from the old DEC VMS code designs, and perhaps, as many speculate, with some of the actual VMS code.

COMPAQ moves in

From 1996 on, there has not been much positive news about Digital. They had run their course and, just as IBM had missed the minicomputer revolution, DEC had its problems in the microcomputer age. In 1995, COMPAQ sought to negotiate a merger with DEC, and they were very well received. These discussions surely influenced Digital's move to Intel Servers as well as technology deals with Intel regarding Alpha processor development and manufacture.

Announced in the third week of January, 1998, for $9.6 billion, Compaq and Digital merged their operations with COMPAQ as the lead dog. IBM no longer had DEC to kick around! (Or was that vice-versa?) This newly resized company, with combined revenues of $37 billion at the time, sporting 80,000 employees, quickly became the second largest computer company in the world.

The DEC identity?

A question at the time was: "Who really knows what is going to happen to the Digital / DEC identity? They had been a dominant force in minicomputers since they broke ground with their PDP-1, back in 1959." The answer of course was nobody and the final answer is that the DEC identity was dead. Gone!

DEC was always a worthy IBM competitor as I recall the times I battled for business against them. In some ways, DEC was victimized by some of the same issues as IBM - coping with new technology which came from outside the Company.

For IBM in the Watson Sr. years, it was computers. Then with Watson Jr., it was minicomputers. Finally with Cary and Opel and Akers, it was microcomputers. For DEC, it was the microcomputer. But perhaps as much a factor in

DEC's demise was a midrange size system from IBM known as the AS/400. This was IBM's VAX killer, and it was very effective.

Did the best company win?

There is much irony in the COMPAQ acquisition of DEC. The greatest minicomputer manufacturer of all time was taken over by the greatest personal computer company of all time. COMPAQ was about a $25+ billion dollar company when it acquired DEC. They had come from humble and risky beginnings as a company who made a compact PC which pretended to be an IBM unit. It was just like the IBM PC, maybe even better, and it was portable.

Unlike DEC, an innovative engineering and development company who designed and marketed its own processors in its own systems, COMPAQ bought the same components as IBM, and assembled computers for sale to the general public.

COMPAQ did nothing special in fabrication, but they marketed to the consumer quite well. They clearly did beat IBM at its own game... on the marketing front. Last time I checked, other than getting the IBM BIOS right on the money, COMPAQ is not known for any advanced technology. They clearly beat DEC in the marketplace. And they went on to beat IBM.

COMPAQ began as a pretender to IBM, and did so well that they became the largest PC Company in the world. They became more successful in IBM PCs than IBM itself. Of course, as we will discuss, IBM could have prevented this, for almost no cost, at the time. Compaq's $25 billion in sales prior to the DEC acquisition puts a value on how big a dollar squander IBM made in the PC area. And Compaq at the time was just one of the big PC players.

DEC or Digital as they began to call themselves in later years was the most innovative of all the minicomputer vendors. Though none of the minicomputer vendors were schlocks, DEC was a real nemesis to IBM.

In the early days, IBM had no clue how to compete against them. They were not the only ones to make life difficult for IBM in the minicomputer arena. Two other notables were Hewlett-Packard and Data General. They both became major players in the minicomputer segment of the industry, though they did not have the impact of the truly original Digital Equipment Corporation built by Ken Olsen, from its humble beginnings in the old mill.

Considering the IBM PC was not brought forth until August, 1981, DEC operating as this 1957 startup company surely gained nothing from IBM using DEC as a subcontractor. IBM neither asked nor did DEC refuse. Regardless, DEC, and its principals Olsen and Anderson gained a lot from IBM's focus on large customers and large transactions.

Though Olsen is with the Saints and Anderson is busy in his post DEC life, their multimillionaire status got a boost from IBM permitting them to be successful even when Big Blue could have changed their opportunity pattern into something less definite.

IBM clearly had better technology at the time and it already had a marketing force ready to crush any company that it perceived to be a competitor. In the minicomputer formation years, IBM did not see this marketplace as a problems that could not be snuffed out. In fact, in its efforts to avoid being declared a monopoly, IBM enjoyed the fact that DEC and other minicomputer vendors claimed they competed effectively against the IBM Company.

Meanwhile the government claimed that there were no competitors because IBM was a monopoly. Yet. IBM competitors were always pleased to steal what would have been IBM business. If we look at this idea objectively, unfortunately for IBM we find that IBM gave the business to them all long before they had a chance to steal it.

DEC made some great minicomputers along the way including their groundbreaking PDP-8 and their ever popular PDP-11, a machine which many analysts suggest is the most popular minicomputer ever. We have previously noted that if DEC were paying attention, it could have had a PC 15 years before IBM. The PDP-8 was so small, it could have fit on a desktop or beside a desk at a minimum.

It was just about portable and it could have surely been made portable. To repeat, Ken Olson, DEC CEO at the time is quoted as saying he could find no use for a computer in the home. That explains why DEC did not invent the home PC. Later after IBM got in the market, Olsen's DEC joined in the push with its own IBM compatible unit.

Ken Olsen was as great a visionary unlike IBM's CEOs after the Watsons. He directed DEC well in the early days of the minicomputer revolution. Ultimately, it was the PC that brought his company down, and it was the PC that he categorically denied had any market significance until it was too late.

In the book, Broken Promises: An Unconventional View of What Went Wrong at IBM, Ken Olsen had his reasons for being upset with an IBM that tried to use its marketing advantage instead of its technology to win its battles. Here is

a direct quote from the book by Daniel Quinn Mills and G.
Bruce Friesen:

"Ken Olsen, the engineer who founded and led Digital
Equipment Corporation, may have been as bitter as Eckstein
about IBM, but he expressed it somewhat differently:
"When technology leads the information technology
industry," he said, meaning when new products and services
were emerging from development into the marketplace,
"then we at Digital do very well. Our sales are strong and
our profitability high. IBM does poorly in that environment.
But when technology is stable for a while, then marketing,
not technology, leads the industry and IBM does very well.
We get hurt."

Chapter 21

Hewlett-Packard Enters Minicomputer Arena

Fishing for your computers

Just one year after the PDP-8 made its big industry splash, another established electronics firm decided to throw its hat into the minicomputer ring. Hewlett- Packard was founded in 1934 by two engineering classmates, Dave Packard and Bill Hewlett. They got together after a camping and fishing trip in the Colorado Mountains.

This high tech company entered the computer foray in 1966, with their first computer (the HP 2116A). The machine was initially designed as a controller for some of the Company's test and measurement instruments. Today, HP offers a full range of computing products, and continues to be a major player in minicomputer sized systems (though minicomputers per se, were phased out years ago). HP is still in PC's big time, both client boxes and servers, as well as laboratory instrumentation, desktop printers, scanners and digital photography.

At the end of 2015, Meg Whitman split the company into a business enterprise unit and another unit to sell PC's PC printers and scanners. HP Inc. will sell personal computers and printers; Hewlett-Packard Enterprise will sell commercial computer systems, software and tech services.

CEO Meg Whitman will run HP Enterprise, while PC industry veteran Dion Weisler will lead HP Inc. Each is designed to be independent, with flexibility to respond to a constantly evolving market. We'll see.

William Hewlett and David Packard - beginnings

Hewlett and Packard had formally filed their Hewlett-Packard partnership on January 1, 1939 with just $538.00 capital. Thus, the Company was well established by 1966 when they entered the minicomputer game. Their "innovative" name pre-merger had long ago been decided by a coin toss. As you might suspect, there were only two options.

In 1938 this team, which operated from mutual trust, released their first product, even before they formally were a business. Their resistance capacity audio oscillator (HP200A), was, in simple terms, an electronic instrument used to test sound equipment. It used an incandescent bulb as part of its wiring scheme to provide variable resistance, which, at the time was a breakthrough in oscillator design. This marked the beginning of a series of innovations that would propel HP to where it is today.

The design of the resistance-capacitance audio oscillator was developed by Hewlett when he was in graduate school. If success could be measured in who your customers are, HP met with early success as Walt Disney ordered eight oscillators (HP 200B) in 1938 for the production of the movie Fantasia.

A one-car garage behind 367 Addison Avenue in Palo Alto, California marked a very humble beginning for the Hewlett - Packard duo. But it served them well. They never got to take anything for granted. The garage doubled as their workshop as the young men started their business together. With just

$538.00, their first tools were obviously quite simple: a bench, vise, drill press, screwdriver, file, soldering iron, hacksaw and some purchased components.

Figure 21-1 HP garage—humble beginnings for a dynasty

But they worked hard. After just a year or so, the partners had outgrown these humble beginnings and they went "big time" by renting part of a small building on Page Mill Road. They also hired their first employees to help them in the production of instruments, their main product line at the time.

William Hewlett was born May 20, 1913, in Ann Arbor, Mich. After attending Stanford University in Stanford, Calif., where he received a Bachelor of Arts degree in 1934, he was awarded his master's degree in electrical engineering from the Massachusetts Institute of Technology in 1936. It is amazing how many of America's technical pioneers achieved college/university degrees at some level from MIT. Hewlett also received the degree of Engineer from Stanford in 1939, another of America's finest schools.

David Packard was born Sept. 7, 1912, in Pueblo, Colorado. He also attended Stanford, and received a Bachelor of Arts degree in 1934 and a master's degree in electrical engineering in 1939.

Hewlett was involved actively in management of the Company until 1987, with the exception of the years he served as an Army officer during World War II. He was on the staff of the Army as a Chief Signal Officer and then he headed the electronics section of the New Development Division of the War Department Special Staff. During this latter tour of duty, he was on a special U.S. team that inspected Japanese industry immediately after the war.

In 1947, shortly after his return to Palo Alto, Hewlett was named vice president of Hewlett- Packard, whose nickname was always HP even before HP became the formal name of the Company in the Fiorina days.

Hewlett was subsequently elected executive vice president in 1957 and president in 1964. From 1969, he served as Chief Executive Officer. Hewlett resigned as president in 1977 and retired as Chief Executive Officer in 1978. He then served as chairman of HP's Executive Committee until 1983, when he became vice chairman of the HP board of directors. In 1987, he was named director emeritus.

William Hewlett had a wonderful life. He died after David Packard at 87 years of age in 2001 at his home in Portola Valley, Calif. When he passed on, the Hewlett Foundation, which he established with his wife, Flora Hewlett, in 1966, had an endowment of $3.5 billion. Mr. Hewlett and Mr. Packard loved their Stanford education so much that together they contributed more than $300 million to Stanford University. Some of the dollars that both Hewlett and Packard earned came from IBM's reticence to take advantage of its technology superiority in minicomputers, PCs, and servers. Thank you IBM but not for all of the Hewlett Packard fortunes.

Packard served as a partner in the Company from its founding in 1939 until it was incorporated in 1947. In 1947, he became president, a post he held until 1964, when he was elected chairman of the board and chief executive officer. Just as Hewlett, Packard did his time for the good of the country. He left the Company in 1969 to become U.S. Deputy Secretary of Defense in the first Nixon administration. He served in this capacity for almost three years until he resigned his post in 1971. Upon returning to California, he was re-elected chairman of the board.

Packard also served on a number of commissions for President Reagan in the 1980s, including the Blue Ribbon Commission on Defense Management, and the Trilateral Commission. In 1993, Packard retired as chairman of the board and was named chairman emeritus. He served in that position until his death on March 26, 1996.

One of the notions about David Packard that I picked up when I read his obituary was that he was a sworn enemy of executive pomposity. Packard's team of employees saw him as a great leader, not as a guy for whom they would have disdain.

The HP Way

Just like Watson Jr. with his basic beliefs book, Packard wrote a book in 1995 titled: "The HP Way." Harpers Business published the book. Packard wrote that one of the objectives of his company was "to maintain an organizational environment that fosters individual motivation, initiative and creativity, and a wide latitude of freedom in working toward established objectives and goals."

From its early years, just like IBM, Hewlett-Packard was at the forefront of the movement to make the Company more responsive to workers' needs. HP embraced a broad-based profit-sharing program, flexible scheduling and an open-door policy with senior executives. Having worked for IBM for 23 years, this looks a lot like IBM. IBM's TJ Watson Sr. of course picked up many of his ideas of how to run a company from NCR, where he was an executive before coming to IBM (then C-T-R).

HP pioneered several management techniques that have become widely followed in the corporate world and can be found in many business school textbooks. One was "management by walking around," a method by which senior executives stayed in touch by making themselves visible and accessible on the shop floor. Another was "management by objective," the concept that people want to do a good job and will if managers establish what they want done and let people do it.

Everything I have heard about Hewlett Packard is positive. For years, my next door neighbor worked for HP and we would share technology notes when he would come home for the holidays. He loved HP like I loved IBM when I began my career. I have always thought the world of HP.

Even Apple's Woz found it hard to leave HP to become a multimillionaire. Until IBM ran into difficulty becoming a $100 billion dollar company—a bad promise by an ineffective executive, IBM was HP at the management level and HP was IBM. Either company would have been great to work before the 1980's.

For native Californians, and for those of us travelers who love the awesome beauty of the west coast, who have walked the piers and tasted the crab cocktails, the prawns, the clam chowder, and the sheer delight of Monterey, we can thank David Packard and the Packard family for helping make our enjoyment more possible. For example, Packard played a prominent role in establishing the Monterey Bay Aquarium. This $55 million philanthropic project was made possible by the generosity of the Packard family.

Both William Hewlett and David Packard were revered both inside and outside of Hewlett Packard. As a point of note, as I have said previously, Steve Wozniak, co-founder of Apple loved his job at HP so much that he had a real hard time leaving the Company to become a multi-millionaire. Think about that.

Both Hewlett and Packard received many honors for their industry work as well as their work for the good of humanity. Just as an example, in addition to being awarded the National Medal of Science, the nation's highest scientific honor, by former President Reagan in 1985, Hewlett held 13 honorary degrees from American colleges and universities.

These include: honorary doctor of law degrees from the University of California at Berkeley, Yale University, Mills College, Marquette University and Brown University; honorary doctor of science degrees from Polytechnic Institute of New York and Kenyon College; honorary doctor of engineering degrees from the University of Notre Dame, Dartmouth College and Utah State University; and an honorary doctor of humane letters from Johns Hopkins University.

Packard held honorary degrees of doctor of science from Colorado College; doctor of law from the University of California, Catholic University, and Pepperdine University; doctor of letters from Southern Colorado State College; and doctor of engineering from University of Notre Dame. Both Hewlett and Packard were world class players, the best in their game. They were principles in one of the world's most successful companies in one of the world's most competitive industries. It is only for such distinguished individuals, that the country's most renowned universities would present their most prestigious honors.

A successful succession

After he had been elected president and chief executive officer and a member of HP's board of director's in1992, the board elected Lewis V. Platt to succeed David Packard as chairman when he announced his retirement on Sept. 17, 1993. Platt had joined HP in 1966 as a process engineer in the Medical Products Group. In 1992, Platt became HP's CEO, and the Company's revenues have since grown remarkably by 187 percent to $47.1 billion twenty years ago, while its earnings grown during the same period a whopping 436 percent.

On July 19, 1999, Hewlett Packard announced that Carleton (Carly) S. Fiorina had been named president and chief executive officer, succeeding Platt, who retired as Chairman at the end of 1999. Platt was succeeded in the Chair briefly by Dick Hackborn, a long-time HP Veteran and industry innovator.

Hackborn became the non-executive Chairman at year end, 1999, at the request of Fiorina, upon the retirement of Platt. Shortly after that, there were some tough times for US industry and tough times for Fiorina at HP. But, she pulled the Company through and is responsible for HP being the world leader in IT product sales today.

Prior to joining HP, Fiorina spent a total of nearly 20 years at AT&T and Lucent Technologies. In her last two years, she served as president of Lucent's Global Service Provider Business, and saw the division dramatically increase its growth, revenue, and market share in every region across every product line. Fiorina is no slouch for sure in business and it is nice to see somebody with her talents and chutzpah running for the US presidency.

More or less a folk hero at Lucent, in addition to leading Lucent's success, Fiorina spearheaded the planning and execution of Lucent's 1996 initial public offering and subsequent spin-off from AT&T, in one of the largest and most successful IPOs of all time. Prior to Lucent, Fiorina had been a senior executive at AT&T. She began her career with the Company as an account executive.

Before she reached success, Fiorina eked out a living as a secretary for Kelly. Carly Fiorina was in fact a "Kelly Girl." A guy named Brian Kelly, your scribe, finds that nice. HP at this early stage of her career was just another business that hired Kelly Girls and Fiorina was at HP long before she was its CEO. That is a nice American rags to riches story...don't you think?

When brought on board, Fiorina was always focused on leading HP to achieve continued success in the year 2000 and beyond. She looked forward to even more growth in revenue and profitability; greater innovation and inventiveness, and she planned to abide by the founders' credo of giving the best total customer experience. With the emphasis on eBusiness at the time of her tenure, Fiorina positioned the new HP as the Company that makes the Internet work for its customers.

HP - A thriving organization

HP has a phenomenal track record. It is well documented.
With a substantially smaller base from which to start, during
the time period that IBM was stagnating, HP was booming.
Once upon a time, HP could be looked upon as a little fly
buzzing around a mighty elephant, IBM. Now the fly has
grown up to be a still-growing, Jurassic Park style mammoth
capable of consuming a stagnant IBM.

HP's early business

During the Second World War, the US government relied
on HP's technology in the microwave and signal generator
field to produce a well-needed radar-jamming device. HP
followed the war with a complete line of microwave test
products and became a recognized leader in signal
generators.

As HP's corporate revenues grew to over $6 billion by the
mid 1980's, HP's resources, knowledge of the marketplace,
and technology philosophy helped the Company grow in
mindshare as well as revenue. Unlike IBM, HP would
continually bring out leading edge products with lower cost
points, even as their older lines were on the shelf, still in
their wrappings, waiting to be sold. Indeed, it is an
interesting notion.

The Watsons had staked IBM with billions of dollars' worth
of assets in the form of plant, cash in the bank, and rental
equipment. Only an act of God, an act of war, some really
bad luck, or poor management could have separated IBM
from its huge horde of cash. IBM's post Watson caretakers
frittered away the eggs, killed the goose, and almost bought
the farm.

HP's only other caretaker to have a history with the HP
Company is Lewis Platt, and Platt might as well have been

Louis V. Hewlett-Packard, because he guarded the assets like they were his own, and he multiplied both the HP bounty and the HP return. Meanwhile the top brass at IBM did not take HP very seriously. After all, IBM was in the mainframe business.

HP invented the first PC – OK, maybe not!

Just as DEC's trunk-sized PDP-8 of 1965 could have been made into the world's first PC, if Ken Olsen had only opened his mind, HP thinks that they invented the PC in 1968. They called their device the HP9100 Programmable Desktop Calculator. They did not call it a computer. It was built without integrated circuits and had no disk drive. It was programmed via a simple magnetic card. One can only speculate that if this machine were named the HP9100 Personal / Home Computer, and it were sold at a PC price, history would respect this claim.

Even before HP had built its first computer (not the faux computer HP9100), while the rest of the world was watching the introduction of IBM's System/360 family of computers, HP was making some history of its own... but in a different field. In 1964, they built the first "flying clock." Perhaps it was not truly a flying clock, but that is what it was called. HP's innovative cesium-beam atomic clock was flown around the world to check worldwide time standards. Not necessarily like IBM in computer technology but nobody could deny the original HP its original greatness.

This almost perfect atomic clock, based on cesium-beam frequency standards, was designed to maintain accuracy for 3000 years with only one second of error. In 1991, HP outdid itself with the introduction of a new and improved version which included groundbreaking Cesium II technology. This was the world's most precise commercially available time-keeping device at the time. It continues to maintain time consistently to a one second variance in 1.6 million years. HP clocks are invaluable in time-critical applications such as the space shuttle, airplane collision avoidance systems and telecommunications.

One of the key components of the Global Positioning System (GPS) which now determines ultimate timing accuracy, is composed of a number of ground reference stations and a ton of satellites. You guessed it! All of the frequency standards deployed at the individual ground reference sites are HP cesium-beam standards. Many sites worldwide monitor the GPS and almost exclusively, these use HP cesium standard models.

HP PCs, Inkjets, and Lasers... the 1980s

As the "me too" crowd were moving in to duplicate IBM's PC, HP was not going to be caught without its product. Thus, the HP 150 personal computer emerged, but with a unique feature which separated its capabilities from most of the units available in 1983. It featured a touch-sensitive screen that allowed users to activate a feature by touching the screen. It ran MS-DOS like all other PCs at the time and its engine was the Intel 8088 microprocessor.

HP devices last. There are many folks out there still making good use of early 1990 LaserJet technology, which cost about $2,000 in 1992. These units still run like new but they are very, very, heavy. In 1984, HP introduced its first LaserJet for a whopping $3,495. But, there was nothing like it at the time. It was small, fast, flexible and reliable, and it delivered high-quality printing at an affordable price. The introduction of the LaserJet created a totally new printer market. MY HP printer was as reliable as an IBM mainframe.

While HP was making a killing in printers, IBM was answering the competitive threat by selling off its small printer division to Lexmark. The Company also had its large printer division up for sale to earn some well-needed cash right before Lou Gerstner called a halt to IBM's self-directed dismemberment.

HP & Intel rolling for 64-bits

In 1994, as IBM was preparing to introduce its 64-bit RISC-based AS/400 and RS/6000 lines of computers, HP recognized the major expense involved in building a 64-bit processor by itself. Yet, with only 32-bit units in its minicomputer stable, the Company understood that it either had to forge ahead or throw in its chips.

In a historic move, HP and Intel began a cooperative agreement to develop a common 64-bit microprocessor architecture to be introduced after the turn of the century (Y2K). The two chip designs that were to come from this effort were the Merced (Itanium), and the second stage McKinley chips. Many industry analysts at the time believed these HP/Intel innovations were going to define computing in the 21st century. Too bad for both Intel and Hewlett Packard, they did not.

Other companies at the time were more innovative, and they stretched their existing technology to far exceed the Itanium, which was just a design notion at the time. Among the 1st of those not willing to give the game up to the Merced, was Intel itself, AMD, and even IBM.

What about today?

As most other technology oriented companies, the onetime second largest computer company in the world, Hewlett

Packard, became # 1 as HP. If we count non-computer related parts of HP, this company was positioned to hit the stars. Hewlett-Packard as many others decided to take fortunes to the Internet.

Some would say that they planned to better capitalize on the Internet. HP called its Internet strategy E-Services. It originated from HP's belief that the Internet would evolve from a collection of Web sites accessed via PCs to a virtual marketplace of Internet-based services that could be invoked, on the fly, from any device. As a conscious marketing organization, HP aimed to be a leader in the evolution of the *Net*.

Its intention was to create a new generation of e-services, by inventing a new breed of devices, and by building the next-generation IT infrastructure. The goal was to flawlessly support a world where billions of devices generated trillions of transactions using HP technology and services. In many ways this sounds like Lou Gerstner's original notion of pervasive computing. And to think, HP got to its mammoth size, mostly unnoticed by the mainframe oriented IBM. Both HP and IBM made their mark with the Internet.

HP has not shut down its product engine. It has more and more products in the growing digital imaging area. From scanners to digital cameras, this new technology is targeted for HP customers to become more inventive as they capture, create, share, and print images.

HP's objectives in this area are that people's online experience of creating, viewing, posting, managing and e-mailing photos to friends, family and business associates will become as easy as "point and shoot." Even when they do point and shoot, there will be an HP offering for them to use. For HP, this has been accomplished while IBM has basically been absent. At the client side, Apple has co-opted the IBM symbol, "I" and every handheld that matters sends its stuff with a notion that it was sent by an "I" something. HP is in that game big time on the server side.

HP has proven that you can be diverse and successful. In 1999, HP spun off its Agilent Technology Company (instrumentation) in the biggest IPO in Silicon Valley history. The intention was for Agilent to focus more on computer instrument related challenges, without worrying about PCs etc. Meanwhile, until the recent 2015 split, HP continued to make a wide and varied set of products for the consumer. That is their deal.

IBM was not able to be successful in small markets as HP has been. When products cost less than about $10K, IBM would not succeed. HP has proven to me and many others that a company can have lots of products, some with competing goals, and yet still be successful.

There is a lesson here for the one time largest computer company in the world. IBM are you listening? I bet Mr. Hewlett and Mr. Packard would not have a problem thanking IBM for the millions they earned while IBM was not watching the store. Both Thomas Watsons however, would be very upset at IBM's performance.

HP - A company capitalizing on its big future

Though I once thought of HP as a minicomputer company, I do not see them in the same light anymore. The HP which I see on a regular basis makes the best printers, the best scanners, the best tape backup systems and re-writeable CD ROM units in the world. Despite my own limited perceptions, HP has become a big computer company, and through their HP 3000 and HP 9000 lines, and their Net Servers running Windows NT and later MS OS versions, for years they continued to be very much in the computing business. Nobody was able to write them off.

HP PC peripherals...not from IBM

In 1984, three years after IBM introduced the PC, Hewlett-Packard pioneered small scale inkjet printing technology with the introduction of the HP ThinkJet printer. Today's HP inkjet printers continue to provide technological breakthroughs with ever decreasing prices. In 1984, HP also introduced the HP LaserJet printer the Company's most successful single product ever. I know HP makes good printers. I used a 1992 vintage LaserJet III for my business for many years. It weighed a ton but would not break. My new HP does Faxes copies, etc. There is no question that today's HP LaserJet printers, are considered the world standard for laser printing.

HP makes billions of dollars from its printer sales and they get very positive recognition from their customers. This helps the Company in other sales areas, such as scanners, and backup tape drives and system, etc. IBM is AWOL from this field of endeavor. Having sold its entire office and small printer division to Lexmark, the IBM Company has seemingly abandoned the huge peripheral market. IBM for a while continued to make some PC sized printers, and scanners, but no longer. HP has the honor of market leader. IBM could not beat HP.

IBM gave up the peripheral market when the P.D. Estridge PC team went to Epson and not IBM to get a printer for the original PC. They did not do much more than re-label an Epson printer as if it were one of IBM's own printers. Customers learned very quickly from their computer retailers that there was no reason to buy that IBM printer when they could get the same thing with the Epson label for at least a hundred dollars less.

Estridge and company did its best to stay away from all IBM trappings when they built the first IBM PC. They did not trust big IBM. They were afraid that if they depended on IBM for any parts of the PC, the new PC more than likely would be delayed.

Even though the IBM Company made some of the finest typewriters (printer mechanisms were part of typewriters) in the marketplace and thus, had the small printer technology in-house, this group gave up the farm by giving their printer business to Epson to start. HP was not invited to the PC party by IBM, saw its own back door opportunity it positioned itself to capture a printer market which IBM had not defended and seemed all too willing to give up.

IBM clearly could have been the leading peripheral supplier in the market that the Company created. With HP making many of their billions per year in this marketplace, and with Lexmark, the IBM small printer spinoff of IBM, pushing well past the $13 billion mark, IBM's folly in printers and other peripherals is a matter of opportunity and dollars lost forever. If IBM had the $13 billion that Lexmark now makes with the old IBM printer business, it would be well above the magical $100 billion mark that the company has longed to reach.

HP exits minicomputer business

Along with everybody else in the industry, HP attempted to get out of the minicomputer business completely twenty years ago. However, it could not convince its loyal customers. HP thus could not exit as it desired. It stayed in to please its existing customers.

Its very popular HP 3000 models had large physical cabinets with front panels, while its later models fitted nicely into desks. In 1984 HP brought out its HP3000 Series 37, the first minicomputer model which ran in offices without special cooling or flooring requirements. This line was extensive in that some models in the range could be used by a single user, whereas other models would support well over 2,000 users.

The HP3000 itself was one of the last of the proprietary minicomputer systems. It had outlasted DEC's famous PDP-11. Of course HP eventually owned DEC, which was acquired by Compaq and then of course Hewlett Packard acquired Compaq, becoming HP. Yes, historians like to say Compaq and HP merged but few Compaq folks stayed on. The Compaq name died just as the DEC name died.

At some point HP rechristened its 3000 as the HP e3000 Series and after almost 30 years, the new HP decided to announce a five year phase-out in November 2001. The Company actually extended the phase-out twice at customer request. HP customers liked their 3000's and did not want to give them up and have to convert to PC servers or IBM boxes.

Today, no more new e3000s are being sold by HP, although used systems will not go away and are continually sold for upgrades on an active third-party reseller market. It's like the 1957 Chevy's in Cuba before Obama. You could not find a newer car. Same with the HP 3000.

HP continued to support its customer base through Dec. 31, 2010. Then, third party firms continued to provide needed support for customers throughout the world. For those that for their own reasons still ran 3000 type minicomputers, they had an option to move their applications to a compatible box built by Stromasys. This compatible unit is equipped with full HP3000 hardware emulation on any Intel i7 Core PC, including laptop versions.

HP got dragged back into the HP 3000 business again in 2013 to help its one-time loyal customers. They demanded that HP sell a license for the 3000's operating system for their new Stromasys units. This cost HP little and gave some revenue to the Company. It permitted its former 3000 customers to run HP 3000 software on the Stromasys product, known eventually as the HPA/3000. And so ends our story of HP, the minicomputer vendor.

HP merges with Compaq

Backing up now to pre-merger days, Hewlett-Packard basically acquired Compaq Computer in a stock swap worth about $25 billion. At the time, the two companies announced the stock-swap deal worth $25 billion. Because of fluctuations in the stock, the value changed but in the end it was more like $22,177,941,500.

Carleton "Carly" Fiorina, who ran for Governor of California in 2012, and for the US presidency in 2016, was the chairman and chief executive of Hewlett Packard at the time. She became the new company's chairman and CEO. During the campaign, Fiorina disclosed that her net worth is $59 million. Thank you, IBM. Fiorina leveraged her outstanding CEO skills in the 2016 Presidential election. IBM had helped make her rich.

Compaq's Chairman and CEO Michael Capellas became president of the new entity. Capellas and four other Compaq board members joined HP's board. Capellas did not have a year under his belt when he took the top job at WorldCom on a three-year deal valued at signing at $20 million. Capellas was only a bit player at HP and he goes down in history as one of the computer industry's multi-millionaires. Thank you, IBM

Though Compaq at the time of the "merger," was the world's second largest computer company, HP, with its revenues back then approaching $50 billion per year, was right on the heels of Big Blue. Based on HP's growth track record pre-merger, it was not inconceivable that before the next decade, HP would have surpassed the somewhat stagnant and ambivalent market-watching IBM.

HP proved that market leading pays off. IBM has always been known for all of the hidden technology which its $5 billion per year R&D budget produced. The Company is also well known for much of its technology that passes muster in design, but is never built.

IBM has always chosen not to let a new product take away its opportunities for any existing products. The new IBM is just the same as the old IBM in this regard. You may recall that Watson Sr. demanded that tired old inventory of huge electromechanical gear live on for years as part of his rental stock inventory. IBM has always chosen not to cripple its existing products with new, innovative, market-leading offerings, as HP often does.

We use the term cash cow to describe this phenomenon. Unfortunately, it gets in the way of real innovation for companies to be sucking off the spoils of old products. Eventually, it clouds the minds of entrepreneurs who begin to think they no longer need to be entrepreneurs.

IBM's ultra conservative, cautious, and timid approach to leading the IT industry for many years has left $billions and $billions on the table for companies such as HP, Microsoft, Cisco, Apple, Oracle, and many others to snatch while IBM enjoyed its many market naps and its lucrative cash cows.

HP researches, creates, innovates, announces, and builds top quality products, which its customers want. HP is market driven. IBM uses the market-driven slogan but then "competes in the markets which it chooses". Perhaps IBM will one day learn a business lesson from HP. In recent years the "HP Way" seems to have tremendous momentum while the IBM way and its basic beliefs seem to have gotten stuck in a pothole someplace.

It might be a good time for IBM to dust off a copy of its often cited basic beliefs and dust off Thomas Watson Jr.'s great book: A Business and Its Beliefs: The ideas that helped build IBM. IBM needs to look deeper into what has made its rival HP such a great company, when for years, HP could not touch IBM in the top technology tier. If IBM rereads Watson's book, I think they will find that T. J. Watson invented the HP Way!

Compaq was never heard of again though at the time of the merger, it was the second largest computer company in the world. This deal was the largest ever in technology history. At the time, HP and Compaq were the two biggest names in personal computers, printers and together they had total revenues only slightly less than that of IBM, who at the time was the largest computer company in the world.

Three years after the merger in 2005, criticism of the Company and the merger reached discordant proportions. Carly Fiorina's 2015 assertion in the first Fox presidential debate noted that much of HP's issues in her tenure had to do with continual brawling in the board room. She was 100% right.

During this time, it was often reported that HP directors had refused to be in the same room with one another and openly accused each other of lying, leaking, and betrayal. How could any CEO function in such an environment? In 2005, the board picked a scape-goat, the CEO that had saved the company. They blamed it all on Fiorina and fired her.

In 2008, after having startup issues with the mega company following the Compaq merger, HP finally eclipsed IBM as the # 1 tech firm in the world. Ironically, shortly after Fiorina left HP, the Company announced that it was the Fiorina-induced merger that helped them achieve the #1 spot in the computer world. Without Fiorina in charge to effect the merger, today we might be reading about Compaq beating IBM out for the top revenue spot.

Nothing lasts forever. HP's # 1 position lasted until 2012 when Apple topped HP's earnings by a hair. One can argue that Apple is now an appliance maker rather than an IT company. Today, semiconductor makers that supply all the phone and small device chips have taken over many spots in the top ten of tech companies. Samsung and Apple go back and forth now in the # 1 position. Apple, a company that IBM could have bought and sold fifteen years ago now earns more than twice the annual revenue of IBM. Thank you, IBM

Oh, by the way!

The detached one-car garage at 367 Addison Avenue, near Stanford University, which over 60 years ago doubled as William Packard and David Hewlett's workshop, was re-acquired by the Company for $1.7 million. In 1987, this property was officially designated a California State Historical Landmark. Recognized as HP's birthplace, and the site of their earliest inventions, this garage is a treasured Silicon Valley milestone. Check out Figure 20-1.

Chapter 22

Data General Formed as a Minicomputer Company

Nothing but minis

Three years after DEC created the minicomputer industry, and two years after HP expanded its business scope to include minicomputers, the Data General Company was founded in 1968 by Edson deCastro. He is a well-known defector from Digital Equipment Corp (DEC), who left with a few ideas of his own.

His company wasted no time building its first minicomputer, the NOVA, based on the integrated circuit technology of the day. It was a technology with which deCastro, a former DEC engineer with a slew of great inventions, was quite familiar.

Edson deCastro ran DG successfully for 21 years and when he left the Company he was a multimillionaire, which in a very public divorce, he split with his former wife. Like most minicomputer pioneers, deCastro owes IBM a big thank you for letting his company be!

The DG Nova

The Nova was the industry's first 16-bit minicomputer and came with 32 kilobytes of memory standard. It had an almost PC-level barebones cost of just $8,000.00. From 1968 to 1980, DG introduced successive generations of successful 16 bit minicomputers. The Nova series were very popular and became known for high performance and excellent price/performance

The Company followed its 16-bit success in the years 1980 to 1988 with successive generations of 32 bit minicomputers. One of DG's claims to fame is that a DG system was the first machine chronicled in Pulitzer Prize winning book by Tracy Kidder, ``The Soul of a New Machine"

DG moves to open systems technology

In 1988, DG changed its strategy from custom built processors with proprietary operating systems to an open systems strategy based on industry standard microprocessors (Intel), operating systems (Unix), and storage components. At the same time, DG changed its role from manufacturer to fabricator/integrator.

NUMA architecture

In addition to the transition to Unix, in 1996 DG entered the Windows NT Server "me-too" crowd. However, the Company took "me-too", one step further with their innovative "cluster-in-a-box." This solution was highlighted by multiple, clustered Intel processors operating together in a one-box clustered system.

In order to get more aggregate power from combining processors, DG moved into the NUMA (non-uniform memory access) environment in 1997. NUMA is a very advanced architecture which permits multiple processors to access memory much more efficiently than previous techniques such as clustering, and symmetric multiprocessing (SMP.)

DG & IBM

DG's Nova Series proved to be another nagging competitor to IBM, though mainframe IBM mostly ignored the annoyance. Those minicomputer sales which DEC or HP did not get, typically went to DG. Considering that DG was able to come from literally no-place, using deCastro's know-how from DEC, and easily enter the minicomputer marketplace, and actually be successful, further indicts IBM for not taking the minicomputer marketplace seriously enough to grow with the industry. IBM clearly lost the opportunity to capture or even share the successes and the revenue of the minicomputer marketplace.

Unlike HP, which already had a successful business with many different successful product types when it entered the minicomputer marketplace, DG had no other real products to sell. The Company sold only its new minicomputers. It can be argued that if IBM had stopped DEC before it got going, by building a better minicomputer, there would not have been a DG.

However, there was no IBM Armada keeping the competitors out. If fired upon, IBM would not fire back. In other words, there was no IBM presence anywhere in sight that was prepared to defend its own assets. To IBM, minicomputers did not count.

IBM just let more and more business slip away. If the Company was anywhere at the time, its focus was not on the minicomputer marketplace. It is possible that IBM was so comfortable in its mainframe closet that it was in la-la land as its competition grew strong. IBM did not as much as fire a shot over the bow just to prove that it was watching, or that it cared.

Ironically, though DG is no longer a major computer player, for a number of years, IBM still found DG to be a thorn in its side. Most recently, DG was a major competitor to IBM in what at the time was the brand new NUMA market space to which the IBM Company had pointed its big blue ship. IBM was already in this new market space, and it attacked NUMA as if it were a mainframe opportunity.

IBM seemed to expect that NUMA was one new area in which it could receive some payback. IBM itself had conducted pioneering research in NUMA technology for years in its Rochester Minnesota labs, long before the idea became popular. True to the mark, IBM did not act expeditiously on its early opportunity.

Engineers in IBM's Rochester Labs had built NUMA prototypes and had published technical papers on NUMA in the early 1990s. However, the mainframe oriented IBM was on-again / off again with the technology. IBM could have been the unchallenged leader in NUMA.

Unfortunately for IBM, a corporate dictate said there should be no NUMA. Instead, the IBM corporate direction demanded that multi-system solutions use clustering and SMP multi-system technologies, which were the predecessors of NUMA. Conservative IBM had again decided to stay with what had worked, rather than use its own-built newest and best technology available.

IBM had the designs and the ability to have built NUMA machines long before DG or anybody else. The Company should have been perceived as a technology innovator. However, for mostly unexplained reasons, IBM managers watched as the two big NUMA stars became Data General and another company known as Sequent Technologies. Thank You, IBM.

IBM liked NUMA

Moving towards today. After watching for a while, the new Gerstner style "agile" IBM felt it was time to get out its big wallet. In a knee jerk reaction to feeling out-staged and outclassed again, and seeming to have forgotten that it already had the technology in-house in Rochester, Minnesota, on September 24, 1999, after three months of finalization details, IBM purchased Sequent Technologies, the publicized leader in NUMA for $810 million.

Considering that, with a little more vision, and by paying attention to its own R&D, and industry trends, IBM could have built its own NUMA solution years sooner, and saved $810,000,000 at the same time, we see the results of IBM management incompetence again and again. IBM had the NUMA opportunity in-house already, but it did not capitalize on it.

Shortly after the acquisition, Sequent (really IBM) posted this nice little note on the Sequent Web site to explain what had occurred:

NUMA Q... The leader in Intel based data center solutions... We're very pleased to announce that the merger between Sequent Computer Systems and IBM has been completed. The two companies are now joining forces to provide NUMA Q technology as a leading platform for e business, customer relationship management, business intelligence, and enterprise resource planning. Customers can expect continued delivery of quality service and customer care.

In the coming months, this site will be in transition to reflect our new relationship as the NUMA Q brand at IBM. Check back often to find more information on NUMA Q products.

IBM reacted to a technology threat, gained mature technology, and perhaps eliminated a competitor through acquisition. But, it is well known inside and outside IBM that the Rochester, Minnesota Labs, home of IBM's AS/400 midrange computer at the time, had pioneered this technology. Yet, IBM spent $810,000,000 on technology which its own labs had pioneered? If I did not believe IBM was above board on insider profits, I would have suggested that somebody made some money on this deal; but it was not IBM.

Shortly after this, IBM was set to implement NUMA in its RS/6000 line of RISC-based processors, and the Company was also staged to offer NUMA in the PC Server space. Though IBM's on again / off again love affair with Microsoft and Intel are sometimes understandable in light of the fact that just about all small to mid-sized companies chose Wintel over IBM, even Big Blue forgot that it was IBM and not Wintel that made the most powerful mainframe and midrange computers in the world. IBM forgot that its systems were built with Power technology and not with Intel processors. Only IBM's Netfinity (xSeries) eServer at the time of the NUMA acquisition used the Intel processor as its heart.

Regardless of where IBM had intended to use NUMA, it did not use the $810,000,000 acquisition for anything productive. In July 1999, when the deal was ready to be finalized, both companies were touting how great it would be with NUMA being found in most IBM technology. It wasn't. It never was. Another IBM acquisition was killed by IBM.

By May 2002 a decline in IBM sales of the models acquired from Sequent, among other reasons, led to the retirement of Sequent-heritage products. Thus IBM's investment in NUMA, like many other acquisition investments over the years went bust in just three years. Since almost a $billion was lost, I suspect the whole computer industry rejoiced when IBM gave up again on a great idea. Thank you, IBM.

Chapter 23

EMC Buys DG; Enters the Minicomputer Marketplace

EMC was a traditional disk storage company

EMC Corporation was founded in August, 1979 by Richard J. Egan and Roger Marino in Newton Massachusetts. As a computer electronics company, one of EMC's first ventures was to build the 64 KB memory boards for Prime Computers, a former front-line minicomputer manufacturer. Following this, they began to make a killing selling high tech disk drives. EMC beat IBM in a business area that IBM had invented and that IBM felt it could control. IBM let EMC dominate the high-powered disk drive industry and eventually IBM lost the battle with EMC and got out of the business. This is a familiar pattern of IBM defeatism. EMC won. IBM lost. Thank you, IBM

So that nobody is deeply concerned that I have included Richard J. Egan as a guy who should thank IBM just because you may never have heard about him, consider this: In its 2005 list of the Forbes 400, Egan was ranked as the 258th richest American, with a net worth of approximately, 1.3 billion, That is a lot of net worth for a disk drive entrepreneur that nobody knows. FYI, to say it differently, Egan in 2005 had a net worth of $1300 million. That makes the founder of EMC a technology billionaire and a technology multimillionaire. Thank you, IBM. In 2009, Mr. Egan, still a billionaire passed away after a fight with lung cancer. He was 73 years old.

Oh, and if you think $1.3 billion is a lot for a thank you to IBM, you may completely excuse Roger Marino, EMC co-founder as his net worth is a mere $1.2 Billion. Yes, that is $1200 million but it is also $100 million less than Richard Egan. Many of us would agree to take that scant $100 million difference to even the account. It's probably time for Roger Marino to issue a brief press statement: "Thank you, IBM."

EMC first enjoyed success in the memory market, another of IBM's innovations. In 1985, the Company was the first to ship new memory upgrades using a 1-megabit chip design. In addition to this success, the Company also went public in a very successful offering. Their success was also marked with a revenue doubling year of $66 million.

Later in the 1980's EMC began to develop the disk technology which would soon become its niche. In 1989, for example EMC announced a set of disk drives for IBM's workhorse System/38 units. These units also worked with IBM's newly announced AS/400 midrange business computer. Obviously the act of making components for IBM's systems, and being able to sell them to IBM's customers as replacements for IBM's own technology, did not initially endear EMC to the IBM management team.

EMC Corporation now has over 70,000 employees worldwide and, is the world's largest provider of data storage systems. This is another way of saying EMC sells a lot of disk drives and other kinds of storage solutions such a storage area networks.

Accounting for the DG acquisition, which in retrospect was like a dot in space, EMC currently brings in over $25 billion in annual revenue. All of this revenue ($25 billion) would be IBM's if IBM knew how to compete. EMC bills itself as the world's leading supplier of intelligent enterprise storage and retrieval technology, designing [storage] systems for open system, mainframe, and midrange environments.

The Company has been doing very well in its industry efforts, and is especially active in e-Business. EMC was recognized by Fortune Magazine on December 6, 1999 and designated one of the 50 top Internet Elite. Since then, they have gained many additional honors but moving from $17 billion to $25 billion annual revenue in the last five years is their greatest honor.

EMC views their mission as making information accessible across the full business enterprise, regardless of the source or the target system. EMC has been very successful in its storage business. In late, 1999, however, they were looking for more, and DG was out there just waiting to be found.

A funny thing happened on the way to Data General becoming a successful NUMA vendor. They were bought out by EMC Corporation late in 1999. And so went another formerly successful minicomputer vendor. The DG logo, along with the DEC logo, are being carried by others. In many ways this signaled the end of the minicomputer era.

IBM and EMC... mutual storage nemeses

For years, IBM has been attacked from all sides and all angles by EMC as this aggressive market oriented organization gained a foothold in IBM's midrange and mainframe accounts. EMC simply would not give up. IBM was not prepared to build a big enough fly swatter to take them out.

Fifteen years ago, with IBM becoming a major advanced disk parts supplier in a $3 billion deal with EMC in the spirit of coopetition, many viewed the EMC DG acquisition as EMCs way of getting its hands on DG's CLARiiON disk array business. Moreover, the Company got a little boost with the technology rich NUMA based DG servers.

But there may be a lot more to the EMC DG merger. IBM lawsuits may have come back to haunt them. Rather than settle long-standing patent infringement lawsuits and counter suits with DG, before EMC's takeover, IBM sat back while EMC acquired DG. The lawsuits have been reinvigorated by EMC. The subject matter of the lawsuits is storage technology patents, and associated infringements, which is just the ticket for a storage company like EMC, who were expected to win this fight.

In November, 1994, DG sued IBM for infringing on a number of its patents. DG claimed that some of IBM's major products, including AS/400 and mainframe servers had included technology patented by DG. Not standing still, IBM countersued claiming a violation of seven IBM patents. In 1996, DG kept the suit alive and raised the stakes when the Company included IBM's RISC based AS/400s. IBM quickly returned the volley.

In December, 1999 IBM took its coopetition partner, EMC to court. Having believed the DG suits were dead, now in the hands of its coopetition partner, IBM learned that EMC had transferred the DG disputed patents in such a way that it kept the patents from coming into IBM's hands.

IBM and EMC; a good deal?

We all know how long court cases drag out. Thus, it could have been a long time for this deal to be worked out. There were at least three obvious solutions to the problem. IBM and EMC could have waited it out and gone to court somewhere in the middle of the decade, or they could have called it a wash and cross-license the patents, or IBM could have chosen to buy out EMC and be the unquestioned leader in the lucrative storage business, with no potential crushing lawsuits to carry on its back.

There were a number of analysts who believed that the latter option made the most sense for IBM and was much smarter given the facts that the worldwide storage business was growing at more than 20 percent annually compared to a few points a year for servers. Considering that the storage component in systems represents half the value of a fully built, complete system (servers, storage, memory, and software) these days, there certainly was a lot at stake.

There were fears back then that IBM could end up winning the battle but losing the larger war against Sun Microsystems, Hewlett Packard, Dell, and Compaq. Buying EMC was calculated as a very expensive option, given its market capitalization of $110 billion. IBM would probably have had to pay at least $140 billion for EMC—if not more.

And considering that IBM itself only had a market cap at the time of about $200 billion, EMC managers and shareholders would have ended up with a big say in how the resulting IBM EMC Corp. would be set up and run. Can you imagine the extent to which IBM, the Company that invented the disk drive had lost its edge to permit a non-entity just a few years back to hold it up to gain a steal.

IBM and DG - A Better Deal!

Sometimes it seems like when IBM is supposed to make the right decision, all the brains have left town for the week. Knowing that this threat was out there, it would have been far cheaper for IBM to have bought Data General for $1 billion, and kept its lawsuits out of EMC's hands. Considering that one of IBM's prime microelectronic businesses at the time was the disk storage and assembly parts business, the Company could have had the undisputed edge for 145 times less money than they would have had to pay to get EMC.

Of course history tells us that IBM failed in the disk drive and storage business anyway. Hard as it is to believe, IBM was the leader and held the dominant position at the time in disk technology. Big Blue unfortunately did not know how to make an easy buck even when it was obvious to its competition.

IBM dominated the marketplace, yet a company—EMC— with none of the great managers that IBM bred with its blue ticket management classes, was able to kill Big Blue in the disk drive and storage areas. How could this happen? Many have scratched their heads that the modern IBM somehow wins in none of its attempted ventures.

Ironically, the time period of the DG deal was the 1990's. IBM was in fact building new facilities to make disk storage system parts to OEM. IBM was not only going to make its own storage; it planned to sell its groundbreaking technology to others.

IBM had the patents and the way to make the best internal parts needed in modern disk storage devices. Yet, despite this, in just a few years, IBM gave it all up for a pittance in cash. IBM could not make a buck in the disk drive space so it sold out to Hitachi at the time for $2.05 billion. Hitachi gained what had become IBM's money-losing hard disk drive (HDD) operations.

Clearly IBM had the best disk technology. The Company had invented the disk drive with the 305 RAMAC in the 1950's. It also invented the floppy disk drive in 1969. It once owned the CD-ROM and DVD businesses. The IBM Company has a huge patent library full of disk inventions which it owns. IBM again led the industry when it invented the highly successful Winchester technology in 1973.

IBM Research had figured out how to take advantage of giant magneto resistive (GMR) head technology right before it bailed from the industry. Big Blue was the unprecedented technology leader; yet it pulled out of the business. It was just 20 years after the discovery of the potential of the GMR disk head, that IBM Research scientists devised processes to easily and economically build GMR microstructures and harness the power of GMR. By using GMR structures in the Magnetic Recording heads of its disk drives, IBM introduced products with the highest areal densities in the world. Yet, it failed in its marketing efforts.

When it got out of the disk business, the Company that once would do anything to save its people from layoffs, also announced it would lay off 1,500 employees from its Microelectronics Division, a move aimed at supposedly increasing operational efficiencies. IBM needed a Watson that was a real human being at the time but none were showing up for work regularly.

In 1996 D. Quinn Mills and G. Bruce Friesen in their book titled Broken Promises—An Unconventional View of What Went Wrong at IBM took a hard look at what caused IBM to experience major financial losses and the need to reduce its staff by half. These authors hit the nail on the head. Ironically, I was writing the first version of this book at the same time they were writing theirs.

In their book promo, these authors capture the essence of what was going on quite succinctly:

Virtually overnight, IBM went from being one of the most respected firms in the world to one widely condemned. This book describes how the Company's violation of two well-established contracts led to its most serious problems. The first was its long-standing relationship with customers, where the implicit agreement was IBM's guarantee of high-quality technology and close-service support. The second was between IBM and its employees, with the implicit commitment to employee security. When IBM abrogated both contracts in the 1980s, its business began to fall apart. Quinn and Friesen describe IBM's experience in terms of broader historical and contextual patterns, and they look at the strategic tasks that IBM now confronts during its comeback.

In the summer of 2015, I went back to my book—this book; dusted it off, made what was there much better. I took incomplete stories from twenty-years ago and brought them up to date. In examining the Broken Promises book, though it does not make me happy to see an affirmation of my own observations, it is nice to find others thinking the same way.

In 2015, I authorized the first printing of the book at 564 pages. Paul Harkins, a great IBM Systems Engineer in his time with IBM bought the book in its first printing and he reminded me that I had left out IBM's major losses in application software as well as a number of billionaires, multimillionaires, and millionaires who did quite well in the application software business. In this, the second edition, I added a Section V to the book which fully addresses this omission.

Back to DG for a wrap-up!

When we consider that IBM paid over $800,000,000 to acquire Sequent Technologies in mid-1999, so that the Company would have leading edge NUMA technology for its RS/6000 and PC Server lines, it was simply a bum deal. If IBM had purchased DG instead, for 1.1 $ billion as EMC did, they would have gotten back all their patents from a disputed status, and they would have acquired DG, a leading NUMA vendor. The Company could have saved the $800,000,000 it paid for Sequent, and been free from EMC patent problems. What was IBM thinking?

There was legitimate concern at the time that we might see IBM over the next few years making a move for EMC with its capitalization of over $100 billion. The cost of such an IBM blunder would be through the roof— $139 billion more than IBM could have closed the deal for in 1999. How's that for bad luck?

IBM had a lucky day in 2000. My call was to buy some IBM stock on May 12, 2000. On this day, IBM settled its lawsuit against EMC for a pittance. In IBM's words: it was a "great outcome" and the amount the Company paid to EMC was "negligible and far less than it would cost us to litigate." Taking such $139 billion dollar chances, adjusted for inflation, may very well be more risky, than T. J. Watson, Jr.'s $5 billion dollar gamble. On the other hand, it was nice back then seeing IBM taking any business risk and winning every now and then.

"Today's settlement amicably resolves all outstanding litigation ... with no findings or admission of liability," a joint statement from the two companies read. The companies will extend their patent cross-licensing agreement, as well as institute a five-year moratorium on patent infringement lawsuits.

Moving from minicomputer vendors

Though there were other minicomputer vendors, which emerged, competed, and withdrew, during the minicomputer era, DEC, HP, and DG were known as the leaders of their day. Even TI took a crack at being a minicomputer vendor with its TI 900 series. But they were not very successful.

After a stop to examine IBM's minicomputer offerings in the next several chapters, we will move from these successful minicomputer hardware vendors to the software which made these unique inexpensive machines successful. This operating system software–Unix—has certainly survived the minicomputer revolution and it can now be found on just about every platform. Since some historically significant minicomputer software was derived from very early research using IBM mainframes, we will cover this along the way as we move forward. Yes, you will find that IBM could have owned Unix; if it had not mismanaged its relationship with MIT.

Chapter 24

IBM's Non-Minicomputer Minicomputers

IBM's "small business computers" were in the minicomputer technology class.

Some think that IBM had several minicomputers in the 1970's. The company used its System/3 and later the System/3X, and AS/400 product lines to compete for commercial business against the minicomputer competition that had morphed their systems to provide business solutions.

In the real-time processing arena, shortly after it introduced the IBM System/3, the IBM Company brought out an inexpensive sensor based product with a mainframe like architecture and a high-end minicomputer price. It was called the IBM System/7. Tom Watson Jr., T.V. Learson, and Frank Cary shepherded the System/7 during its lifetime. Nonetheless it was not a very successful product in terms of IBM revenue.

Though reasonably inexpensive, because it was a mainframe type machine in structure and size and in architecture, it was not viewed by the industry as a minicomputer. I know of no IBM customers who used a System/7 for anything other than process control, real-time applications. If Payroll were the application, a System/7 would not be the solution.

The IBM System/7 as it was introduced to the world in 1970 was a rugged and highly reliable computer that could measure, test, analyze and control industrial and laboratory events as they occurred. The sensor-based system, which rented for as little as $352 a month, was IBM's lowest-cost computer at the start of the 1970s. It cost less than a System/3.

System/7 performed quality control on TV set faceplates.

I was the IBM Systems Engineer for Owens Illinois in Pittston PA during the 1970's. My job was to support Ken Huffman, the DP Manager in his use of the IBM System/3 Model 15. Ken managed the system and wrote production data reporting programs. OI used two System/7 machines on the production line to sense whether their newly manufactured TV faceplates were OK or not OK. The System/7s reported their data to the System/3 for further analysis.

Metal plungers would form molten glass into TV faceplates. Sensors would then measure the formed glass at many different points to assure that it was neither too thick nor too thin. If it were too thick the TV picture would be distorted. If it were too thin, radiation could leak.

The System/7 would decide whether a piece of faceplate glass continued through production or was taken off the line, smashed, and re-melted for another go. The System/3 would take the sensor readings from the System/7 by plunger ID and if a faceplate were rejected, the system would tell the production engineers the locations of bad spots on the plungers and how much should be shaved off to make the next run with that plunger a good one. It was a very advanced application for sure. Neither System/7 rarely if ever went down.

Though technically superior to its minicomputer competition, the cost of not looking and feeling like a rack-based minicomputer while sporting a larger price tag than the minicomputer competition, did not help make the System/7 successful for Big Blue. It was, however, one heck of a capable system.

In the real-time computing arena, a marketplace which IBM had not defined, the System/7 was often rejected as a suitable platform. Though the products were excellent, IBM's efforts in delivering a total solution were half-hearted. IBM's marketing team of sales personnel and Systems Engineers such as I, did not understand the notion of real time computing enough to differentiate it from competitive minicomputer offerings.

The IBM Company initially did not view the minicomputer marketplace as a threat to its bread and butter mainframe business. Thus, it took few bold steps with any of these "sideshows" to avoid product erosion in its other mainline computing areas.

The bottom line is that IBM introduced System/7, an excellent technological marvel but invested little in making it successful. Thus, it was rejected by IBM's own internal team of field marketers and by customers time and again. IBM's marketing force did not understand the machine or the sensor-based marketplace; yet they were charged with selling it. It was therefore a lost cause.

IBM took another shot at the minicomputer marketplace with its introduction of the Series/1

Chapter 25

IBM Introduces the Series/1 as a Bona Fide Minicomputer

IBM builds great systems

In the mid to late 1970s, IBM finally took notice that the bona-fide minicomputer marketplace was doing quite well without its lead or presence. In a knee-jerk reaction, the Company developed and rushed to market a phenomenally rich hardware architecture, which was completely open and extensible. It was far better than the competition's entries. IBM really knows how to build great computer systems when it chooses to do so.

In many ways, it was a huge PC; but the PC had yet to be introduced so it could not be compared well at the time. Not ever having been in this market space as a leader, IBM made a lot of mistakes in launching its showboat minicomputer hardware product.

The machine was called the Series/1. It was brought forth by IBM's General Systems Division (GSD) on November 16, 1976. It was a small, general purpose computing system offering both full data communications and excellent sensor-based capabilities. In many ways its hardware was so excellent that it exceeded the capabilities of all of the minicomputer competition. It replaced the IBM System/7 in IBM's hardware catalog.

The machine also allowed users to attach a large number
and an enormous variety of input and output devices,
including custom-built devices for special application
requirements. If IBM's field force understood the
competition, and were prepared to be successful with this
first class product, IBM would not have had to *cry uncle*
again in this new arena. IBM's branch office marketing
teams were simply not ready for this great product.

Figure 25-1 Two IBM Series/1 Minicomputers

Though the hardware and the hardware architecture were as
good as could be, at the time of its announcement, there was
no software for the Series/1, thereby making the machine
unusable for the masses. IBM had not even taken the time to
create a real operating system for its new unit. No top grade
operating system was ready to run on the new Series/1 for
some time to come after the hardware was available.

Moreover, because IBM had a thing against Unix, the most
successful non-IBM operating system of the day—which ran
on all other minicomputers, Big Blue would not support

Unix on any of its hardware platforms, including Series/1. This too was a big mistake that kept the Series/1 as an also-ran machine.

Unix was the major open operating system supported on most other minicomputers in the industry. Thus, as one might suspect, the Series/1 initially floundered because regular businesses were not inclined to write operating systems for any hardware systems they deployed. IBM's Series/1 was adopted by only those companies that did not need industry-standard-ware.

Just as IBM did not understand its System/7, the Company's traditional marketing force, deployed in major metropolitan areas as well as remote urban areas such as Scranton, PA and Utica, NY, by and large did not understand this powerhouse machine. Thus, they were not comfortable selling it.

Series/1 sales results reflected this fact. Though IBM pressured its sales force with measurements and incentives, the Series/1 never really sold well in the general marketplace. Customers of the normal IBM marketing team bought business mini-computers such as System/3, 32, 34, etc., not minicomputers per se.

As the Series/ 1 product matured, however, IBM kept the hardware alive and enhanced it. In this time, IBM's best operating system architects built a completely new operating systems for this new system. It was called the Realtime Programming System (RPS), a very sophisticated OS. IBM's internal labs loved the Series/1 and they wrote their own OS known as the Event Driven Executive (EDX). They ported this OS from the System/7.

Coupled with the very basic Control Programming Support (CPS) operating system, third party software houses and large companies with many branch offices found that the Series/1's hardware architecture and its very low price made it an ideal product for a build-once—install-many, environment.

Plus, as a big incentive, the box came with IBM maintenance. It became the perfect branch office machine for companies with hundreds or thousands of branch offices. Additionally, the IBM Series 1 had great data communications capabilities. So, the machine was also deployed frequently as a powerful communications server. It fit in well in corporate America.

No computers for National Book Company

At the time, IBM had a device called the 3741 which had light programming capabilities. The unit was a key to diskette machine and would typically not be used as a central computer system.

However, I had a client, the National Book Company, a division of W.W. Norton & Company. Its management had a New York consultant who liked the 3741. At the time the IBM Series/1 was announced, they were planning to use the programmable model of the IBM 3741 data entry machine to prepare invoices for printing. The Company had a number of excellent typists in its office and it was not inclined in these early days of computing to automate all operations fearing a mass exodus of skilled personnel.

Just as the 3741 did not evoke a computerized environment, the name Series/1 did not immediately make one think of a computer system. National Book decided that it would use a Series/1 with multiple display stations to enter the invoices for printing. It was a simple application. Because the local office was very interested in making its Series/1 sales numbers, I was asked to assure that this application was written and that it worked.

As a technical guy, I got to learn EDX and a program called PROMPT by Mid-American Control Corporation. In a month or so, Barbara Keegan, a sharp National Book employee assigned to the project and I had the application running and the WW Norton officials were quite pleased.

With this new capability of the Series/1 as a business and/or communications machine for independent software vendors and large companies, the box ultimately became a success, but not for the purpose of which it was built. Ironically when the PC was introduced, this very model for developing computing applications would work quite well.

On February 1, 1991, ten years after the PC was introduced, after a very successful run, and with its replacement minicomputer product (RS/6000) already doing well in sales and installations, IBM withdrew the Series/1 from marketing. By this time, IBM was trying to categorize all of its systems. The Company never liked the term minicomputer as it almost always meant the competition, so IBM relabeled its minicomputer systems as midrange systems. They were mid-range between a PC and a mainframe. See Section IV for a more detailed discussion of RISC hardware and the IBM RS/6000

Chapter 26

MIT, IBM and the Early Development of Unix

IBM and MIT

Though the best operating system for minicomputers from its first clean release was Unix, this world famous operating system actually started out as a time sharing system for big mainframe computers.

Editor's note. I have all the references for the quotes in this section if they need to be examined for any reason. In the 20 years since I wrote this section, things have changed and so I have changed this section substantially to make it better. Any quote in this chapter can be plugged right into your browser and you will find its context and the author of the quote.

Through its Cambridge Branch Office, at the same time as DEC's major successes, IBM was working with MIT in support of its efforts in time-sharing, but in a somewhat clandestine fashion. IBM still was not back on the track with Harvard after the Howard Aiken snubbing debacle. The Watsons had been snubbed by Harvard after a major investment in Mark I and they had never forgotten this.

Yet, IBM valued its MIT relationship, since it gave the Company access to one of the greatest brain trusts available in academia. MIT is as good as it gets. Behind the scenes, the local IBM Office would provide hardware as MIT needed it, and they would also modify IBM's standard offerings to meet MIT's unique requirements. In fact, the local IBM office was performing tasks for MIT which were contra-strategic to the corporation. As long as nobody told anybody in HQ, the locals continued to please their giant customer—MIT. Ironically, to be successful, the local IBM office had to go around the IBM mother-ship.

MIT and timesharing

To say that the principals at MIT were activists regarding timesharing is an understatement. MIT was "hell-bent" on developing a viable timesharing operating system. If there was one leadership niche that MIT had determined would be theirs, it was in sophisticated operating systems. Whereas Harvard, buoyed by the Harvard Mark I and subsequent Aiken and Grace Hopper ventures, focused mostly on hardware, MIT, Harvard's cross-town academic rival sought to gain and keep its leadership in the operating system software field. MIT was very good at it.

MIT's engineers were not able to find a machine that could readily address their peculiar hardware needs in any vendor's standard catalog. They had discovered that to share hardware effectively, they would need hardware enhancements to existing computers. With these enhancements, their time sharing operating system would be able to divide the systems resources efficiently among multiple users sharing time on the system.

The MIT engineers asked IBM for a number of hardware enhancements to their installed IBM 7090 computer. (The 7090 was a transistor based late 1950's high powered scientific computer). IBM's Cambridge Branch Office team and a corporate IBM liaison team were pleased to oblige.

Without the enhancements, the 7090 could not be used for timesharing.

Of course, whenever IBM altered MIT's systems locally, it made the MIT unit, a "one-of-a-kind." Thus, when MIT finished its great work, no other computer in existence could run its software. MIT was not pleased. It wanted to be able to offer its new developments to other academic institutions across the world. Though IBM was very accommodating, not being able to duplicate the capabilities was a major drawback for MIT doing business with IBM.

CTSS Compatible Time Sharing System

In the early 1960's MIT had three programmers, under the leadership of Professor Fernando Corbato. All three were working on the university's time sharing operating system project.

Figure 26-1 MIT Datacenter for the CTSS project

IBM 7094 at MIT
ctss-compatible-time-sharing-system

The operating system they designed was called the
Compatible Time Sharing System (CTSS). They had
prototyped an early version of CTSS and had even
demonstrated it using an IBM 7090 at MIT in November,
1961, some ten months before DEC's PDP-1 time sharing
venture.

But since IBM was not really paying attention to time
sharing at the time, the IBM Company made no hay about
it. Thus, history credits DEC and its PDP-1 Operating
System, as the first timesharing system. This is another time
when IBM was in through the front door but they let a
Johnnie Come Lately take the prize.

IBM misses recognition for an industry first

Though there was no quantifiable dollar value in this
recognition, when we consider the cost of advertising and
the continual PR race in which all computer vendors are
always engaged, this was clearly another opportunity for
IBM to demonstrate its world class technical leadership.
Moreover, MIT was not in it for the bucks, but for the glory.

Unfortunately, just as many times before, thinking the
proprietary IBM game was more important than matters
outside the Company, IBM would ignore such industry
events. Thus, in time sharing operating systems, as in many
other important technologies, IBM became an also-ran in
technology, which the Company had pioneered or the
Company could have easily owned.

To help or not to help?

IBM's support of MIT is an enigma. Though Thomas
Watson Jr. had personally donated the initial machines to
MIT (and it was known that Watson Sr. had more than a
little disdain for Harvard after the Aiken snubbing), nobody
at the IBM local level really knew whether corporate

management wanted to continually respond to MIT's requests for help. IBM was having its share of communications problems among its management hierarchies. Rather than find out (calling Watson), the Cambridge Branch Office just gave MIT help as they requested it. But nobody really knew how long Mother IBM would allow this special support practice to last.

Digital Equipment Corporation, on the other hand, had a formal relationship with MIT that was open and steadfast, and Digital engineers responded well to their neighbor's requests. Already this new startup (DEC) was out-foxing the best marketing organization in the world.

IBM's distractions—System/360

While IBM was in a half-hearted semi-sponsorship of the CTSS effort in Cambridge (Corporate IBM had no interest in timesharing systems), the Company had its own major event going on in Poughkeepsie, New York. In the early 1960s through its introduction in 1964, IBM had been preparing its new family of computers—the System/360. The Company had staked its future on the success of this new family and nobody in IBM was interested in getting in the way of S/360's success. IBM spent $5 billion on the deal and would be out of business if it failed

MIT, for its part was well into the time sharing game by this time and, though they had not perfected their act yet, they had already begun to provide time sharing services to several other New England Universities, in addition to their own users. This was a very prestigious undertaking for MIT to help enable remote computing at these neighboring institutions.

With this much exposure in a lead role to other academicians, MIT was not about to give up time sharing for anybody. And no reasonable company would have expected that they should. Though happy that it could make time sharing work on the modified IBM 7090, MIT wanted their innovations to be generally available to all universities and institutions needing time sharing.

MIT expected S/360 to have what it needed

MIT was anxious for the introduction of IBM's new System/360 as they were hoping the next generation of computers would have even more hardware innovations, which would make time-sharing systems even more useful. Meanwhile, the Systems Engineers and Customer Engineers in the Cambridge office knew that IBM designers had built special hardware for MIT's IBM 7090, and they were concerned that the functions provided by this special hardware, would not be part of the new S/360 family design. Their fears were well founded.

For MIT to be able to use the IBM System/360, IBM would at a minimum, have to include the special hardware as an orderable feature of the System/360 line. Without this, MIT would not be able to continue their CTSS project with "state-of-the-art" IBM S/360 mainframes.

To be sure that MIT's needs would be accommodated, the locals arranged for IBM's lead S/360 designers to visit with Professor Corbato at MIT. In this way, IBM could benefit from MIT's research, and MIT could benefit from the inclusion of time sharing hardware in the base System/360 architecture.

Sorry MIT, it's not in the plan!

Unfortunately, in IBM at the time, there was great resistance to the notion of timesharing, interactive systems. Not only was their no intention of fulfilling MIT's wishes, it was not even a market in which IBM planned to enter—ever. IBM again was not ready to embrace the future when the past was selling so well. The Company intended to continue its "batch is best philosophy" by optimizing these new machines for multiple levels of concurrent batch processing.

IBM and timesharing

One could only imagine that IBM saw a marketing threat to its business if companies were able to share time on one computer, rather than having to buy their own IBM system. IBM's consistently myopic view would greatly interfere with its ability to prosper, missing one opportunity after another under the guise of protecting its business from internal cannibalism.

On April 7, 1964 when IBM announced System/360 without the address relocation hardware necessary for time sharing, MIT and other leading edge IBM customers, were understandably dismayed, and even angered. The IBM Company seemed undaunted by what appeared to be a small setback. IBM had delivered batch processing at its best. Ever onward IBM!

Project MAC at MIT but no Steve Jobs

MIT had just bought a second 7094 (A bigger 7090) in the fall 1963 to initiate a new project intended to move the notion of timesharing ahead many fold. This effort was known as the Project MAC. They would use this new 7094 system for the Project MAC while the other 7090 would continue to run the CTSS. The objectives of Project Mac were to use the lessons learned from CTSS to produce the finest time sharing system possible.

The name CTSS was abandoned as the name of the new operating system became known as Multics. This would become another major MIT project, and IBM's failure to have the right hardware for MIT would come back to haunt the IBM Company in a big way.

It is not really known for certain what the term "MAC" actually meant. There is no definitive answer in history—just a few possibilities. Some think it stood for Machine Aided Cognition" or "Multiple Access Computing" or even "Man and Computer. If it were twelve years later, it could have been the Apple Macintosh!

As a springboard from CTSS, MIT devised Project MAC to design and build Multics, an even more useful time sharing system, partially based on the CTSS prototype. The basic goal of the Multics project "was to develop a working prototype for a computer utility embracing the whole complex of hardware, software, and users. It was to provide a desirable, as well as feasible, model for other system designers to study."

IBM misreads the MIT scenario

In February, 1964, only a few months from angering MIT with its intentions for the System/360, IBM, seemingly oblivious to what was about to happen to what had been an excellent relationship with MIT, initiated what was to become the Cambridge Scientific Center. The objective of the center was to work even closer with MIT and other academics. This center was intended to help IBM gain a presence in major universities. The specific mission of the center was to develop instructional solutions and devise means to help create more computer-literate individuals and computer-competent college graduates.

As luck would have it, the Project MAC project headquarters was in the same building as the IBM Scientific

Center. After the System/360 was announced and the
Project MAC team believed their needs were intentionally
ignored, the IBM Scientific Center personnel and the MIT
folks remained on speaking terms as they met in the halls
etc. But they were not especially friendly. IBM had delivered
a death-blow to MIT and did not realize how substantial the
hit actually was.

Considering that IBM was planning to use its formerly
excellent relationship with MIT as a springboard for getting
business at other universities, the insult to the MIT team
was a major blunder. IBM followed this by investing money
in facilities and people to capitalize on a relationship which
they had just destroyed. MIT put the kibosh to any further
love affairs with IBM. This was not the IBM Company's
finest hour.

A wounded relationships bring no bounty

Later in 1964, the Project MAC group went to the
marketplace again looking for better computer hardware.
IBM had steadfastly refused to give an inch on generally
available time-sharing hardware of its System/360. MIT
was telling IBM that its chances were over. IBM had set
back MIT's project and from MIT's perspective, the
schmoozing did not matter as much as the lack of delivery
of necessary function. MIT had no love for IBM from this
point on. For IBM, Harvard hated the company and now
MIT hated the company.

The 7090 generation had become old and passé. The group
let out a request for proposal (RFP) for a new system which
would have to be better and substantially faster than their
7090. Additionally, it would have to include all of the
hardware necessary to support the MIT expanded view of

time sharing. Moreover, the system would require third generation hardware such as IBM's System/360.

MIT had already become aware that IBM competitors, namely GE and RCA would be pleased to incorporate the necessary hardware as standard features of their new generation boxes, which they had positioned to compete directly with System/360. MIT thus had more choices than to blindly pick IBM as its vendor, and they were inclined to look elsewhere after being embarrassed by IBM's System/360 introduction.

IBM had placed Harvard in the corner for snubbing them, and MIT put IBM in the same place for the same type of action. IBM never recovered from this at MIT nor in all of academia. With no leading academic sponsor, IBM's efforts in colleges and universities over the subsequent years had little success. As the Higher Education Specialist for our local branch office in Scranton, PA, I saw the disdain for IBM in Academia first hand. The Company lost more than the timesharing market by upsetting its former friends at MIT.

It really did not matter to MIT why IBM had not included address relocation hardware in the new System/360. They would find another vendor to provide exactly what they wanted. And, just as IBM harbored poor feelings for Aiken and the Harvard experience, MIT was not particularly concerned about continuing with IBM hardware or with IBM people.

Good reasons can still make it wrong

Besides not having a love for time-sharing, IBM believed the introduction of new hardware in the basic System/360 architecture would have delayed the already late S/360 project even further, and would have made the project even more risky. Knowing he could not explain it away to his

MIT constituency, the IBM Cambridge Scientific Center manager, Norm Rasmussen tried to do all he could to repair relations with MIT.

IBM's repair efforts fail

As the new manager of a group whose purpose was partly to capitalize on the IBM / MIT partnership, only to find that his company had destroyed the relationship, Rasmussen was extremely embarrassed. Hoping to get the System/360 blunder behind him, and still believing he could get the MAC business, he immediately assembled a group to put together IBM's best bid for the MAC project.

The IBM group worked very hard and finally proposed a solution calling for the modification of IBM's System/360 architecture to include address relocation and whatever else was necessary. This was the same approach the Company had used with the 7090 system. This hybrid machine fit the specifications for the Project MAC bid, but it was not a standard offering and was not ever to become a standard offering. At the same time, Bell Labs was also looking for a major time sharing system. IBM conveniently proposed the same hybrid machine for Bell Labs.

MIT sends IBM packing

Ostensibly because they wanted their output to be usable on a mainline computer, (one which anybody could purchase - not a unique hybrid as IBM proposed), the Project MAC committee rejected IBM's proposal. Despite Rasmussen's best efforts, IBM had failed. The egg on IBM's face hardened even more quickly in light of IBM's investment in the Scientific Center. IBM did not look very good to the very same education community in which they had just invested a substantial sum.

Of course, there is much speculation that MIT was still quite annoyed at IBM for neglecting its needs. Some feel MIT was so upset, they would have bought from a street vendor rather than IBM. IBM had missed yet another opportunity. The Company was further disappointed when Bell Labs also rejected their proposal for the hybrid solution.

This moment defined the solidification of IBM's reputation as not being worthy of academia. IBM had been snubbed by Harvard, and then went on to snub MIT. Such snubbing's had more of a role in the history of computing than one would ever imagine.

MIT returns IBM's snub

MIT's Professor Corbato, who was not known for being an irascible man, added even more fuel to the fire. He published a Project MAC Report containing a crushing analysis of the weaknesses of the System/360 as a machine on which to implement a time sharing system. Corbato was not the only one complaining about the System/360 hardware limitations. Soon, IBM had to face a number of irate customers who had mobilized under the auspices of the SHARE Users Group.

IBM executives unscathed—surprise!

Though executives in IBM kept their jobs after this major blunder, this was a major loss for the Company. Its ramifications continue to haunt the Company to this very day. Seldom after this would IBM systems be the machines of choice for leading edge academic computer science research. In higher education, IBM was o-u-t! Since the smaller, higher education institutions would often take the example of the leading edge institutions, they chose to move to DEC and HP, and DG and others. Anything but IBM! IBM has suffered a business drought in the academic community since this time. And, from my vantage point as a college professor, there is still no end in sight.

The impact on IBM & academia

Having spent twenty-three years working with higher education institutions as a Senior IBM Systems Engineer, followed by six years as an internal consultant for a local university, and seven years as an IT faculty member at a different local university, I can attest that there is still no love lost between academia and IBM. Whereas in business, the IBM name on a product most often helps the sale. In academia it is just the opposite. I have seen academic managers more than willing to spend more on less... just to avoid having to work with IBM.

This ultimately spills over to the students who graduate from these institutions, and those in the community who are touched in one way or another by the students and the professors. Students leave with the computer bias of their professors. It is not until graduates take jobs in IBM MIS shops within mainstream businesses, that they lose these biases. Those who build their own shops in smaller companies or dotcom ventures, most often build without any bricks or mortar or help from Big Blue.

Since colleges typically do not teach about IBM systems, though most businesses continue to use IBM systems, it makes it much more difficult for students to gain a foothold in such organizations, since they require substantially more training than should be necessary. They have a tougher time being assimilated. This is one of the reasons that today, computer majors are more likely to take jobs in the PC area, even though these are typically lower paying than positions in an IT shop using an IBM business system.

So, IBM lost its opportunity to be a leader in time sharing systems. Moreover, in snubbing its best academic partner of the day, the Company also squandered its opportunity to shape the minds and hearts of new computer technicians to have a favorable opinion of IBM products upon graduation. But, perhaps neither of these are the most severe consequence of this blunder. It actually gets worse.

IBM squandered first rights to Unix!

IBM lost the business at MIT to a GE 645. The Project MAC would eventually implement Multics on the 645 and they had the software in general use at MIT by October, 1969. It had been a five-year effort. At the same time, in 1969, Bell Labs (The organization that was initially interested in the same System/360 hardware as MIT), began the work which would ultimately become the Unix operating system.

Bell Labs, rather than IBM was able to use MIT's research in both the CTSS project and the Multics effort to set this project underway. Unfortunately for IBM, this project would not even use IBM systems. IBM was o-u-t. Unix would first be built for GE hardware and DEC Unix was right around the corner.

MIA IBM helped its competition

It is interesting to note that before there even was a Windows NT, IBM's greatest nemeses were the many hardware vendors who used a derivative of Unix to drive their competing machines. It never had to be. For just a couple thousand dollars' worth of hardware development for System/360, IBM could have avoided the snub, and would have been the platform upon which Unix was developed. One might say that if IBM played its cards right, for a very small investment, the Company could have owned Unix and all associated rights. Can you imagine?

IBM would eventually build a system with the proper hardware for timesharing. The Company would also get over its aversion to timesharing and develop its own time sharing software system. They called the special box the System 360 Model 67. Anybody could buy it. Ironically, the time sharing operating system that IBM built without MIT would become known affectionately as the Cambridge Monitoring System (CMS) from the US locale of MIT.

Later, as if the problems had never occurred, in the great spirit of Orwellian changes, though CMS would continue in IBM, it would be re-christened as the Conversational Monitor System (CMS). It was an integral part of IBM's Virtual Machine (VM) Operating System. VM of course ran only on IBM mainframes whereas Unix was designed to run on all systems. Was IBM really clever?

I think IBM should have eaten a lot of crow and gotten back into MIT's graces no matter what it had to do. Arrogance killed a goose ready to lay many golden eggs for IBM but IBM's plans overrode the plans of this goose. VM would never be ubiquitous enough to beat Unix, no matter how good it was.

Unix became the time sharing operating system which defined the rules of the game. IBM never recovered and Unix gave life to a hundred thousand paper cuts by IBM's many Unix competitors. IBM could not beat them because Unix actually was that good.

Additionally, it was too late for MIT. MIT wanted its own operating system, not IBM's. It was also too late for computer science students, and this faux pas cost the IBM

Company dearly by creating and bolstering IBM competitors, such as DEC, and all subsequent Unix computer manufacturers.

One might ask, "How many systems over the years did IBM lose to one form of Unix or another?" The number surely would be staggering! When we consider that Unix may never have been developed for competing platforms if IBM had incorporated address relocation hardware in its System/360, this was an expensive mistake indeed.

Bell Labs, the ultimate inventors of Unix, based on Multics, based again on CTSS, would have had no perceived need for a GE or DEC machine if IBM had maintained its relationship with MIT.

Bill Gates loves Unix

Guess what platform Bill Gates cut his eye teeth on? If you said the DEC platform and Unix, you would be correctimundo! Guess what operating system DOS was modeled after. Right again, Unix! Paul Allen snuck a few Unix-like features into DOS as it was being made ready for the PC announcement. Guess what operating system Microsoft and just about every other development shop uses to build its software. Right again! Unix!

So, can we say that, with Windows NT and subsequent Microsoft OS versions, having come to life from their development on Unix machines—that without Unix, Windows NT and its successors would never have come to life?

What could have been never will be!

Wouldn't you love to see the movie where Tom Watson Jr. and the Indian Brave, who we've all seen tearing as he looks at highway litter in the distance, are in a conversation? Both are tearing, as they overlook the Cambridge skyline... for different reasons. Watson speaks and says that he wishes that he never made the decision to deprive the System/360 from having time-sharing hardware. The Indian Brave turns out to be a Genie. Watson's wish is granted.

Can you imagine the impact on IBM history? With no Unix competition to distract sales efforts, John Akers would have been able to finish his tenure as IBM's Chairman as the most successful chairman of all time. IBM mainframe operating systems would be running on the desktop. Lou Gerstner, of course, would still be a multi-millionaire, but he would never have been motivated to coin the term "eBusiness", since that would never become an item on Nabisco's strategic plan.

The effect on IBM's future business

But that wish was never granted. There are no such things as Genies! Both the Brave, and Tom Watson Jr. would be forced to continue to tear for years.

Who is IBM's competition today? It is Unix boxes from assorted vendors and Windows x86 servers with operating systems developed on Unix machines. Perhaps, if IBM had paid more attention to business in 1964, it would not have ever had to deal with Bill Gates—ever! This little oversight has certainly had cascading ramifications.

Open systems software – Unix

In the late 1960's the only thing that seemed to be going slow from a technology standpoint was IBM's reaction to change. The System/360 had filled a major void in 1965 and, from its power-thirsty customers, IBM got back its $5 billion gamble and then some. Things were so good for IBM that, in many ways, the company began to believe that it was invincible. Nothing had ever been as successful as System/360. In reality, for IBM, nothing again ever was!

IBM's primary business - mainframes

Unfortunately, the success with System/360 was all IBM needed to help the Company believe that it was in the mainframe computer business and not in the computer business in general. All of the Company's success had come from "big iron," and the Company operated as if "big iron" was all that mattered.

IBM's Data Processing Division (sold mainframes) lorded over the Office Products Division (sold typewriters) as the corporate sales champ. The perspective of the computer folks at IBM regarding the Op Division was that IBM advertised, and then the OP guys went around and picked up orders and the OP techs merely plugged the typewriters into the wall. IBM mainframe people thought that was all there was to be successful in things that were not mainframe.

IBM had an army waiting

Perhaps for this reason, IBM never looked to its highly polished Office Division sales force to help solve its minicomputer problem. If the Company chose to notice, it already had the best trained army of field force typewriter salesmen just waiting for some exciting new products to sell. Moreover, these salesmen made regular calls on the very customers which the mainframe sales culture of IBM did not even want to meet.

These small account IBM sales personnel had learned to manage many different accounts and were able to make a good living besides. There was a large gap between the typewriter and the mainframe, but, unfortunately, nobody in IBM was asked to pitch in to fill that gap.

As a side-note, as IBM was deciding about whether it wanted to have a direct marketing force for typewriters and small computers, it folded the highly successful Office Products (OP) Sales Force into a new IBM division known as the National Marketing Division (NMD), but IBM spent way too much time trying to get these great salesmen to leave the company rather than help the company be successful.

The former head of the Office Division of IBM got the job as the head honcho for the new computer division. The former typewriter salesmen were being assimilated (force - fit) as computer salesmen. It was way too late.

But I remember the simple battle cry which the new chief used to send his new division to war against the competitors of the day. He said that in order for the division to be successful, and to meet its objectives, everybody had to do just three things: 1. Sell, 2, Sell, and 3. Sell. It sure would have been nice if IBM management sent in a few good plays every now and then. Exhortations did not do the trick for IBM. And, firing IBM's best salesmen did not help either! IBM management did IBM in!

I never forgot that. Nor did I ever forget what great salesmen those OP guys really were. I always thought of the OP crew as IBM's only real salesmen. When logic failed to win a sale, they immediately switched to emotion, and they would close the business. One of my favorite OP salesmen, Tom McDonald had a simple philosophy: "Every day you try to start something, move something else along, and close something."

These OP guys and gals visited tons of IBM customers every day. They knew the secretaries' nieces' names, and they were familiar with the executive's golf swing. This was a great waste of talent... a squander of a major opportunity for sure. IBM could have used this talented team to stop the leakage caused by minicomputers first, and Unix second. Last, but not least, with OP reps leading the charge, IBM could have won the business PC game.

Chapter 27

What is Unix and Why Does It Matter?

Bell Labs brought Unix to the world!

From the time Bell Labs chose to not move forward with the hybrid System/360 timesharing solution with IBM, it began collaborating with MIT and GE on the development of the Multics Operating System. They bought a GE mainframe just like MIT instead of a System/360.

In 1966, Ken Thompson joined the computing science research group at Bell Laboratories, which had been the research arm of AT&T. Soon, Ken Thompson, who is now known as "The Father of Unix" was seriously involved in the Multics project. Unix came from all of the work of CTSS as well as Multics, and may be described as an evolutionary natural progression from these earlier timesharing efforts.

Bell Labs talent perseveres

The Multics project was intended to improve the performance of multi-user time-sharing computer systems. Unfortunately, after a substantial effort, Bell Labs withdrew from the project, as more and more Bell developers recognized that Multics was going to fail in its objectives. Not only was it not going to be the beat-all, and end-all of operating systems, but it would no-way-soon deliver any sort of usable system. It was a good second try at time sharing but no cigar!

A, B, C languages

At about the same time, two highly motivated and talented programmers from Bell Laboratories, Brian Kernighan, and Dennis Ritchie created the C Programming language. Just as Unix was the third iteration of time sharing with CTSS and Multics its immediate predecessors, C Language came naturally after A and B language ran their course.

Though many argue that C is not really an English-like, high level language, it is substantially better, and more productive to use, than low level assembly languages. The C language's pointer arithmetic, and low-level approach gave the language enough facility that it could actually eliminate the requirement for assembly language on most machines.

Thus, the C language's high level characteristics mixed with low-level (machine oriented) facility, allowed it to be used for the most primitive functions, such as developing most of the internals of an operating system. Additionally, the high level attributes of C would permit an operating system to be developed which was machine independent - not tied to a particular piece of hardware. This would come in handy as the Multics team moved on and they wanted to take their work with them to the next box.

Good things spawn good things

Ken Thompson and Dennis Ritchie were two of the last Bell researchers on the Multics project, and they did not want to see all of the good notions dry up. They had been using the Multics system for their own work as they tried to make it perform better. They had used the CTSS system even before that. With the close of the Multics project at Bell Labs, they realized that their major resource, a GE 645, was going to be taken from them. They needed to come up with something to replace what they had been using for the past several years.

Thompson left Bell Labs before Ritchie. Since 2006, he has been working at Google where he co-invented the Go programming language. Ritchie, who died in early October, 2011 worked for a long time for Bell Labs and its morphing into other companies. He summed up his thoughts on Multics at the time the project was just about over on the AT&T Web site.

> *"We didn't want to lose the pleasant niche we occupied, because no similar ones were available; even the time sharing service that would later be offered under GE's operating system did not exist. What we wanted to preserve was not just a good environment in which to do programming, but a system around which a fellowship could form. We knew from experience that the essence of communal computing, as supplied by remote access, time shared machines, is not just to type programs into a terminal instead of a keypunch, but to encourage close communication."*

As the 645's days were numbered Thompson and Ritchie created numerous proposals to persuade the organization to fund their project. But they were continually unsuccessful. The two were not famous then... just a few blokes trying to get their jobs done. They wanted to find an alternative to Multics, if for nothing else, their own productive use. Thompson eventually found a little used PDP 7 computer which had a very necessary component - a quality display processor. This single station system had been used infrequently as a Graphic II terminal, and the two pioneers were able to rescue this machine from this mundane task.

There's Rube Goldberg in many creations

The development team had some difficulties early on with the DEC PDP-7 and they were forced to use some Rube

Goldberg techniques to get their programs into the box. Eventually an assembler was developed. This made it much easier for the team to support itself. Thompson invented the file system, then there were user utilities (copy, print, delete, etc.) and a simple command interpreter which they called the shell.

The name game

Thus, a new operating system was born, which went unnamed until well into 1970, when Ritchie's partner in the C language project dubbed it Unix (UNICS vs. MULTICS). The PDP-7 was a single station unit, and so Unix was first used for single station work.

Making the first Unix

The first cut for a multi-user time sharing operating system ironically was on a single user version of the reasonably small PDP-7. But more facility was clearly needed. Only a bigger machine would do. Where there is a will, there is always a way.

Thompson and Ritchie found a need in the Bell Labs internal patent office for text processing and were able to persuade management to bring in a PDP-11, a more reliable and modern system, to complete the project. The first job was to port their new operating system to the PDP-11.

Thus, the 16 bit PDP 11 became the second UNIX port, and enabled multi user facilities because of the PDP-11's inherent memory management hardware. The patent office loved the end result. They were able to use required symbols, and the custom editor would even number the lines on their reports.

The patent office liked what they got and decided to keep it. They chose to adopt the end product, which was a multi-user Unix (Maybe it should have been called Multics?). This was the defining moment for Unix. From this day, the use of Unix at Bell Labs began to spread.

Putting the "C" In Unix

The icing on the cake was when this talented team later rewrote the Unix operating system itself in C language. Other than a few hundred lines of assembler code, the new C language based Unix was completely portable.

This portable build with C enabled the first port of UNIX onto a non-DEC computer, a 32 bit INTERDATA 8/32 minicomputer system, which looked a lot like an IBM System 360/370. This work helped them learn about portability issues to help make Unix's portability better each time.

Unix begins to spread

As Unix became perfected, it was offered by Bell Labs free of charge for academic institutions, and it was offered to commercial firms for a reasonably expensive price tag. By 1974, Unix had been installed on over 600 computers, mostly in academia. From experience I know the mind-set of academia. They like what is good and leading edge. However, the combination of free + good is much better. Unix fit the bill perfectly.

Unix was designed by low level techies for low level techies. It couples a combination of a program development environment and the use of a high level language (C) to code systems software. Unix continues to be popular and has been enhanced significantly over the years. It has been ported to many platforms, even microprocessor systems such as Z80, Motorola 680X, Intel 808x etc., as well as to a variety of mini (DEC, HP) and main frame systems, including IBM mainframes.

Unix has also been ported to x86 machines but Bill Gates would prefer you had not heard that. Microsoft does offer its own Unix derivative called Xenix. Additionally, Unix is the prime operating system on IBM's PowerPC chip based RISC System/6000 (RS/6000), which has been re-christened as The IBM Power System. IBM chooses to call its Unix, *AIX*, for Advanced Interactive Executive, but it is Unix for sure.

The Berkeley influence on Unix

The life of a Unix prognosticator became more difficult when the University Of Berkeley (BSD) became a prominent figure in Unix development. Berkeley began to offer software support and useful extensions to the system. Not too coincidentally, Ken Thompson had spent a couple of years at Berkeley as a visiting professor.

Soon, Berkley began to make its own extensions to Unix. Because of the tight relationship with AT&T, the more useful advances of Berkeley, e.g. TCP/IP were brought back to the AT&T versions of Unix. But the Berkeley personality overall grew to be different from the AT&T version.

With two versions, BSD & AT&T, Bell Labs began to get commercial pressure to license the code to enable OEM's such as Microsoft with ZENIX, and many others to port Unix for their specific platform considerations and for platform stabilization. The side benefits of making the operating system become "vendor provided" and "vendor supported", were seen to be better documentation, training, and other factors.

One would not expect Unix to be used commercially without the proper tool set, which one would expect to be included in a commercial version. Thus, again for Unix and the industry, this was a win-win proposition.

Nobody, including Linus Torvalds emerged as the Unix standard caretaker

Unfortunately, everybody who touched Unix, seemed to "enhance" it for their own purposes. When one system is enhanced and others are not, the end result is simple incompatibility. Thus, Unix no longer was Unix. It seemed that all of a sudden there were too many different Unix's. There were various flavors of a similar operating system, all claiming to be the one, true, and of course, the "best" Unix.

Too many different flavors of Unix

The quandary for the industry was "how to bring them together." Bell Labs and Berkeley and the rest of the Unix ports continued to make changes to their respective versions, and the Unix "standard" no longer was a standard. The IEEE / ISO standards organizations got in the game to try to make some sense out of the new mess. They developed a neutral standard for Unix called POSIX. This standard included kernel features of both BSD & Bell Labs. It could have worked if it were accepted by all. But all were not ready for it. Self-interests ruled the day.

POSIX to the rescue?

The beauty of the POSIX (it still exists) standard is that it translates POSIX compliant calls to the calls of the target operating system. Thus, if an operating system vendor chose to be "open", and implemented the POSIX calls properly, any of the "compliant" applications, which would run on that system, could theoretically be on the list of supported

applications for any other POSIX compliant Unix
implementation.

The Open Group over the last twenty years has emerged as
the official caretaker of the Unix standard, which happens to
be a superset of the POSIX standard. The Open Group is
the most famous certifying body for the UNIX trademark,
and it has published the Single UNIX Specification
technical standard, which extends the POSIX standards and
is the official definition of a UNIX system.

For this book, this is more than enough for us to know. It
does help to know that AT&T basically sold its rights and
after a long chain of holders, those rights are now held by
The Open Group. www.opengroup.org

Original intent of time sharing emerges as Unix

Hopefully by now you can see that the whole idea of Unix
was to build a portable, less cumbersome version of Multics.
What actually resulted was substantially better than the
original idea. Unix ultimately eclipsed Multics, in part
because of its portability and adaptability to readily available
computers.

C Language most certainly helped this. Unix (all flavors)
became an elegant time sharing software system for
minicomputers. It could be used for text editing, general
computing, switching system operations and trouble
reporting. It later became the foundation operating system
for the Internet. .

Chapter 28

Among Many Unix's, Another Unix—Linux

Some heroes become billionaires—some don't

Every war has many heroes. If we hypothesize for a moment that the Information Technology Industry is a war unto itself, fraught with many battles for the innovative edge, technological superiority, and marketing leadership, we will find many heroes. Some of these heroes are now legend in their own right, and pure and simple champions of the computer Industry. This book is filled with them:

From Bill Gates and Paul Allen to Steve Jobs and Steve Wozniak, from Terry Waitte to Michael Dell to Rod Canion, to Bill Joy, to Larry Ellison, Ray Noorda, and many others. Most of these industry heroes were little more than kids when they began to move on their special idea. Many of them today are mega billionaires or multimillionaires and are still relatively young in age. They became mega-forces in the IT industry.

Linus Torvalds

Linus Torvalds, the father of Linux, is a relatively new industry hero and still a young man. Unquestionable hero that he may be, Torvalds for a while was the exception to the billionaire rule. His story has been told many times before. We'll tell it again here in case you have not heard it. As of now, Torvalds is surely not a pauper with a net worth of $150 million and he makes about $10 million per year.

Figure 28-1 Linus Torvalds Creator of Linux

As the Linus Torvalds story most often begins, he lived in Finland for many years on a road called Kalevagatan, about ten minutes from downtown Helsinki. In the late summer, 1990, Torvalds, then a 20 year-old student at the University of Helsinki, was taking his first Unix class.

Eventually, seven years later, after getting his fill of all the computing delicacies the University had to offer, he would achieve a master's degree in Computer Science. Long before he received his degree, however, he would make computer history by spearheading the development of a Unix-like operating system.

His work, dubbed Linux for not so obvious reasons, quickly became the most favored alternative to Microsoft's Windows x86 versions and mother Unix herself. Linux today powers your Android phone and it powers most of the internet

A PC for Unix?

As Torvalds was getting ready to get back to the University in the fall, 1990, he discovered that one of the required books for a Unix course he was taking was Andrew Tanenbaum's Operating Systems: Design and Implementation. Tanenbaum was a former hack himself, a professor of computer science in the Netherlands, and a mini-pioneer in the computer revolution in his own right.

Tanenbaum had built a baby Unix, which he called Minix, and he designed his book to use Minix as a vehicle to teach operating systems to university students. This was a defining moment for the young Torvalds as it served as a motivation for him to break down and buy himself his first PC. Until he witnessed Minix and the power of Unix, Torvalds had resisted becoming a PC User. In his own words:

"That's when I actually broke down and got a PC... if I had gotten a PC [before Minix], I'd have gotten this crummy architecture with this crummy MS-DOS operating system and I wouldn't have learned a thing."

As intrigued as he was with Minix, he found it very limiting. What Linus Torvalds really wanted was the whole banana. He wanted a machine which had the full Unix operating system ready to go. He wanted to run Unix at home on his own computer. Minix was not the answer because it was incomplete. Unix was not the answer because he could not afford to pay $5,000 a copy for an OS for his home. In addition to the steep software cost, Unix did not like to run on Intel PCs. It preferred $10,000+ computers, which again diminished its appeal for home, hacker use.

Part of Unix was simply not enough

Tanenbaum never intended for Minix to be a full Unix. However, when it was released to a technology starved hacker world in 1987, within two months, there was a newsgroup with over 40,000 users worldwide. This teaching operating system was not enough for Torvalds, though it served as both a foundation for learning and as a base from which he was able to begin tinkering with the notion of building a real operating system.

Eventually, as Linus Torvalds chose to proceed and he got more and more into his OS project, he encountered Andrew Tanenbaum in the Usenet (like a faceless Facebook) and the two began a series of spamming offenses. Torvalds, the young neophyte took on Tanenbaum, the seasoned professor, in a battle of words. Each noted the superiority of their respective approaches to operating systems. It was a duel of honor fought with words over the electronic media.

The high road was far too high for their exchanged word blasts. They both drove the low road. It was very much a kiddie-like encounter. At one point, Tanenbaum, rather than attempting to continue with logic, even offered that Torvalds' operating system conception was so poorly structured from the get-go, that if he had turned it into Tanenbaum as an academic project, the professor would have been compelled to give him an "F" grade for his efforts. A low blow in academia!

Tanenbaum was continually approached to make Minix into much more than he ever intended. Users wanted more and more capabilities. Though he freely admitted that Minix was not the answer to Unix, he received hundreds of emails each day asking him to add this feature and that feature. Tanenbaum acknowledged that many users had gotten frustrated with his constantly saying, "no." There was definitely an opportunity for someone willing to build the OS which Minix never would be. Linus Torvalds was that person.

After about a year of Unix and chewing on the perceived deficiencies in Minix, in August, 1991, this 21 year-old student from Finland began a post to the comp.os.minix newsgroup with the words:

"Hello everybody out there using minix - I'm doing a (free) operating system (just a hobby, won't be big and professional like gnu [recursive gnu's not Unix]) for 386(486) AT clones."

The beginning of Linux

This was the beginning of an effort which would culminate in the building of a complete Unix-like operating system which now carries the name Linux. It would become a freely distributable version of UNIX. Unlike BSD and AT&T Unix, at the cost of $0.00, this operating system would be completely affordable to the ordinary computer hacker.

Unlike BSD and AT&T Unix, however, the kernel for this operating system would be developed primarily by Linus Torvalds at the University of Helsinki in Finland. Because the kernel was not being lifted from AT&T, this new Unix would be free for anybody. Torvalds would see to that.

Though intimately involved in every step, Torvalds did not write all the operating system code by himself. He had plenty of help from many UNIX programmers (they like to call themselves hackers) and other computer wizards across the Internet.

Torvalds created a development environment in which anyone with enough know how and gumption could develop new pieces or even change the operating system. Ultimately, Torvalds was and continues to be the final arbitrator as to which pieces make it into the distributed operating system and which ones go into the "efforts" bucket.

How Linux got its name

It is not coincidence that Linux is very similar to Torvalds' first name, *Linus*. Indeed he reluctantly gave the operating system his first name, since he was concerned he would not be taken seriously if he gave the perception of being an egomaniac. Linus Torvalds had in fact given his early operating system the name "FREAX." Though he admits today that this was a bad name choice, at the time he saw a combination of free and freak and the infamous Unix X – the *"ecks"* sound—which most versions of Unix carry--(such as AIX, XENIX, UNIX).

Linus is thankful that his friend Ari Lemmke who ran the University FTP site took it upon himself to change the "FREAX" label. Linus had been using Linux as his working name, and Lemmke thought this name was more appropriate and posted the work under the Linux label.

Considering how brand names take on so much meaning in marketing, the name FREAX would certainly not have helped people get the warm fuzzies for this new Unix. "FREAX" has so little marketing appeal by itself that one might presume it was created by a focus group behind closed doors in the hallowed halls of, ok, I'll say it --- corporate IBM. I couldn't resist the shot.

Free software begets free software

An operating system kernel doth not an operating system make. It takes much more. In many ways the development of Linux is like a perfect story which has a manifest destiny to complete successfully. Even before Linus was being frustrated in getting a cheap, fully functional Unix for his PC, in 1984, Richard Stallman, President of the Free Software Foundation had put together a project which he cutely called GNU. Recursively named "GNU's Not Unix," this project was begun by Stallman as a counteraction to the rules and encumbrances, which software vendors were imposing on the software user community.

Stallman is an advocate of total software freedom. In many ways, Linus shares the same basic philosophy. The Free Software Foundation isn't only interested in software being free. Stallman and company are most interested in all aspects of freedom regarding software. Stallman says: "The word 'free' doesn't refer to price; it refers to freedom." Stallman sees all of the caveats and rules associated with software typically selling for hundreds of dollars, as a form of repression.

From Stallman's perspective, you get to use the software, but you are inhibited from making the slightest change. Everything about the program from its design to its source code is kept a tightly guarded secret. Stallman's idea for software freedom would have software with no secrets. Source code would be provided.

Users would be able to take the software apart, see how it works, and make whatever changes they wish. The world of the Free Software Foundation is a different world indeed. People can share free software with their friends - just by making a copy - no royalties, no shareware fees, nor any restrictions at all. But the world of commercial software remains rule infested.

With Linus Torvalds and Richard Stallman's GNU project, there is a definite chicken or the egg dilemma. Long before Linus took his Unix course, Stallman had been building a Unix, -- GNU Unix if you will. His aim for the GNU project was to write a complete "free" version of Unix, including the kernel and all the associated elements. The objectives of the GNU project were to give users the freedom to share and change software but not add restrictions and impose them on others.

Fully aware of the GNU activity, including the fact that Stallman's project had yet to develop a kernel for his operating system, Linus saw this as a great opportunity. There was a large bevy of fully functional software just waiting for his kernel. Rather than hope that someone might decide to write applications designed specifically for the kernel in his operating system, Linus tweaked Linux to work hand in glove with GNU's pre-existing Unix (waiting for a kernel) applications.

It was a marriage made in heaven, with results, not expectations. Linus never had to port programs to Linux. Instead, he ported the kernel to work with the programs. Linus notes that "Linux was never the primary reason for anything - user programs have always been the reason." With a kernel and the supporting software for a complete POSIX compliant Unix operating system, the whole deal added up to a complete system. There is no doubt that a big part of the reason why Linux took off so spectacularly, and was almost universally accepted from the get-go, is that by the time version 1.00 came out, thanks to the GNU project, just about everything else needed for a complete OS was there waiting.

Open source Linux: the many contributors

Much of the software available for Linux was developed by the Free Software Foundation of Cambridge, Massachusetts. Linux development is championed by the GNU project at the foundation. But Linus Torvalds and GNU are not the only pieces of this grand Linux puzzle. Though Torvalds and the GNU project get substantial credit for Linux software, programmers all over the world have contributed to the growing pool of Linux ware.

Throughout the years, this work has culminated in Linux receiving major attention from the commercial software world. IBM and others, including Microsoft, have become contributors to the growing Linux software pool. The Linux Foundation, http://www.linuxfoundation.org is now the storehouse for Linux.

Building Linux: how it got done

Giving credit where credit is due, however, we come right back to Linus. He developed the Linux kernel more or less as a hobby project, after being inspired by Andy Tanenbaum. In fact, as noted above, the first discussions about Linux on the Internet occurred on the Usenet newsgroup comp.os.minix. Linus's intention for these discussions was the development of a small, academic UNIX system for Minix users who wanted more than Minix had to offer at the time.

The most detailed work involved in building the core functions during the early development of Linux was all written in 386 assembly code. In other words, the toughest part had to be developed in the toughest way. Very few people ever get good at writing assembly code and very few people get to build the foundation of a new operating system. For the techies, a good part of this early work dealt with writing functions such as task switching and memory management using the 80386 protected mode interface.

Linus explains the rest of the project in these words:

"After that it was plain sailing: Hairy coding still, but I had some devices, and debugging was easier. I started using C at this stage, and it certainly speeds up development. This is also when I start to get serious about my megalomaniac ideas to make 'a better Minix than Minix.' I was hoping I'd be able to recompile gcc (GNU's "C" language compiler) under Linux someday...

Two months for basic setup, but then only slightly longer until I had a disk driver (seriously buggy, but it happened to work on my machine) and a small file system. That was about when I made 0.01 available [around late August of 1991]: It wasn't pretty, it had no floppy driver, and it couldn't do much anything. I don't think anybody ever compiled that version. But by then I was hooked, and didn't want to stop until I could chuck out Minix."

Is it ready yet?

Linus never announced his version 0.01. In fact, the routines were hardly executable. In order to use the Linux operating system at this stage, a user would have to have a Minix machine to get it all set up. Even after setup, the user would have to play with the operating system to make it function.

These were the humble beginnings of something which has grown from just a few thousand lines of code twenty-three

years ago to over 15,000,000 lines today in Linux 3.0. When
a clean Linux was finally released for real on March 14,
1994, at kernel # 1.0.0, it had 176,250 lines of code.
On October 5, 1991, Linus introduced his first "official"
version of Linux. He called it version 0.02. It had a shell and
a C compiler, but it wasn't capable of very much. However,
it was something which computer hackers (the good kind)
could really get into. There was little effort placed in the
areas of user support, documentation, or even code
distribution and configuration in this early version.

The bulk of the effort was extended to produce a strong base
(kernel) operating system. Though these areas are important
for commercial systems, the Unix community has always
treated such ergonomic issues (user support, documentation,
code distribution facilities etc.) as secondary to kernel
development. Linus and the rest of the Linux community
were no different.

As the hacker add-ons and change offerings kept coming in
and Linus kept tuning the operating system, soon there was
a version 0.03. And as even more folks worked on the
system, Linus skipped the next set of 0.X releases and
moved to 0.10.

After more revisions, Linus knew that he had something,
and was preparing for a release of a usable sanctioned
version. To reflect this, in March, 1992 Linus pushed up the
version number to 0.95, giving the notion that version 1.0
was just around the corner. This would be the signal that the
software was considered theoretically complete and free of
known bugs.

Linus was apparently a hard man to please. As the versions
of the operating system were getting closer and closer to 1,
but never reaching 1 (asymptotically approaching) in

December, 1993, Linux was sitting at .99.pl14 –
mathematically reflecting that it was getting better but it was
not quite there.

It was twenty + months after version 0.95 signaled that
Linux was coming. Yet it still had not arrived. Version 1.00
would not be released until Linus knew it was highly stable
and rich in function. This was not Microsoft code. Linus
wanted it to actually work. In March, 1994, Linux came out
the front door at version 1.0. Linus was finally pleased, but
not pleased enough to stop or to call the project complete.

Free as a bird!

One of the nicest parts of Linux (there are lots more), and
one of the main reasons why it has received so much
attention from users and from the press is that its kernel uses
no code from AT&T or any other proprietary source. Linux
was developed by programmers, for programmers who
wanted a nice operating system to use on the Intel (PC)
platform. They did not want to deal with the cost of Unix
and the control of Unix by so many fragmented outside
sources.

At last: a real operating system

When Linux was released in March 1994, in many ways it
was Linus Torvalds's stamp of approval on a phenomenally
complex project performed by semi-disconnected
developers. The user base for the unofficial Linux had
already grown large, and the detached development team
had grown substantial.

Linux supports POSIX standards

Most industry experts agree that Linus did a reasonably
good job in creating a POSIX compliant Unix brand OS.
Most of the utilities that come with Linux were not written

from scratch. A large number were BSD ports. They were readily adaptable to Linux because the APIs are so compatible.

A new Unix... a Unix clone from scratch

In many ways, Linus Torvalds et al., did for Unix in 1994 what Compaq did for BIOS in 1982. He freed it from vendor domination. If IBM were willing to sell their PC BIOS code in 1981, they could have made a ton of money from the clone manufacturers just like AT&T sold its Unix.

Unfortunately, IBM was not willing to share this part of the system since they believed it made their PC non clone-able. IBM wanted to keep it a secret, a notion which is anathema to the open software community.

AT& T, however, was not held back by trying to keep Unix a secret. Nor did they mind making a ton of money by holding the rights and selling it. Considering that Unix was really an internal project for AT&T, things worked out pretty well for them, almost by accident. They sold Unix to whoever would buy it, and they made a nice buck on it, despite it being just a side venture for them.

Since IBM refused to share its BIOS, like AT&T, by selling it and profiting from their sharing, they forced their imitators to build it themselves. Compaq used IBM's extensive documentation and they were able to reverse engineer IBM's BIOS. They were able to fabricate a set of specs which many believe were better than the original. From the specs, Compaq created their own BIOS, in much the same way as Linus created Linux.

IBM got nothing for COMPAQ's efforts. AT&T got nothing for Linus's efforts. Eventually, keeping the secret, cost IBM much more than they ever could have imagined. Compaq overtook IBM as the largest PC manufacturer in the world. In many ways, IBM's once closed door on an open PC platform may be diagnosed by historians as the Company's reason for losing control of an industry, which it had created.

For IBM and Linux, IBM has probably lost as much on Linux if not more than it lost by not being the owner of Unix. It is hard to believe IBM had all this and simply gave it up.

With the same frugal attributes as Apple founder Steve Wozniak, who would not pay the price for the Intel 8088, or the Motorola 6800 and selected the $25.00 6502 instead, Linus hated the thought of paying anything for the operating system. He viewed the fees exacted for using Unix as donations to a kingdom, of which he was not a citizen.

Besides being unaffordable to the common person, the fees were outrageous in themselves. Unlike Compaq, Linus did not have to reverse engineer Unix since its source was always available, though subject to licensing fees. He just figured out how it ran from the source.

For building the Unix kernel from scratch, the name Linus Torvalds is forever etched in the computer hall of fame. Once Linux was built and the utilities were ported, a free Unix came into being. The rest is current history.

Chapter 29

The Microcomputer Revolution

Chipmakers galore!

IBM deployed unique solid logic chips in its System/360 for sure but the company did not have an exclusive lock on the micro-chip industry. In fact the chip—aka the integrated circuit—was invented in parallel by Jack Kilby of TI and Robert Noyce of Fairchild in the late 1950's. The integrated circuit paved the way for all microchip manufacturers. In essence it involves making all parts of a circuit, not just the transistor, out of silicon.

IBM therefore was not the only company that hired smart college graduate computer technology engineers to craft innovative chip designs. There were lots of chipmakers. Such companies included Zilog, Motorola, Texas Instruments, Fairchild, and even Bell Labs. It was not until further advances with integrated circuits that Intel's Ted Hoff invented the microprocessor (4004) in 1971. A full microcomputer chip system was invented in 1972.

Let's define microprocessor and microcomputer now before we get too far into this history. A microprocessor is a simple central processing unit (CPU) on a single chip (remember the term 'Single Chip'). It includes Arithmetic Logic Unit (ALU), Control Unit (CU), Registers, Instruction Decoders, Bus Control Circuits, etc. All parts noted would be on a single chip. A microcomputer chip includes a microprocessor. In essence it is the merging of a microprocessor with the peripheral I/O devices, support circuitry and memory (both data and program) memory. It is not necessary to be on a single chip (remember this point, not necessarily in a single chip). However, it did not take long for microcomputers to become single chip entities.

Just as today, science professors at academic institutions such as MIT invented many useful tools in the 1970s. The first microcomputer for example was invented in 1972 by a team led by Bill Pentz at Sacramento State University. Their unit was called the Sac State 8008. It took a while for the single chip microcomputer to be invented.

The computer-on-a-chip patent, called the "microcomputer patent" at the time, U.S. Patent # 4074351, was awarded to Gary Boone and Michael J. Cochran of Texas Instruments in February 1978.

Other laboratories created other models of the microcomputer using multi-chip designs. Their devices were more successful than the original Sac 8, and are responsible for setting off the industry. Chips such as the Altair 8800 and TRS-80 top the list. The Sac State 8008 never had real marketing success.

Introduced in 1975, the Altair 8800 was designed by the Micro Instrumentation and Telemetry Systems group in Albuquerque, N.M. It was powered by an Intel 8080 microprocessor. Memory was too expensive then so the Altair chip real estate contained no memory. The Altair 8800 opened the door for other microcomputers, such as the TRS-80 or Model I, which Radio Shack introduced in 1977.

And, though these companies, including IBM made great chips, they too were not the only chip makers before IBM offered its PC in 1981. The Intel microprocessor line was in full play at that time and it was eventually selected by IBM to power its first PC. There are a lot of rumors about Apple's "Woz" wanting to use an Intel 8080 to power the first Apple, rather than the bargain basement MOS chip that was selected. There were lots of choices in the semiconductor chip industry—that's for sure.

I find it strange that neither Tandy Radio Shack nor Apple, the two kings of the home computer marketplace, which erupted after integrated chips were perfected in the mid 1970's, looked to Intel for their home computer chip solution? It makes one wonder what IBM knew that they did not. Or was it just chance?

Before we look at the Home Computer marketplace in the mid-1970's, we will examine many of the major chipmakers of the day. Chips come before systems. These companies all had a major impact on the hobby / home computer marketplace long before IBM's PC. One thing for sure; no home computer was built by any company that did not depend on a microprocessor built by one of the chip pioneers that we are about to discuss.

IBM of course had its own microprocessors for its own use but chose not to deploy any of these in its own PC. Over time, IBM used its own designs in imbedded controllers and eventually built enough chips that it sold them commercially.

Let's now take a hard look at those successful chipmakers that made microprocessors for the home/hobby computer industry pre IBM PC and post IBM PC. Because their stories are so interrelated with the home computer vendors, whose machines they powered, in this section of the book, we will dip in and out of silicon back to home use so that this section is not confusing and it can remain entertaining and informative.

Besides Gordon Moore and Robert Noyce of Intel, there are other billionaires and a ton of millionaires in the list of people who helped make this micro computer technology revolution happen. They deserve all of their own plaudits. Every now and then, big IBM would use one of these great companies as a subcontractor for controllers or major processors in its devices. The point is that even before the IBM's record breaking PC, these chip entrepreneurs were out there. They were trying to break into a technology market that was very new to everybody in the early 1970's. Opportunities were endless and the chip makers did not have to worry about IBM as a competitor. Thank you, IBM.

Most of the microprocessor stories that we tell in this section took place prior to John Opel's tenure as Chairman and CEO of IBM. One company's microprocessor prowess that we do not spend much time talking about is IBM's own semiconductor business. IBM could have been the best microprocessor company of all time if it had chosen to sell its chip products in the System/360 era. Instead it kept its chip technology to itself.

IBM used most of its own microprocessor chips and other chips until the late 1980's and 1990's for its own internal system production. IBM manufactured lots of systems, controllers, and devices requiring its own chips. In the 1990's IBM moved into the Power Line of microprocessors, which it chose to sell on the open market.

IBM eventually decided that it was as good as it got in the chip marketplace and so it began to compete and sell chips from its foundry. The Company also sold chip designs from its engineering specialists inside its labs. IBM was a great engineering company that once was also a great marketing company.

The Microprocessor changed the world

There is a major difference in the types of businesses run by the systems produced in their day by minicomputer and microcomputer vendors. Most minicomputer vendors in their heyday built "killer" equipment and then hoped to sell a system to a business, whereas, microcomputer / microprocessor vendors were often hidden in back rooms, creating their products as components for the full-line computer manufacturers of minicomputers or personal computers.

Chipmakers other than IBM

As noted, IBM did not invent the integrated circuit. Jack Kilby from TI, Robert Noyce, cofounder of Intel, and other contemporaries get credit for the creation of the integrated circuit though industry historians always mention Kilby from Texas Instruments as the inventor.

IBM always had tremendous marketing power in the data processing industry, even when it had no computers per se in its product line. When IBM did choose to get into the computer industry, it took less than ten years for it to become one of the premiere semiconductor (chip) makers in the world.

The IBM Supercomputers using the Company's Power chips are a result of IBM's superior research and design. Despite all of its magnificent technical accomplishments in areas from disk drives to database to telecommunications to computer chips, IBM seemed to always be able to snatch defeat from the jaws of victory. The industry analysts are speculating today that IBM is contemplating getting out of the hardware business completely. That would be a shame for many reasons.

IBM has had a lot of good years. Though one time in the early 1980's CEO John Opel predicted that he would make IBM a $100 billion dollar company by 1990, it did not happen. Opel made a lot of bad mistakes and IBM paid for them in John Akers' tenure. His projection was not even close. In fact it was not until 2011 that IBM hit $105 billion in revenue and now the company has faltered back to the $92 billion mark.

Coincidentally, 2011 was IBM's 100th year of operation as the International Business Machines Corporation. IBM fumbled on many opportunities, mostly in the Opel years and beyond. During the Learson / Cary years, IBM steadily grew revenues and despite the weight of the US Government's antitrust suit, did quite well for itself. After Cary and Learson, things began to go downhill.

As we take a look at the chip makers and microcomputer manufacturers in this section and then we segue into home and hobby and personal computing, you will see that there were many companies that got pretty good at the microprocessor game.

Many bright engineers and scientists worked for companies other than Big Blue. IBM was not alone in being able to innovate. But, IBM had the marketing force and a corporate team of marketers focused on the largest businesses in the world. IBM therefore could have done substantially better in terms of revenue with its massive opportunities. Along the way, many entrepreneurs got rich but few got rich by working for IBM.

In this part of Section III, we focus on many different chipmakers. In the next few chapters, for example, we examine several well-known companies, such as Texas Instruments (TI), Intel, and Motorola. Additionally, we examine some not too-well-known companies, such as

Shockley Electronic, Fairchild Camera, MOS Technologies, and Zilog.

Until the wave of foreign chip foundries from the 1980's forward, we could say that all of these companies from the 1970's, plus two of the major chip innovators of all time, IBM and Bell Labs, were responsible for building just about every computer chip that was ever born.

Some of these companies are known because every now and then they have been in the consumer marketplace with items such as radios, watches and home computers. Others are well known because they are the companies that built the computer chip processors for IBM, and IBM compatible computers - IBM, Dell, Gateway, HP, Compaq, Lenovo a well as the many Apple and Radio Shack units produced over the years.

Some of the companies build or at one time built semiconductors but more or less stayed in the background while others would venture out occasionally. Still other chip manufacturers, such as Intel are on the forefront continually with their relationship with Microsoft. Intel also makes a lot of other products such as mother-boards, and memory, for which they are paid handsomely.

Many in the industry chortle as they still refer to the Windows and Intel combination as Wintel, as if it were a company by itself. In many ways it is. However, to be exact, "Wintel" is a portmanteau (blend) of Windows and Intel, referring to personal computers using Intel x86-compatible processors running Microsoft Windows.

TI and Zilog and Motorola were quieter in their day. Their only recent forays into the computer marketplace was when they provided processors for somebody else. TI at one time operated a chip foundry for Sun's microprocessors in much the same way as Intel provided the foundry for Compaq's DEC/Alpha processors before DEC and Compaq became part of HP.

There are two companies, which belong in any examination of semiconductor technology. However, we are not including them in this section. They are IBM and Bell Labs. Neither of these companies have had a major influence in the commercialization of semiconductors. They are both major technology development pioneers and major producers, but the fruits of their labor have not typically been offered for general sale. Instead, companies used their innovations to help gain the competitive edges in their respective industries. They did not sell chips per se.

Bell developed transistor, signal, and switch technologies which eclipse all other players in the telephone switch market. IBM, while preparing for the System/360 days, became a major developer and manufacturer of chips used in its System/360 and later proprietary systems, controllers, and devices. Neither Bell nor IBM were known for selling chips. They made the best designs for their products for their respective industries so that in their industries, they could retain their # 1 status.

The microcomputer / semiconductor industry is very exciting with many of the pioneers, including Intel's Gordon Moore, A Bell Labs graduate, still very much alive to share in their company's glory. Let's start our microcomputer adventure by first taking a look at the Texas Instruments company.

Chapter 30

Texas Instruments—a Micro Tech Pioneer and Eternal Innovator

TI was once the in-home computer champ.

Every now and then we hear about Texas Instruments doing something special which affects our lives. One of my first introductions to this company was when they tried their hand at digital watches in the 1970s. They were neat. But they were not as neat as the TI/99 4A home computer which could be bought for $50.00 at Wilkes-Barre's Boscov's Department Store in 1982.

At the time, the TI/99 and the 4A machines had been out from the late 1970's and TI had them in fire-sale mode. When released in the 1978 time frame, the TI 99 sold for $1150.00. Later the 4A, an enhanced version was introduced and it sold for $525.00. At these prices, the TI 99 models were affordable. At, $50.00, they were literally a steal.

The "99" had a TI-developed speech synthesizer chip unit that would work with many of the TI/99 game cartridges which were available for kids and adults back then. Does the term: "Hunt the Wumpus" ring a bell? It was TI's big game for years, and it was a lot of fun for families.

Of course, some of the game cartridges were not game cartridges at all. They were clever little programs which made kids think that learning was fun. My son Brian thought such learning was a lot of fun. Brian had a love affair with calculators from when he could barely speak.

Figure 30-1 TI 99 4A Hunt the WUMPUS!

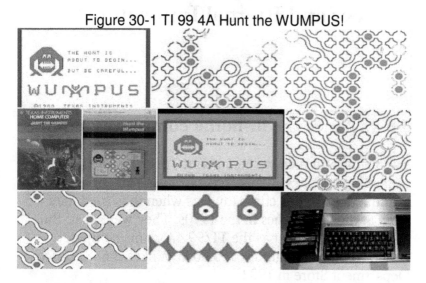

During the 1982 Christmas season, at 2½ he was speaking pretty well and he had become a whiz with his calculator, which, before he had begun to speak properly, was his "kuh-shah-shun." That's the phonetic spelling, of course. Eventually, he could say calculator, just like you and I, but mom and dad kept using "kuh-shah-shun." because we thought it was so cute.

Santa and the TI/99 4A

Anyway. Santa gave the 2½ year-old the TI 99/4A complete with speech synthesizer for Christmas. Santa had set up the unit in the family room, two rooms away from the tree so he left a note for Brian by the tree. He could read the note and he made a b-line to the family room.

You know the look in his eyes when he saw it! Before we knew it, he was sitting down in front of the biggest TV in the house, working one of the math cartridges for kids. For some reason, he selected the hard problems. They started off with the machine speaking: "Two plus four plus one equals." When it finished, it paused and in a deep, slow voice said, "Your turn!" Brian quickly "plugged-in" a "7" and the machine rewarded him with a series of happy sounding tunes and small fireworks images.

Then the machine said "twelve plus seventeen plus nine equals." Again, the machine said, in that same deep voice: "Your turn!" Brian thought for a while and then when he was ready to "plug-in" the answer, he heard a buzzing and an unhappy sound and the machine read the problem again and gave him the answer... "38"... which he already knew but was too late! He had not entered it in time. That would never happen again to my Brian!

The 2½ year old paused the machine and left the room. He came back in a minute or so with... you guessed it, his "kuh-shah-shun." The next time the machine said: "Thirteen plus fifteen plus seven," Brian was plugging the numbers into the "kuh-shah-shun" as it spoke. When the machine said: "Your turn" He plugged in the value "35" right from the display on the "kuh-shah-shun." He was never wrong again! We loved the TI home computer. As an IBMer, I thought it was a toy but it was as much a computer as the big guys I worked with in IBM client offices.

TI products were very likeable

I never met anybody who had a TI digital watch or one of their "99" computers who did not enjoy the experience. In the 1970s, TI also made complete minicomputer systems, but they chose to not stay in any of these three businesses for very long. As an IBM conversion engineer, the TI business computer users who I met, were forced to move to another platform, but they still liked TI. They were moving only because TI was getting out of the "minicomputer" business.

TI and IBM

Though TI would typically not be lined up on a chart as a competitor of IBM, because they do not fabricate competitive products to IBM's, they continue to be a major force in the information technology field. They make many of the base components for computers and they are very good at it. Moreover, if TI ever decided to become a full computer vendor again, they have the engineering skill to make the venture successful. If they found some marketing somewhere along the way, they would be quite formidable.

TI has a number of other firsts to its credit, including the first commercial silicon transistors; the first integrated circuit—Jack Kilby of TI and Robert Noyce of Intel share the industry honor—; the first microprocessor; the first single-chip microcomputer; and the first electronic hand held calculator. And for those who like to hear machines speak, they also invented the first single chip speech synthesizer, the reason why everything from toys to greeting cards can talk to you and me. And, of course, the TI/99 voice was the motivation for my son to get out his calculator

TI is just about a $15 billion company today. They have had some recent divestitures and acquisitions which have positioned them better for the future. Their company direction has been focused for the last decade or so on digital signal processors (DSP) and analog technology. TI acquired National Semiconductor in 2011, laying the groundwork for its next-generation signal-processing technology.

TI's innovative analog and DSP technologies, along with its other semiconductor products, help its many customers meet real world signal processing requirements. TI is the world leader in digital signal processing and analog technologies. IBM is lucky that TI was marketing constrained and not technologically constrained or TI could have given IBM a run for its money.

Before flat screens became the rage, TI had invented DLP Technology. I have a DLP machine and its picture is as clear as being there. TI began its DLP Products division in 1993. This division is committed to developing innovative, best-of-class technology for products ranging from the first iPod docking device with built-in DLP Pico™ projector to the Pittcon Gold Editor's Award-winning DLP NIRscan™ evaluation module for the field of spectroscopy.

To unleash the unlimited possibilities, TI's world-class digital technology also empowers leading electronics manufacturers, scientists, and engineers to develop innovative products from the world's brightest, laser-based IMAX® digital projectors to proven solutions for measuring and sensing. TI keeps making money and every now and then it breaks away with a neat idea like a computer for a kid or a wrist commando watch or a speech synthesizer.

The Company uses highly programmable and flexible technology and therefore it continuously enables breakthrough developments in consumer, medical, industrial and automotive applications ranging from mobile projection to optical sensing and DNA synthesis. We should never discount TI.

TI has no thank-you's for IBM nor should it have. Perhaps IBM, recognizing Jack Kilby's groundbreaking work at TI has in fact benefitted from TI, and maybe IBM should be thanking TI.

Before TI found its niche, IBM's R&D budget was almost as much as TI's gross sales. Yet, it is tough to find negatives about TI technology, since it is and seems to always have been leading edge. I guess the only thing I might suggest, as an avid IBM rooter, is that Virginia "Ginni" Rometty, IBM's CEO never forgets to send a nice holiday gift and warm singing greeting card to Ralph W. Babb, Jr., TI's leader. Your Turn!

Chapter 31

Shockley & Fairchild Semiconductor—the Pioneers

Microcomputer pioneers

Before we go to the next chapter to discuss bigger entries in the microcomputer field, such as Motorola, a long-time electronics corporation which provided a lot of roots for the Microcomputer revolution, let's first look at a few pioneers in the industry and a few of the earliest companies

Shockley Semiconductor— Pioneer's Pioneer

When William Shockley was ready to leave Bell labs to found his brainchild, Shockley Semiconductor in 1955, as one of the first companies in the newly forming semiconductor industry, he took with him a legacy of invention and eight of the most talented young men who would ever work anywhere and anytime in the computer electronics field.

Shockley decided to form his company to build transistors. After all, eight years had passed since he, John Bardeen, and Walter H. Brattain had invented the transistor for Bell Labs. It was a time to celebrate at Bell Telephone Laboratories in December, 1947 with this historic introduction. But the celebration had long passed.

The devil made me do it!

Shockley was a brilliant man. He was very aware of all the industry buzz about computers and what they would mean in the future, and Bell labs was a pioneer in building computer components for their huge telephone switches. There were lots of highly technical people to talk with and lots of bright Bell employees who were willing to jump ship for the right opportunity to make it big. It makes me feel honored that I was offered two different jobs at Bell Labs before I chose IBM.

Before he made the jump, Shockley knew that he needed some financial help to get through the startup phase of a new business. He received some funding from Beckman Industries and he formed his new company in Palo Alto California, which is near Stanford University.

This is right smack dab in the heart of what is now known as Silicon Valley. Shockley Semiconductor was thus the first semiconductor company to arrive in "Silicon Valley," California. In many ways William Shockley gave birth to Silicon Valley.

He pulled his group together, to get on with their work, not too long after leaving Bell Labs. The team he worked with are well known in the industry today, especially to computer scholars. They have often been referred to as the greatest collection of electronic geniuses ever assembled.

Good things do not always last!

Unfortunately for Shockley Semiconductor, they would not be assembled for too long. His company did not last long. It never did make it big, and after just a few years, Shockley sold out to Clevite Transistor in April, 1960. While it may not have been a success financially, its industry impact was felt big time.

Shockley himself was recognized as a genius as an engineer, but his management style was in conflict with the group. He drove eight of his key employees away within the first year. For twenty years after the traitorous eight left Shockley, they proved they were special. These eight of Shockley's former employees started 65 new enterprises. Now, that is impressive.

The founding of Fairchild Semiconductor

This list of men who left Shockley sounds like who's who in the history of computers. These men, who became known as "the traitorous eight," were: Robert Noyce, Gordon Moore, Sheldon Roberts, Eugene Kliner, Victor Grinich, Julius Blank, Jean Hoerni and Jay Last. They left Shockley semiconductor in 1957 and together formed Fairchild Semiconductor, which became an "independent" business unit of Fairchild Camera.

Fairchild Semiconductor did pretty well for itself after some innovations by Jean Hoerni were implemented in the 1959 time period. During Fairchild's heyday, the number of employees ballooned from a handful to about thirty thousand, and sales rocketed from a few thousand dollars to about 150 million dollars per year.

Fairchild experts go elsewhere

As Fairchild and the semiconductor industry grew, many of Fairchild's original eight saw opportunities elsewhere. The two most notable, Moore and Noyce left Fairchild in 1968 to manage a small start-up company which they had named Intel (Integrated Electronics). Noyce was the general manager of the Company and while there, he invented the integrated chip—a chip of silicon with many transistors all etched into it at once. Along with Jack Kilby of TI, Noyce is credited with this first.

Robert Noyce had left Philco Corporation (TVs et al.) where he had been able to perform research on leading edge electronics. Gordon Moore left his chemistry research position at Johns Hopkins University's applied physics lab. They both set out to do something special with their lives. They had issues with Shockley, almost immediately, and chose to move out, along with the other infamous members of the "traitorous eight." Shockley was upset with the whole bunch of them leaving at the same time and the notion of a large scale mutiny is conjured up with his "traitorous eight" label.

Life was not that bad

Moore and Noyce did very well for themselves at Fairchild Semiconductor. Noyce had become general manager, and Moore was head of Research and Development.

While at Fairchild, as noted above, Noyce made semiconductor history by independently inventing the integrated chip. However, at the same time, as previously noted Jack Kilby was involved in a similar project at TI, where he also, independently, invented the integrated silicon chip. History credits both men with this invention.

Though Moore and Noyce were doing quite well at Fairchild, what they received was not exactly what they had bargained for. There were major changes in management at Fairchild Camera and strange things were happening in the business. Some believe that the Fairchild Camera board was diverting funds from the semiconductor group to areas outside the business. Noyce and Moore were not pleased with the situation and they decided that they had enough. These two soon went out again and formed another company, Intel Corporation.

Chapter 32

Motorola the Chip Maker with Different Roots

From Galvin Manufacturing to Motorola

Long before Moore and Noyce began to build their fortunes at Intel, The activity had begun for the future Motorola. At 33 and 29 respectively, Paul V. Galvin (1895-1959) and his brother Joseph E. Galvin (1899-1944) were a bit older than some of our modern day billionaires such as Jobs and Gates when they began their entrepreneurship by purchasing the battery eliminator business of the bankrupt Stewart Storage Battery Company in Chicago. On September 25, 1928, the Galvin brothers gave name to their enterprise as they incorporated the Galvin Manufacturing Corporation.

Motorola's first product

The name was really no surprise as they quickly rid the new organization of the remnants of the Stewart Company. But they kept the five employees, while renting new quarters on 847 West Harrison Street. Of course wages were not that steep back then, but even the first week's payroll of $63.00 taxed the fledgling company.

Their hard assets were meager, consisting of $565.00 in cash and $750.00 in tools. However, there was a prize hidden in this company, the design for the Company's first product, a battery eliminator. Today, we might call such a device an AC adapter.

This clever device, when it was developed, enabled battery operated home radios to operate on ordinary household electrical current. It wasn't too long before the Company had to tackle its next big problem. As electronic tube radios took over for these battery units in households, battery eliminators would soon become obsolete.

Before having to tackle an obsolescence problem, however, the Galvin's were already on their way to their fortune. By 1930, after just two years, their net annual sales rocketed to over a quarter million dollars. At the same time the Company diversified and built the first practical and affordable automobile radio. Now we are starting to see why they became Motorola.

Since radios were not an option provided with an automobile at the time, the Galvin's had an instant success on their hands. Way back then, Paul Galvin recognized some value in a future company name change and he coined the term Motorola for the Company's new product line. Motorola brings with it the connotation of both motion (motor car) and radio (Victrola). As you might have expected, it was not long before Galvin's share of the auto radio business grew so rapidly that it established the Company as a leader in the U.S. market.

New products, nice growth for Motorola

Product line innovations came fast as the Company invented the "Police Cruiser", an AM auto radio pre-set to receive police broadcasts. This was Galvin's first entry into the new field of radio communication products. Of course today the Company is a leader in pager products and many wireless computer devices.

By 1940, net sales were almost $10 million and the employee population had grown to almost a thousand, as Galvin Manufacturing became a pioneer in FM radio communications. During the same period, the Company developed the first hand held two way radio for the U.S. Army Signal Corps. The portable "Handie Talkie" two way AM radio quickly became a World War II symbol.

Galvin / Motorola in the WWII effort

Just like all of the other electronics companies and business machine companies of the day, Galvin committed its full resources to the war effort. Once the war broke out, the Company did sell 125,000 already built radio units for home use. But, they were the last shipped until the Company went back to peace time production in 1945. It certainly must have been hard to get a radio back then.

New name, new directions for Galvin Manufacturing

By 1947 when the Company offered its first public stock offering at $8.50 per share, the Motorola trademark was so widely known that Paul Galvin changed the Company's name to Motorola, Inc. By 1948, as IBM and Univac were duking it out for computer champion, Motorola made its initial entry into the TV business with its $179.00 "Golden View" offering. Considering that black and white TVs currently sell for less than $100.00, we can get a sense of how privileged one had to be in 1948 to be able to buy one of these. On top of that, Motorola's "Golden View" was the least expensive TV of its time.

Motorola begins a semiconductor group.

While computers were being built with tubes, in 1952, Motorola began a semiconductor development group. Their first efforts were in the manufacture of a 3 amp power transistor. Being a technology developer and a product manufacturer, the Company eventually used its technology to build a commercial product. The auto radio which incorporated transistors for the first time was introduced in 1956. By 1959, Motorola technology had gotten so good that their new, smaller and more durable, all transistor auto radio, quickly became considered as the most reliable in the industry.

After a while, Motorola got good at making components as well a consumer products. Though initially, the Company manufactured transistors and other semiconductors for exclusive use in its own radios, televisions, and communications products, in 1959 Robert Galvin, son of founder Paul Galvin decided to reduce its costs of component production by becoming a commercial producer and a supplier of semiconductors for sale to other manufacturers. Motorola was officially in the semiconductor business.

By 1960, net sales had climbed to just about $300,000,000 and the employee count was approaching 15,000. The Company became a leader in all facets of the electronics world. One of Motorola's chief customers during this period was the US Government as the Company built a transponder for the Mariner II for its flight to Venus.

This unit provided a radio link spanning 54 million miles. When Mariner IV hit the sky's in 1964, Motorola was there again with a transponder used to send images of Mars all the way back to earth. Motorola remains a major supplier in the space program and has been active from the Gemini program through the Hubble Telescope to many top secret efforts underway today.

Like Texas Instruments, Motorola has been in all aspects of the electronics industry from semiconductors to home products to space equipment. The Company even had a major role with the Hubble Space Telescope. Surely Motorola must believe their parts had worked on the Hubble, since management proudly highlights their participation on the Company's web site. The Company also likes to highlight its consumer product accomplishments on its web site. A quick look and, if you don't know already, you'll find the Motorola name associated with many diverse products such as the following:

- Rectangular picture tubes
- 8 track tape players
- "Pageboy" radio pager
- Low cost plastic encapsulated transistors
- "Quasar" line of color receivers.
- America's first all transistor color television sets
- Portable FM two way radio "Handie Talkie"
- Components for battery powered quartz watches
- Integrated circuits, quartz crystals, and miniature motors
- Short range radio frequency radio telephone system
- Electronic engine control modules
- Pocket Bell pagers
- Instrumentation for cars and trucks
- Control modules for engine transmissions.
- Secure telephone terminal
- "Micro TAC" personal cellular phone
- Lightweight Satellite Terminal (LST) radio
- Wireless In Building Network (WIN)
- etc.

High Technology

Though the Company became well known for its consumer products, over the years, Motorola moved out of a number of consumer areas to focus on its main interests—technology.

Figure 32-1 Motorola Car Radio

For example, in 1974, it pulled out of the TV business, selling the Quasar brand to Matsushita Electric. In 1987 Motorola produced its last auto radio. At the same time, the Company also divested itself of its display systems business as well as its automotive alternator and electro-mechanical meter product lines.

Motorola has also acquired a few companies along the way to strengthen its presence in technology areas in which it wanted to better participate. These include Codex Corporation, a leading manufacturer of products and systems for data communications networks, and Universal Data Systems, a maker of moderately priced data communications equipment.

The reason Motorola is in this book is not because of most of the items on the list shown above. It is because they were and continue to be a major player in the semiconductor arena. Hundreds of companies have used and many continue to use Motorola processors and semiconductor components in thousands of products from coffee makers to controllers for mainframe computers.

Motorola's microprocessors

Motorola has been in the microprocessor business for a long time, having introduced its first microprocessor, the 6800 in 1974. This unit contained approximately 4,000 transistors. The specs at the time were unbelievable as the chip needed only a single 5 volt power supply and was supported by a range of RAMs and ROMs, and other devices, thus making it an ideal chip to select for mid-1970 era computers or controllers – such as the Apple I and II.

The early 6800 customers came from various heavy industries, such as automotive, communications, industrial, and business machines sectors. It is also a fact that Apple's other Steve, Steve Wozniak loved the 6800 so much that he wanted to make it the engine for the Apple I. However, as the story goes, the "Woz" was a great shopper and he found the big blue light special on at MOS technologies, a Motorola break-away company who were charging just $25.00 per 6502 copycat chip vs. Motorola's $125.00 for the original 6800. Though one might say that the 6800 was an inspiration for the Apple I, none of these chips found their way into Apple's PCs in these early days.

Moving from technology generation to generation, in 1979, two years before IBM's PC was introduced, Motorola introduced its first 16 bit microprocessor, the 68000. This was a hummer of a machine and its power and facility was great enough that Apple would begin a relationship with Motorola that continues to this day with the 68000 becoming the base microprocessor for the Macintosh. The 68000 was capable of completing two million calculations per second, and Motorola touted its architecture as enabling the unit to be used both to run and to write programs for scientific, data processing, and business applications. And thus, the Macintosh.

In 1984, Motorola upped the ante again with the first true 32 bit microprocessor dubbed the MC68020. This unit had over 200,000 transistors with access up to four billion bytes of memory. By 1986, more than 125 companies, including IBM, were producing systems or controllers that used this processor.

Despite Motorola's major success in microprocessors, though the Motorola 8-bit 6800 chip was available in 1981 when IBM launched its PC, Big Blue chose not to use the Motorola unit. IBM had been using Motorola for other components over the years such as for outboard processors for its minicomputers, mainframes, modems, and network gear.

IBM, Apple, & Motorola (Freescale)

About ten years later, looking for some chip business of its own, IBM made a sales call on Apple, a company with an affinity towards Motorola, and it offered the PowerPC RISC processor as an option for the waning power of the Motorola 68000 series. Apple promptly informed IBM that it did its chip business with Motorola's Freescale operation.

Undaunted by the setback, IBM packed up and went over and made a sales call on Motorola to see if there was something there. The result of course was that IBM, Apple and Motorola formed a partnership on the IBM-developed PowerPC chip line.

And so, through a Motorola division known as Freescale, Motorola did its own thing with the PowerPC while IBM was using its PowerPCs in stronger strengths. Apple of course used (Apple IBM Motorola) AIM Consortium's PowerPC in Macs until 2005 when Intel made a sales call on their company.

IBM uses derivatives of the PowerPCs today in their computers and controllers. IBM's Power 8 processor is recognized as the best in the industry. There is a new partnership with IBM and Apple just formed so time will tell how this arrangement works out.

Unfortunately for IBM followers, the arrangement with Motorola for the older PowerPC chips was dissolved and the companies went on their separate ways. IBM enhanced its PowerPC research and eventually created iterations of the chip that had immense processing power. For years, in fact, what IBM now calls its Power line of microprocessors have been so powerful that they are used to power systems in the IBM line, such as the Power Systems that rival mainframe performance levels.

The oft-cited reason that Apple pulled out of the arrangement and went with Intel instead of staying with IBM or moving to AMD, was that Apple didn't believe it could get the requisite performance per watt from processors being supplied by IBM and Freescale--formerly Motorola's chip-making arm. This translates into Apple (aka Steve Jobs) being worried about IBM's and Motorola's ability to deliver competitive processors for laptops.

Apple complained many times about IBM's problem, from their perspective, with dissipating heat in laptops; and eventually the Apple Organization became convinced that Intel would be a better choice. A less cited reason for Apple to break its hardware bond with IBM was that Apple simply wanted a better pricing deal on chips. Who really knows?

Back to Motorola and its ascent into being a technology leader in microprocessors and chips. There was never a question that Motorola's developments were leading edge. Displaying its penchant for high quality processes in making its chips and processors. In 1988 Motorola was declared the winner of the first of the very prestigious Malcolm Baldridge National Quality Awards, given by Congress to recognize and inspire the pursuit of quality in American business. IBM's AS/400 system lab in Rochester Minnesota, a few years before it had adopted the Power Chip was also awarded the prestigious US Malcolm Baldridge Award for quality.

During the first decade of the 21st century, cell phone popularity raged. Many are not aware that those chip companies able to drive cell phones were able if the time were right, to be able to drive a US expedition to the moon with just one IBM cell phone Power processor. Most of the processors in the cell phones over time were designed and manufactured by Motorola.

In 2004 Motorola introduced its own RAZR V3 cellular phone, an ultra-slim, metal-clad, quad-band flip phone. The 13.9mm thin phone used aircraft-grade aluminum to achieve several design and engineering innovations, including a nickel-plated keypad.

Most of us regular folk called it the "razor," but we loved the phone in its time. Motorola was not in the consumer retail cell phone business for a very long time but its processor chips become well known in the cell phone industry.

Life continued for Motorola and many of its successful divisions. For example, Motorola Mobility Holdings, Inc. (Motorola Mobility) on January 4, 2011 announced that it had completed its previously announced spin-off from Motorola, Inc. and its shares began trading on the New York Stock Exchange (NYSE) under the ticker symbol

"MMI." And, so, in the future, Motorola will not always be known as Motorola.

Unfortunately, just as IBM has had its share of financial issues since the Watson's stopped running the Company. Motorola has not done so well in the past five years. The Company's recent issues began before 2011, but they got worse shortly after January, 2011.

After years of discussions, the Company split into two parts: Motorola Solutions, an enterprise- and government-facing wing, and Motorola Mobility, specializing in handsets and set-top boxes. Then in August 2011, Google announced that it would be acquiring Mobility for around $12.5 billion a deal that took about nine months to close after it was first made public. Three years later, Google got out of the business and now simply holds Motorola patents. Lenovo bought the rest of Motorola Mobility for just about $3 Billion.

For the record Motorola is now known as Motorola Solutions, Inc. It has had its ups and downs for sure. In 2013, for example, it was on its way up again with revenue above $8 billion for the year but it slipped to just over $5 billion in 2014. As far as we see in 2015, the Company was holding its own on a similar trajectory to 2014.

Also like IBM, Motorola seems to enjoy spinning off pieces of the Company and selling as much as it can of one time money making technology areas. The other part of the 2011 spinoff, for example, Motorola Solutions sold its Networks division to Nokia Siemens Networks early in 2011. On October 27, 2014, the Company sold its enterprise solution business to Zebra Technologies for $3.5 billion.

Of course we know that in 2003, Motorola basically got out of the semiconductor business. Eventually, it seems that all the parts will be gone and there will be no more pieces of Motorola to sell. I hope I am as wrong about Motorola, a one-time strong US company as I hope to be about IBM, the one-time leader of computing in the entire world.

IBM and Motorola, big time in chips

Considering that IBM was a boom company at the beginning of the 1980's and a bust company at the end, it is clear that Motorola was doing something very right during this same time period. IBM for years in the 1960's and 1970's viewed itself the largest chipmaker in the world. Ironically, the business area (commercial chip-making) which Motorola entered and excelled during this period, was one in which IBM chose not to compete. Growing from $3billion to $30 billion could have had a very positive impact on IBM's income statement.

Today IBM is out of the chip making business per se as is Motorola. However, IBM still has its Power chips which it no longer manufacturers but the Company tightly controls the design of these chips known today as Power 8. The Power 8 is the fastest chip in the world. It is so fast that it doubles the performance of the chip used in IBM's Watson Supercomputer.

Chapter 33

The Founding of Intel

Andy Grove, Gordon Moore, and Robert Noyce... that says it all!

As discussed in the Microcomputer Pioneers section, the two most notable Fairchild Semiconductor employees to leave were Gordon Moore, a chemist, and Robert Noyce, A Physicist. Both left in 1968 to manage a small start-up company which they had named NM Electronics for Noyce Moore, and later changed the name to Intel (Integrated Electronics). Noyce, who had earlier invented the integrated circuit, was the general manager of the Company and Moore was the Executive Vice President. They selected Andy Grove as Director of Operations and their first employee. Grove was a dynamo.

Robert Noyce had left Philco Corporation (TVs et al.) where he had been able to perform research on leading edge electronics. Gordon Moore left his chemistry research position at Johns Hopkins University's applied physics lab. They both set out to do something special with their lives. They started with Shockley and moved to Fairchild when Shockley became too much of a boss.

Life was not that bad

Moore and Noyce did very well for themselves at Fairchild Semiconductor and could have had great careers but something was not right at Fairchild as they had a tough time keeping promises. Noyce had become general manager, and Moore was head of Research and Development. While at Fairchild, Noyce made semiconductor history by independently inventing the integrated chip. History credits both Robert Noyce and Jack Kilby with this invention.

While working at Fairchild, there were major changes in management at the parent company, Fairchild Camera and strange things were happening in the semiconductor business. Some believe that the Fairchild Camera board was diverting funds from the semiconductor group to areas outside the business. Noyce and Moore were not pleased with the situation and they decided that they had enough. They went out and formed another company, NM Electronics, later to become Intel Corporation.

Moore and Noyce put together a business plan for Intel (rumor has it Noyce typed it on a single sheet of paper) and they went off to conquer the world. Their objective was to make complex integrated circuits. That was what they did best. They wanted to make something complex, which could have universal applicability. They each put in $250,000, and they received $2,500,000 of investment money to get the Company off the ground. As I said, life had been good at Fairchild Semiconductor.

I addition to creating Intel, Both Noyce and Moore have made their mark in history in other ways. Noyce, of course, with the invention of the integrated silicon chip, and Moore for having made an often quoted prediction know as, "Moore's Law."

Moore's Law

To be technically accurate "Moore's law" is the observation that the number of transistors in a dense integrated circuit has doubled approximately every two years. Having been in the semiconductor business for years, while at Fairchild, Moore took notice to the fact that the growth of computer power was so regular, that you could set your watch by it. You can still predict it that accurately. He observed that microchips were doubling in circuit density (and thus in their potential computational power) every two year or so.

It was back in 1965, that Gordon Moore published a paper entitled 'Cramming more components onto integrated circuits'. In it, Moore made an historic technology prediction to which historians have attached his name. It boils down to a simple statement: 'The number of transistors incorporated in a chip will approximately double every 24 months'.

This recognized geometric growth in power over time has been "canonized" as a law known as "Moore's Law." Thus, future expectations of computer power have been and continue to be simply extracted from past growth. And it is right on the money... a smooth curve on a graph. Though Moore expected his law to be in force for just ten years, it seems that human accomplishment in the field of computing is still buoyed by it, or constrained by it, whichever. The curve does not stray from the law.

Moore recognized that physical space will ultimately determine how long increases in densities can be achieved. After all, from his point of view, the law expired in 1975. But, as the separation between circuits gets to within atoms, without a technology that goes even deeper than atoms, Moore's law is expected to expire someday. Right now, nobody knows when that will be. However, the grand prognosticator himself, Gordon Moore in 2015 suggested that foresaw that the rate of progress would reach saturation: Moore noted: "I see Moore's law dying here in the next decade or so."

Memory first at Intel

When Noyce and Moore brought Intel on-line, they were building memory semiconductors for the industry. They wanted to do more, but they needed customers for these yet-to-be memory wares. At the time, electronic calculators were coming into being and they were rapidly replacing the old electro-mechanical models. They tried to find some established calculator companies with which to partner. However, it seemed like all of the calculator companies had already teamed up with a semiconductor company for their new lines. Eventually, they found a company called Busicom, which was a Japanese firm, just starting in the calculator business.

Busicom wanted to build both business and scientific calculators. Busicom had already designed the 13 chips which they wanted fabricated. These chips would form the basis of 13 different calculator models. The Intel engineers at the time were very busy making memory circuits and the Company really did not have the engineering resources to take the Busicom design and build all 13 chips. But Intel really wanted this business.

Why not build a computer?

As they examined the issue, one of the engineers, Ted Hoff, burrowed through the design and looked at what they were really trying to accomplish. After he understood the objectives, Hoff suggested to Moore and Noyce, and others at Intel, that all of Busicom's objectives for the 13 different calculators could be achieved with one general-purpose computer architecture, rather than thirteen unique solutions.

Hoff knew he was on to something good. When he was discussing the potential of this undertaking, he told Gordon Moore that he could see this type of chip being able to be a major component in such things as elevator controls and traffic light controls. In addition to a general purpose computer, this unit would also serve as a general purpose controller.

Most folks in the industry at the time believed that a single chip computer was something that might be achieved in the "someday" time frame. Ted Hoff thought that "someday" had come. He understood that to build anything on one chip, you must be very hardware efficient. Having had considerable experience with the hardware of the DEC PDP-8 minicomputer, a very hardware-efficient machine, Hoff thought that without much more complexity than a memory chip, a simple processing unit could be built.

Intel builds the 4004, the world's first microprocessor

After getting the approval of Busicom, Hoff and four other engineers completed this project (design and creation) in four months. Completed in 1971, they had created the world's first microprocessor. The end result was the 4004, which goes down in history as Intel's first commercial microprocessor. The project was a big success. The future would be even bigger.

The 4004 was not much larger than a fingernail and it was smaller than a thumbnail (3mm x 4mm). On this one chip lived 2300 transistors. Intel sold the chip for $200.00 at the time. This one 4-bit computer chip delivered as much computational power as Eckert and Mauchley's prized ENIAC. However, the 4004 didn't need 18,000 vacuum tubes or the space of a small warehouse to get its job done... just a little less than a thumb.

Who owns the end product?

Not only was the project a big success, but the R&D was paid for by Busicom. Such a deal! But that created its own issues since Intel was constrained from selling the fruits of its labor. Busicom partially owned the end product. Through negotiations, concessions, and money, Intel was able to get back the rights to their development, and as some may say... the rest is history.

Today, Intel is the most successful personal computer chip maker in the world. They are continually building plant capacity for their semiconductor business as well as other businesses in which they engage. They are a major market force to be reckoned with by all.

More Intel microprocessors all the time

From the 4004, the Company then built the 8-bit 8008 (200 KHz) in 1972. Then, in 1974, with the introduction of the 8080, Intel increased the chip density from that of the 8008 by a factor of 2 (5000 transistors) and tweaked the speed to render 20 times more power than the 4004. It did not take long for this full-bodied processor to find itself as the main component of the first kit computer - the Altair. From here, the home computing phenomenon was born.

Intel's processors get even more power

In 1976, Intel had already begun to refine the architecture of its systems as they introduced the 5MHZ 8085 microprocessor. At about the same time, one of Intel's big competitors back then, Zilog, released its famous 2.5 MHz

Z80 chip. IBM became a valued Intel customer when it chose the 8085 for its 5280 Intelligent Data Entry Unit, a replacement machine for the popular IBM 3741 key to 8" diskette unit.

In 1978, Intel used the 8085, its 8-bit entry as the basis for the introduction of the more powerful 16-bit, 4.77 MHz 8086 microprocessor. When IBM later introduced its Displaywriter Word processor, they chose the Intel 8086 as the engine to drive their new unit. This machine had a similar cycle time to the 8085 but, as a 16-bit machine, it worked on twice as many data bits internally at one time.

Intel's 8088 was a hybrid 8085/8086 unit. In essence it was a cheaper version. Like the 8086, it processed sixteen bits internally. But, like the 8085, it processed 8 bits externally when it went to the 8-bit bus for input/output operations. Within two years, the 8088 chip was destined to become the most pervasive computer chip of all time, when IBM selected it as the engine for its first PC.

The introduction of the IBM PC and its clones positioned Intel as a dominant player in the semiconductor industry. One can only speculate where IBM would be today if the Company had selected a home grown chip? Where would Intel be? Intel was already successful so it would have grown independently of IBM but surely it would not have grown as large. This was a very big and nice gift from IBM to Intel, worthy of a big thank you for sure.

Gordon Moore's net worth in 2015 is about $7 billion. The net worth of Robert Noyce who passed away in 1990, checked in at just about $4 billion. As I like to say, no IBMer ever became a billionaire by being the Company's best employee. I include myself in that long IBM list.

It was the selection of the Intel 8088 as IBM's PC engine that got Intel into being one of the largest chipmakers in the world. Intel was already a billion dollar company so it does not credit IBM with all of its success.

IBM at the time had a machine sold through its normal sales channels called the IBM 5100. It was PC-sized but cost about $10,000 with all the accoutrements included. PCs, when fully equipped cost close to $5,000.00

IBMers in the know, have suggested this small unit in the late 1970's was a machine with the power and architecture of a mainframe System/360 model 30 built-in under the covers. That was why IBM did not have to rewrite the APL language to run on the 5100.

What if IBM had used this same engine in its PC instead of the 8088? Noyce and Moore would have surely become millionaires regardless because of their personal talents, but multi-billionaire status may have been tough to achieve. By the way, Andy Grove's net worth, thanks to his great work for Intel, holding no technology patents hit the $400 million mark. Grove was not a founder so that is not a bad take for an important employee.

Intel did not need IBM to continue its success nor did it need IBM to be successful in the first place. But, the 8088 would be the engine for so many PCs that Intel people could not help becoming multimillionaires because of the IBM contract and then because of all the compatibles' contracts.

In 1980 Intel introduced its first 32-bit microprocessor, the iAPX-432 as well as a math coprocessor known as the 8087. IBM concentrated on large scale integration and high powered processing whereas Intel incrementally moved the dial. Intel impressed IBM substantially in the data entry area, word processing, and finally the PC. If IBM was not going to choose a microprocessor from its own stable, Intel was its best choice for a stable technology solution. Intel made good stuff.

Intel on the move - more microprocessors

Intel was not to be stopped. Once IBM got them going at top speed, they ran and ran and ran... mostly to the bank. They are still running. Thanks in part to startup "gifts" from IBM, Intel is now approaching becoming a $60 billion company. They are moving up on IBM itself in terms of annual earnings.

Just one year after an Intel chip was selected for the IBM PC introduction, Intel introduced its 80286. This removed the hardware limitation of 1MB which had been the constraint of the 8085/86/88 processors. With 20 address lines the 808X units, the processor could reach only 1 million addresses.

Microsoft's DOS, the prevalent operating system at the time, had split the 1 million addresses available on the 8088 at the 640,000 mark. Below 640,000 was DOS usable memory, and above 640,000 was where the memory on adapter cards for sound and video and networking would be addressed. That's why 8088 based machines never had more than 640k of memory.

The 80286 used a larger address and was able to reach 16 MB of "real" addressable memory and 1 GB of virtual memory. To put the growth of this processor in perspective, it consisted of 130,000 transistors and ran at a speed of 12 MHz.

In 1985, Intel introduced the 80386, a real 32-bit computer system. The Company clearly solved the problems prevalent with the 80286 architecture and built a fine unit. This processor would bring powerful computing to the masses. Again this power was achieved by the execution of Moore's Law, as Intel was able to jam 275,000 transistors on a little piece of silicon - the 80386, a.k.a. the 386.

In 1989, Intel again raised the bar. The price/performance curve continued its steep climb following Moore's Law. Their new 80486 was substantially faster and featured more than a million transistors, an unprecedented density, at the time, for any processor.

In 1990, at the early age of 62, Robert Noyce, co-founder of Intel, and good friend of Gordon Moore, of Moore's Law, died of heart failure. Noyce held 16 patents for semiconductor devices, methods, and structure. He is in everybody's microprocessor hall of fame.

Intel introduces its Pentium line

In 1993 as it was obvious that Intel was becoming a large, successful company, other microcomputer manufacturers such as AMD and CYRIX were doing a reasonable job of cloning Intel processors, and selling them for less and less. Moreover, these chip cloning companies had begun to use the numbers 486 in their product names so it made it easier for the public to understand there was 486 equivalency in their clone units.

Rather than introduce an Intel 80586, as expected, to avoid the confusion and resulting lost sales, Intel took the 5 in the middle of 80586 and called their new line the Pentiums. Numbers could not be trademarked. But the word Pentium could. These chips added system level functions to the chip and promoted a major increase in raw computer power. The Pentium supported multimedia, graphics, fast I/O, and communications facilities new to the PC arena. And while designing the powerful Pentium processor, Intel followed the laws of their co-founder Gordon Moore, and produced a unit with over 3 million transistors.

In 1995, Intel was at it again with the introduction of the Pentium "Pro", which featured dynamic instruction execution and other performance oriented features such as more integrated cache memory... all included within the chip package. And, again, no laws violated, the Pentium Pro checked in with 5.5 million transistors.

In 1997, Intel introduced yet another Pentium Processor. This one got the handle, the Pentium II. It included Intel's MMX video technology and blasted over 7.5 million transistors on a single chip. It also offered cache enhancements and delivered somewhat faster processing than previous Intel units. It was surely fast enough and powerful enough to support the editing of digital pictures as well as multimedia productions such as music or home movies.

In early 1999 the Company announced the Pentium III family of high speed processors with 8.5 million transistors and 70 new machine instructions to assist in the use of the Pentium in multimedia and games processing. The 500 MHz Pentium IIIs benchmarked at approximately 10% faster than the 450 MHz Pentium II.

Thus, Pentium III's by themselves did not deliver substantially more power than Pentium II processors. However, when applications were written specifically for the new advance instructions buried on the chip, Pentium IIIs run substantially faster than the older Pentium IIs.

Since October, 1999 when Intel juiced up the Pentium line again, perhaps in response to Advanced Micro Devices' (AMD) 700 MHz Athlon chips, which had for the first time eclipsed Pentium chips in performance, a game of leapfrog began in x86 processor performance.

In March, 2000 AMD passed Intel again with the introduction of the 1st GHZ processor (1000 MHz). Intel gained the lead again and the game continued. Intel's newest chips at the time achieved densities of over 28 million transistors using a new .18 micron spacing process. Dr. Moore's law continues as the chip law of the land.

What's next for Intel?

In 2000 and beyond to today, Intel had been offering an even more souped-up version of the Pentium III known as the Xeon processors with better structure and even more cache. These processors were better performers and were typically used in servers which needed all the gas they could get in the day's server-centric environment.

The Intel big future...

Though Moore's Law has done Intel well, they began to prepare for the day that "more" Moore could not be gained from the current architecture. In the mid-1990s, Intel partnered with Hewlett Packard to build the next generation 64 bit processor (code named Merced and announced as Itanium or IA 64). This joint effort was to use the latest in variable length instruction word/group (VLIW/VLIG), or what HP/Intel calls EPIC (Explicit Parallel Instruction Computing).

For the 2000 - 2010 decade, we saw more Pentium III type machines introduced to continue to leverage corporate Windows application software investments. However, companies prodded by HP, a major player in servers were jumping on the Intel Itanium and what were hoped to be the follow-on *McKinley* 64-bit application bandwagon.

In 2014, the end-of-life writing was on the wall for Intel's high-end Itanium chip, with the launch of the high-performance usurper, the chip maker's 15-core Xeon E7 v2 chip. As powerful as the chip may be, if nobody uses it, it does not matter. But, that won't happen!

Intel's Itanium was found mostly in Hewlett-Packard (HP) servers running the HP-UX, OpenVMS or Linux operating systems. But the Xeon E7 v2 chip, which is based on the x86 instruction set architecture, had been slowly encroaching on the market speed occupied by Itanium. With Intel positioning it now as a high-performance alternative that can run both Windows and Linux, the new preferred Server Operating System, the Itanium is being urged to vacate the stable and go to the open lands.

With the E7 v2, analysts see the Itanium as a step closer to meeting its eventual end. The new Xeon E7 v2 chips have been built to have the throughput and performance to run in-memory applications, and also RAS (reliability, availability and serviceability) features, which were originally introduced by Intel just for its Itanium line.

Intel will surely survive but in the 2014/2015 era, Itanium should always be referred to as past-tense. Itanium's success along with a full Intel commitment could have destroyed the IBM Power chip line. Another thank you, this time from IBM is in the cards.

A June 2015 update on Power 8 v Intel Xeon Haswell.

The IBM Power 8 processor has begun to appear in financial applications where compute-intensive loads are expected. How does IBM's powerhouse stack up against Intel's highest-performance CPU offering – the Xeon Haswell – on such a typical workload?

The benchmark results show that in certain workloads the Xeon is twice as fast as IBM's Powerhouse but in double precision computing, the gap is almost removed. Perhaps more importantly, IBM's mean time between failures makes Big Blue the cleaner performer and it lasts lots longer without having to be replaced. When the frog leaps again, we'll have to go back to both IBM and Intel. Maybe they should merge?

Will Wintel survive?

Over the many years in which Intel and Windows have been big buddies, both firms in the Wintel partnership have attempted to extend their monopolies. Intel made a successful major push into the motherboard and chipset markets—becoming the largest motherboard manufacturer in the world and, at one stage, almost the only chipset manufacturer—but badly fumbled its attempt to move into the graphics chip market, and (from 1991) faced sharp competition in its core CPU territory from AMD, Cyrix, VIA and Transmeta. Intel after enduring such threats may be the only game in town for those with an aversion to Power.

Wintel is not as dominant as they once were. Linux is really taking off in the enterprise and the desktop. Linux is in fact ubiquitous in data centers, mostly because of cost, but also security. Once everyone decided they needed a website, web hosting companies started coming to life overnight. Linux cost them a lot less in setup and support. Cheap web hosting at less than $10.00 per month was made possible by Linux. Even though there are tons of Windows servers, it isn't what it used to be.

Desktop computers do not seem to matter as much. Browsing is done on our phones, PDAs and tablets. This makes Wintel worried because more PCs are sitting in the corner collecting dust in most people's homes.

I do keep wondering when the game PCs will be running home applications without having to pay through the roof for software??? Maybe never!

Whichever way the market goes, Intel is quite resilient and they know they have to hire the best to get the best... and they do!

Chapter 34

Zilog: Great Microcomputer Pioneer

Champions do not last forever

W.C. Fields, when asked if he croqueted in one of his famous movies, scoffed and then bragged that he had once been the "champion of the Tri-State League and the Lesser Antilles." Then as he walked forward, he fell hard to the ground. He questioned: "What lazy lout left all these wires all over the lawn." Wires on the lawn of course, are part of Croquet!

Unlike Fields, Zilog was once the real champion, but it was more than little wires that got in its way. When all the other chipmakers were forming their businesses, Zilog was claiming victory after victory and they took their money to the bank.

Many, who lived through the beginning, who went through both the minicomputer revolution and the microcomputer revolution recall the Zilog Z80 Microcomputer as a formidable competitor for the pleasures of the microcomputer world. As a champion, the Z80 microprocessor is the undisputed largest-selling 8-bit chip of all time.

Z80 standard

In many ways, the Z80 chip and an operating system from a company formed by Dr. Gary Kildall, known as Digital

Research, along with a bus known as the S100 were the standards in hobby and home computing in the mid to late 1970's. This was even before Radio Shack and Apple's ventures into the new easier to use home and personal computer arena.

Most of the companies who engaged in the home computer business were startups, but one company eventually took the Z80 chip big-time well into the big leagues.

The Z80 was chosen to be the main engine for the Radio Shack TRS-80 line of computers which became very successful in the late 1970's before IBM's famous PC was introduced. Radio Shack was so close to the notion of the Z-80, that they named their prime machine after it - The Tandy Radio Shack -80, a.k.a., TRS-80.

After it broke ground with its 6502 based Apple I, which was little more than a board prepared to become a computer, Apple came out with its highly successful Apple II home computer. This one was complete with casings, a pleasing look, and an option for a color monitor.

During this period, Steven Jobs, the marketing guy on the Jobs / Wozniak team, was seen scrounging around for some software to help buoy the unit sales of his new Apple II. To this end, Bill Gates' fledgling Microsoft organization led the efforts for Jobs by building a "softcard' containing a Zilog Z-80 processor and memory. This was not charity as Microsoft expected to make a bundle.

It was extremely innovative. When an Apple II was equipped with one of these Microsoft softcards, all of the software written for the Z80 microprocessor, most of which was free, was immediately usable on an Apple II machine. There was lots of it. How about that? These guys could do almost anything they chose.

This was a technological coup for Microsoft, and a marketing coup for Apple, and a big winner for Zilog as it strengthened its place in the early chip race. Despite these successes, the big IBM company snub in 1981 would make life difficult for Zilog, a very innovative company. IBM chose the Intel 8088 and ignored the already successful Kildall endorsed Zilog chips, which already ran the CP/M operating system.

Where did Zilog come from?

Zilog was founded in 1974 by Federico Faggin, one of the inventors of the microchip, whose name is on the patent. Faggin used his resources with some help from others to launch the Company with the chip as its main product. Though we have been recognizing Zilog's contribution to early personal and home computing, it was not the premier company in the industry. But it was really something.

Forbes suggests that if Federico Faggin did nothing in his whole life after leading the Intel team that developed the first microprocessor in 1970-71, his place in the technology hall of fame would be assured. They have concern for why his name is not a household name, like Jobs or Gates? Maybe because he did not own the Company for which he worked. Maybe that is why he formed Zilog?

For most of the Company's history, its devices had been used in the back room, out of site from the logo-seeking public. The type of chips in which Zilog actually exceled were humbly found on microcontrollers, well out of sight and under the covers of the actual piece of equipment which was being controlled. These were the chips that got placed into things such as television sets, remote controls and similar electronic products. Their programmers were known at the time as engineers.

If it were not for IBM's selection of Intel's 8088, the popular 8-bit Z80 chip could have helped spur spectacular growth for many of the industry's players, especially Zilog. However, this did not happen. Though growth was steady for Zilog, it was not raucous, and there was always a problem area with which the Company had to deal. Competitors such as Intel, Motorola, Texas Instruments and Mitsubishi became too powerful and made it tough for Zilog to mount any sustainable efforts to win the game.

Selling the Zilog Company

Faggin did not keep the Company very long, selling out to Exxon in 1981. Exxon, not a tech company in any of its incarnations LBO'd the Company to Warburg, Pincus. They brought Zilog public again in 1991. Faggin surely started something good with Zilog.

For a while in the 1990's Zilog began to do well again as revenues grew at a nice 18% per year. During this period, the Company diversified into modems for satellites and they formulated a marketing strategy of going after relatively small semiconductor custom orders.

Never on top of the pile for too long, Zilog quickly found more bad luck. By 1997, they were barely avoiding red ink on $261 million of sales. By this time, the stock had slumped to less than $20. The death spiral had to end or it would take them under.

After these years of unexceptional performance, the Company still had survived and was intact well enough to be acquired in 1997 for $527 million by the Texas Pacific Group, who after a brief period, took the Company private again. This acquisition breathed enough life into the Company for it to make a full recovery and to be able to grow again.

Spirited management

Zilog first disappeared, and then recovered and began to grow again. In 1998, the newly energized Zilog Company hired Curtis Crawford, who had been Lucent Technologies Inc.'s Microelectronics Group President. As its CEO, Crawford was brought on to move the ship towards successful waters. No company in the microcomputer industry dies forever. It simply slides in with another successful group effort.

Chapter 35

MOS Technologies / Commodore

Pennsylvania company makes good!

Funded by Allen-Bradley, MOS Technology, Inc. (not to be confused with Mostek) was founded in Norristown, PA in 1969 to develop calculator chips. Unlike a lot of other pioneer companies of the day, MOS was not founded by a notable person like Bill Gates, though key people certainly contributed to its success.

MOS Technology, Inc. ("M-O-S" being short for Metal Oxide Semiconductor), also known as CSG (Commodore Semiconductor Group), got into the semiconductor design and fabrication business. Commodore International acquired MOS early in the chip game and used its 6502 microprocessor and various designs for its range of home computers. Those of us with white hair remember the Commodore PET, Commodore's Vic 20 and Commodore 64 models quite well.

Though I have researched for many hours and hours, I have found just two names from the group of former Motorola engineers who were instrumental in the creation of this new company. One is Chuck Peddle, an engineer who became CEO. Peddle was Jack Tramiel's right hand man at Commodore. The other name is Bill Mensch, who helped build the Motorola 6800 and worked on the 6502 team led by Chuck Peddle. He was also the designer of the 16-bit successor to the 6502, known as the 65816.

The 6502 created a revolution in chip processor technology as MOS Technologies sold the unit for just $25.00 while lesser capable units from Intel and Motorola were selling for as much as $179.00. It was so inexpensive that it could be included in popular video game consoles and would not make the price much different. For example, it was used in Atari, Apple II, Nintendo Entertainment System, Commodore 64, and others. All used a variation of the MOS 6502 chip.

History shows that the 6502 was so cheap that many believed the chip and all its hoopla was just a marketing scam. This was manifested clearly at a major 1975 technology trade show. The 6502 was not at first given much play. Attendees had not been made aware of MOS's superior chip masking techniques. Therefore when they added things up, it did not compute. In other words, when they calculated the price per chip at the current industry yield rates, it simply did not add up. They concluded that it had to be a scam.

What made believers and buyers out of those checking out this new phenomenon was when both Motorola and Intel dropped their prices on their own designs from $179.00 to $69.00 at the same show in order to compete. The move by these MOS first-class competitors legitimized MOS and the 6502, Rumor has it that at the end of the show, the wooden barrel full of 6502 sample chips was bone dry.

The 6502 would quickly go on to be one of the most popular chips of the day. A number of companies licensed the 650x line from MOS, including Rockwell International, GTE, Synertek, and Western Design Center (WDC).

Microprocessor lore

The 6502 unit quickly attracted the masses, not as much for its facilities, but for its price. When there may be more future chips with a family resemblance, sometimes companies replace the last # in a product such as the 6502, with an X, such as 650x.

The 650x chips were not only loved by the masses, many big corporations quickly got into the love affair. Soon the 6502 began to be found in video game cartridges and video players as well as some top flight home computers. They were as good as Motorola's chips, at only 20% of the cost. Few could deny that!

Just in time for an Apple

In 1976, Apple (Jobs and Wozniak) put together their first computer. They called the unit the Apple I, and, with Wozniak's shopping talents, Apple chose the MOS Technologies' 6502 processor as its engine. Their Apple I was not much more than a single-board computer for hobbyists. However, along with the 6502, the unit also had a built-in video interface and in-board ROM which was used to get the machine fired up so that it could run other programs from external sources.

In 1977 Apple put a nice case on the Apple I, fixed some problems, added some more goodies like a color adapter, and the Company introduced their very successful Apple II line of computers. As you would probably bet and be correct, the Apple II came equipped with the same 6502 processor as the Apple I. Both Apple and MOS technologies (then Commodore Semiconductor) were well on their way to the bank.

Unlike the 8080 and Intel's bulkier offerings, the 6502 (and the Motorola 6800) had very few registers. It was not much more than an 8 bit processor, with a 16-bit address bus. Inside was one 8 bit data register, two 8 bit index registers, and an 8 bit stack pointer. The 6502 was a technician's dream.

One of its secrets was that there were actual secrets built into the machine. In other words, there were some undocumented instructions which the techno-geeks could discover and have fun with while others used them to extend the capabilities of their devices.

Besides Apple and Radio Shack, there was another home consumer oriented computer company stirring in the 70's, which liked the 6502. Commodore would soon become a big company before it ultimately fell by the wayside in the mid 1990's.

Though the Company really was not in the same market as Apple, it was interesting for Apple to have chosen a chip that would become controlled by a company that could have been one of its competitors.

The Burroughs of home computing

I have admitted that I am a 23-year retired veteran of IBM. I worked for IBM for over 23 years. As such, I did not escape IBM without carrying out of the Company a number of hard coded prejudices, some of which I still hold. One of them was a penchant against The Burroughs Corporation.

Correctly or incorrectly, from a competitor's viewpoint, I had Burroughs pegged as a technology laggard and as a company, which sold lots more performance and capacity than its machines could possibly deliver. It may not be true but it sure was my perspective all the while I was with IBM.

Without knowing my disposition towards Burroughs, while I was lamenting my own problems with Commodore while writing my first book titled, The Personal Computer Buyers Guide, published by the Ballinger Division of Harper Collins, one of my best friends, Al Komorek, RIP, who was an ardent hobby and home computerist at the time, had just attended a Commodore seminar at a local Boscov's Department store.

Once I gave him the cue from the trouble I was having getting accurate information for Commodore, he weighed in with a quote that I will never forget. It says it all: "Commodore is the Burroughs of home computing." I do not think that I ever had discussed my Burroughs negatives with my buddy Al.

In the mid 1980's, along with Dennis Grimes, the best friend a man could have, I wrote another book specifically about Commodore along with five other books published by John Wiley & Sons, in a Buyer's Guide Series.

Our author's agent Mike Connolly contracted for us with John Wiley and Sons to publish the books. The five other books were also about other popular computers and computer companies of the early 1980's. It was a six-pack deal with the publisher, and of course to do such a large project we had lots of help.

In the six months that it took for Dennis and I to put all the books together, Commodore had really made some big changes... not for the good, and not all were disclosed to us or to the public.

Commodore made creating this book series a bigger problem than it should have been. Just trying to get information about the Commodore product line was like pulling teeth. We could not discern which product IDs were products or developer's ideas for products.

It was not as easy as dealing with Apple or other mainline companies. And Commodore was less than 100 miles away from our offices in PA. Finding a technician in Commodore with whom to talk was just about impossible. We would have driven to talk to somebody who knew something.

As previously noted, Commodore was less than 100 miles from where Dennis and I were writing the books. I had asked the Company for all of the information on their current product line as well as those products, which would be released shortly.

There were a number of systems which Commodore included in their information and press packages including the B128, which never saw the light of day. It was the hardware equivalent of vaporware. I actually saw pictures and brochures of machines which were never released— ever.

When Dennis and I were ready to submit material to John Wiley for publishing, we tried to verify the technical information they had given us on the new product lines. There was nobody home no matter how many times Dennis or I or my sister Nancy, who ran the office for us, would call.

Nonetheless with the information we had, we submitted a complete book to Wiley for publishing about Commodore but we (Wiley and Kelly/Grimes) agreed that it would not serve us well to have unsubstantiated products presented as if they actually existed.

Moreover, Commodore had been sliding in the press as a reflection of the turbulence in the Company after their President Jack Tramiel resigned and sold off his controlling shares. Tramiel's departure fostered a distorted vision and created a major management hole that was never adequately filled,

There never would be a Kelly/Grimes Commodore Book from Wiley, though it had been fully written. I wish I had kept the submission material so I could put it on the Web now. That alone speaks volumes about Commodore's demise in such a short period.

From Commodore to Atari

Jack Tramiel took his wad and bought Atari Computer, whose graphical computers quickly became a favorite of my friend Al Komorek. Not to be outdone, Commodore reacted by introducing the Amiga line of PCs, a technology the Company had acquired by outfoxing Jack Tramiel in the acquisition of a small startup.

Even Tramiel admitted at the time that the Amiga architecture produced far superior machines than his Atari units. Nobody could explain however, what had happened to Commodore. It reminds me of a song by the Buoys, a local group that sounded like the BG's with a hit about "TIMOTHY." Nobody knows what happened!

As the plot thickened, Commodore believed they were a home computer company and not a chip manufacturer. With the move to the Amiga, there was no longer a need for the 6502 chip set since the Amiga was built around Motorola's 68000 base. Eventually, Commodore abandoned its MOS Technologies business as it focused primarily on its prime market.

Apple, once tied to the 6502, for its part began to purchase more powerful and more expensive CPUs from Motorola and then IBM, and then both.

Bust time in the Bahamas!

Eventually Commodore, after having reached a cool billion dollars in sales, could not sustain its product line or its corporate life. After changing the corporate headquarters to the Bahamas, for tax purposes, the big Bahama Mama went bust in 1995. Along with the bust, went Commodore's control of the 6502 chip and its follow-on chip "x" devices.

Though there were attempts to resuscitate the Company and its Amiga line, these mostly failed. Commodore et al is now well decomposed in the bone-yard of computers and the bone-yard of business. What a flop for the Burroughs of Personal Computing.

The Amiga survives Commodore

Nobody knows what good will come of things that have gone bad. Though Commodore was long in the rotting, the Commodore developed Amiga proved to have a life of its own.

After being tossed around from company to company for many years, in and out of the hands of such stalwarts as Gateway Computer and others, Amiga again resurfaced in two forms—hardware and software.

The hardware version, called Amiga One was available through various hardware manufacturers while the software version, designed to run natively on machines or even under control of other OS platforms such as Linux, has been championed by a new organization known as Amiga Inc. It almost makes me want to cheer!

The Commodore Semiconductor Group (formerly MOS Technology, Inc.) itself seemingly has survived under new circumstances. It was bought by its former management and in 1995, the Company resumed operations under the name GMT Microelectronics, utilizing the recognized troubled facility in Norristown, Pennsylvania that Commodore had closed in 1992.

By 1999, this rejuvenated group had $21 million in revenues and 183 employees. However, in 2001 the United States Environmental Protection Agency shut the plant down. GMT ceased operations and was liquidated.

Maybe it was a real violation and not just EPA overreach. One day in a future edition of this book perhaps we can clear this all up. The EPA gave them no second chance and they are gone. It was too late for Commodore Semiconductor to survive in any form. Maybe they made chips that spied on the EPA… Just kidding!

Ownership of the remaining assets of Commodore International, including the copyrights and patents, and the Amiga trademarks, were held by a company called *Escom* but they quickly passed to U.S. PC clone maker Gateway 2000 in 1997. Gateway retained the patents and sold the copyrights and trademarks, together with a license to use the patents, to Amiga, as one might expect.

Amiga as a Washington based company, was a Commodore derivative but this new derivation came from former Gateway subcontractors Bill McEwen and Fleecy Moss in 2000. On March 15, 2004, Amiga, Inc. announced that on April 23, 2003 it had transferred its rights over past and future versions of the Amiga OS (but not yet other intellectual property) to Itec, LLC, later acquired by KMOS,

Inc., a Delaware company. It seems nothing ever dies in the chip world.

Shortly afterwards, on the basis of some loans and security agreements between Amiga, Inc. and Itec, LLC, the remaining intellectual property assets were also transferred from Amiga, Inc. to KMOS, Inc. Isn't this like reading a detective novel?

On March 16, 2005, KMOS, Inc. announced that it had completed all registrations with the State of Delaware to change its corporate name to Amiga, Inc. The Commodore/Amiga copyrights were later sold to Cloanto.

AmigaOS (as well as spin-offs MorphOS and AROS) are still maintained and updated. Several company's produce related hardware and software today. Nobody starts from scratch as the IT world is already full of chip inventions. It is an interesting tech story which reads like a poorly written novel.

The principle machine (Amiga) & the home computer market never seemed to go away!

IBMers such as I. from the late 1970's wondered about IBM's reluctance to enter the Home Computer marketplace. Why not? IBM was the best technology company in the universe or so we thought; so, why not?

Over the years, many computerists as well as those just interested in computer folklore have learned the story of Apple. It is a neat story. Two guys who were nobodies in life made it really big. We'll tell some of their story in the next chapter to help properly position Apple in the Personal Computer arena, as a predecessor to IBM's emergence, and partly because it is so interesting.

Of course, along with the Apple Story, just as with the
Radio Shack story, are a number of areas where IBM had a
major business opportunity, but did not see it, chose not to
act, or were not able to succeed, and others had to get
tractor trailers to haul out the IBM gold that Big Blue left
behind.

Chapter 36

Radio Shack – The first Personal Computer Company

Embroidery to Personal Computers

Tandy Corporation began in 1919 in the Leather Business and the Company was very successful. Tandy had a landmark year in 1961. Tandy Leather was operating 125 stores in 105 cities of the United States and Canada and expansion was the name of the game. Tandy had just acquired the assets of Merribee Art Embroidery Co.

Charles Tandy, the CEO became intrigued with the potential for rapid growth in the electronics retail industry during 1962. By April 1963, the Tandy Corporation owned the Radio Shack Corporation, which, at the time was a virtually bankrupt chain of electronics stores in Boston. Within two years, Tandy's new acquisition turned a profit under Charles Tandy's leadership. Charles Tandy did not get any help from IBM at this time and thus did not yet owe the IBM Corporation a "Thank You."

Just ten years after starting with nine Boston outlets, the Tandy Corporation began to enjoy unprecedented growth. The Company was opening two Radio Shack stores every working day. By 1988, the peak of the Company's heyday, there were more than 7,000 Radio Shack stores operating. As a point of braggadocio, according to Tandy estimates, one out of every three Americans was a Tandy customer. I know that I was and I miss my close-by Radio Shack store.

Tandy hired good people. When Charles Tandy died in 1978, there seemed to be nobody who could fill this aggressive and thoughtful manager's role. Philip North, boyhood friend and administrative assistant to Charles Tandy for years, took over the reins of the Company. North was not a technology guy so he looked to John Roach, a 1967 hire and a favorite of Charles Tandy to handle the technical side of the business. Roach had been hired in 1967 by Tandy as its Data Processing Manager. It was not long before Roach was the Chairman and CEO and he led the Company through its most prosperous times. Roach understood technology.

Today, John Roach is a Fort Worth Texas retail legend? The former IT Chief was charged with ushering RadioShack into the computer age as the top executive at Tandy Corp. Roach is still in the news and recently he predicted that "nanotechnology will create the next revolution to make things go faster and higher."

It was Charles Tandy and John Roach, through their Radio Shack stores and with the help of the Tandy research and manufacturing arm, who brought the first business oriented Personal Computer to America and the world in 1977. It was not the IBM PC. It was technically not Apple. It was Radio Shack.

Of course Apple had introduced the first hobby / home computer, which Apple co-founder Steve Wozniak (The Woz) hand built in July 1976, and so Apple technically beat Radio Shack to the punch. Additionally, Apple brought forth the Apple II in June 1977 so those if you count the Apple II as a business personal computer v. a hobby / home computer then Apple was the first. Additionally in that same year, Commodore introduced its famous VIC 20.

The Apple I, of which only 200 were ever built and which 63 are confirmed to still exist, is not and was not ever a Personal Computer (PC). It was a fairly complete set of integrated components that could be finished off into a functioning computer system by the purchaser. If you were not a tech, you would not enjoy the Apple I as a helpful tool for you or your business.

The Apple II was a Personal Computer and a home computer. It could also theoretically be called a hobbyist machine. The first of these units was sold on June 10, 1977. Tandy brought forth its Tandy Radio Shack-80 (TRS-80) computer on August 3, as a Personal Computer. It was technically not the first home / hobby machine, but with all of the Radio Shack stores selling the unit, it quickly become the most popular, and it held that position for another five years.

Radio Shack outsold Apple by a five to one factor until 1982. In August, 1981, IBM announced its PC and the game changed for all PC vendors. Since IBM could not make enough machines to satisfy its demand, the folks at home as well as corporate America enjoyed buying TRS-80 units and Apple IIs for quite a while.

Not all good things last. In 2015, Tandy Radio Shack filed for bankruptcy. At the time, it formally announced the 1,784 specific stores that were to close by the end of March 2015.

Stores from all around the nation were closing from Warwick, Rhode Island, to Redondo Beach, California. It was reported that most were offering going-out-of-business sales. That is a shame.

Bankruptcy protection does not necessarily mean that RadioShack intends to go out of business completely. It does mean that hard times are here for the Company and management has a certain period of time to rebuild itself and shield itself from creditors.

What were Tandy's PC Products?

The Tandy Radio Shack 80 was powered by a Zilog Z80 microprocessor chip. The term personal computer was not yet in vogue so this unit was announced as a Home Computer. In my day as an IBM Systems Engineer, I saw many TRS-80's used in my client accounts but few Apple II units. The TRS-80 was discontinued in January 1981 when the next model was introduced. When IBM helped launch a host of IBM compatible PCs after 1982, Radio Shack built models that were 100% IBM compatible and so for a time it gave up its Z80 niche and it sold PC clones in its stores. For this, we have another company saying: Thank you, IBM.

The TRS-80 Model 1 was not IBM compatible. It was out long before IBM got the guts to put out a PC. The TRS-80, was no slouch by the standards of the day. By 1979 it had the largest selection of software in the microcomputer market. Until sometime in 1982, this unit was the best-selling Home Computer, as noted, outselling the Apple II series by a factor of 5 according to analysts.

Radio Shack eventually answered the IBM PC challenge with its own clone version. It was known as Tandy Radio Shack's Model 2000. It was introduced in the fall of 1983. The Model 2000 was intended to outclass the IBM PC with twice the speed, more storage, and higher-resolution graphics. Tandy had used a more powerful processor known as the Intel 80186, which could run rings around IBM's older 8088. Unfortunately for Tandy, most potential PC compatible purchasers did not seem to look to Radio Shack to find an IBM Compatible Unit.

If nothing else, the microcomputer era was really exciting, even if you knew nothing about computers. Radio Shack was a big player.

Chapter 37

Apple Piqued the Home Computer Aficionado in Us All

A computer named Apple?

The Apple II really stirred things up when it came out because it was not only seen in tech outlets, it was sold where people bought normal things. I can remember being at an IBM training school in Philadelphia in late 1977, hoping to learn more about the new IBM System/34. Along with a few other students, I walked around town at lunch time and we were all intrigued by the window of an electronics store, featuring an Apple II. We all thought it was really neat, but somewhat odd at the same time. To a person, the loudest thought was "What goof would call a computer an Apple?"

All of my co-workers at IBM and the IT people in the IT shops that we covered had what could be called universal wonderment as to where IBM was in all this new miniature computer stuff. As an IBM employee, I know IBM never counseled any of us about where it was. IBMers wondered if we should look at this new machine as competition or as a home consumer appliance.

Nobody at IBM chose to give its marketing force any direction on home or personal computers, or microcomputers. We, IBM's tech employees who helped the largest IBM customers sort out technical issues were given no guidance by mother IBM so we understood what this thing was all about. IBM said nothing so we had to sort it out ourselves.

In 1977, no Home computer was competing against what IBM saw as its territory. It was apparent that Big Blue figured it would watch and see while we employees were also watching and seeing.

As noted above, on a particular day in Philadelphia, a group of IBMers who hardly knew each other found an Apple personal computer in a store window. Like the rest, I was in awe. The notion of a home computer was very appealing, but none of us really knew what to make of it... or whether in the business context, we should.

Of course, at that time, we thought the IBM brass knew better. Though amused, none of us felt compelled enough to step inside the store. In retrospect, at the time, perhaps we, the computer experts of the day, were somewhat intimidated with a machine we clearly did not understand.

Apple, founded by a couple of regular guys, who just happened to be geniuses

Steven Jobs, an adopted orphan, along with Stephen Wozniak, a brainiac techno-geek, founded Apple Computer on April 1, 1976, - about forty years ago. Jobs, who passed away after making his mark on the world on October 5, 2011 was just twenty-one years old, and Wozniak was a youthful twenty-six. The pair had first met at Homestead High School in Los Altos CA. Jobs was thirteen and Wozniak was eighteen. Both had a deep interest in electronics.

Early technical collaboration

Long before they even thought of Apple, the two were collaborating on electronics projects, one of which was their infamous "blue box" project. Wozniak perfected the blue box and Jobs got him customers. They stopped production because they were concerned of possible arrest.

Their crafty little blue box when attached to a phone would give the caller free long distance service. Though there was a big marketplace for their illegal units, for fear of prosecution, they ceased production. They pursued their separate interests for some time after this.

Figure 37-1 Wozniak and Jobs

The college years

Both decided to attend college after graduation from Homestead. Wozniak had been out about five years before Jobs graduated in 1972. Both were very smart, but when they moved on to college, they were not necessarily prepared for the full academic trip. Wozniak, because of his light hearted demeanor, prankster nature, and partly because he just wasn't ready. Jobs, because he was a dreamer, fascinated with life, and just wasn't sure.

Eventually, Wozniak would make good on his college start and graduate from Berkeley in 1982 with both his engineering degree (electrical) and a B.S. in Computer Science. Ironically, he received his degree five years after he had made engineering and computer science history with his invention of the Apple I and then the Apple II. Steven Jobs would never find the time to go back for his degree, but any of us would be proud to take a college or graduate level course from this master of invention who happened also to be a master of marketing.

While Steven Jobs was still in High school, he would attend electronics lectures given by Hewlett Packard. He would eventually get a job at HP as a summer hire. Not many years later, in 1973, Stephen Wozniak, who had recently dropped out of the University of Berkeley, took a position as an engineer with the same Hewlett Packard. He loved HP, and he loved his job.

Jobs chose Reed College after high school, where his declared interests were Physics, Literature, and Poetry. He lasted a full semester and then dropped-out, never to return again. Though officially a drop-out, Jobs reportedly "hung-around" campus for another year basically having fun... Like, wow man! I can relate to that! But somehow, I never got to do it! Jobs enjoyed a nice philosophy course here and there while he was getting his spiritual life sorted out.

Woz: the electronics "nut"

The "Woz", as he still likes to be called, was always an electronics "nut." From the moment when dad gave him a crystal radio kit, when he was just seven years old, he was on his way. Steve and dad built the radio, and "it actually worked." While in high school he used his dad's minicomputer manuals and he started putting chips together to make computer designs. All by himself, Woz learned how to design and fabricate computer systems.

In his spare time, he decided to improve the design of the Data General Minicomputer model known as the Nova, (DG Nova,) a minicomputer level machine, which he particularly liked. The Woz never got the opportunity to present his design improvements to DG. Before he and Jobs teamed up for the big kill, Woz would design computers alone in his room.

Since he was not too gregarious, he used his electronics talent as a vehicle to show folks how smart and likeable he was. It helped him as a social equalizer... an ice breaker.

If the task at hand were an electric or electronic design, or even a computer, or a BASIC interpreter, a shell operating system, or a "blue box" tone generator, with a no-arrest safety switch, Steve Wozniak was up for it. He made it work, and he felt better for it. At the time it seemed like everybody in the world gained.

Jobs resurfaces; goes back under; resurfaces

After his year-long hiatus, milling around Reed College where he had dropped out after his first semester, Steven Jobs was about to resurface. This time, in early 1974, he was looking for fun and money. He took a job as a video designer at Atari, Inc., While working off and on, Steve Jobs created the video game "Breakout" for Atari, with a little help from "the Woz",

The Apple I, a product of iterative design

Woz wanted more than anything to build a computer. The end result of his efforts and Jobs' help with the funding was the "Apple I," a board computer. Hobbyists loved it. It was by no means the beat-all, and end-all of computing, but it was easier to use than the 8080 based Altair kit. To make the computer even easier to use, Wozniak also built a keyboard attachment into the box, using a teletype-like adapter, rather than use the even less expensive, but more difficult to use panel switch notion from the Altair.

Jobs influence on the "partnership"

Steven Jobs became especially interested in the prospects for this new computer which Wozniak had built. As "Woz" completed his Motorola 6502 based computer and displayed the enhancements or modifications at the bi weekly Homebrew Computer Club meetings, a place where techno-geeks met and compared notes, Jobs was plotting his marketing strategy.

As a mere visitor of the Home Brew Computer Club, Jobs made suggestions during the design phase which helped shape the final product. For example, he suggested the newer, less expensive dynamic RAMs for main memory, rather than the older, more expensive, static RAMs. He also suggested getting printed circuit boards made for the design and to sell duplicates to Home Brew members for them to assemble at home. Jobs thought big while Wozniak enjoyed the game.

Jobs was the contact man. He was the "marketing" person. He was the business side of the duo. He also understood technology so he was not a schloff. Though Steve Jobs knew something about engineering himself, he was so smart that he deferred to Wozniak's expertise. In a word, Jobs was a very "gutsy" individual. In a second word, he was also very resilient.

He would prove to be the spider who would eventually get the first strand across the chasm. He was the little engine that could. After he talked Stephen Wozniak into leaving HP to co-found Apple with him, he needed every bit of this chutzpah to become a success.

The seeds of the Apple Organization – Home Brew

With lots of help from Home Brew Club friends, the Apple I assembly line was in place. It was successful but with just 200 units produced, it could not take them too far across the world, but it could attract investors; and it did!

This financial success of the Apple I began to attract investors. Jobs spearheaded this part of the action. One of the early investors was Mike Markkula who, contributed somewhere between $80,000 and $250,000. It is believed that 80,000 was for equity, and the rest was given as a loan. For his major stake, in May, 1977, Markkula became Apple Computer's Chairman. Not too long after Markkula became chairman, Michael Scott, who had been an executive at Semi-Conductor, Inc., became President. Markkula's net worth today is $1.2 billion.

The Apple Company was now a company. With Markkula on board, Apple was able to gain a line of credit with the Bank of America, as well as $600,000 in venture capital from the Rockefellers and Arthur Rock. How about that?

"Woz" designs the Apple II

Wozniak seemed to never rest. He and Jobs had gotten ahead of the pack, and the "Woz" was going to keep them ahead of the pack. There was no machine quite like the half-built Apple I, other than the low-budget computer kits of the day using Z-80 technology.

Despite the odds, and no reason to think they would be immediately successful, the two boys from Homestead High were nowhere close to done. Wozniak was always studying, testing thoughts, and building. With the Apple I design frozen in printed circuit boards, the "Woz" took the rudiments of the Apple I and redesigned it. He made it even more than it was ever supposed to be. He was and even today is "the Woz!"

Completed in 1977, the Apple II was by anybody's standards at the time, a great piece of work. Though it was loaded with piece parts inside, and was not as integrated internally as it appeared externally, it more than fit the bill for the day. The Apple II was packaged in a professional looking beige plastic case, and one of its most salient points was that it could display color graphics.

This good look and its fine function would allow Apple to ask substantially more for this box than the Apple I. It was a marvel in the industry. As noted above, I saw one of the first in a store window in 1977 and was duly impressed.

"Woz" gets a real memory problem

During this period, Apple had become a big company, with revenues exceeding $100 million. All was going well for Jobs and Steve Wozniak, until one day in February, 1981, the "Woz" was taking off in his Beechcraft Bonanza, and the plane had engine failure. The crash gave him some facial injuries and a lost tooth, and for a while, he had a difficult time with his memory. It made him look at life a bit differently.

The Woz did not have amnesia, but he could not remember a conversation just minutes after having it. We know, and he knew, that he was lucky. Understandably, this shook him up, and he was very inactive at Apple during a several year period of reevaluation. Thankfully He fully recovered.

Apple moved from the Apple II to the Apple III and it also put forth a machine that it called the Lisa, and then came the Macintosh, designed by Jobs. The Apple III and the Lisa never took off. The Company continued selling Apple II 'e" units, a better Apple II, until the Mac took off big time. Over time, Jobs got very interested in music and micro-gadgets, and notebooks with small display units (iPads,) and then into phones with iPhones. Steve Jobs kept pushing Apple's envelope to be the best in things that never existed before he dreamed of them. Meanwhile the Woz was enjoying life. Apple is now the # 1 tech company in the world.

The IBM PC impact on Apple

On August 12, 1981, IBM announced its PC and gained a larger share of the computer business than Apple had lost. IBM's PC announcement and its PC Story is given in Section IV as it happened during the John Opel years at IBM.

Coincidentally, Apple suffered a real debacle with a failure of the Apple III line. It did not have the things that Apple II aficionados liked about Apple.

Markkula and company reorganized and tried to fix the problem. President Michael Scott terminated a number of employees because of the problems. He did not survive himself, and was replaced by Mike Markkula as President. Steven Jobs later moved into Markkula's seat as Chairman, but eventually, the business people in Apple led by John Sculley, fired Steven Jobs. They put their creator out on the street. Jobs came back after having major success with Pixar, a filmmaker that produced 16 films including "Toy Story."

Ironically, Apple II models were selling like hot-cakes, even after the IBM PC was announced. The January 1983 release of the $1395 Apple IIe, brought another power and capacity increase to the line. Powered by a suped up 65C02 processor, the IIe ran at 1.02 MHz. Standard Ram was 64K and ROM was up to 32K. The IIe lasted for quite a while. It was a better Apple II, and was nothing like the Apple III. It worked for Apple until it was discontinued in mid-1993. It was the only Apple ever to last ten years or longer.

The graphical user interface (GUI) of the Lisa and Mac—on its way!

No IBM PC had a GUI interface. Ironically Xerox, the great copier company, had the lock on GUI development at its Xerox Palo Alto Research Center (PARC). Steve Jobs visited PARC and was welcomed. He got his first look at the Xerox Alto, a Xerox test computer with a real graphical user interface (GUI). This was unheard of in the 1970sand 80's.

One of the key players at Xerox at the time was another historic figure, Scott McGregor, who was writing the Xerox windowing system and who later was pirated by Microsoft for its Windows project. While IBM was focusing on mainframes, other companies were moving technology innovations on an un-plotted curve.

Always a project, but never a product, Xerox never brought their Alto or GUI technology to market. They were not convinced that it would sell. They felt that it was too revolutionary for the times.

After his visit, Jobs was convinced they were wrong. He was more than impressed. He knew for sure where he wanted to take Apple. Almost immediately upon his return, Jobs strengthened the attention of Apple with this GUI notion and major hardware development began.

Because of this visit, It would appear that Apple "stole" a number of XEROX engineers who came on down to Apple to build a real GUI for a real machine that was actually going to be built to be sold. Though Apple did hire a number of these engineers, in all fairness to Apple, the Company had been working on the "Mac" operating system prior to Jobs' trip to PARC.

Jobs visit to Xerox PARC would come back to haunt him more than once over the next few years. For example, when Jobs initiated a lawsuit against Microsoft for stealing GUI secrets from Apple, since ruthless Bill would do what he needed to win, Jobs' position was weakened by having visited the Xerox PARC and having witnessed the Alto in operation.

Bill Gates had no problem challenging Steven Jobs that the reason Microsoft and Apple each had a GUI was because they both had the same source—Xerox PARC. Many still do not believe Gates as he also had insider information from Apple, as he was a lead contractor for the Microsoft applications that ran on Apple. Could Gates be so callous? Who knows?

When Jobs accused Gates of stealing the Mac GUI for Windows version 1, Gates retorted: "No, Steve, I think it's more like we both have a rich neighbor named Xerox, and you broke in to steal the TV set, and you found out I'd been there first, and you said. "Hey that's not fair! I wanted to steal the TV set!"

During the Apple GUI project, Job's visit would haunt him again. Mike Markkula, Apple's President at the time did not find Steven Jobs to be a very good project manager, and he relieved him of all his duties on the corporate GUI project. Jobs, who owned 11% of the Company at the time, was able to find another project in the organization. It just so happens that the goals of his new project became the same goals as the corporate GUI project: design and build a GUI based computer which could be mass produced.

And so, on his own, Jobs began Mac development and because of Steven Jobs and his departure and return to Apple that the Company is now recognized as the best technology company in the industry, especially with their "i" innovations. Who knows where Apple would be if Jobs was able to survive his treatments? One thing for sure, at $200+ billion gross revenue in 2015, it would have been hard to top.

As we are evaluating IBM's many gifts to so many technology companies, by either intentionally not competing or not, Apple is one of the few companies that did not use IBM's technology to win its game. At more than twice IBM's annual gross revenue, can anybody deny Apple the distinction of being the top technology company in anybody's lifetime? Wow!

Apple with Steve Jobs in command, could do no wrong. From the Mac forward, Apple kept its laptop and desktop industries strong while investing in smaller and smaller expensive gadgets such as iPads, iPhones, and a host of other technologically elite gadgets. Everything Apple tried, it sure seems, was successful. Today Apple is reaping the rewards of all its fine work. It is the most valuable company in the world with the largest market cap ($740 billion), as well as the largest sales ($200+ billion), profits ($45 billion), and assets ($260 billion). It is the world's #1 technology company.

For 2015, Apple lorded over rival Samsung Electronics into first place, and it killed American giant companies Microsoft, Google, and IBM.

When IBM introduced its PC, which today brings in well over $1 trillion in revenue to many companies from different market segments, it easily topped Apple, Radio Shack and all other home computer manufacturers of the 1981 era. Steve Jobs' mind, however, kept working and working and he never gave up.

There is clearly a difference in attitude when you feel that you own the company v you are merely a caretaker in the CEO position. IBM settled and settled and settles whereas Apple innovated in product design as well as marketing. Apple is beating everybody worldwide with more than twice the sales of IBM.

Unlike Microsoft, Apple did nothing to hurt IBM. IBM could have had a lot of Apple's business but it was not interested in such competition. Shame on IBM. Apple simply outperformed IBM, the one-time IT-champion in its own technology industry.

For the record, IBM holds a lot of patents for cell phone technology such as gallium arsenide chips, yet the IBM Company has never really done well introducing anything like a consumer product. IBM even blew it with its PC, the smallest IBM mainline product of all time. Can you imagine if IBM had a guy like Steven Jobs running the show?

Chapter 38

A Key IBM Software Invention: Relational Database (RDBMS)

E. F. (Ted) Codd invented the relational database management system for IBM

IBM is credited in computer history with the invention of relational database. When IBM's Santa Theresa labs were conducting research in the notion of relational database in the 1970s, Edward "Ted" Codd defined the basic principles of relational database and codified the famous Codd rules for Relational Database. He first published information on this new concept in a 1970 technical paper.

Figure 38-1 Ted Codd Inventor of Relational Database

Edgar Frank "Ted" Codd

"A Relational Model of Data for Large Shared Data Banks"

IBM's first relational database product was announced in 1978. It was given no name. It was part of a whole new system being announced at the time. Not many are aware that relational database was a standard, integrated feature of every IBM System/38. It was shipped "free of charge." as part of the OS.

More & more programs to maintain

In the 1970's, though the minicomputer was making inroads, the mainframe was still king. However, life in mainframe shops was getting more and more difficult. The number of programs needing care and feeding was growing and growing. Program counts had increased from just a few hundred in the 1950's to thousands and thousands in the "typical" mainframe shop during Codd's day.

Moreover, as more programmers were hired and trained to cope with the ever-expanding work load, they created more and more programs which required more and more periodic maintenance. In many ways, the solution (more programmers) actually helped exacerbate the problem. Moreover, there had not been any major software productivity breakthroughs in years, so the old tools and methods had to suffice.

There were not even any major items on the horizon which would help increase programmer productivity. The so called 4GLs were not the panacea many believed they would be. Programmers did not even like to use them. It was just more and more COBOL, on top of more and more COBOL. In fact, as interactive programming began to replace batch processes, programming with CICS type monitors for display-oriented programs actually became more difficult, not easier.

In the past, functional processes were handled in nice little batches and then reconciled to be exact. Preparing for a user to be working with a terminal, interacting with the program, was a far greater challenge for analysts and programmers than reconciling a batch of transactions at a time.

With the new video (CRT) terminal technology, programmers had to anticipate the types of mistakes which online users would commit, and they had to build clever ways of recovering from these somewhat predictable human errors. Interactive programs grew bigger and bigger and more and more complex. If programmers chose to ignore errors, users would be frustrated, and their programs would permit bad data to enter the system. This, of course would lead to the half-accomplished programmer looking for a new job.

Program data definitions—time consuming

One of the biggest parts of programming in the 1970's was defining and dealing with data. As analysts were getting better in designing systems, they built more and more data files, which added substantial flexibility and control to their systems. Unfortunately, the better the systems were designed, the more programming routines had to be written to enable these new facilities. Instead of programs having two or three file definitions, it became common for programs to require ten or more files to be defined and processed. Thus, more and more programs were being written at the time, and each program was more complex.

Computer programmers were struggling with the many ways to deal with data. To build long lasting systems, programmers and analysts had to do much more than just worry about processing techniques. They had to factor in the notion of data and structures and views, and they had to become concerned with advanced concepts such as data normalization in order to assure an enduring data file design.

As ever increasing amounts of programmer time were required to deal with the many facets of data, the industry had awakened that something needed to be done. Eventually, the study of data and creating information became a science in itself. IBM introduced the concept of a database as its attempt to make working with data, a more productive experience. The first IBM databases in the 1970's were hierarchical in structure, with no foundation in science or research. They were merely implementations. But they were a start as the concept led database developers to the right solutions.

Though database work with these new tools was complex in and of itself, the resulting structures made life somewhat easier for programmers. Detailed structures could be copied intact from the database, saving the programmer the painstaking work of defining every data item again and again in every program. Moreover, since the overall data design was produced by data specialists, rather than by programmers on the fly, the end results of data base design would produce systems which were typically more cohesive and which were not fraught with anomalies requiring programming work-arounds. In this regard, database technology indeed helped make programmers substantially more productive.

Hierarchical databases

IBM used various names for its database products and packages such as DL/1, and IMS, in these early years. These two mainframe hierarchical database packages had very good success rates with large, corporate customers. The basic notion of the 1970's database constructs was that data elements typically had hierarchical relationships. In other words, there would be parent / child relationships between data entities. An order record for example would be a parent and a transaction record would be a child.

Said differently, for example, a customer order would consist of order information and line items. One order would have many line items. The line items had no meaning without the order information. Database designers would put the order information in a record type designed for this purpose. They would put the order line item information in a record designed for its purpose. There could be one order record and many line items. In this scenario, the order record would be the parent of the line item records (children).

To get to the line items, database programmers would "navigate" through the order record, which would point to the first line item, which would in turn point to the second line item. The pointers would be embedded in the records.

Hierarchical databases provided efficiency in dealing with data. However, they brought their own level of clutter and complexity with which to deal. Many in the data sciences did not appreciate the complexity of these implementation-only databases. Moreover, there were more problems than just pointers. Highly skilled and intelligent and costly database technicians were needed to set up the new databases and to maintain them.

Additionally, since the implementations did not have their foundations in mathematical science, the hierarchical structure design was sometimes a force-fit upon an application. Thus, many systems had work-around programming for areas which the database could not be made to handle. Since this is not a DB class, we have already said more than enough about hierarchical databases.

Developing the ideal database system

The data sciences community in various universities and labs across the country were wrestling with the notion of taming data once and for all. One such lab was located in Santa Theresa California.

In the late 1960's and 1970's in this Santa Theresa lab, Ted Codd, an IBM software engineer at the time, was working through mathematical models to come up with the "ideal" database, a database which could be perceived as a simple collection of rows and columns, no matter how complex the underlying implementation.

When Codd completed his research and proved that his new theorem would work, he called this model the relational database, and systems using this methodology became known as relational database management systems (RDBMS).

Dr. Codd introduced the relational data model for structuring data as well as two database query languages using relational algebra and relational calculus. He presented papers to fully describe these concepts: *"A relational model for data for large shared data banks"*, CACM, 1970, and *"Relational completeness of data base sublanguages,"* in: Database Systems, edited. by R. Rustin, 1972.

The newly developed relational database notion needed an external language for the manipulation of data. Codd and the team in Santa Theresa came through again. The SQL (Structured Query Language) language was originally developed by Codd and company at IBM in a prototype implementation of what they called a relational database management system. The Codd implementation was dubbed, System R, in the mid-1970s.

One can only suspect that the "R" stood for relational. Through this prototype, IBM proved that the Codd theorem was practical. The language was designed to work with the relational structures also defined by Codd. The original SQL language (SEQUEL2) was described in the November 1976 IBM Journal of R&D. System/R would become the basis for IBM's largest mainframe relational database known as DB2.

Meanwhile developments continued in the relational database field with Michael Stonebraker and E. Wong developing the Ingres Relational Database Management System (RDBMS) at UC Berkeley in 1973. This DB was not commercialized until 1983. Later, Ingres evolved into something called PostgreSQL, a free software OODBMS (object-oriented DBMS).

The biggest event that was happening at the time, however was that Larry Ellison founded a company in 1979 that eventually becomes Oracle Corporation. Ellison released Oracle V2 is in 1979, followed by Oracle V3 in 1983. And, of course for all of the work of others in releasing great RDBMS's, Ted Codd was awarded the ACM Turing Award in 1981.

Chapter 39

Oracle Announces the First Commercial Relational Database

IBM toyed with RDBMS; Oracle was serious

In 1979, though IBM had created the Relational Database Model years before, Oracle Corporation introduced the first commercially available implementation of SQL and relational database. In 1978, IBM's rogue Rochester Lab had already announced its System/38, which included an integrated relational database, Unfortunately, IBM could not make the System/38 work on time and the machine was not shipped until mid-year 1980. Thus, Oracle's entrée' goes down in history as the official first commercial relational database management system.

IBM finally got something going as a separate product in 1981 with its first implementation of SQL and relational database for its smaller mainframe line. The product was known as SQL/DS and it was released to run under both the DOS/VSE and VM/CMS Operating Systems.

In 1983, IBM finally was convinced enough to release its Database 2 (DB2) Relational Database to run on its largest operating system known as MVS. Rumor at the time was that IBM was selling its hierarchical database offerings so well that it was reluctant to release a relational database offering (DB2) that would compete directly with its IMS and DL/1 products. Big Blue's strategy was to sell DB2 as an additional database product for query purposes and to leave the hierarchical database products in place for fast transaction processing.

Today, IBM's invention, SQL, is widely implemented and is accepted as the industry standard database access language. Despite how well IBM did in the research pit, however, it was clearly beat in the marketplace by Oracle. Considering that Oracle, which for years sold nothing but database products, made about half ($40 billion) of what IBM made last year ($92 billion), IBM gave up quite a bit by pulling its punches with DB/2 and SQL. Oracle's revenue is going up while IBM's has shrunken for the last three years.

Oracle Founder Larry Ellison's net worth is now $54 billion. His wealth is only surpassed by his long term disdain for Microsoft's Bill Gates. Gates has Ellison by $25 billion in the net worth category. In many interviews, Ellison has been heard saying that he hated Microsoft and its products. Rumor is that he even hired private detectives to dig up dirt on Microsoft. No confirmations but that is some of the folklore in the industry. Ellison is an entrepreneur and he had no problem beating professional CEOs such as those at IBM.

Chapter 39 Founder Larry Ellison Serious about Oracle

Oracle co-founder Bob Miner passed away in 1993 leaving $600 million to his family. Ed Oates, another Oracle co-founder, retired in 1996 as a multi-millionaire and he leads a private life. Oates often volunteers his time as a board member of the San Francisco Zoological Society. Some people made a lot of money from IBMer Ted Codd's invention. Thank you, IBM.

Ted Codd, the inventor of Relational Database Management Systems (RDBMS) worked for IBM for over thirty years. He passed away in 2003. I heard him speak at a database convention in San Francisco years ago. He was amazing.

Dr. Codd is not recognized as being in the millionaire's club but his net worth when he passed away more than likely put him in the club but not by much. Life sure is not fair. Larry Ellison should be giving Ted Codd, his silent mentor over the years, a big and continuous Thank you IBM, for his

(Ellison's) great wealth. It was all IBM's for the taking but Big Blue did not want it. As we go through all of these industry segments in chapter after chapter, think about all of the dollars IBM left on the table. Industry entrepreneurs had no problem grabbing the cash.

For many, other than industry watchers and IBM marketing employees in the 1970's, it was a conundrum as to why IBM chose to neglect relational technology as designed by its own Ted Codd. IBM had the keys to the kingdom and the gatekeeper himself, Ted Codd worked for the Company. Big Blue had every reason to succeed big time in RDBMS.

During the 70's despite IBM's reticence, Codd continued to be employed by IBM and he continued his work in relational technology. Codd later coined the term and developed the theory of OLAP—an acronym for Online Analytical Processing. It is a computer-based technique for analyzing business data in the search for business intelligence. For the record, Oracle has great respect for Dr. Codd and the Company now imbeds OLAP in its standard database offerings

As noted, many believe that IBM was so heavily invested in its existing high speed non-relational database product IMS and was so anxious to preserve the revenue from that product, that it ignored relational database at its own peril. IBM itself was initially quite unreceptive, and even hostile to Codd's relational ideas.

As a consequence, the void created by no IBM action after Codd defined RDBMS in papers and conferences helped convince other vendors, including Relational Software Inc. (later renamed Oracle Corporation) and Relational Technology Inc. (later renamed Ingres Corporation), to steal the day from IBM and bring relational products to market well before IBM.

Some suggest that IBM management had to be dragged to the relational table kicking and screaming. IBM was losing for years in a market in which it deliberately chose not to compete. As the Company finally took notice that the database winds were blowing against them, senior IBM management decided in the late 1970s that IBM should build a relational product of its own.

As noted, that decision resulted in the announcement of SQL/DS for the VSE & VM environments in 1981 and then IBM finally released DB2 for the huge mainframe MVS environment in 1983.

It is truly amazing that the Company with the greatest computer minds in the world and the greatest R&D facilities would not be able to capitalize on its own inventions. Maybe IBM was spending too much money on R&D, such that the brass could not properly evaluate the merits of all of its lab creations and their potential market appeal. Maybe like HP dis for the second time in 2015, the company should have created smaller independently managed companies. Surely the big blob we know of as IBM could not manage all of its successful businesses or its opportunities.

IBM is reported over the years to have discarded 90% of its potential product discoveries. Just 10% made it out of the labs. There was apparently no effective scoring system to assure the best ideas were introduced. How else can we explain how one of IBM's top inventions ever—relational database—would take so long to emerge from the labs as a product?

At least IBM woke up and is fully engaged today in the RDBMS market. IBM now is almost # 1 in relational database sales by a skosh. Starting in 2001, according to the Gartner Group IBM's DB2 sales have seen more IBM

licenses than Oracle. Whether it can be sustained or not is
the question. IBM's DB2 is a powerful offering that
competes quite well with Oracle, the market share leader by
far. IBM has a long way to catch up to the leader.

History will not judge the IBM Company kindly on its
publishing all the details of Codd's relational database
definition in 1970. Considering that the Company
introduced no products using the technology until the early
1980's, telling the competition how to build relational
databases was not something that was very business smart.
Why tell the competition how to build a product designed to
blow your own future products away?

For Oracle, however, it was the difference between
struggling and a bright future. Thank You, IBM. IBM's
reticence to be successful in the relational database market
could not have made Oracle more pleased. It was just what
the Company needed to get the bragging rights forever of
being the first company to capitalize on the notion of
relational database, a notion, almost ten years earlier
invented by IBM.

How Oracle got started

Oracle got its start in Santa Clara California, in 1977. Larry
Ellison, Bob Miner and Ed Oates together founded the
System Development Laboratories (SDL). The three had
been inspired by a research paper written in 1970 by an IBM
researcher titled "A Relational Model of Data for Large
Shared Data Banks." Of course we know that the innocuous
IBM researcher was none other than Edgar F. (Ted) Codd,
cited above.

His work first appeared in Communications of the ACM,
Vol. 13, No. 6, June 1970. Thus, Ted Codd, of IBM is
credited with inventing the relational database. In his ACM

article, he described the 12 characteristics of a relational database system. This was just the beginning.

By 1990, at about the time relational database was well established and Codd was no longer with IBM, he carried relational database to the high sciences as he wrote his classic reference book, The Relational Model for Database Management, (Addison Wesley, 1990). This expanded on his work of twenty-years past, and defined 333 characteristics of a "pure" relational database system.

Using Codd's manuscripts of how-to directions, the three Oracle programming buddies decided to take a shot at building this new type of database called a relational database management system (RDMBS). Meanwhile, IBM continued testing or at least toying with Codd's theories with a minimally funded project known as System R.

After Ellison, Miner, and Oates formed Software Development Laboratories, SDL, they very quickly got some work, for which they would be paid (a very important factor). It was a top-secret project for the CIA, code named *Oracle*. SDL won the bid.

The work on this contract continued until the government pulled the plug on the funding, but the three visionaries saw the marketable value of a system that could store and retrieve a large amount of data in a consistent and reliable format.

The SDL team, became enamored with the name Oracle, meaning source of wisdom. They felt it would be an appropriate name for their project. Not being sure whether the CIA would feel the same, they asked for and received permission from the CIA to use the name Oracle.

In the late 1970's there was not much knowledge of database in the industry as a whole. Database itself was an anomaly. As if predestined for success, in 1978 the new Software Development Laboratories moved from their office in Santa Clara to a new one on Sand Hill Road in Menlo Park, the very heart of Silicon Valley.

Since their name was so generic, however, very few companies understood the business in which they were engaged. In an attempt to better explain their company function within their business name, SDL changed their moniker to Relational Software Inc., or RSI.

Oracle V2, the First Commercial Relational Database

After two years in the making, RSI shipped its first commercial SQL database, called Oracle V2 in 1979 (there was no V1). By this time in 1979, IBM had been testing its System R product for better than twice as long as it took SRI to build and release its product.

In fact, in 1978, IBM had already announced its first relational database management system, which was given no name and was introduced without any database hoopla. The database was buried in something called the Control Program Facility (CPF), the poorly named operating system used on IBM's System/38 "business computer."

The S/38 was the predecessor system to the midrange AS/400. As it turns out, IBM never shipped its first S/38 until 1980, with a database, which was a subset of Codd's initial definition, making Oracle's claim of being the first company to introduce a relational database ring true.

Looking for an even better company name, RSI changed its company name to Oracle Systems Corporation in1982. Later they shortened it to Oracle Corporation. They had also named the product of their project, *Oracle*. Naming the

Company after their one major product helped the
Company gain immediate name recognition. Sales quickly
were recorded in the $ millions.

Another Oracle

In 1983, hoping to leverage their success over many more
system platforms, the Company decided to make their
relational database management system (RDBMS) portable.
Introduced as Oracle V3, they rewrote their product 100% in
"C" language. In this way, ports to other systems became
easier to accomplish.

One of the most successful ports was to the DEC VAX
system. Thus, Oracle became the first portable database to
run on minicomputers and mainframes. This became their
hallmark. In a few more years, their database would also
run on the PC (microcomputer) platform. IBM at the time
wrote systems programs that would run only on IBM
computers. IBM chose not to migrate its software to run on
non-IBM systems. This arrogance cost the IBM company
tons and tons of dollars.

Moving On Up!

From this humble beginning, Oracle Corporation became
one of the world's leading suppliers of software for
information management, and the world's second largest
software company. With annual revenues approaching $40
billion, the Company continues to offer its database,
application server, tools and application products, along
with related consulting, education and support services. As
an IBM stockholder, I hope IBM wishes it had paid
attention but the arrogance factor is big at Big Blue, and so I
would bet that IBM has not learned any lessons from
competing and losing.

Having been viewed as a database company for many years, midway through its life, Oracle began to build business applications for its database, and subsequently, it acquired software packages for reselling that used its DB as a prerequisite.

In this way, if the Company were planning to compete against IBM and its DB2 database in a given situation, and there was no applications software for the alternate platform which operated on Oracle, the Company would be able to offer its own software as a solution.

With the advent of the Internet, Oracle quickly recognized the importance which database and database scripts and programs play in the eBusiness world. As a preemptive strike, Oracle built a series of offerings for the Internet, as well as a ground-breaking Internet database. A client could thus purchase Oracle, without application software, and be able to create a solution.

Will Oracle's customers stay loyal?

Oracle did so well in the applications business that the Company chose to compete against its own developers and customers, such as SAP. IBM stayed stuck in the mud and would not budge into this area. Oracle's revenue is rising and IBM's is falling. You make the decision as to the best strategy. There were some industry concerns that Oracle was taking business from its own customers. Yet, with increasing sales year to year, repercussions have not been exacted against Oracle in any meaningful way.

Larry Ellison, the flamboyant, out-spoken Oracle CEO obviously thinks the risks are worth it; but as he began this venture, many believed there would be a fallout. One example of such fallout did occur a while ago. In late 1999, SAP, a long-time Oracle proponent, suddenly cozied up to

IBM and began to move its applications from Oracle to IBM's DB2 platform. The public reason SAP gave was that IBM's DB2 is supported on more platforms than Oracle. But was that really the reason? This is an important question for Oracle's future and for IBM's.

Microsoft disease

Many industry experts believe that Larry Ellison has had the same disease which afflicted a number of other Silicon Valley billionaires. Ray Noorda from Novell, and Scott McNealy from Sun are two others who have long been diagnosed. The disease, of course is the deep distrust, and dislike, and preoccupation with bringing about the demise of Bill Gates. Back when Microsoft moved into Web TV, the disease overwhelmed Ellison into getting Oracle involved in an unsuccessful deal to deliver over 500 channels.

Then there was the time Gates retaliated and cut Ellison from Microsoft's preferred database vendors list. There is no love lost so Ellison has been looking for a way to cut Gates out of the whole pie, especially the client pie.

In this vein, twenty years ago, Larry Ellison announced the concept of the network computer (NC), an Internet appliance, thin client with its own local memory, a fast microprocessor, and no disk drive. More importantly for this 1996 architecture, was that it did not need MS-Windows. The NC went to the island of bad ideas and forgotten toys years ago and Microsoft not only survived, Gates is still the richest man in the world with Ellison in third place. I must admit, I loved the notion of the NC, and was sorry to see it did not make it.

Overall nobody (Novell, IBM, or Oracle) has been very successful to date in fighting the Wintel juggernaut or

Microsoft disease in any fashion—whether it be at the client or server level.

Ellison for many years spent much of his time as a very loud critic of the way the biggest software company, Microsoft conducted its business. With Gates taming down his involvement, the two have been seen several seats away at games. In one picture that I saw recently, John McEnroe, not known for temper tantrums of any sort, was sitting in between these two supposed arch rivals. Time cures all ills.

Oracle doing well while hedging Its Bets

Ellison sees Oracle as being a big-time player in traditional database activities as well as those database related opportunity activities on the leading edge, such as Web Information Management. Ellison and company are always looking for acquisitions to further their leverage.

Regarding the Web, Oracle has filled the bill with all of the necessary underlying components, including electronic commerce, data warehousing, application integration, manageability, mobile computing, and online transaction processing. They have either built it or acquired it.

As the trend has been to more server-based computing, and as more and more companies transform themselves to use e-businesses as well as brick and mortar, Oracle's back-end Internet-enabled solutions are designed to give the Company an opportunity to further expand its market opportunities.

Success in new areas

Oracle has had real success in the applications area. Larry Ellison has often put out the puff when there was no substance. Unlike Microsoft, however, at Oracle, results are what actually count. The fact that Ellison talked about leveraging Oracle's database core to expand into new eBusiness areas and other areas did not create much of an industry stir until he actually achieved positive results. Show me the money!

Even though the results are in to Oracle's betterment, Ellison is still talking about the next move. He does not stop. His efforts have been a clear success. Larry Ellison sees his plans being accomplished and they have been paying off for Oracle for years. Its future is bright. That's why in 2014, Mr. Ellison decided to "relax" a little bit and he stepped down as CEO to the Chair and some "light" technical duties.

Ellison is successful in database and software as Apple is in everything it touches. The late Steve Jobs and Larry Ellison had always been engines that would not stop when the mission was in front of them. Oracle's e-commerce initiatives have been quite successful. I think that differentiation is important. The entrepreneur will beat the paid CEO any week of the year!

The Oracle Company is now viewed as a major force on all application software fronts, including e-commerce. Oracle's big competitor in the ERP space (most importantly, SAP as Oracle purchased PeopleSoft a while back) has still not fully caught up with Oracle in its e-commerce efforts. PeopleSoft, of course never will as it is now a part of Oracle from a 2005 acquisition. The bottom line folks is that Ellison never sleeps.

Thus, Oracle is no longer just the traditional database / applications software vendor as its roots had positioned the Company for so long. Though they continue to be strong in the database area, they are now a viable, leading-edge provider of Internet-based eBusiness and ERP solutions. They are a company that seemingly can do it all.

Did Oracle cost IBM?

Students of relational database know about the beginning of this science in the IBM Santa Theresa Labs. IBM had been working on the notion of relational database in the late 1960s and throughout the 1970s. As we related above, a key IBM employee, Ted Codd, a recognized genius, would define forever the basic characteristics of a relational database system.

Unfortunately, he was ahead of IBM at the time. When Codd initially published his work in the Journal of the ACM way back in 1970, IBM formally was credited with inventing relational database. But IBM just took its time in bringing products to market. In the mid 1970's the Company had a few relational prototypes, which were doing as research projects in the Santa Theresa facility.

The System "R" project had even become famous along the way. With relational database pinned down from concept through implementation, why IBM could not capitalize on it, as we have discussed, continues to be an enigma.

Meanwhile, three programming grunts—Larry Ellison, Bob Miner and Ed Oates did no original research. They did not have to do any. Instead, they got their hands on Codd's paper and recognized the value in his work. How convenient?

They were so inspired that they began the Company which would become Oracle. Their simple purpose was to develop Codd's notion into a real software product. They started seven years after Codd had invented relational database, and by sheer desire, they were able to beat the laggard IBM Corporation to market.

IBM, the inventor of relational database, is finally doing well in this area, but they had given it all to Oracle even before they had even begun. Perhaps if the Company had introduced relational database at its natural time, rather than tinkering with it for ten years, there would be no Oracle today.

If there were no Oracle today, who would be bringing in the $40 billion + gross revenue which currently goes to Oracle? Would some of it go to IBM, the real inventor of RDBMS? Would IBM's bottom line be $40 billion fatter? Perhaps this is the per annum true cost of not paying attention to business and giving the relational marketplace to Oracle?

One must ask, how many big opportunities like this could any other company lose and still survive? How many times can you squander an opportunity, which you spent millions to create, before your stockholders call for management heads?

Of course, T. J. Watson Jr. was in charge in 1970, and Learson to 1973, and these were the good days. Frank Cary was the guy on the scene when IBM gave up relational database to Oracle and Ingress. IBM was the best company in the world or so it seemed. The Company just had a little trouble knowing what business it was in. The stockholders had no clue. There was no real database marketing strategy in corporate IBM. Database had not really become an industry. The mainframe was bringing in the cash. It seems that's all that mattered!

Chapter 40

IBM and Data Communications: Why Big Blue Failed?

Background information helps

This chapter is about teleprocessing, a term IBM invented, and how IBM failed again in another technology that it had invented. This is another major subindustry in which, at one time, there were no IBM competitors.

Before we tell the IBM teleprocessing story, let's briefly review some things we have already lightly examined. Then we will discuss how IBM lost the teleprocessing industry as it did many other industries. Like many other technology areas in which IBM no longer competes, IBM invented teleprocessing. For a while, the IBM game was the only game in town.

Somehow it became a habit. IBM could not sustain its sole ownership of lucrative industry sub-segments so it would punt when it felt appropriate. IBM had the best punters in the industry. Big Blue had a terrible time maintaining success when it was challenged. Let's review some other IBM failings before we continue on with teleprocessing.

IBM the early leader in computers

After its huge success with the IBM 650 tube oriented mainframe computer system from 1953 onwards, IBM led the computer industry in all facets from that point on. When the Company took a $5 billion gamble on 1964 System/360 in the Watson Jr. years, IBM cemented its lead. It did not give up its lead until it was beaten by the merged HP in 2007. IBM had defined the computer industry. Most IT subindustries that today are big industries by themselves were started by IBM and led by IBM for many, many years.

For a good number of those years, especially in the beginning IBM led the disk drive industry; the tape drive industry; the computer memory industry; and for some time, it led the computer chip industry. IBM also led the card reader industry and the card punch industry, word processing and many others. What happened to IBM as a leader?

IBM began and it led the operating system industry until it insisted that Microsoft take those honors. It also coined the term "word processing," and with its many advanced office productivity hardware and software products, it created the word processing industry. Now it is not even a participant. IBM led the office industry from the day it invented the Selectric Typewriter in 1961 until it gave it up unexpectedly to PC and small printer vendors in the early 1990's, and of course to Microsoft Word.

IBM has a marketing deficiency

IBM's corporate administration once explained to me, when my customer, Marywood University bought 82 IBM PCs preloaded with a free copy of Microsoft Word, why the IBM Company could not afford to put IBM's own word processing software, known as DisplayWrite on each PC instead of a competitor's software.

They told me they could afford to load MS Word because it was free, as a give-away, but the Software Division charged the PC Division several hundred dollars per copy to load IBM's own package on each PC. Marywood was using IBM's office hardware systems known as Displaywriter; as well as IBM's Office/38 at the time.

Marywood was not looking for a Microsoft Word solution. IBM was not wise enough to see that Microsoft wanted to take its word processing business away and so it helped Microsoft many times over by giving their software free on every IBM PC sold. IBM claimed it could not afford to give its own word processing software away. A few years later, IBM was out of the word processing business because IBM was dumb and Microsoft was smart.

Within one year, their neophyte PC users at Marywood fell in love with Word, and the University adopted Microsoft Word as its word processing standard. There would be no more IBM Displaywriters and no more IBM Office/38 for email or document preparation on campus ever again.

Actually, IBM simply did not realize that it could not afford to not load its own software on each PC because it lost this account and every other account to Microsoft. Bill Gates knew that his next upgrade charge for Marywood would more than make up for initially giving away the software to get a customer hooked. IBM insisted on making a dime even if it would not get the business, rather than making a dollar each time by smart marketing.

A losing record!

IBM also created the small business computer industry with such products as System/3, System/32. System/34,

System/38 and AS/400. IBM invented RISC technology but offered products only after others, such as Sun Microsystems had captured that industry segment. IBM invented hierarchical and relational database industries. The Company owned the hierarchical DB industry at the very time that it invented relational database.

IBM did not enter the Relational DB industry until Oracle was already the de facto leader. IBM created the Personal Computer and the PC industry as it added a new dimension to Home computers for professionals. IBM was snookered by its major partners in the PC industry and ultimately lost its lead and then it lost its ability to compete, and then it had to exit the industry that it had created.

IBM was also the big gun in the development of the most popular programming languages. The Company developed RPG, FORTRAN, PL/1, APL, Event Driven Language, and SQL.

In 2013, IBM created the Corelet Language, which is now the most advanced language ever. It mimics brain functions on supercomputers. IBM as a company loves Java but this language was developed by Sun Microsystems. I could never figure that one out. It surely helped Sun but not IBM.

The focus of this chapter is yet another industry, which IBM created and lost. IBM coined the term teleprocessing. It was the first company offering teleprocessing and yet it could not build a marketing image to sustain its fine products.

Before we get into some history, I will take the time to make some new assertions and summarize some points made in other chapters so we can get a perspective on why IBM lost the teleprocessing industry to many fine companies, but especially to Cisco.

IBM's penchant for protecting mainframe business

The bottom line reason for just about every IBM marketing failure over IBM's entire history is mainframe myopia. There is a secondary reason—fear of government antitrust action. This was most in play during the beginning of the PC revolution. In the PC debacle, IBM lost to companies that at one time could not even spell c-o-m-p-u-t-e-r.

In this chapter, we discuss decisions based on IBM arrogance and its love of mainframes for positioning the Company to be behind the pack regarding the biggest teleprocessing opportunity of all time—the Internet. The reason we talk about all the other big losses is because there is a pattern. IBM has not been able to handle success in any other part of its business areas other than mainframes.

Now, if IBM chooses to exit the hardware subindustry completely as analysts are speculating, some of us are wondering if Big Blue will even be able to drive to work. Can anybody expect IBM to be the least bit successful if it no longer is the mainframe company and if it cannot force mainframe customers to buy its other stuff?

IBM for years marketed minicomputers successfully without using the term. It referred to them as midrange System/3X machines one day and small business computers the next day/ But, IBM never called them minicomputers. Who knows why?

IBM would not introduce a minicomputer because it had not created the notion of minicomputers. Minicomputers sold for a lot less than IBM priced its wares. When the Company finally came out with a supposedly traditional minicomputer, it would not use the same definition that had been defined by HP, DEC, DG, Wang and other stalwarts in the minicomputer industry.

Big Blue would not permit its software to be used on competitive machines and for many, many years, it would not permit Unix, a popular industry standard OS on minicomputers to be used on any IBM systems. If you did not work for IBM, you would think that IBM had a marketing death wish.

Yet, IBM kept bringing in huge profits from mainframes, and though stockholders should have been complaining, the dividends were always there. The IBM Board surely should have known better, but they took life a little too easy.

Minicomputers were very inexpensive machines that were able to perform mathematical functions and control processes such as traffic light systems, monitor processes, etc. Bell Labs used DEC minicomputers to create Unix and then rewrite Unix in C language. IBM had an aversion to Unix and C language because neither were invented by the mainframe folks at IBM.

Moreover as Unix flavors emerged, the favored BSD Unix was the darling of Academia and it came with a rich TCP/IP and a host of applications such as FTP, Telnet, SMTP, etc. These were known as the *TCP/IP well-known applications*. IBM refused to permit TCP/IP and these well-known apps to be used on any of its hardware product lines.

The IBM System/3x line did not run Unix and it did not run TCP/IP. IBM mainframes did not run Unix and did not run TCP/IP. When IBM came out with its Series/1 minicomputer in 1976, it did not even have an operating system. Therefore, IBM's first theoretical minicomputer built for sensor and process applications, did not run Unix nor did it run TCP/IP or its well-known applications. Where was IBM's industry research on this?

Why was this? As you have read many times in this book, it was because a dominant fact in IBM history is that IBM simply wanted to protect its mainframe business. Big Blue hoped to control the entire industry with its silly rules intended to help IBM—not its customers.

IBM's operating systems from S/360 onward, included a derivative of its System/360 DOS which in later years was known as VSE for Virtual Storage Extended. Larger mainframes ran Virtual Machine (VM) (developed by IBM to show MIT it knew how to write time sharing software) or Multiple Virtual Storage (MVS), which was a derivative of System/360 OS modified many times over the years to support huge workloads.

When IBM's customers built applications for VSE, they did not run or migrate to MVS and Vice Versa. Nor did they run on Unix or System/3. That was the idea. So, when Linux came out, nothing in the IBM stable of software immediately ran on Linux. IBM did not want its customers to be able to switch to portable operating system flavors (Unix or Linux) that ran on many other hardware platforms. The issue was that somebody might choose to no longer use a mainframe.

IBM's internal teleprocessing protocol was called Systems Network Architecture / Synchronous Data Link Control or SNA/SDLC. It sometimes was shortened to SNA.

IBM did not want its competitors to become experts in using its SNA/SDLC *teleprocessing* protocol developed for mainframes. Moreover, IBM did not want its bread and butter systems to use TCP/IP even though it was the industry standard teleprocessing protocol built for the

Internet by the Defense Department. IBM by policy kept itself out of the successful parts of networking.

IBM did not want it to be easy for its customers to switch computing platforms from IBM. Big Blue, in these instances did not have the best interests of its customers in the forefront. Many would conclude that IBM was not even making decisions that would benefit IBM.

IBM protects mainframe revenue at all costs

To show the extent that IBM would go to protect its mainframe revenue, here is a recent story that gives a great perspective. We have reported in this book that IBM has dominated the mainframe computer business since the category was created over four decades ago. Big Blue still gets about one-quarter of its almost $100 billion in annual revenue from sales, software, services and financing related to the mainframe machines.

Clearly IBM is not about to give up its mainframe business for anybody. Consider in 2009 when a rookie in the IT business, a company known as Platform Solutions in Sunnyvale, CA, developed software that turned standard Intel servers into systems that emulated expensive IBM mainframes. IBM brought out the reserves to fight back. Legal action nonetheless failed so IBM resorted to its bank account.

Big Blue bought the Company for $150 million. It then terminated the threatening product. On my own, I would have believed that IBM had already well-tuned mainframes so that no competitor's product jury rigged for x86 servers could touch the mainframe in reliability and performance. Maybe the mainframe is a big puff piece? Who really knows?

Why would IBM spend $150 million on something that would run applications at 1/10 speed and break two to three times as often? I would like IBM to answer that one. Can there possibly be corruption in IBM like there is in a mismanaged government that has gotten too large and too powerful.

IBM hated its competition with a major passion. It therefore hated minicomputer vendors—Unix, TCP/IP, and anything that smelled like a loss for mainframe sales. Next to the System/38 and then the AS/400 advanced computer lines, there was only one thing that IBM saw as a bigger threat to the mainframe—minicomputers and later x86 servers.

Where did the tough IBM go?

And, so, in the 1980's to get rid of minicomputers, IBM temporarily took the governor off its AS/400 product line. Mainframes were unarmed competing against minicomputers so IBM brought in something that could finish them off. IBM wiped out most of the minicomputer products in the world and it brought DEC to its knees with its AS/400 product launch.

I have often wondered "Where did that IBM go?" The competition did not know what hit them back then. Soon, however, IBM stopped paying attention to the AS/400 after having lost its shirt in the PC marketplace. Instead, IBM invested resources in a product line that was already lost— the PC.

IBM tried to get it back by thinking the general public would give up their compatible PCs so that they could enjoy the ambiance of a nice PS/2 with OS/2 as a one-two product punch for the client desktop. IBM did not understand the market. If Big Blue had reduced prices to 80% of the competition, it could have saved development dollars and won back the industry.

To those of us working the sidelines in those days, the one-two punch turned out to be much less awesome than a pillow fight. Microsoft, Intel, Compaq, and others knew IBM had guns loaded with blanks with its marketing approach for PS/2 machines and the OS/2 operating system. These 100% interested competitors went on to reduce IBM's PC market share to almost nothing and eventually they forced IBM out of the desktop PC business. IBM, the big boy was slaughtered by a bunch of ants.

IBM stumbled big-time in the 1990s again trying to make up for Chairman Opel's recklessness. John Akers almost sold the corporation to the Grim Reaper piece by piece, losing $14 billion in his last two years.

Many of us believe that if it were not for Chairman Lou Gerstner's arrival and his quick focus on services and software, HP would have been able to take over IBM in 1995 for chump change. Lost in the shuffle was this fabulous AS/400 box that had killed the minicomputer and DEC and when permitted to be deployed was still knocking them dead in what was known as the "midrange" market.

The PC was not the only battle IBM was losing during the PC period. The venerable and venerated SNA/SDLC communication architecture and protocol that we will discuss in this chapter was never really adopted by the government or academia, though it has been wildly successful in the business community since 1974.

The AS/400 as a "new box" and of course the IBM mainframe were all SNA/SDLC oriented. Both also had IBM's killer teleprocessing application which was a defined SNA facility implemented as Advanced Peer to Peer Networking APPN).

By the way, IBM's teleprocessing protocols were great. SNA/SDLC was tops. If IBM ruled the world as it thought it did in teleprocessing, all would be good today. But, IBM ruled nothing in data communications. SNA/SDLC were discarded by all other computer vendors because IBM kept the protocols proprietary and did not attempt to make them universal.

Besides, the protocols required a lot more difficult setup work than the real industry champion, which came from Berkeley—TCP/IP. Only huge corporations needed everything SNA/SDLC had to offer. And so, again, IBM pleased its mainframe customers rather than the world of IT.

The rest of the world including all world governments including the USA, were looking for more from TCP/IP. Meanwhile IBM mounted campaign after campaign about how TCP/IP was second-rate against SNA/SDLC. Nobody expected IBM to ever choose to be a leader in TCP/IP, and to be honest, it made IBM look silly

So nobody could say a politically incorrect word against IBM. Big Blue did have a me-too TCP/IP "product" available for the AS/400 and the mainframe. The AS/400 version was written in Pascal and it was simply terrible. IBM intended the package to be terrible to show how bad TCP/IP was but instead IBM proved how bad its systems were in a TCP/IP world.

For a small system, the price tag on an AS/400 for TCP/IP was $26,000. Without this feature, IBM could not even bid on government and academic projects. IBM's TCP/IP was so bad, however, that if it were ever essential for the success of the installation, IBM would not bid as it would never be able to implement successfully—and it cost $26,000 with no exceptions for tiered pricing.

IBM decisions kept the Company from competing

Unfortunately, IBM had made the AS/400 an SNA-only machine at its heart and even with the TCP/IP add-on expensive product, most of what one would expect in a viable TCP/IP stack was not to be found.

As you may recall historically, at this time, the Internet was coming into its own and then-Vice President Al Gore was pushing the notion of the "Information Superhighway." Of course, the highway was paved with TCP/IP, so the AS/400 was a non-participant in the early 1990s.

The IBM mainframe TCP/IP stack was not well regarded either. Basically AS/400 and the mainframe were out in the cold with regard to accessing TCP/IP networks including the Internet. None of this seemed to bother Chairman John Akers at the time.

Additionally, the client/server revolution had arrived. Both Unix and NetWare servers brought forth file and printer sharing for a PC-crazed neophyte business user class. Additionally, Visual Basic and other visual languages permitted users to benefit from the same point-and-click interface they had come to enjoy with Windows 3.0, 3.1, and then Windows 95 and later versions. To choose not to satisfy these needs could indeed be the death of any platform.

For both the Internet and client server, the IBM corporate strategy was to keep the AS/400 and the mainframe as non-players in this critically important application area (TCP/IP applications).

IBM's rationale was simple. The Company already made two platforms—the RS/6000 running Unix, and PC servers running Windows for Workgroups, then Windows NT, as well as NetWare—so its executives believed that two out of its four product lines were enough to satisfy its customer's TCP/IP needs. IBM has been paying the price in lost sales for such a dumb strategy to this day.

No sane person would have made such a decision. John Opel and John Akers kept IBM out of the Internet as it was being formed, though IBM did have a role in infrastructure activities. You and I would not have made such a decision. It was insane. Lou Gerstner spotted the insanity on his first day of work.

Do Cadillac owners need a second car?

Would a GM executive decide that the Oldsmobile, Buick, and Cadillac owners would not need automatic transmissions since the Chevy and Pontiac lines offered these features? Would they forbid their premiere divisions to retool for this convenience when the less expensive models already had this stuff built-in? Would they think their customers would simply buy a cheaper second car if they wanted an automatic transmission?

You and I can see that those who would have ordered Cadillacs, of course, would not have bought a Pontiac as a second vehicle just to get an automatic transmission. Instead, they would have opted for a GM competitor's nice Lincoln Town Car with an automatic transmission or a Mercedes and said the heck with GM's philosophies on what I need and do not need.

Why did IBM CEOs not see the obvious?

GM would not get the lost sales for those who went to Ford or Mercedes because they could not get what they felt they needed from GM. So also with IBM and its AS/400 line and its Cadillac mainframe line. IBM had its head in the sand not permitting mainframes or AS/400 systems to have first class TCP/IP stacks to use.

You know that. I know that. And Lou Gerstner knew that on his first day of work at IBM. If the machine you wanted could not run TCP/IP, and you bought it, then you could not sell your stuff on the Internet. Lou Gerstner knew that even before he was briefed.

Lou Gerstner was a first-class merchant. He understood why things sold. It was because they appealed to customers. Making products appealing was second nature to Gerstner. He knew how to sell anything—including cookies!

Mr. Gerstner made a great decision shortly after his arrival at IBM on April Fool's Day, 1993, that would help stop the AS/400 and mainframe product line erosion (remember the mainframe was even declared dead for a while). Yes, as hard as it is to believe, IBM had also decided that its mainframe division did not need a robust internet capable TCP/IP stack or client server facilities.

Somehow, a guy who had just spent a part of a lifetime working with cookies and cigarettes, somehow saw something that the cream of the crop IBM executive team had not seen and without Gerstner's help never would have seen.

Gerstner immediately called for the retooling of all IBM systems to fully support the Internet and client/server. He not only saved the IBM Corporation with his services and software strategy, he personally saved the AS/400 and mainframe divisions by forcing the line executives to add the missing (and unbudgeted) TCP/IP stack and client/server facilities to their product lines. Lou Gerstner would not be put off. He was the only executive in IBM at the time who saw things clearly and who had the guts to make it right.

So, in 1994 IBM introduced a new, no-charge TCP/IP stack for the AS/400 and for its mainframe operating systems. The AS/400 stack reportedly performed 700 percent (eight times) better than the former chargeable stack. The same team that built the stack for the AS/400 (operating from Endicott, New York, under the able direction of Armando Fratezi), built the same stack for the mainframe.

At the same time, IBM introduced Client Access/400 and an inboard Intel server to help its AS/400 customers with the client/server revolution that by then had just about completely passed IBM by.

Nothing happens overnight in IT and so it took until the late 1990s for the full stack and all of the well-known TCP/IP utilities to be available with expected function. The 1994 offerings were quite buggy as IBMers new to the TCP/IP protocol were implementing to specifications and not to how the Unix players in the industry had actually shaped the protocols to perform.

As noted, nothing happens overnight and thus, while the dot-com revolution was in full swing and companies were spending huge amounts for Internet servers, both the AS/400 and the mainframe were just being made able to participate. Can you imagine the lost sales to Sun Microsystems and others who championed the dot-com day? Yet, other than John Akers himself, no IBM manager of whom I am aware was released from duty.

Dot com not for IBM minicomputers?

Meanwhile, AS/400 developers and development teams
were disenfranchised from participating in the dot-com
revolution. It eventually became a dot-com bust for sure, but
there were some great days and there are some great
companies that got their roots during this period. Just look
at Amazon, Yahoo, and Google. These companies were not
able to enjoy the benefits of an AS/400 or mainframe at the
time, since IBM's decisions about TCP/IP had kept their
systems incapable of meeting their needs.

Finally by the year 2000, most of the TCP/IP artifacts
necessary for a real Internet server found their way into
these IBM computer product lines. Most of the new
development work on the systems was still green screen,
despite the fact that the system could now support TCP/IP
and all its wonders.

Why was this? With Gerstner no longer paying attention
and perhaps believing that all systems were enfranchised for
the Internet and client/server, he issued no more technology
decrees. Yet, the last step of the metamorphosis had not
taken place--the ability for AS/400 developers to develop in
an AS/400 style and have their end-products usable on the
Web.

Why did this not happen? Corporate IBM began a new love
affair with a software language that it had not created. It
was known as Java and it continues to light up IBM's light
to this day in one form or another.

It's like somebody in IBM actually thought it was OK to tell
the AS/400 developers to learn German when they already
spoke only Spanish. Somebody in IBM thought, and
apparently still thinks, this is OK. Meanwhile the AS/400 is
now called the IBM Power System with IBM I, and Big
Blue knows it is not necessarily a mainframe.

It was philosophies such as these that swept the teleprocessing sub-industry from IBM and made IBM's competitor's successful. It also opened up the door for huge companies to be formed that made productivity in teleprocessing products their major mission. Thank you, IBM.

Chapter 41

Teleprocessing: the Next Step beyond Card Readers and Printers

How should computers handle processing in remote branch offices?

Early computer systems consisted of a processor, which could compare values, add, subtract, multiply and divide. To give the machine the values to compare or to apply mathematics, an input device such as a paper-tape reader or an 80-column card reader, was required.

Computers built in the 1950's had no real direct input capabilities other than a console used for operator communications with the computer system. It was not used for data input. There were no terminals. There were no display stations. There were no attachable PCs.

Computers in the 1950's, 1960's, and 1970's could attach printers and card punches directly with big fat cables so that data could be punched into cards, and it could be printed in reports or forms such as invoices.

Let's suppose that companies that had their corporate HQ in Pennsylvania, required that operations such as payroll accept input directly from branches in California. When the mainframe was first invented, there was no device available to get the data from California to Pennsylvania. One inch sized huge wires for each card reader or printer were prohibited by cost to be able to be stretched across the country.

The US mail was not a good option for immediate responses that were required. Email was not available yet. Sending in a report from California via email about employee hours even if it could be done would take a lot of time to arrive and payroll deadlines might not be met. There were no faxes or copiers to expedite the process either. We were at the very beginning of the technology explosion.

Would it not have been nice if there were an inexpensive device that did not have the bells and whistles of a real computer system—substantially less expensive—that could be installed in California? Would it not be nice if this unit could provide data input to the big HQ computer simply by making a phone call?

If this were possible, the big computer in PA could process the payroll, for example, and provide a report for the less expensive unit in California to print? Would it not have been nice if this process could all happen in minutes instead of days?

Since the answer to that question was and still is a resounding yes; it sure would be nice. IBM figured out how to remotely connect 80-column card readers and typewriter keyboards to computer systems and they also figured out how to connect 80-column card punches and typewriter type printers and regular higher speed printers to the same computer systems—even when the distances were not measured in feet but in hundreds or thousands of miles. But, how?

Getting data from point A to point B across the country

Since no company wanted to stretch a big wire across the country for their own use as it would be unaffordable and wires would be all over the countryside even if they could, they asked the big long-distance phone company AT&T for some help. AT&T aka Ma Bell at the time, had wires already set up for communication across the country and parts in between.

Since there was a huge opportunity for AT&T to make a big buck on some new technology, they were quite interested. The combination of the phone company along with computer companies selling long distance data processing solutions came into being. In many ways, that is why the research and development arm of AT&T, Bell Labs became so proficient in computer technology.

The first four letters of telecommunications and teleprocessing denotes that telephone lines outside or in many cases, hard wired telephone lines inside buildings, were used to send data and receive data from computers. This would be called host computer to/from terminal data communications.

Phone companies provided wires and IBM provided "terminals." FYI, A computer is an electronic or electromechanical hardware device that is used for entering data into, and displaying data from a computer or a computing system with processing of data in-between input and output. The word terminal means end point and in the early days, a computer would speak to just one terminal or end point device at a time.

IBM Introduces the 1050 Data Communications System

IBM's best entrée into the terminal equipment marketplace in the beginning was the IBM 1050 Data Communications System. It was introduced to the world on March 12, 1963, a year before the IBM System/360. It featured asynchronous communications (aka asynch.)

Figure 41-1 IBM 1050 Data Communications System

Using this method, each character (A. B, C, etc.) was serialized and synchronized individually for transmission over telephone lines). Techies like to call this method of serialization asynch. Instead of fat cabling carrying multiple letters or numbers at a time, asynch enabled the data to be sent out as bits of a number or letter at a time so that the data could be crammed into a skinny phone line or like wire.A typical 1050 system had a control unit with limited intelligence, as well as a keyboard/printer which often was nothing more than a re-worked IBM Selectric Typewriter (1052 Printer/Keyboard. With other options, the 1050 could also read and write paper tape, and it could read and punch 80-column cards.

It performed all of its tasks very slowly—typically no faster than 300 characters per second minus the overhead. Since phone lines often had static in the early days, the overhead included retries. Each time a synchronized message was sent, it had to be acknowledged. If the acknowledgment was not received, the data was retransmitted.

Let me say that again as it differentiates terminals from directly attached card readers and printers which have no static or signal interference. Telephone line overhead was a major factor as telephone lines in the 1960's often had lots of static (interference) and retries were frequent. Retries took up a lot of bandwidth. Additionally synchronizing each individual character and assuring its successful arrival took up a lot of the already small band width available on a telephone line. Things seemed to take forever, but they took a lot less time than the mailman.

No green screens or color monitors

To envision how this worked, it helps to remember that in the 1960's, there were few green screens. Color monitors had yet to be invented and CRTs were just hitting the marketplace. But, there were lots of card readers and card punches and printers.

For years before the 1960's, card readers and printers and the like were directly attached via huge cables which transmitted loads of data characters in an instant. We are not trying to be technical here but a character such as an "A" in computer signals requires eight "bits" aka electrical pulses plus a check bit, a ninth "bit" to send that A to the computer or for a printer to receive an "A" for printing.

Those big thick cables would send all of the data "bits" of an A at the same time along with probably three to eight to sixteen other characters, *A, B, C,* etc. at the same time. These cables thus sent all pulses in parallel since each pulse needed its own little wire inside of the big shielded cable about the size of a ½ inch to ¾" pipe.

The cables between the computers and these devices were so thick that most data centers were built with false flooring about nine inches to a foot high and the cables were stuffed down under the floor.

IBM had long ago perfected how to get clean data to the computer from peripheral devices such as card readers. For example, a card reader might read cards at 1000 cards per minute with 80 characters per card, and all of those signals were sent and processed by the computers of the day as each card was read over these huge cables.

To me that is still impressive. Likewise when printing, the computer would send out one line of print at a time, often 132 characters per line, and there would be no problems. The lines would be printed at speeds often over 1000 lines per minute.

So, to effect remote communications, AT&T and other phone companies were asked to get into the computer act to take the place of those extremely thick cables. How would this work? Phone cabling has two wires but sometimes four. So, there are not enough wires to send data characters (A. B, C, 1, 2, 3) in parallel. Remember letters and numbers have 8 parts called bits. So, if an "A" has eight parts, it is impossible to send all of the "A" pulses on eight wires when there are at most four telephone wires.

Attaching a card reader or printer remotely therefore involved engineers first figuring out how to make data flow serially rather than in parallel. There just were not enough wires to send a whole character at a time on a Ma Bell telephone line. If you can imagine all of the pulses of a character lined up in the machine on top of each other with each pulse having its own wire, how does the computer get these 8 bits out over the telephone line? The first thing that the engineers did is decide to use just one of the four wires in a telephone line to send and the other to receive. The rest is logical.

Parallel cables; Remote=serial phone lines

The eight data bits in parallel were in the form of pulses all arriving at the same time on different wires. The engineers created a hardware device that would capture the eight bits at one time and temporarily stop receiving any more pulses in parallel. Their device would then take each pulse from the top wire to the bottom wire and send the pulse one at a time out over the telephone line. When it sent the last of the eight pulses, it would receive another eight bits from the computer and repeat the process until the whole message was sent.

By converting the bits one at a time from parallel to serial, some analysts in describing what they had done called their device a bit tipping unit as it took vertically aligned bits, tipped them, and sent them out horizontally or as it is called, serially. In computer terms, this bit tipping unit device was called a transmission control unit. It was also known as a *serialize / deserialize* (SERDES) unit. The *deserialize* part came on the other side of the transmission, say in California, where the SERDES (bit tipping unit) would receive the bits serially and send them out vertically / parallel.

When the full character reached the other end, in order for the computer or terminal equipment to recognize the A, it all had to be brought together again with all pulses in parallel. How this actually happened would be a great conversation with an electrical engineer. I do not plan to have such a conversation so I gave this high level view so that you can understand the logic, not the electronics involved.

It would be nice if that were all that were needed to place a remote terminal someplace and make it work. Unfortunately, in addition to requiring data to be transmitted serially, phone lines cannot handle digital pulses. A digital pulse is an electronic signal of a certain, say amplitude, for an instant in time. If there is a pulse for that instant in time, then the bit is said to be on. In the next instant of time, there is not a pulse, then this next bit is off. In computer terms, an off bit has a value of 1, and an on bit has a value of 0. You may recall seeing international on/off switch markings on computer equipment that say 1 for on and 0 for off.

Because the phone company cannot send on and off signals on a phone line, the digital / data pulses must be converted to analog / voice signals. We have discussed how a computer serializes its characters, called bytes in computer terminology, and how it *deserializes* the bits in the byte at the receiving station.

If the objective were to print a 132 character print line, the terminal or computer would have to have a small amount of memory (known as a buffer) to be able to store the full line of print before it was printed.

Need for modulation / demodulation

Unfortunately, Bell Telephone in the 1960's and its tech arm Bell labs did not originally engineer their lines for anything other than nice clear talk with highs and lows as somebody raises their voice and then lowers it. Data was not on their minds. Talk was not transmitted over phone lines as bits, but instead, as wavy signals representing the person's voice. The equipment to handle the fluctuations in voice are referred to as analog components. The many changes in voice signals in technical terms must be carried by what are known as analog signals.

Voice conversation transmission devices from the start were able to transmit voice over these lines in an analog form with no conversion at all right from one phone to another. The receiving phone recognized the analog signal and sent it to the speaker in the receiver which provided the sound of the voice. One person speaks and another one, on the top end of their phone hears what was spoken. Voice transmission is thus known as analog.

Computer signals are very discrete. There are no fluctuations as in voice. They are represented by the absence or presence of a pulse in a timed slot in serial mode. So computer vendors wanting to communicate over phone lines figured how to chop up a second of analog bandwidth into 2400 individual parts, and thus, they were able to send 2400 discrete signals. The signals by some were called bits, and by others were called baud.

Regardless, it takes 8 data signals to send a character of data. The term baud came from how many pulses per second could be sent on the telephone line equipment. And, so, a very technical explanation would be that in telecommunication and electronics, baud is the unit for symbol rate or modulation rate in symbols per second or pulses per second. It is the number of distinct symbol changes (signaling events) made to the transmission medium per second in a digitally modulated signal or a line code.

Consequently, most novices and many pros consider baud and the notion of bits per second in early transmission technology to always be the same value. Later as faster modems permitted more than one bit to be carried per baud, the notion of a bit equals a baud no longer held true.

Computers speak in discrete pulses while home line voice requires continual and variable signals recognizing the fluctuation in the human voice. So, how could data in pulse (digital) form even if serialized to fit on the wire, be able to use such a flawed analog electrical scheme? The answer is that computers would not be able to communicate over telephone lines no matter how well they tipped their bits. Some other technique was needed. The experts came through again.

Modulation solved the bit problem in data communications

The engineers went back to work and figured out that voice was what they would call a modulated signal, and data would be what they called a de-modulated signal. So, when computer signals would be serialized and ready to go out on the phone line, there was one more step necessary. The signal had to be modulated. And, thus, a separate piece of hardware was necessary to achieve this.

Modem is a term we all know by now

The extra piece of hardware was needed to take the digital (demodulated) signal and modulate it so that the analog phone lines could handle the traffic. On the receiving side, the modulated signal would reach another box whose job it was to demodulate it into computer bits. Once demodulated, the digital pulses (bits) could be sent serially to the SERDES or transmission control unit and be put back as parallel pulses to be received perfectly by the data processing equipment (computer or terminal).

The piece of hardware that we are discussing is known today as a modem. Modem of course stands for modulate / demodulate.

Now that we have the bases covered for how data processing devices talk to each other over telephone lines, let's move on with IBM's role in teleprocessing / data communications / networking, since Big Blue invented just about everything in the early days of computing.

Early modems were provided by the phone company while the SERDES was provided by the computer vendor. Over time, companies such as IBM made more powerful, faster, and more accurate modems and the phone company merely provided the phone line. Data communications equipment from modems to great terminals are included in IBM's invention list. Too bad for IBM stockholders that Mother IBM did not decide to be really successful in any of these "fringe" areas.

IBM kept improving the devices and protocols for data communications

For a company (IBM) that has been losing revenue from 2012 through 2015, one would expect that if it had captured some of these marketplaces, such as data communications that it had created, it would have fared much better over time and perhaps have a big wad of cash in its corporate pocket.

While IBM was getting the protocols in order, it was also improving the terminal devices that could talk to computers for great distances over phone lines.

In 1965, IBM improved the 1050 system by using its knowledge and creating the IBM 2741. Both used *asynch* protocol. In 1967 IBM invented a better data transmission methodology than *asynch*. It was known as the binary synchronous protocol. Techies called it *bisynch*. The IBM 2780, first shipped in 1967 to communicate with second generation IBM computers was a far superior machine than either the IBM 1050 or 2741.

The 2780 used the new binary synchronous protocol and was much faster in throughput. It optimized the most precious resource, the slow, 2400 baud / bits per second, telephone line. Instead of one character at time, binary synchronous devices transmitted blocks of data such a full 80 column card image or a 132 character print line.

Figure 41-2 IBM 2780 Data Communications Terminal

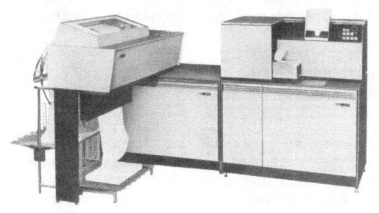

IBM 2780 Data Communications Terminal

IBM kept improving things. Later it introduced its 2770 terminal line and then its 3780 line, a much better technology than the 2780. As phone technology and modem technology improved, the speeds of the devices benefitted accordingly. Today, we see the Internet measured in millions of bits per second. Back then 9600 bits per second was very high speed.

IBM invented another protocol as it discovered the limitations of binary synchronous communications. And, so, in 1974, the Company introduced the IBM 3770, a Data Processing Division (DPD) product terminal which supported the newly invented SNA Architecture and a new data communications protocol known as Synchronous Data Link Control or SDLC.

Whereas *asynch* was one character at a time with two devices talking to each other, and *bisynch* was blocks of characters at a time with two devices talking to each other, SDLC permitted many different devices to communicate with each other at the same time over one telephone line. It is the most sophisticated; most efficient; and most complex communication protocol of all time. It was not and is not for the faint of heart.

Since 1974, Systems Network Architecture (SNA) has been IBM's proprietary networking architecture. It is really special. It includes a complete protocol stack for interconnecting computers, terminals and their resources. The architecture creates a blueprint and in the blueprint it describes formats and protocols. It is in itself, not a piece of software. It is a major design document implemented in devices and computers and it uses the SDLC protocol for the sake of remote error free computing.

The implementation of SNA still takes the form of various communications packages, most notably on mainframes, a low level notion called the Virtual Telecommunications Access Method (VTAM). VTAM is the mainframe software package for SNA communications.

Despite all of the difficulty in setting up mainframes for data communications for large enterprises, IBM simplified the notion and deployed SNA and SDLC in its small business computers—the System/3X line. IBM technicians in the IBM labs and plants predefined the specifications so that gurus in small IT shops were not needed.

Small business computers using such integrated technology thus had no problem talking to big IBM iron. The only problem was that very few if any non-IBM vendors used IBM SNA and so there was little to no heterogeneous device capabilities.

For communication with large mainframes, for example, an IBM System/34, or System/36, or System/38 or AS/400, or later IBM i systems devices, could be implemented in hours, not weeks or months. All of these small systems were built at the OS level with SNA fundamentals, and it was no charge.

IBM adopts TCP/IP to connect all computers

IBM had in many ways blocked its competitors from being viable in the SNA arena, hoping it would hurt the competitor's ability to sell their computers to IBM customers—especially mainframe customers. So, instead of SNA, IBM's competition adopted the government developed TCP/IP protocol standard for their data communications projects. TCP/IP became a part of UNIX so it was natural for minicomputer vendors to adopt it.

The Internet was on its way

While IBM was avoiding Unix and the Internet to save the mainframe, they were both becoming very successful. The Internet's been around in some form for decades. Lots of things happened over time that brought the dot com domains in wide use by the mid 1990's. It was before this, however, in the mid-80s, though, that the Web as we know it started coming together—and those precious dot-com domains started getting snatched up.

In the spring of 1985, getting ready for commercial enterprises, the first dot-com domain was sold and registered. A domain named symbolics.com was booked on March 15, 1985. The site at the time belonged to a company known for its Open Genera Lisp and Macsyma computer algebra systems.

The Company, Symbolics, unfortunately went bankrupt. However, somebody bought the name. Thus symbolics.com is the Internet's oldest continually functioning dot-com domain. Take a look at it and you may think you are back in 1985. It is cute.

The first dot com domain and the dot-com bubble, are two different things. The dot com bubble is when many companies became rich selling products on the Internet. This lightly began in 1995 and was in full play by 1997. The bubble began to burst in 1999 and the bubble ended about 2000-2001. Some companies made lots. Some lost lots. Some made lots and then lost it.

IBM eventually moved into Ethernet and TCP/IP networking products in the 1990s after ignoring them for a decade too long. With TCP/IP as the major communications protocol for the Internet, it was the end of a bright future for SNA. IBM products continued to use it but it made little sense for two robust protocols to have to be supported in one IT shop.

IBM was late to the game but it developed and/or or resold some fine functioning families of Ethernet switches and TCP/IP routers. Where it had no time to develop products, it resold its competitors' ware. As an also ran, however, IBM never gained top spot in the popular TCP/IP game, and thus was never the big gun in networking as it was in the days of the 1050 and 2780. The one word that describes IBM and TCP/IP is rejection.

IBM's competition loved TCP/IP and consequently almost all IBM computers for years could not talk to any non-IBM system that used TCP/IP anywhere in their network. This was not a good enterprise strategy for IBM from the beginning. When IBM finally was forced to work with TCP/IP when Lou Gerstner adopted the Internet for eBusiness, it enabled all IBM systems to participate in open networks and broadened the chances for IBM systems to be adopted. Unfortunately, IBM had already poisoned the well for its own data communications opportunities with TCP/IP. But, things did get a lot better.

This increased IBM opportunities; but it would have been better if IBM had built first class open architecture products from the beginning. Because IBM was not part of the scene for so long, IBM's marketing team had a difficult time convincing non-IBM small customers who used DEC, DG, Prime, etc. to look at IBM's TCP/IP.

Being an employee of IBM at the time, I noticed that there were no excuses; there was no apology; there was no apparent reemphasis on TCP/IP broadcast to IBMers or customers. Only those following the issue or with a pressing need to be on the Internet understood how far off the mark IBM had been with its SNA-only strategy. IBM lost a lot of business and a lot of good will with its marketplace stubbornness. All of IBM's competition should thank it for giving it such unchallenged opportunities in the marketplace. Cisco owes IBM the most.

I saw it first hand before IBM chose to create bona fide TCP/IP stacks within their systems. For one of my customers to communicate with other vendors using

TCP/IP on a small System/38, for example, they were expected to spend about $26,000 for a very poor performing and buggy implementation of TCP/IP while there was no charge for SNA. IBM customers did not forget this.

Lou Gerstner set IBM free in "teleprocessing."

When Lou Gerstner took over in 1993, he solved the IBM problem with TCP/IP. What Cary, Opel, and Akers, would not do out of ignorance to the marketing issue, Gerstner got done. Gerstner set IBM straight in data communications so in this chapter, there are times when he must be discussed. The other CEOs with their SNA and mainframe myopic stance regarding IBM business, almost assured IBM no place in Lou Gerstner's eBusiness world. Thank you Lou Gerstner.

We are examining technology that began in the Watson, Learson, and Cary years, but the whole notion of networking continues to the present time, and so we will finish what we began in the section and this will take us to today.

There is more to go in this data communications area as it is a major opportunity almost 100% missed by the IBM Corporation. For years IBM missed its chances in DC regardless of who was the CEO.

Despite inventing the notion of data communications and networking in the 1960's, and in fact coining the term teleprocessing, IBM basically floundered in telecommunications in the 1990's until 1996.

At the Fall Internet World show, then IBM Chairman Louis V. Gerstner, Jr., unveiled the notion of the "new killer apps," a world of transaction-intensive, networked applications delivered to a world of connected individuals by all of the world's most important institutions.

They all ran under TCP/IP so it was no wonder all IBM systems were ordered by Gerstner finally to be equipped with rich, not ho-hum, TCP/IP stacks.

At a time when the conventional wisdom casted the Internet as the home of games, information and e-mail, Gerstner's Internet World speech reoriented the debate around the more profound vocational implications of networked computing.

Gerstner listened to the thumping outside of IBM as much as he heard IBM advocates suggesting the Company stick to its SNA guns. IBM would be a $30 billion company today instead of $92 billion if the TCP/IP naysayers had their way. There was so much pride in SNA inside of mainframe IBM that I would bet there were many high ranking IBM executives unhappy that Gerstner saved IBM but took down SNA. Gerstner had the guts to make this decision heard all around the world after he heard all of the input.

And, so, in addition to his 1993 decree on TCP/IP, in 1997: IBM Chairman Louis V. Gerstner, Jr. announced to all IBM employees the debut of a major strategic campaign built around the IBM-coined term "eBusiness."

Gerstner was not a computer guy per se and IBMers internally joked about him being not much more than the "Cookie Man" from his days at Nabisco. Yet, here he was in his first major customer address on e-business—a speech considered by many as the first "wake-up call" to Wall Street on the implications of the networked world.

In the speech, Gerstner described to the Securities Industries Association, the Internet's ability to challenge centuries-old business models and transform the nature of all important transactions between individuals and institutions. He was 100% on the mark.

Unfortunately, as in many areas in which what could have been was not, IBM had not prepared itself to reap the benefits of Gerstner's level of e-Business. Yet, here we are just about twenty-years after Gerstner's eBusiness launch and the world has changed just as Gerstner had predicted. It is now a place where e-Business and hand held devices are the natural way of conducting business.

All first-rate companies have major eBusiness presences on the Web and most have many apps to make the millennials of today and those of any age with an i-something want their app more than any other.

IBM surely could have done better with terms it had coined such as eBusiness, word processing, and teleprocessing. Of course this is the overriding message of this book. The Company had many opportunities but its management structure did not permit divisions to make real decisions, and top management after Watson and before Gerstner, was reluctant to make the big decisions.

Some of us think drones with AI abilities that could have digested the Watson's decisions and looking at the input they had available, would have made much better decisions than Cary, Opel, and Akers. They were all scaredy-cats in pinstripe suits and wingtips. Gerstner, the "cookie man," had real guts and the courage of his convictions.

Gerstner would have liked IBM's General Systems Division

After its dissolving of the General Systems Division, a very effective, and truly autonomous division in IBM in the late 1960's into the 1980's, IBM used a top down model to manage corporate business. The Corporate Management Committee made too many decisions. Voices from outside central command were not welcome.

Nobody expected IBM to give up central control of anything but when the anti-trust division of the US Justice Department was breathing down the necks of top IBM executives for a complete breakup of the Company, IBM figured it was better for the Company to have the split occur its way.

So, they created a new division in 1969. The new division, the General Systems Division (GSD) was the Company's first and last totally integrated division. It was like a company within the IBM Company. GSD had the responsibility to design, develop, and manufacture its own new systems. It also had responsibility in the United States to market and service the resulting products. In many ways, it made its own decisions. Folks in Mainframe IBM did not like another group in the Company selling computers of any kind.

IBM in Rochester Minnesota was the center of the universe for the new division. If you took a trip to Rochester, with its lousy winter weather and mosquito infestations in the summer, you would see these particular engineers and scientists had nothing better to do than concentrate on the best notions for the IBM Rochester product line. They were dedicated to Rochester's success.

People came to Rochester either to learn about IBM's excellence or to offer help to IBM. Of course some came to be cured by the Mayo Clinic, and we wish them all wellness. I would bet there were never any Olympic swim champions from Rochester or surrounds. Only the ducks in the warm waters of Silver Lake seemed to think Rochester was like the tropics. Regular people who were not 100% IBM solution freaks or patients went south for the winter.

When GSD was formed, this new alignment gave IBM Rochester a singularity of purpose: IBM's center of development for its low-cost general purpose systems (business minicomputers) and their programming and sales support. Rochester people loved being the best and IBM eventually forgot about that and shut down their operation. IBM's mainframe bigots did not like being upstaged by regular people who happened to be very smart—even if it were good for the Company.

As an integral part of this discussion it helps to know that all of IBM's systems produced by GSD were equipped with IBM's flagship SNA communications architecture and the SDLC protocol that it required. IBM Rochester's systems were thus great communicators. They too were prohibited from participating in Unix ventures or TCP/IP because IBM's mainframe oriented leadership had a deep hatred for both.

Feel free to take a Web trip into IBM's archives to get a great picture of how special GSD and the Rochester Lab and Plant site was to the IBM Corporation. http://www.cbi.umn.edu/hostedpublications/pdf/IBMRochesterHistory.pdf

IBM kept GSD on until there was no threat that the government would spit the Company. John Opel, as CEO did not make many good decisions but disbanding GSD was a bad decision made under the guise that IBM's largest customers did not want to hear from different IBM Salesmen selling small business computers, office systems, and mainframes. The theory was that customers wanted one voice from IBM. Opel unfortunately has been proven to be a dunderhead from his many other IBM-diminishing decisions.

Having lived through many major reorganizations, the one that disbanded GSD made a lot of people in the Company feel *what's the use.* Those with a GSD heritage did not give it up. We always hoped IBM would see the light in things that were keeping the Company from a greatness it was assured with proper execution.

IBM also prematurely wiped out the people who worked for its Office Products Division. With minimal training, it released them to become computer salesmen or technicians and they often could not handle it. So, those with an Office heritage most often took the suicide pill offered by the Company as it wiggled out of the word processing business. It was not a good time in the Company seeing people disappear.

Those in the mainframe camp were still just interested in mainframes and were glad to see GSD, a possible competitor taken out by IBM Execs. Mainframe marketing reps looked to a former GSD product solution only if the customer refused to take their mainframe business offering, and otherwise, the customer was heading to the competition.

It was a disaster as most of IBM's great reorganizations have been over the years. My wonderful father, who was the smartest man alive in my life, would have said that if John Opel had another brain, it would be lonesome.

And, so, though TJ Watson Jr. loved wild ducks, he did not give his successors the same mindset. IBM post Watsons, never liked autonomy and thus there was little of that to be found in the corporation other than GSD, which they eliminated as soon as they could. IBM had to get rid of GSD because GSD would one day take over IBM because IBM at the top and in the mainframe camps had forgotten that customers had always driven IBM's business fortunes.

Since arguing with the IBM-defined solution was no longer permissible in the post Watson politically correct IBM world, everybody in IBM quickly piled on to any idea that looked like it would be favored by the top brass. *Yes* was always the word. *No* was stricken from the IBM hand books and sales songs. I was always on the fringe for I was never a "yes-man."

Few innovators who had families (and could not afford to be held in a poor light) brought anything forward. It was too dangerous in the Opel years. Post Watson, it was OK to be a lapdog because the wild ducks that Tom Watson Jr. admired so much had gone extinct from IBM.

Little got done without the top brass having to know it all. IBM joked when I joined in 1969 that more great products had been placed in the trashcan of technology, because their sponsors simply could not sell the idea or because a more powerful entity in the Company with a less marketable idea chose to destroy their project's opportunities. The joke had come back to dominate the Company. The joke had become the Company. Whereas Sun suggested that the network is the computer and they said they were the dot in dot com, the IBM Company had become a joke with a lot of cash. But, then it lost the cash.

Said differently, IBM theoretically fostered competition internally because that was a Watson wish, but when a better method came forth, the political power brokers who were mostly represented for years by the IBM mainframe aficionados, shot it down.

IBM did not see teleprocessing as an industry

IBM had invented the term *teleprocessing* as a *cutesy* idea when nobody dared to try to connect IBM to IBM other than IBM.

Admittedly, IBM's goals were not for company personnel to become teleprocessing experts or data communications experts. Big Blue put forth all this research and resulting products simply to make its mainframe products be able to talk to other IBM loving products such as other mainframes, IBM terminals and any computers that could pretend to be them (emulation). IBM did not have a winning instinct even though it coined many of the terms; owned the marketplaces; and SNA is still the best communications design protocol of all time... but not for the Internet.

And, so like many IBM side businesses, as data communications hardware and software became big businesses unto themselves, the IBM business planners were AWOL. They simply missed it. IBM did not jump in and claim its share of the business from the marketplaces it had created.

Yes, that means IBM was absent without leave {AWOL). It's like IBM did not know what hit them. IBM had forgotten how to win. IBM did not even realize teleprocessing and data communications were industries unto themselves and that as the principle supplier of processing power to that industry, IBM could have easily dominated the purchasing choices of its mainframe and small business customers.

It chose not to lead the industry in anything but large mainframe computers, since the mainframe was typically very successful, IBM created many stock market millionaires along the way. For many, this seemed to make up for Big Blue's inability to lead. The IBM Company also created multi-millionaires in competitive companies that got to run roughshod over IBM. None of the millionaires however, worked for IBM.

IBM's desire to survive after Opel caused it to continue its fire sales of IBM divisions, and telecommunications was in its crosshairs. In 1999, it almost got the job done but somehow it was not a completely done deal. IBM was squirming to get out of the networking business.

IBM could not make it work

On August 31, 1999, IBM sold a ton of its proprietary telecommunications products to Cisco, a company that IBM had enabled to be successful by not engaging fully in the industry. Without IBM's expressed permission, over the years, through aggressive marketing, Cisco grabbed market share from IBM.

In the 1999 deal, Cisco got substantial portions of IBM's networking intellectual property. This ended for a time at least IBM's tinkering into industry standard protocols v SNA and token ring.

IBM was not known to love Ethernet or TCP/IP and so it was a late entry into Ethernet and a vast array of TCP/IP networking infrastructure products. Lou Gerstner spent much of his efforts positioning Big Blue into a services company.

Yet, because it was rethinking in which markets it would compete, IBM at the time chose to support and leverage its networking business from a server and storage systems perspective as well as from its consulting and services business. Looking at it as an observer, I would suggest that nobody in the business world cared what IBM was going to do. Even Lou Gerstner could not change that.

Before Gerstner offered a lifeline to IBM, the other players in the data communications industry along with many other segments of the technology industry expected IBM to go under. It helps to recall that this section of this book is about IBM's lack of success during its history in what had become the data communications industry or the networking Industry. Take your pick!

The IBM Company seemed to either not recognize that there was an industry there or it chose to disengage and not compete. Either way, IBM lost $billions in current annual stockholder opportunity. When IBM invented teleprocessing and data communications, Cisco did not exist. When IBM exited data communications, Cisco's annual sales were approaching $50 billion per year. How is that for mismanagement? IBM had once owned the whole deal.

Much has changed for IBM since 1999

All of a sudden, complicated notions regarding IT and networking have emerged such as server virtualization technologies. These were once predominately a mainframe capability but IBM did not capitalize on it when it was theirs to own. It did not take long and such capabilities were available in almost all server environments and they grew in popularity due to their ability to improve operational efficiency, flexibility, and systems availability.

IBM had once focused on providing customer solutions but it forgot most of its major missions as John Akers, after taking over for John Opel, IBM's worst CEO, had moved IBM from a position of leadership to a concern for survival.

IBM had a lot of firsts in teleprocessing / data communications and yet it did not capitalize on those firsts.

Worse than that, the products and architectures that IBM created formed the basis for new sub-industries within the computer industry. For example, among many other innovations, IBM invented the disk drive. Yet, it did not dedicate the resources to be # 1 in the disk drive / storage business.

And, so like many other technology business areas that IBM created and originally dominated, the Company gave up its disk drive business. IBM claimed that the business was no longer profitable enough.

When you do not make the storage devices for the computers you sell, many businesses would deny you the opportunity to even be considered a storage vendor. IBM believed it could get out of storage hardware and become the smartest team on the field for storage solutions. Too bad for IBM that its customers did not think so. They bought their storage solutions from storage vendors who took their industry seriously. Big Blue positioned itself as an also-ran. Whether IBM wanted to admit it, disk drives were becoming part of the networking scene.

During this period, storage networking notions, including Fibre Channel Storage Area Networking, was experiencing very-significant growth rates. Though IBM was never an Ethernet Champion, it signed up as Ethernet bandwidth, which started at 10 million bits per second (Mbps), grew through Fast Ethernet (100Mbps) and Gigabit Ethernet (1 Gbps to 10 Gbps and even 40 Gbps today, with 100 Gbps in the near future.) Though a part of the foray, IBM was not a leader, and to many, IBM seemed disinterested in the fight at all.

Is IBM making a networking comeback?

Recognizing so many marketing failures. IBM got the notion that it should position itself to become a household name in networks and systems which depended on networks. Both areas of technology have continued to become increasingly interdependent. IBM, despite seemingly selling out to Cisco in 1999, recently has come back into the mix as increasing server virtualization strains the capacity and flexibility of networks to support it. What are we to expect?

IBM's huge performance advantage, gained from its expertise in mainframes and super-computing, over everybody else in the industry, still helps Big Blue. Ethernet technologies are now so advanced that they can provide a viable converged alternative to separate storage and data networks, and token ring is basically non-existent in what once was once called the LAN environment.

If we all face the reality, storage networks, in which IBM is no more than an also-ran, have grown to where the costs of running separate networks are very significant. Therefore, IBM solutions in this area have recently become an attractive target for IT operational cost-cutting initiatives.

These initiatives most often target IBM at the data center. Most people in operations do not call IBM when they need help. But, at one time, they did. That is why IBM's gross revenues have declined for four years in a row.

IBM knows that the evolution to a dynamic infrastructure requires a fundamental rethinking of the relationship between the network and the IT infrastructure. Organizations deploying such solutions need a holistic approach to plan and design the network along with servers, storage and applications.

This is the only way to ensure the flexibility, performance and manageability to deliver optimal value. The big question of the day after scores of IBM failures in more simple technology: "Does IBM have what it takes?" Revenue is still going down after four years so maybe so; maybe not!

Back to the future: Never rule out anybody in the IT Business. Historically, on April 28, 2009, we would find IBM reentering the networking business as part of its "Dynamic Infrastructure" initiative. Whatever it gave up to Cisco was put on hold for the time being. So, now what?

IBM, a big company for sure, but not one on an obvious growth trajectory, still offers software, hardware, and services to help clients build and manage more dynamic system networking infrastructures. But, can IBM win the business in these areas?

At least now it appears that Big Blue is trying to win. Maybe it has no choice. Check your local papers for the results. I would vote today that IBM's competition will win as IBM will get sick of competing if big results do not come instantaneously.

That's that for IBM's chances for a reconstitution of its once assured network business. Now, most of the prior discussion was about remote teleprocessing and data communications.

Again, this is not a technical book but to discuss marketing failings in technology we have had to dip into some simple technology explanations. We are about to do that again as we examine local area networks and we look at how Robert Metcalfe, the man who invented Local Area Networks with Ethernet is enjoying his farm.

Chapter 42

IBM and Local Area Networks

What is a local area network?

The simplest definition of a local area network (LAN) is "A computer network that links devices within a building or group of adjacent buildings."

There are a number of devices that make up a LAN such as the network card that fits into the PC and connects it to the wired network and a central device to which the pc and other device wires are connected. The central device is often called a hub or a switch.

Technically all devices on a network have one of these cards which is known as a network interface card or NIC. PC NICs plug into the system bus and have connectors for network wires on the back end.

Every network has a topology with high speed switches and/or hubs, which interface to the wires and provide the LAN protocol. There are other parts and devices but the most important of course is the internal cabling which must be high quality to avoid any interference and signal distortions.

Today, more than likely you would select cat6a type cabling. It is 30% more expensive than category 6 and 60% more expensive than cat5 cabling. However, it handles all types of speeds today and it means if you laid cat6a cabling today, you would not be redoing the job in a few years.

Though PCs did not exist in the minicomputer era, you can envision a LAN by thinking of fifty PCs wired together via hubs and switches. When each PC is wired to a hub or switch, it is the same logically as if each unit is connected to every other unit. Because of the physical infrastructure and the network card (NIC) in each computer, any of the PCs could thus "talk" to any other PC.

LAN rules are the same as protocols

To make this all happen, rules must be agreed upon. Rules in IT are known as protocols. Before local area networking became a big deal with PCs, it became a big deal with minicomputers in companies that could afford lots of them. They would put them all in the same building or the same campus of corporate buildings. The network would permit minicomputers to talk to each other as well as to larger machines such as mainframes.

Each computer in such a network needed to be able to access the network physically via a NIC and then be able to send and receive data to/from other "nodes" on the network. The nodes in the early days were other minicomputers or mainframes. Eventually, the network consisted of PCs, minicomputers, mainframes, intelligent printers, and other devices such as a smart TV.

What needed to be invented for this physical set of components to work together? Well, as noted, each computer needed to have a compatible network attachment mechanism called a network card (NIC) that would attach in a compatible fashion to the network. This card was inserted into the PC or minicomputer bus on one side and the network wire on the other. It enables the computer to

transmit and/or receive data from other nodes on the
network.

Thus, in addition to the physical cards, there are protocols
needed at the physical layer of the network, where the actual
bits and bytes are trafficking. There also must be logical
processes that enable the physically attached nodes to
communicate data to each other.

Robert Metcalfe invents Ethernet

And, so, LAN pioneers, who did not necessarily know they
would become multi-millionaires at the time came forth to
assure all would work first at the physical wire layer. Robert
Metcalfe was one of these pioneers. He is credited with
inventing Ethernet, which to those in the business is a LAN
protocol.

The Ethernet Local Area Network (LAN) as created by
Metcalfe in 1973 was a direct result of his trying to devise a
way to permit several computers to share just one printer. At
this time, Metcalfe was working for the Xerox Palo Alto
Research Center (PARC).

Nobody invents anything in a vacuum. In fact, Metcalfe got
the idea of a LAN from the ALOHA network at the
University of Hawaii. Their system used radio waves
instead of telephone wire to transmit and receive data.
Metcalfe decided to use highly shielded coaxial cables
instead of radio waves to limit the transmission interference.
Today, Ethernet is the most widely installed LAN protocol.

Crow as a meal makes later meals better

Before Metcalfe brought Ethernet to life, he recalls having to
eat crow in his early technology life. His predicament

required that he call up the inventor of the minicomputer, Digital Equipment Corporation, in the early 1970's to tell them that the $30,000 computer that they had kindly loaned him had been stolen.

Ironically, in some strange way, this became good news for DEC as up to that time, computers had been far too big to steal. When Metcalfe informed DEC of his predicament, they thought it was the greatest thing that had ever happened. Metcalfe relates that "Because it turns out that I had in my possession the first computer small enough to be stolen! And they made a big PR deal out of this!"

Metcalfe ultimately went to DEC for more help to popularize Ethernet. His protocol provided a carrier sense / multiple access / collision detect / collision avoidance (csma/cd&ca) technology for local area networks. Any device via its NIC could send at any time. Other devices delayed sending when the line was busy (collision avoidance). Yet, when two devices sent data at the same exact time, collisions occurred and no data was delivered.

So, collisions still occurred but the Metcalfe protocol was equipped to detect the collision (collision detection). It would then start a pause on the network that all other NICS would "hear," and they would stop to provide time for a data transmission retry. He called the protocol Ethernet but techies knew it as csma/cd&ca.

Like everything else, net protocols evolved

Metcalfe was not the first to toy with networking protocols and topologies. In the early 1970's David Farber at the University of California saw the opportunity to connect minicomputers over a high speed network. He knew that normal telephone wire was not going to do it. He devised a scheme called token ring, which depended on much better shielding for the cabling to achieve 2 megabits per second transmission speeds.

His idea was mimicked by many who made changes to his idea to make it better. Along the way to being a product brought forth by IBM's perfections in 1985, there was the Cambridge token ring and there was also a token ring devised and promoted by MIT.

Token ring is a protocol just as Ethernet but it demands a physically different wiring and network topology and a different network interface (NIC). You cannot mix Ethernet and Token Ring devices on the same network segment. Token Ring has always been seen as the better technology for LANS but somehow Ethernet won the day, mostly because it was less expensive.

If IBM were paying attention to what was happening on college campuses at the time, it would have been aware of the need for LAN technology. IBM could have owned all networking during this period but it was putting it off without giving a reason.

First of all, it took IBM forever to come out with a product and secondly, its token-ring product was very expensive compared to Ethernet. Finally, any reselling vendor wanting to incorporate token ring had to pay IBM's exorbitant licensing fees. Few were therefore incented to build token-ring products. Customers chose Ethernet over token-ring because it looked a lot better on their bottom lines. IBM again lost in the marketplace. There are millions and millions of network cards today and none are IBM.

With minicomputers being very affordable for large companies, just as Farber had noticed in the university environment, there was a big need for high speed building and corporate campus network communications technologies. With minicomputers in play, the easier these smaller scale machines could talk to each other, the more likely a number of them could replace a bigger machine such as perhaps even an IBM mainframe computer.

Could LANS possibly hurt IBM's mainframe business?

IBM did not initially see LANs as a threat. At least they did not instruct us in the sales Branch Offices that LANS were a threat. And, so, these little machines and their networks took off in a big way, without any IBM interference. When high speed local networking and software was added for easy intra building communications, the mainframe as expected became a big target for minicomputer vendors.

IBM still did not react in a meaningful way and it has been paying the penalty for its inaction for a long time. IBM eventually got interested in the local networking game with token-ring, but with its exorbitant pricing, despite the superiority of token-ring, IBM lost another marketplace.

The major IBM thank-you beneficiary for local networking protocol hardware devices is Robert Metcalfe. Born in Brooklyn, Metcalfe is not yet reported to have publicly thanked IBM for his success.

Metcalfe began his career as an engineer. Then he became a technology executive and on the way, he made a ton of money and for a while he took a run as a venture capitalist. All in all, Metcalf is best known for inventing Ethernet, the protocol that has always been the most cost effective method on local area networks.

Metcalfe was not a regular guy.

Robert Metcalfe was very creative and he decided to do what he wanted to do in any given year. He went on from inventing Ethernet, the networking system which allowed computers of all sizes to communicate with each other in the 1970s, to found the multibillion-dollar company 3Com.

This networking company was involved in all facets of telecommunications. Metcalfe certainly could have taught IBM a bit about marketing LANS and network products while he was at 3Com, but then again IBM did not ask. Later, some suggest Metcalf simply dropped out of hard technology to become a technology pundit.

In recent times, Metcalfe has been writing a nationally syndicated InfoWorld column and often the Ethernet inventor makes brash predictions about the future of the Net at industry conferences.

In 1979, Robert Metcalfe started his career as Robert Metcalfe, entrepreneur. He left Xerox PARC, where many techno-geeks got their start to launch 3Com, a firm devoted to selling commercial versions of Ethernet and other networking products.

His company went public in 1984, at which time Metcalfe became a multimillionaire. If IBM were on the watch, Metcalfe might have become a one millionaire; but IBM's dozing off gave Metcalfe and his ideas more opportunity to prosper. One must wonder where was IBM—the industry watcher and the stockholder protector?

Eventually, Robert Metcalfe took his multi-millions from his inventions and his time in corporate America and along with his wife started a farm in 1993. They raise rare breeds of pigs, chickens, sheep, goats, horses, and cows. Metcalf can do whatever he pleases with his millions. Thank you IBM!

Ethernet defeats token-ring

Eventually, after many years of stubbornly waging a useless war, in the mid-1990s, IBM relaxed its intolerance towards Ethernet. One day, it was OK, even for IBM, to sell Ethernet equipment. Unfortunately for IBM, by the time it had decided that it was ok, its customers had already been using Ethernet for years, and they had been trained by IBM to not buy their Ethernet gear from IBM.

These once extremely loyal IBM customers, had been forced to go to Metcalfe's 3COM, Cisco and other "networking" companies for their Ethernet network facilities. When IBM blew the whistle and said, "You can stop buying from them ... we can sell Ethernet now," Big Blues' customers politely acknowledged with a "Thanks, but, no thanks!"

IBM lost LAN & SNA—TCP/IP the winner

Innovations in networking were not only occurring on the hardware front with the introduction of LANs, remote data communications was also being extended with still another non-SNA protocol.

IBM had thought that it had sewed up data communications with SNA, a very rich protocol. The US and other governments sponsored a very different protocol. IBM competitors went this way, also. IBM competitors found SNA a bit too rigid for their tastes, and with IBM not permitting them to build products to support SNA without huge licensing fees, for their own business success, they went along with the government standard.

The protocol that could be applied on wide area networks (WANS) as well as LANs was labeled as the Transmission Control Program / Internet Protocol (TCP/IP). This was before there really was an Internet.

Moreover, since data communications on the local side got the label LAN, the logical name choice for wide area telecommunications networking became known as WAN. Just like SNA, the new TCP/IP worked equally well on LANs and WANs.

IBM would not even acknowledge TCP/IP

Just as IBM closed the door on Ethernet, it also closed the door on TCP/IP, the protocol of today's Internet. IBM chose not to see TCP/IP coming. The Company kept singing the SNA/SDLC mantra even as its customers had discovered the many benefits of TCP/IP.

IBM tried to deny its customers the use of this new government developed and sponsored protocol by not providing adequate support for it in their host system software. IBM's customers did not like this.

Consequently, IBM's host systems and big telecommunications controllers did not support TCP/IP very well. In a typical cut your nose off to spite your own face strategy, the IBM developers were not motivated to build a good TCP/IP stack; nor was IBM marketing ready to suggest that they do so. IBM arrogantly would not support the protocol that beat IBM hands down. Nothing kept IBM from winning in the TCP/IP and Internet protocol space but IBM.

The networking community viewed this as a failure of the IBM Corporation to innovate in a marketplace which the IBM Company itself had created— telecommunications.

IBM falls way behind in another market that it created

With IBM's reticence for Ethernet and its late entry into the world of TCP/IP, the Company was not prepared when its customers wanted to run multiple protocols on the same facility, perform LAN switching, WAN switching, IP switching, SNA and IP integration, bridging, etc., etc., etc.

If a loyal IBM customer had a vanilla SNA requirement, IBM could and would do well. But, if there were wrinkles in the requirements set, (wrinkles were those nasty heterogeneous a.k.a. non-IBM systems or devices), IBM probably could not get the job done with its product line. Moreover, with its reduced sales force over the years, IBM did not have enough talking heads to move its customers into the IBM way rather than the right way. IBM therefore was inevitably left without gaining the networking business. Yet, since customers needed equipment, software, and services, somebody got the business and profited from it— just not IBM.

IBM misunderstood the data communications marketplace

IBM got so far behind the curve that companies like ChipCom, Cisco, Bay Networks and Metcalfe's 3Com were happy to fill in the gaps. IBM believed it could win the communications battle by denying its customers the right to run other protocols on IBM machines. The more IBM misunderstood the marketplace, the more IBM's development team produced products that did not fit the needs of the industry.

After a while, IBM not only appeared to have lost its leadership in the communications industry, the Company continually lagged way behind the leaders. In many ways, IBM began to be perceived as a company that did not know what it was doing in data communications. Any company choosing to compete against Big Blue at this time had the upper hand, and they all owe IBM a big thank-you for their successes and their earnings.

Buy v. build?

To solve many of its marketplace misperceptions in the 1990s, since Big Blue had not invested in Ethernet or TCP/IP hardware, the Company was forced to purchase its Ethernet and TCP/IP gear for resale from industry sources who had stayed abreast of industry technology innovations and market acceptance. IBM would examine competitor's products, make small changes, if any, and then slap on the IBM label so that it appeared IBM too was in that particular business.

Unfortunately for the Company, IBM was not real good at this either. In many cases, the companies from whom IBM purchased huge quantities of gear for resale, would save their best products for themselves. These companies would more often than not, have a better product available than the one IBM would re-label and re-sell. They would then compete against IBM's entry and win the business against their own inferior product labeled as IBM's.

Competitor or partner?

IBM was easy pickings for any company interested in success. IBM's biggest competitors were its supposed partners. Wait until you read about how long time IBM ally

Microsoft bamboozled and dominated IBM. The IBM
Company seemed to like giving these gifts of business and
market share to its competitors, disguised as partners. Nice
guy, gullible IBM lost lots of business to its partners over the
years. IBM stockholders should have been making a killing.

While Big Blue had few of its own solutions in the form of
products, while trying to use its marketing force to control
its customer's networking purchases, reactions were not
positive. IBM's once loyal cadre of customers formed
relationships with companies outside of the glass house.
IBM became an outsider, looking in, and the Company lost
lots of customers and it never fully recovered. Its customers
stopped trusting that IBM would do the right thing for their
business needs.

IBM jumps the networking ship

In the late 1990s and early 2000s, IBM jumped completely
out of the major networking business... switches, routers,
etc. This was a major defeat. The Company decided to turn
most of its business over to Cisco for the opportunity to have
a favored status with Cisco regarding IBM services.

The Company simply gave up in data communications.
IBM had invented data communications like so many other
technology methods but could not make it work on the
marketing side. Lou Gerstner, CEO at the time of the Cisco
deal, had a thing about cutting your losses. IBM and Cisco
signed a $2 billion alliance on August 31, 1999. IBM had
already discontinued many of its once stalwart networking
products, deferring instead to industry standards or strong
competitors.

There have been many other product discontinuances as
IBM, with Gerstner at the helm, was trying to figure out
which businesses could work for IBM after Akers' neglect.
The Cisco deal was cut for 5 years but it has been renewed
in different ways throughout time as needed. At the end of
five years, I did not expect IBM to be in the networking
business in a big way, if at all. It really is not and may never
be again.

Chapter 43

Cisco Soundly Defeats IBM in Networking

To Cisco, the spoils

Cisco came into being in about 1984. IBM had been doing teleprocessing since the 1960's. Yet, like many other industries which IBM had begun, Cisco was able to beat Big Blue in a game that IBM had created. Cisco is therefore one of America's greatest corporate success stories and they operate in the most complex area of IT technology. Thank you, IBM.

From nothing in1986, the Cisco Company grew into a global market leader that holds No. 1 or No. 2 market share in virtually every market segment in which it participates. Cisco became a public company in 1990, at which time its annual revenues were just $69 million.

From there, revenues have grown so that their last four quarters show annualized revenue for 2015 of $49.2 billion, an increase of 4% year over year. Cisco is the darling of Wall Street and it should be. It wiped out IBM that did not act as if networking was a subindustry of IT. As measured by market capitalization, Cisco is among the largest companies in the world.

Besides being the major force responsible for moving IBM out of the network industry, Cisco is the recognized leader in all facets of the industry. Not too coincidentally, Cisco's big claim to fame is its top flight support for the Internet from backbone routers to gear that every IT shop buys to connect.

When you think of all of the power and complexity which is necessitated by the network of networks (the Internet), from where we dial in or connect vis DSL, cable, or leased lines, to where our ISP connects to the regional ISPs to the big thick telephone pipes to the National ISPs, there are tons of routes in routing tables processed by Cisco routers.

More Internet messages are moved to their Internet destinations by Cisco equipment than any other company's equipment. It is a Cisco world on the Internet. And the Company literally killed IBM in that marketplace. Ironically IBM was an early player in the Internet and helped build the Internet. Somehow IBM lost its way.

Besides routers, Cisco also makes LAN and ATM switches, dial up access servers and network management software. These products, are all integrated by the Cisco software which they call IOS.

This software has the intelligence to link geographically dispersed LANs, WANs and even IBM networks. Cisco's networking solutions connect people, computing devices and computer networks, allowing people to access or transfer information without regard to differences in time, place or type of computer system.

Cisco history

On July 27, 2015, John Chambers the Cisco CEO finally did it. He stepped down as CEO of Cisco and gave up the reins to Chuck Robbins, a Cisco veteran that John Chambers thinks is a powerful execution machine.

Robbins has the stuff that motivates him to get things done. That's why Chambers was happy to pass him control. Robbins can now take his talent and plot his own course for the Company, one of the most valuable and successful companies in America.

Cisco dominates when it comes to selling networking equipment to everybody from small Joes to universities to ISPs, to big corporations and governments. It is an undisputed fact that if you walk into any data center, you will not find IBM gear running the networks. Chances are close to 100% that you will find Cisco hardware.

Cisco is the worldwide leader in networking for the Internet. As much as eighty-five percent of Internet traffic travel across Cisco's router systems. Moreover, Cisco supports, manages and operates business systems for various major third parties. Cisco is the big kahuna in networking.

John Morgridge from 1988 to 1995 as CEO, Chairman, and now as Chairman Emeritus, got Cisco started big time. Chambers arrived in 1995. After two decades and meteoric growth and success, John Chambers finally decided to move on with his life, though he surely will always be watching Cisco and he hopes he will not be missed too much.

Whenever many of us think of Cisco, we think of John Chambers, its recent CEO who seems to have been with the Company forever. However, he was not. He joined in 1995, long after Cisco was founded and had already become immensely successful.

Cisco actually got a somewhat shaky start when founded in December 1984 by Leonard Bosack, Manager of Stanford's Undergraduate Computer Science Lab and Sandy Lerner, of Stanford's Graduate School of Business Computer Lab. They were not necessarily the top two IT people at Stanford at the time, but they were very knowledgeable about networking and both were aggressive enough to start a company that today is worth more than $300 billion in capitalization.

There were three others from Stanford who were co-founders of the original Cisco though not necessarily at the level of Bosack and Lerner. They too deserve entrepreneurial credit. These founders include Kirk Loughheed, Greg Satz, and Richard Troiano.

There was almost no Cisco

In case you are wondering, the name "Cisco" was taken from *San Francisco.* Before being fully born, this company named after San Francisco almost was killed before it was able to breathe because of some checkered activity by the founders as they prepared to launch their new company.

Stanford University almost ended Cisco's chances for success for what the university believed to be major asset misappropriations. Cisco's first product was in fact, an exact replica of Stanford's self-created "Blue Box" router.

Moreover, the Cisco released product, a multi-protocol router, ran a stolen copy of the University's multiple protocol router software. A Stanford research engineer, William Yeager, had originally written the code. Good things may not have happened to Cisco if the rest of the world had not been waiting for such products for so long.

Despite having started Cisco, while still employed, the deeds of Lerner and Bosack were not immediately discovered.

And, so Bosack and Lougheed, another founder who was also a Stanford Programmer, both kept working for the University until the problem was discovered. Both gentlemen were then forced to resign from Stanford over the Cisco trouble to avoid a criminal complaint.

To finally resolve the matter, in 1987, Stanford licensed the router software and two computer boards to Cisco. There were other concessions over the years. Money was also part of the initial settlement. Nobody paid a big price and the beneficiaries of Stanford's kindness have never been fully identified.

Cisco—a company with a product

As noted, John Morgridge became Cisco's first CEO in 1988. He was the 34th employee at Cisco Systems when he signed up to be President and CEO in 1988. Morgridge joined Cisco even though there were issues of legitimacy and revenue was only $5 million annually. Morgridge changed all of that and as he concluded his time as CEO when Chambers came in 1995, he had taken sales to over $1 billion and 2,250 employees were working for Cisco worldwide.

After John Chambers became CEO, during Morgridge's term as Chairman, Cisco continued its meteoric rise to become the world leader in networking technology and grew to more than $25 billion in revenues and some 50,000 employees in 77 countries (2006.) When things were going crazy in 2000 at the height of the Internet bubble, Cisco temporarily became the most valuable company in the world, with a market cap of $555.4 billion. Over time, the cap has gotten to a reasonable size of $131.75 million.

Taking Cisco public created millionaires

On February 16, 1990, Cisco was doing quite well and the founders took the Company public with a market capitalization of $224 million. The Company was listed on the NASDAQ stock exchange. All of the founders and a number of employees became millionaires.

When Sandy Lerner was fired for undisclosed reasons on August 28, 1990, her husband Leonard Bosack resigned in protest. The happy couple walked away from Cisco with $170 million. They committed 70% to their own personal charity.

In the nineties before Chambers, to 1994, Cisco acquired several companies who specialized on Ethernet switching – Kalpana, Grand Junction, and Crescendo Communications. Together these three formed the Catalyst Business Unit, and they kept Cisco moving and growing.

As noted, all of Cisco's founders have become millionaires. Chambers and Morgridge are billionaires. If only we would have known that with all the splits, a share of Cisco bought in 1990 would be worth $14,000 today. Thank you, IBM.

By the year 2000, John Chambers and Cisco helped make at least 2,500 of Cisco's 23,000 employees at the time stock-option millionaires. This of course convinced the rest of the employees that they too would be millionaires soon through hard work.

Cisco strengths

The Company provides what is known as end to end networking solutions that customers use to build a unified information infrastructure of their own, or to connect to someone else's network or the Internet. An end to end networking solution is one that provides a common architecture that delivers consistent network services to all users. The broader the range of network services, the more capabilities a network can provide to users connected to it.

If you need it, the word on the street is that Cisco has it. They made well over twenty acquisitions in their early years and even more recently to bolster areas in which they did not have a leading solution. Thus, the Company offers the industry's broadest range of hardware products used to create networks or give people access to those networks. They are the Microsoft of Networking. Cisco also has a software set, IOS, noted above, which provides the glue for these network services and it fully enables their networked applications.

Cisco personnel are well known for their expertise in network design and implementation. They offer technical support and professional services to help their customers maintain and optimize network operations. As today's largest networking company, Cisco is unique in its ability to provide all these elements today, either by itself or together with partners. IBM needs Cisco today much more than Cisco needs IBM

John Chambers, President & CEO, Cisco

John Chambers, another outspoken individual as many of the other relatively young leaders (multimillionaires and billionaires) in the technology industry, served the Company as its President & CEO until 2015. He joined the Company as the second in command when Cisco had $70 million in annual sales. During the past twenty years as President and CEO, Chambers has grown the Company from $1.2 billion in annual revenues to its current run rate of $47 + billion.

Chambers has been key to the growth. He established leadership in key technology sectors of the networking industry and aggressively pursuing new market opportunities. Having had an IBM background, Chambers knew what he had to do to win against IBM, and he did it.

Now that there is a strategic alliance between Cisco and IBM, IBM is more or less off the hook from having to keep up with it all in the networking area. As its market share dwindled, networking became more and more of a sideline at IBM, and it could not afford to stay abreast of all of the changes in the industry, and so being a leader in networking was out of the question.

As IBM's part of the strategic alliance, the Company is positioned to capitalize on the services business, which is IBM's fastest growing area. IBM customers and Cisco customers will now be able to turn to IBM Global Services for all of their Cisco support needs — from network consulting and design, to procurement, implementation and maintenance.

In 2015, as we have discussed, Cisco pre-announced that its next CEO will be Chuck Robbins, a 17-year Cisco veteran who was leading the Company's global sales and partner team. He took over on July 26, 2015.

Chambers retires

In 2014, Cisco talked about the eventual retirement of its longtime CEO, John Chambers, who is now 66. The Company announced that it had about 10 candidates in mind and Robbins was among them. Well, it is now done and Robbins is the guy.

Cisco has a long history of skipping over those that were heir apparent to the crown as Chambers had been talking about — and pushing back — his retirement plans for years.

And heirs have either gotten sick of waiting and left or were politically pushed out.

Chambers is not Bill Gates or Larry Ellison but unlike many of the billionaires who must thank IBM in their sleep if not in public, John Chambers steps down as CEO of Cisco from a salary of $22 million per year. Will he thank IBM? Who knows? One thing for sure, he is registered already as having a net worth of over $1 Billion. Nice Job John! Thank you IBM! You ran a great company!

Cisco IBM alliance

When the two companies released their press reports a while back about their August 31, 1999 alliance, there had to be some agreement on the following two statements. IBM, the one-time leader in corporate networking, and a company which boasts about its participation in building the early Internet infrastructure, had to examine statement (1) very carefully.

1. Cisco is the worldwide leader in networking for the Internet. For more information, please visit www.cisco.com.

2. IBM is the world's largest information technology company. For more information, please visit www.ibm.com.

Ellen Hancock's role

Though Lou Gerstner at the time probably did the best he could in a trying role in networking during the Ellen Hancock years, the Company seemed to get so far behind that there was no catching up technically, and no catching up from the mindshare which had been lost. When we consider that Cisco did not exist in 1985, it is quite remarkable that they whooped IBM in a business which IBM created and owned for years before Cisco was born.

Ellen Hancock was known to play the IBM line and not take many risks. She watched EMC take on IBM when as technology manager she had a big say as to how IBM would respond. She did not respond. IBM lost its entire storage business to EMC. When Gerstner came to IBM he quickly noticed that Ellen Hancock was running the high profile yet dysfunctional IBM networking business. IBM under Hancock could not make anything work and she had the biggest say in IBM's demise in networking.

One thing for which she takes full credit is the disposing of the Rolm Corporation, an IBM acquisition that lost more and more money from IBM mismanagement year after year. Rolm had a different culture than IBM and a different work ethic—not bad, just different.

Rolm folks worked in our IBM office in Scranton, PA. They were sharp people. They were alive and sought out every business opportunity. Rolm had become a successful company with these people. IBM gave these free spirits so many rules that they could not do their jobs. IBM killed Rolm by force fitting a curmudgeon culture on a bunch of real people. What a shame.

Ellen Hancock sold the business. Eventually, her decisions to back SNA/SDLC rather than move towards Internet technologies had to be foremost on Gerstner's mind when he forced her out of her prestigious position.

If you are a Cisco fan, just as you would give Hancock and "F," you would give Chambers a big "A". But in terms of giving gifts to Cisco, IBM gets low marks. It seems that nobody can defeat IBM better than IBM itself. In Networking, the Company did exactly that! Moreover, the

$47 + billion which Cisco hauls in every year comes from business which IBM could have had and should have had.

If there were a parallel universe, the business would have rightfully gone to IBM, the inventor of computer based data communications... if only IBM had played its cards right! Who will be the next to choose not to say: Thank You, IBM!

Section IV

CEOs John Opel & John Akers Together Almost Sunk IBM

John Opel ushered in the 1980's as the new CEO of IBM after Frank Cary stepped down in 1981. One can summarize Opel as a chairman with lots of spirit and opportunity, but failure followed his legacy into the next CEO's (John Akers) tenure. Opel made a lot of stockholders happy but he mortgaged the future to do it and Chairman John Akers was the guy left to pay the mortgage.

Mr. Akers took over a company that had apparently been very successful right until the day that he took over. As we look deeper into the John Akers years, we see a guy who was dealt a hand from his predecessor from which few great CEOS could recover. John Akers never recovered and IBM almost was dismembered on its way to insolvency.

During the Opel / Akers years there were lots of exciting things happening in the industry and also in IBM. For example, IBM introduced its famous Personal Computer product line. Additionally, IBM developed a great chip known as the Power chip and a great system known as the RISC System/6000 to finally leverage IBM's invention of RISC technology.

An IBM Engineer John Cocke had invented RISC technology and during this period, after an unsuccessful attempt with an underpowered machine called the RT/PC, IBM released its very powerful best of breed RS/6000 in 1988. This was the best of RISC. IBM became well known in RISC technology circles. So far, after its long overdue start IBM has done reasonably well with RISC. But, IBM is now contemplating getting out of the hardware business.

By the time IBM entered the fray, the field was getting crowded with Sun Microsystems having taken the RISC technology lead. Without Sun making the IBM-invented technology so successful, some wonder if IBM would have ever announced a system based on RISC technology.

IBM for years had an aversion to Unix but with the RS/6000, the Company got over that and announced a full function Unix implementation that it labeled AIX for Advanced Interactive Executive. Eventually, the same Power architecture used in the RS/6000 machine was enhanced to become the basis for a number of Supercomputer systems, which IBM built during this period.

IBM PC

In John Opel's first year, the work Frank Cary did in marshalling the IBM PC team came to fruition. In August, 1981, Chairman Opel had the pleasure of introducing the IBM Personal Computer to the world. IBM was very successful and formed relationships with Microsoft and Intel, which over the years became very stormy. There was no exclusivity in the contract and so both Microsoft and Intel (Wintel), permitted any computer vendor to make a clone of the IBM PC with the same exact parts Wintel supplied to IBM for its PC system.

During this period, Radio Shack, Hewlett Packard, Compaq, Gateway, Dell, and others copied the IBM Personal Computer and marketed their own clone versions of the systems.

This section is very entertaining as it shows the number of times that IBM had the opportunity to actually reclaim its dominance in the PC industry but as it turns out, IBM no longer is even a player. How this happened is most extraordinary. The irony is that both Microsoft and Intel are huge companies today that together are bigger than IBM. Moreover, Bill Gates the CEO of Microsoft during these troubled IBM times has been the richest man in the world for at least sixteen out of the twenty last years...and he still is.

Chapter 44

John Opel—A Chairman with Lots of Spirit, Opportunity & Failure

Opel was not Watson-trained

Let's immediately begin this John Opel part by discussing IBM and its killer PC. It was brought into the marketplace during John Opel's tenure at IBM. IBM was not in the PC business when John Opel took the reins from Frank T. Cary

IBM only became the recognized leader in PC technology when it finally introduced its groundbreaking PC. This occurred in the first year of John Opel's tenure as Chairman but the effort behind it came from the work of former Chair, Frank Cary.

Before the IBM PC was announced few analysts thought that there would be anything wrong with a mainframe oriented computer company introducing a small hobby, home or personal computers and not making a big push to dominate this new area of endeavor. In other words, it would be OK for Big Blue to try its hand at becoming an also-ran in toy sized computer units.

And, so, the PC marketplace in which IBM found itself in the late 1970's and into 1980 and 1981 was not something the executives in the board room planned to conquer. IBM

did what was expected and was content to be an also-ran in
the diminutive home computer and hobby marketplace.
Hey, it was a passing fad anyway? Right?

It had become embarrassing for IBM Executives in public
speaking engagements that the largest computer company in
the world could not create a computer system that would
operate at the home and personal level. IBM executives read
the papers and answered questions from their grandkids
about what grandpop really did for a living. Did he really
help Santa Claus? And why could Santa not bring a PC with
IBM's name on it?

IBM Executives were making enough money. They simply
wanted to save face at home. Their efforts to produce a unit
to compete in the personal space, were the boldest steps ever
for an IBM that most often waited five to ten years from
idea to product. But, then again, this product was more like
company advertising than something real? It was just a
placeholder to protect IBM as a company that could make
anything. It was not to be taken seriously by the IT industry.

To repeat, few industry analysts at the time thought that Big
Blue's board of directors had big intentions of the Company
becoming the champion in the home computer marketplace.
Just a few geeks were using home computers at the time
though the learning games for kids were getting much better.
This was not real bad thinking at the time. Before the IBM
PC was announced there was apparently no real big, billion
dollar type marketplace envisioned for IBM to capture.
Could IBM have really missed a trillion dollar market? They
sure did!

With little risk, IBM therefore came out with its PC mostly
to prove to the masses that it was a real computer company.
As folklore has it, it was OK to not try hard with the PC
because IBM did not need the business. It was announced
simply because IBM executives were sick of being

embarrassed at home when their grandchildren asked why their PC said Apple, Radio Shack, TI or Atari. Why were there no computers at home made by grandpop's company?

Mostly everybody in the first sixth of the 21st century has a perspective on PCs because they are so dominant today in our lives. For example, according to IDC, over 300 million PC's were sold in 2014, and another 3 million larger pc servers (x86 servers) were sold during the same period. Somebody made a lot of money on those units, and nobody is thanking IBM for their largesse in giving the business to other companies but they should be for sure.

If all this business were IBM's, at $1000 per desktop/laptop unit, the revenue would be $300 billion, and if we suggest that PC (i86) servers go for $10,000, then we would add another $25 billion to the mix. Can you believe that with just PCs, IBM would be a $325 billion company when with its current repertoire of products and services, the Company is less than $100 billion and revenue is decreasing each year. Something has been wrong in Denmark for IBM for some time.

And, of course we are not counting the chipmakers, tablet makers, phone makers, game consoles, etc. all of which were spawned from the acceptance of the IBM PC. If we had a calculator with enough digits, we would find the total value of the PC marketplace over is at least $500 billion and more likely a $trillion dollars in revenue or even more each year. For IBM, it was a big market to lose and today to be left without even a trace of business in this lucrative profit area, is unimaginable.

Before we move into the introduction of IBM's PC during the Opel years, we need to take a look at what the notion of home computing was all about in the 1970's. Since all of this pre-PC activity was begun during the Frank T. Cary regime at IBM, the microcomputer revolution is chronicled in Section III, which you just absorbed. Feel free to read that section again to get the proper perspective.

The computerists of this 1970's pre-PC era would be known as geeks today. Perhaps that is how they saw themselves back then. They were tinkerers and thinkers with big brains and their minds were focused on technology for the sake of technology, and because it was cool! IBM employees may have been in their ranks but until 1981, the IBM Company was not in the marketplace.

IBM ignored Apple in the beginning as the IBM Company seemed to have had nine million Wozniak's working in its zillion labs across the world. It continued to ignore Apple when the PC was the big winner in the marketplace but the Apple II and its derivatives continued to sell big time, and Apple had a following of people, most of whom did not like IBM, Intel or Microsoft.

What IBM never had was a guy like Steven Jobs, who could turn a piece of dirt into success, if he chose to do so. He had that much positive energy as a CEO and as a tech leader. It is well rumored that the IBM Board thought about correcting IBM's stodgy version of success when the Company was ready to replace John Akers for the Chairmanship. Akers of course resigned as was required for IBM to succeed.

Jobs was more than a contender for IBM's CEO job. Unfortunately for IBM, Jobs stuck with his mettle and he and his rejuvenated Apple killed IBM in the marketplace. IBM today and its stockholders wish it could be Apple. Apple revenue is 2X IBM today. Apple will never have to say thank you IBM as it won victory over IBM by its own capabilities, not by IBM's weaknesses. I admit that the gains may not have been as great if IBM were paying attention to business.

Apple people never got a special gift of instant insider as Bill Gates' people did. Thank you John Opel. In the Microsoft chapter, please note how Bill Gates mother asked John Opel for a favor, and IBM has been paying for that favor ever since.

IBM had no idea that the Home Computer would actually produce a marketplace and if they thought it would, they would never have believed that a big computer company like IBM should ever try to be involved.

As an example of IBM's mainframe myopia, neither CEO Frank Cary nor his successor, John R. Opel would bring a RISC based minicomputer product to the marketplace during their respective tenures. Cary served until Opel's appointment as CEO in 1981. Both resisted making IBM's General Systems Division mainstream even though its technology outclassed the mainframe IBMers in Poughkeepsie.

IBM was so confident, it thought it was supply constrained

Opel, as many CEO's before him, was fully absorbed by IBM's tremendous mainframe success at the time and he believed that if manufacturing constraints were lifted, IBM would move from a $50 billion company to a $100 billion company magically by 1990. Under Opel IBM made a lot of hard hats happy, spending the corporate reserves on major construction projects to increase plant space. The Company was continually building new plants and adding on to existing facilities to help make the Chairman's dream of having $100 billion in manufacturing capability by 1990 a reality.

Ironically, IBM CEOs of the past, especially in the Watson years, set up the Company so that IBM subcontractors took most of the risk of expansion along with the Company and they supplied many of the components needed for manufacturing IBM's finest systems. Why did Opel's IBM think it had to make everything? I still do not know that answer as it was not the IBM way.

Opel was not as cautious as other IBM CEOs but he had no apparent substance for his chutzpah. IBM used up way too much of its substantial cash reserves building Opel's dream factories. Then, there was so little planning for the product line that there were no major products needing to be built in the new huge facility space. IBM had failed to create a marketplace for its new manufacturing capability. What products were on the horizon that needed such space—none!

Chairman Opel's push for $100 Billion was viewed by industry insiders as pure hubris. He set IBM back almost to the stone age financially and the 50-year old John Akers expected ten year term as CEO (until he hit 60 years of age) hardly had a chance. Opel had almost burned the Company down to the ground. Unfortunately, when Akers took over, he could not smell any smoke at all and simply continued the Opel plan.

Ironically, few of the loyal soldiers such as myself understood the damage that Opel had done while it was occurring. We thought everything was la! la! la! When Akers took over and life was no longer good for IBM employees, Akers got the blame. For ex IBMers, it took a while for many of us to see it rightly. We had blamed Akers; but it was Opel.

Peter E. Greulich, of MBI Concepts Corporation, wrote an excellent article titled: "IBM's One Hundred Year History Is about Cash, Culture and Mutualism."
http://seekingalpha.com/article/2933406-ibms-one-hundred-year-history-is-about-cash-culture-and-mutualism

I would recommend this article, written by a 30-year IBMer for those looking for more. It is excellent. Here are the first three paragraphs of his article. These succinctly explain what happened in the Opel years and the influence Opel's dynasty had on John Akers prematurely giving up the Company reins to Lou Gerstner. Here it is:

"When John F. Akers assumed control of IBM, he inherited from his predecessor - John R. Opel - a market expectation that could never be met. Opel had promised a $100 billion IBM by 1990, and a $180 billion corporation by 1994. When Business Week published an article on February 18, 1985 (IBM: More Worlds to Conquer) about his goals, it used the word "hubris." It was.

"As many IBMers of the time - but few of today's analysts - remember, IBM set this expectation by playing its first corporate financial game. Most of the Company's revenue at the time came from its leased hardware install base, which it converted to a purchase model over a few short years at a fraction of its true value. In a fire sale, the Company exchanged a perennial, one-dollar gold piece for a devalued, one-time, two-dollar paper note. IBM's revenue growth was temporarily hyper-inflated to make futuristic predictions look attainable; but IBM was also financially hyper-extended.

"John Akers, in 1985, found himself in the middle of an investment and employment tsunami. He stopped the investing and hiring, and started reducing and redeploying the IBM workforce, but then he was blindsided by the 10th largest stock market decline in history. Even though IBM grew revenue by more than 50% over the next six years, we missed Opel's 1990 revenue target of $100 billion by $30 billion; and in the ensuing three years, IBM would lose $15 billion."

IBM PC came during Opel years

On the brighter side, John Opel's appointment coincided with the introduction of the IBM PC. I do remember it well. I happened to be in Boca Raton Florida, the plant of manufacture for the IBM PC. I was there for an IBM System/38 banking class. Hoping to one day be a writer, I had just purchased an $1800 memory typewriter using my employee discount. At the time, we had just one child so the cost did not really bother me.

Meanwhile, IBM still was not running at a revenue pace that would meet or eclipse John Opel's prediction that by 1990, the Company would no longer be supply constrained and IBM would therefore reach the magic $100 billion plateau. From that vantage point in the Opel plan, IBM would dominate the industry.

Instead, in my observations, IBM was lucky to have survived its many mistakes. IBM stockholders should never thank the IBM Company for the poor performance of the stock while Big Blue gave up one opportunity after another. Yet, somehow IBM has never suffered a stockholders' revolt.

What happened in the Opel years changed IBM?

It started in the Opel years but continued into the Akers years. I worked for the marketing division which ran the IBM branch offices. The IBM Company began to look at salesman and field support personnel, who put together customer solutions that could be purchased from IBM, as a drag on expenses. My buddy Dennis Grimes' father when he got wind of what IBM was doing suggested that only a company that no longer wanted to sell anything would get rid of its sales force.

The new IBM, without the marketing oriented Watsons and their good students: Learson and Cary; did not understand the value of its field marketing and engineering force. For years they had abused it and then abused it more. For proof of this, we need only check the facts. Rather than fix an administrative and computer order processing problem, IBM sacrificed its technical field force to the order processing god.

By the time the Company believed it could not afford its expensive technical field force, IBM had already contorted these highly trained technicians into an army of technical order takers. When IBM pulled the plug on technical support to its customers, there were few customers who missed it. It had been MIA for years. IBM had morphed its best systems engineers into people that its administrators could rely on to apply the right sales codes on an order so the plant would ship a new box with the stuff the customer actually ordered. Another company would have automated such a function and kept its engineers servicing customers.

What brainiac would stop renting machines?

Thomas Watson Jr. almost brought IBM to bankruptcy as he spent $4 billion of the Company's cash reserves, and borrowed another $1 billion in order to build a new computer which in 1964, he dreamed would work, In 1981, John Opel had no clue what products he would be able to sell for IBM to meet his lofty $100 billion sales target for 1990, but he was building the plants just in case.

Frank Cary had begun to sell equipment outright in order to make earnings look a little better. John Opel needed all the sales from the rental inventory so that he could pay for all the plant capacity and human resources he was bringing on to satisfy his $100 billion dream.

Since IBM was spending its extra development dollars trying to bolster its mainframe capabilities, one would surmise that the Company had projected that its stagnant mainframe sales would begin to grow at the pace of the industry or better. Other than the mainframe investments, there was little tangible evidence that the $50 billion IBM Company at the time had any real plans as to how it was going to double in size in less than ten years.

Though they were planning to build mainframes which nobody in the whole world wanted, IBM kept building and building and building manufacturing floor space so that it could meet the demand for the products necessary to meet the Chair's 100 billion dollar projection. Millions of square feet of manufacturing space never saw an IBM product or IBM part in any stage of production. Yet, to finance all of this construction, the Company needed many billions of dollars. The Chairman would not have it any other way.

IBM "willed" that the plants be successful. Perhaps there were even corporate incantations. But there was no plan! Unfortunately, the correct product mix was never offered and the plants, as they were completed, had to be discarded and sold for pennies on the dollar. In addition to plant capacity for the unknown products, to fully assure such growth, the Company had to ramp up its headcount by over 100,000 new employees.

Nobody could increase its staff by 33%, and its plant capacity by 50% without a tremendous amount of cash. How would it be paid? Perhaps nobody even asked. After all, this was IBM. The Company managers displayed wanton disregard for the assets of the corporation as they pursued an expansion program that was not product oriented, and not crisply forecasted.

IBM's almost assured demise, would have been trumpeted by its competitors. Perhaps it was God that sent Tom Watson Jr. to meet Lou Gerstner Jr. at the airport on his first day of work. Watson was not unaware of IBM's troubles. He told the magician that IBM could not continue without good management and he made sure Gerstner knew that he expected a lot from the first CEO hire from outside of the IBM culture. That was a good ten years after Opel was banking on the impossible.

Not planning product demand for the excess capacity was a big mistake. IBM's biggest squander however, was ramping up for its big $100 billion a year achievement without financing plans. It was like the Federal Government raiding the Social Security Fund. IBM had one thing which no other business had, which was big enough that it would come close to financing the whole project.

What do you think that might be? Well remember at that time, other than a bright future in PCs, IBM rented or leased almost all of its heavy iron. John Opel could sell off IBM's rental base and compromise the future of the IBM Company to satisfy his $100 billion plant capacity bet by 1990? But, would a sane person actually do that? Opel would not only do that; he did it, and that is why Akers tenure was so tough! There was no money left for anything.

If you wanted your job in IBM at the time, it was not even a consideration to take on the Chairman about how asinine his goals were. Telling him that his financing plan was even more ludicrous was out of the question. As an IBMer at the time, hoping the executives would give us a few good plays to execute, I recall hoping somebody, who had a brain, was doing all this to the Company knowing would all work out. It just wasn't so.

The value to IBM of its rental base.

When clients rented machines from IBM, the Company's service personnel were at the ready keeping the installed gear in ship shape and fully operational at all times. When they needed more powerful equipment, much more often than not, IBM's loyal rental customers would go back to IBM and for just a few extra bucks a month, they would install their upgrade. That was the hook that IBM had with its rental customers. They were always ready to buy from IBM the next time. Growing the business was easy as there was already an income base year after year. Technically, if IBM sold nothing in a given year, its income would be the same as the prior year based on steady rentals.

With a deep rental base, IBM did not have to be that much better as long as the gear was being rented. Once the customer took title to the gear, the BUNCH, or DEC, or HP, or DG could make a sales call and with sales schmooze, convince the customer much more easily to drop IBM and get their next modern system from them rather than from IBM. Big Blue had always seen its rental business as an annuity as it was. It was an annuity that grew as the customer's business grew. John Opel did not care.

As an IBM systems engineer working with IBM customers every day, I could not believe that IBM would get rid of such a source of eternal profits—its rental base. The IBM Company unfortunately was being run by a guy who was like a cash addict. He needed a lot of revenue to pay for his building projects. John Opel chose to sell off IBM's rental base of computers... the base which literally assured IBM, year in and year out, of sustained large profits.

IBM senior executives at Opel's direction decided to move IBM from this nice, safe, steady rental business into the risky, dog-eat-dog business of selling computer products outright. There would be no steady income coming to IBM forevermore.

In some of the years during the 1980's, especially 1985, which was a peak year for revenue and profits, IBM looked like an unbeatable industry winner. It looked like senior executives had made a great decision. Unfortunately, the more rental equipment that was sold off, the more difficult it became for the Company to attain the next year's revenue objectives. Each year, more and more outright purchases needed to be achieved as less rental inventory was available for sale, and a diminished number of rented units contributed to each year's results.

Here is how bad it got. As a systems engineer, I got to read the sales commission plans for the office and the marketing managers kept us on alert for things that helped our office achieve objectives and which helped the Branch get into the 100% club.

One year in particular, certain pieces of equipment were placed on what appeared to me to be a fire sale. The customers using the gear were not about to discontinue their leases or cancel their rental options that year. However, IBM was so hard pressed for immediate cash that they offered big incentives for salesmen to bring in a check for the purchase of any existing rental machine.

I can recall that the sales pitch for the customer was easy to make. It was a great deal for customers but a poor deal for IBM. The breakeven in many cases for the customer was more often than not, less than a year, and often as little as nine months. In this case, the customer wrote a check and owned the box and never had to write another rental check.

If they wrote a check in say February for a nine month break-even machine, IBM cashed the check and "made a killing" that month. But, even a fool knew that in November, after the breakeven date, IBM no longer would receive any rental income and thus the revenue for the year for that piece of equipment was less than if the client had continued renting the machine.

Year after year, IBM sold off more and more of its success base. By the 1990s, only 12% of IBM's revenue came from rentals. Thus, 88% of the revenues in any given year had to come from services or be recreated from new sales. This was a formidable task for any marketing organization. Not only were few innovative product designs coming for the millions of new square feet of manufacturing space, but there was less and less of a guaranteed revenue base upon which to build.

Thus, IBM's growth slowed to a standstill, and actually began to decline in the 1990s. When there was just about no rental base left, and coincidentally the world slipped into a hard recession, IBM had no fallback plan with which to absorb the shock of such a major decrease in sales. Not only did IBM not reach $100 billion by 1990 (They were about $60 billion) but the Company was in such bad shape when Chairman Akers finally stepped down, the Company came close to bankruptcy.

Because he truly rescued IBM from its own demise, Lou Gerstner will more than likely one day make the business hall of fame. But, IBM, for squandering its lucrative, repeatable, rental business for the sake of creating plants for unplanned products, gets very low marks. This was one big mistake that IBM made from which no one particular competitor benefited. But, a weakened IBM, the biggest computer vendor in the world, helped all computer vendors move against IBM with impunity. IBM had no muscle to fight back. Thank you, IBM!

The revenue was there... IBM just didn't get it!

Though the Company did not achieve Opel's growth forecast of $100 billion by 1990, it was not because the number was unachievable. If we examine the success of startup firms in industries which IBM should have controlled, there was plenty of opportunity for the IBM Company to have reached its goals. Unfortunately, the Company not only planned its efforts poorly, but it suffered tremendous implementation failings. Companies with little resources, but plenty of ideas, beat IBM in market after market.

Despite being beaten by microcomputer vendors and Unix vendors, rather than taking on the challenge with a winning strategy, the Company stubbornly stayed with its mainframe emphasis. Consequently even companies never before hear of beat Big Blue regularly on many new fronts.

When we discuss this failing in this book we note that IBM got beat by everybody from microcomputer vendors to PC vendors to software vendors such as Microsoft. A large part of this major loss occurred during the Opel years. However, the selling off of the rental base made earnings look great.

With IBM today as a $92.7 billion dollar company, knowing that it once reached and surpassed $107 billion—just five years ago—IBM's big mistakes during the Opel years appear even more damaging.

IBM began the PC revolution by introducing the IBM Personal Computer during Opel's tenure. At the time, there were no real competitors so IBM management policies created all of its problems. IBM itself brought on its competition. Neither Microsoft nor Intel, IBM's biggest PC predators, needed to be in the picture at all. Microsoft revenue in 2015 exceeded IBM's for the first time. This shows how damaging it was for IBM to turn its operating system business over to Bill Gates in 1981. If Microsoft were not in the picture, that revenue would be IBM's and there never would have been any clones. Not even one clone!

IBM had the whole PC industry to itself if it moved smartly. It did not. Analysts estimate the whole PC industry brings in between a $half trillion and a $trillion each year. One would think that every IBM CEO at the time and every senior manager, especially those in forecasting, would have been fired for missing out on all that revenue. Yet, IBM's Board of Directors sat idly by as if we had not hired them to protect stockholder assets.

As noted, predecessor CEO Frank Cary had put the PC group together to make it all happen but Opel was the guy who was in charge when IBM had to sell it and make it work for its customers and for IBM. Opel did neither. He blew it big time and worse than that, he could never tell a real IBM partner from a thief.

How bad did he blow it? Opel forecast 275,000 PC units to be sold in the PC's first five years. So, with all his unneeded plant capacity on the drawing boards, the CEO did not reserve any manufacturing space in case the PC was a bit more successful than mainframe IBM had expected. On the very first day of the announcement cycle, ComputerLand, a small computer retailer ordered 250,000 units of IBM's new

PC. On day one, they gobbled up almost the entire five-year forecast. What did they know that Opel did not? IBM's forecast was already way off and just one order had come in and just one day had gone by.

Final thoughts on John Opel

Though Opel was a tyrant in terms of assuring that his unrealistic goals were met; he was a gentleman also and was well liked by most IBMers. Additionally, his numbers at IBM were phenomenal. His gift to his successor, John Akers was a company in which everything had gone negative and was not about to come back. Opel bequeathed a company in unstable condition despite its great record from the great asset selloff during the Opel years.

John R. Opel, therefore is remembered by most as the person who presided over IBM in its final period of dominance in the information-processing industry. He is also the man who oversaw the Company's move into personal computers. Though he did not cause the problem, John Akers took the rap for having destroyed IBM. Of course, Akers surely could have done a better job even with the hand he was dealt.

Things changed almost immediately after Opel left office. In the late 1980s, and early 1990's, with Akers at the helm, IBM went through a painful period of cutbacks as the computer business underwent huge changes. Small computers based on microprocessors and using standardized software increasingly took over from centralized machines using proprietary hardware and software.

Some blame IBM itself for helping bring on the shift when it introduced its first personal computer in 1981 under Opel's charge. They are correct because IBM did not see what it had actually created until the barn door was wide open and the Company had given away almost all of its assets,

The initial issue as seen in Mr. Opel's and Mr. Cary's legacy is that IBM did not design any part of the PC itself. Worse than that, it did not select its piece parts from the existing stable of IBM processors and operating systems available within the Company.

In an effort to make an inexpensive machine that could get to market quickly, it used a microprocessor from Intel and operating system software from Microsoft. IBM did nothing to protect its product from copycats. In fact, it gave away too much control of its PC project to Microsoft and Intel.

The machine was a huge hit. Thus IBM made desktop computing acceptable to corporate America and the IBM PC became the industry standard. Because IBM gave Intel all the rights to the heart of their new product, and Microsoft all the rights to the product's brains. IBM was left with nothing. Even when it should have realized the value of the operating system and micro-processor, it did nothing to stop the erosion of its product line.

In essence, competitors quickly realized they could essentially make copies of the machine using Intel chips and Microsoft software. IBM actually told Microsoft it was OK for them to market the same OS under their name for clones. IBM could not have done this without Opel's permission.

The power in the computer industry shifted to Intel and Microsoft, and hardware became a low-price commodity. IBM eventually sold its PC business because it did not know how to run this business and refused to learn. Now, of course IBM focuses on software and services and of course, mainframes are still the top priority.

During Opel's tenure IBM did not simply hold to its traditional marketplaces. It entered new ones but then did not have the expertise to survive. In addition to the PC, the Company moved into Computer Branch Exchanges (CBX) and it acquired the Rolm Company, which made an advanced telephone switch at the time. IBM also bought a piece of Satellite Business Systems and had to sell that when nothing happened. Big Blue also took a small stake in Intel, reportedly to shore up Intel against Japanese competition. It should have taken a larger stake and did something about Intel selling to clone manufacturers.

After he stepped down as IBM's chief executive, Mr. Opel remained chairman until May 1986 and he was a board member until 1993. Mr. Opel passed away on November 2, 2011.

Chapter 45

A Deeper Look at John Akers' Years

Opportunity accomplished list had no entries

John F. Akers took over for John Opel as CEO in 1985. By the time Akers took office the cash was all promised to pay for Opel's past adventures. The drawing board Akers had to look at demonstrated that IBM was going to have to do a little scraping and some scrapping to keep itself afloat. Under Opel, the Company decided that it was going to be capacity driven, rather than be like the old IBM which was always supply constrained.

In the Akers years, IBM continued to execute better than any other company in the mainframe product area, but the mainframe marketplace was flat, not growing like the exciting minicomputer, PC and RISC processing areas. Five years of building John Opel's plants had given IBM tremendous production capacity, but the Company had focused on the wrong product areas and it forgot how to sell.

To meet the decreasing demand for IBM PCs, and to meet the new but small demand for the RISC based RT PCs, and to meet the unexpected modest rise in Series/1 sales, IBM did not need the huge amount of manufacturing plant capacity, which post Opel was now ready to come on-line.

It takes a mainframe

While IBM was still counting on mainframes to pull it through, its competitors were making a killing in the markets in which the IBM Company chose not to vigorously compete. As the competition advanced, IBM appeared to lay down and accept its plight rather than fight back. Cosmetic changes and face saving were the order of the day.

Rhetoric, rather than a resolve to innovate and prosper became a hallmark of Chairman Aker's regime. Whereas John Opel had built the farm, John Akers took IBM awful close to buying the farm.

During the 1970's and through 1985, IBM had successfully passed through the Watson years, the Learson years, and the Cary years. In the early 1980's, feeling very good about IBM, to the point of being cocky, then Chairman, John Opel forecast that IBM would be a $100 billion company by 1990. Akers took over in 1985.

From the time Opel gave the word to begin expanding IBM to meet his lofty goals, the Company began to change dramatically, and the words "best customer service possible," and "respect for the individual," began to be used sarcastically by many IBMers who could not explain how the new IBM was in synch with its once venerated mantras.

John Akers is given credit by most IBMers for messing up the IBM we knew. Meanwhile Mr. Akers chose to blame the marketing force for his failure. We were not selling enough!

New IBM hires learned a different culture

In the 1980s, in trying to achieve john Opel's $100 billion dream, IBM began to hire again—lots of new people. But the new hires were treated differently. College culture had changed and the college grads hired by IBM expected

something from the Company. They had big-time
expectations. When I was hired, I hoped that I could make
it and do well in the Company. This new crew expected the
Company to give them something whether they earned it or
not. They wanted quick returns simply for having joined
IBM.

In the 1980's, IBM wasn't sure what it was going to do with
its field force, especially systems engineers. Top
management no longer believed that it needed to provide
top quality support to customers. IBM felt it had nursed its
customers into competence over the years. IBM believed
that its customers were not willing to pay a premium for any
free support included in the price of the product.

IBM Systems Engineers, the folks who helped salesmen
know what to sell and helped them sell it, could design a
system on a blackboard to get a sale. They then could help
the customer implement it exactly as designed. These bright
technicians no longer had value in the new IBM world. I
was glad that IBM did not know how to fire us all right
away but there was a lot of stress knowing that Big Blue
would be happy to get rid of us all. It was not comfortable at
all working for Akers' IBM but everybody was happy to still
have a job with IBM.

In the sixties and seventies, every Systems Engineer had to
learn how to write programs. SEs had to get technical to
survive. When a customer had a problem with a statement
in an RPG or COBOL or Assembler program, a systems
engineer would help them resolve it. SEs got good at
programming and often fixed their customer's coding
problems for free. The more programs customers' wrote, the
more IBM equipment they would need to run the programs.

The new IBM never gave new hires the opportunity to mature technically. Instead, they learned how to sell and install packages, and enlist third party help for the technical piece. Some got by merely by knowing how to order large system software. IBM managers were slow to recognize this transition, as the IBM technical force became less and less competent.

A socialized reward system emerged

The Company also lost sight of the purpose of its reward systems. The most coveted award for a Systems Engineer was to be nominated for the Systems Engineering Symposium. Symposiums were awe-inspiring. They were three-day events in a beautiful location. Nominees would hear the best speakers and executives in IBM, and other general interest speakers who were the best in their field.

As a further reward, the attendees would be feted by the best entertainers in the world (Four Seasons, Beach Boys etc.). IBM spared no expense on motivational speakers such as Merlin Olson, Bob Richards, Henry Kissinger, and Walter Cronkite, etc. They were great events. Only the best Systems Engineers in the US would be invited.

In Utica, I watched Nick DeSalvo get nominated every year. Nick was tops in Utica, and everybody knew that to take Nick's slot, you had to get as good at your job as Nick was at his. In Scranton, I saw Tommy Vasil and Tony Opalski get the nod every year. I watched what it was that each did and how they did what they did.

Eventually, I too learned how to be a professional and be respected by my customers, IBM management, and my peers. In 1974, after my fourth year with the Company, I was selected and I soon became a regular at the Systems Engineering Symposium.

In the 1980's, because of charitable back to the field type employee programs to save the jobs of displaced IBM plant people, IBM Systems Engineering managers who were not qualified were put in place. My manager for example had never been a Systems Engineer, yet he was charged with evaluating my technical contributions.

These new managers simply were not as good at differentiating talent, abilities, and real accomplishments. They had a tough time understanding who had done what for whom, and why it was significant or insignificant. Moreover, the marketing managers seemed to be controlling the technical action more and more.

Systems Engineers began to be nominated for the Symposium or they would receive large cash awards simply because they had assisted in a sale, not because they had achieved a major technical feat which resulted in a huge sale or a happy customer.

It no longer mattered that an SE had helped a customer achieve a level of technical greatness, which would have been impossible without his or her expertise. It no longer mattered that, thanks to direct SE assistance, customers were making effective use of IBM equipment.

It only mattered that the customer bought a lot of new stuff from IBM. The new SEs quickly learned with these new rules, that technical proficiency was not as important as marketing awareness.

At the same time, as previously noted, with the merging of divisions, reorganizations, back-to-the field programs etc., individuals without the necessary skills, were often promoted to technical managers (SE Managers). If a person had been a manager in a prior IBM position, regardless of the type of position, chances are they would wind up a manager in the field. Since the Company did not want to risk having these folks become marketing managers without having been marketing reps, the SE manager's job was a good dumping spot for them.

For several years before I took IBM's great retirement parachute, I had the non-pleasure of working for a manager who had never worked in a computer division, and who was mostly computer illiterate. Though he was bright and talented, his Office Division background had not prepared him to manage a team of computer technicians.

It is actually a big negative to the whole IBM field system that a person with such a background was able to survive while his technical team was sinking. IBM eventually asked this manager to rank all employees and cut the ones on the bottom. The truth is that in Akers' IBM, as long as somebody was terminated, and IBM no longer had to pay their salary, it did not matter how good of an employee they ever were.

New SE Managers such as mine quickly became politicians in the Company to survive. They could not differentiate the actual accomplishments of their force, since they had never walked the walk or talked the talk. With social skills and hearsay as their major guiding principle, they began to socialize the recognition system. In these bad times, IBM took back 10 or 20% of SE salaries and then gave year-end bonuses and other recognition awards. Some employees got nothing back. IBM managers began to merely split the rewards, regardless of merit, so that "nobody would get upset."

The cause and effect relationship between hard work, accomplishments, and rewards became very broken. SEs with two years' experience, for example, would be sent to the Symposium simply because management believed that "it was their turn."

Akers could not afford Opel

IBM had decided that its technical and marketing direct field force had become too expensive to sustain. Considering its misuse, it is understandable that the Company would reach such a conclusion. It seemed that John Opel's expansion program had made everything too expensive for John Akers.

IBM begins to emulate its poor competitors

Somehow the advanced vision farm in IBM had stopped producing good ideas. IBM was plum out of thoughts on how to keep the organization successful. In desperation, the Company began to adopt a business model used by its less successful competitors from throughout the years. Though this was a bad idea, at least it was an idea.

IBM competitors were always a dime short in how they dealt with their customers and prospects. They had no expensive marketing team with long-term relationships with customers. Instead of using its own staff, IBM's competition franchised their action through distributors. They did not use a direct sales force.

Though IBM at the time was still the leader in the overall computer industry and had gained customer loyalty because of its support structure, the IBM chieftains decided to abandon their formerly successful formula for employees and for customers. IBM began to emulate its competition.

Akers' IBM stopped traveling the high road

IBM has always had a ton of lawyers ready to defend its practices, right or wrong. Before I left, during the John Akers years, IBM was not a good company, and its lawyers defended the Company's self-serving actions to a fault. I saw some bad decisions by IBM in a number of areas. IBM wanted to get rid of employees, especially older employees who offered the least resistance and who were the most vulnerable.

Akers' IBM squeezed employees and made them feel incompetent in plant and field locations. In this way, Big Blue could thin the ranks by making its employee morale so bad that the people that management were squeezing for *supposed better performance,* would have enough and just quit.

All of their actions during the Akers' years and beyond were not legal but IBM always held the upper hand with its retirement and exodus transition options. I saw firsthand undue pressure on older employees, and other employees who simply happened to be in the wrong place at the wrong time.

Since John Akers was mentioned in discrimination case after case, IBM's lawyers worked to get him a protective court order to block his deposition from being taken in employee action cases. IBM lawyers do not defend regular employees—just IBM executives. John Akers was too important for IBM's continuing business needs to be deposed.

Sometimes it would take a long time for cases to hit the courts. The negative employee policies of today in IBM got their start in the Akers' years. Here are a few stories with that as a backdrop:

Kathy M. Kristof from the Los Angeles Times on August 10, 2003 wrote: "With help from a federal judge, Kathi Cooper has thrown a monkey wrench into the world of corporate pensions. In late July, Cooper, a 53-year-old internal auditor at IBM Corp., won a landmark court ruling that could make it tougher for companies to convert their traditional pension plans into so-called cash-balance retirement plans. U.S. District Judge G. Patrick Murphy, ruling in IBM vs. Cooper, found that the computer giant illegally discriminated against older workers when it switched to a cash-balance plan in the 1990s."

Here's another one: James Castelluccio, a 41-year IBM employee sued IBM in Federal court and won a substantial award. Nothing comes easy when facing IBM, but Mr. Castelluccio had the guts to see it through. This Stamford man claimed that IBM had dismissed him after 41 years because of his age. He is now collecting between $3.5 and $4 million following his federal court trial. The judge said IBM should have been interested in uncovering the truth regardless of whether the employee, James Castelluccio, had taken the severance package or pursued his lawsuit. The judge basically chastised IBM and awarded millions to the plaintiff.

As the story goes, a few weeks before Castelluccio's 60th birthday, his manager Ms. Collins-Smee, in her very first meeting with Castelluccio, asked him his age and if he was interested in retiring. He said he had no interest. The next day, Collins-Smee sent an e-mail to the human resources department saying she wanted to replace Castelluccio and that things were not going well between him and her.

Hey, they had just met! She said that Castelluccio would agree with that point that all was not well. Castelluccio never even knew of this e-mail until the discovery phase of the subsequent lawsuit. As you can see, since Akers, and perhaps before him, IBM did not always play fairly.

IBM decided to defame the employee, make him feel worthless and hope he would cave and take a package as many other beleaguered older employees had done under pressure over the years. The jury deliberated for about a day and then returned a verdict in favor of Castelluccio. Sometimes the right thing happens when you take on the bad guys. In the end, the total of the judgment is between $3.5 and 4 million.

More recently, Mark Lungariello wrote about another lawsuit that accuses IBM of age discrimination. The suit was filed in 2014. Three former IBM employees accused IBM that they and others were pushed out of the Company in favor of younger, recent college graduates. This is not yet resolved. Remember, there are over a million stories in the Naked City! Here is one more:

Jill R. Aitoro, an Industry Reporter for iSeries Network.com wrote about this issue on September 17, 2002: "A band of laid-off IBM workers in Vermont is pointing fingers at Big Blue for what they claim to be some fishy practices. Findings from a study of the June 2002 layoff at the Vermont Microelectronics division spurred some former employees to file complaints against IBM for age discrimination. Another study of the November 2001 layoff at the same IBM locale revealed nearly identical results."

Is a union the answer for IBM employees?

All during my IBM career, there were no unions at IBM because employees felt we did not need them. IBM truly practiced a notion of "respect for the individual." IBM for the most part was a good company until Akers blatantly broke the many promises made by the Watsons to loyal

IBM employees. A union sure would have helped hapless IBMers in the Akers' years.

And, so, today, for the life of me, I have no idea why IBM employees simply do not organize for self-preservation as the Company has been changing long-standing practices ad hoc to save bottom line money. This has had the effect of harming IBM employees and retirees.

This IBM union is worth a hard look. Here is the Alliance@IBM Local 1701's Statement of Principles. From what I have read, they are a principled organization and they already do a lot of good for IBM employees and retirees:

> *Alliance@IBM/CWA Local 1701 is an IBM employee organization that is dedicated to preserving and improving our rights and benefits at IBM. We also strive towards restoring management's respect for the individual and the value we bring to the Company as employees. Our mission is to make our voice heard with IBM management, shareholders, government and the media. While our ultimate goal is collective bargaining rights with IBM, we will build our union now and challenge IBM on the many issues facing employees from off-shoring and job security to working conditions and company policy.*

I never liked unions when I was with IBM as they have a way of homogenizing all employees into the same soup. I did like how in my time with the Company, there were some good IBM managers who made an attempt to fairly evaluate employees and reward them accordingly with bonuses and promotions.

What recourse would I have had if IBM decided to defraud and fast-talk and chisel its employees with negatives and lawyer-speak, as seems to be happening now? I would have been screaming bloody murder looking for my own lawyer or a good union for sure.

In my twenty-three years with the Company, I met very few IBM employees who were not downright excellent. Working with such sharp people and competing for the spoils of a non-union shop at the time was a lot more exciting for me than getting an 87c an hour raise because everybody else got one.

However, in watching IBM's behavior close hand and through the press over the last few years that I was with IBM and since, I would not trust IBM management today to ever do the right thing for me. IBM managers will gladly rule against any employee even if the accusations are untrue and it may ruin the employee's life. If I were with IBM today, I would surely be a member of this reasonably new Alliance. As a retiree, I have already signed up. For employees, it would help even out a game that today is always won by IBM.

The second unbundling

Whereas the original unbundling of 1969 marked the beginning of the deterioration of the customer / IBM relationship, it hit its all-time low in the last few of the Akers' years (late 1980's—early 1990's.) IBM, not having learned from its mistakes of the late 1960's, again unbundled support from system sales. And, in a move, which made the new unbundling as permanent as the end of the rental business, IBM began to retire or fire (lay off without a possible rehire) its field representatives, both systems engineers and marketing personnel.

In another bold move, IBM also changed its sales model from direct to a distributor-driven channel strategy. IBM's customers of the early 1970s had become outraged by unbundling, after IBM unilaterally announced that the

Company was cutting-off free technical support for its products. Likewise, the less trusting, less loyal customers of the early 1990s were similarly outraged.

Unlike the 1970's however, when IBM's customers wanted to complain about the shabby treatment they were receiving from Big Blue, this time, the customers found that there was nobody left home to listen to their complaints other than the competition.

Beginning of the end for IBM's branch offices

Hell bent on separating the customer from the reason they chose IBM in the first place (the best support in the industry), IBM chose a cowardly implementation approach this second time around. Never having forgotten unbundling and the price Buck Rodgers, head of the Data Processing Division at the time, had to pay for his decision, no IBM executive was going to lose anything by *announcing* another cessation of support.

They just did not announce it. They merely eliminated most of the people who populated the local offices. The de-facto result was that IBM customers no longer had any IBMer calling on them. And, nobody in IBM bothered to tell the customer. I am not kidding. I got out as soon as I could under the Individual Transition Option II (ITO II), which was IBM's best deal ever before the axe fell.

For leaving early voluntarily, I got 47 weeks' severance pay; I got paid for all my unused vacation time – over 10 weeks. I got a five year bump to my service from 23.5 to 28.5 years. I was able to receive all IBM benefits, including medical for my wife and family for life. When I reached 30 years from my start date, I began to collect my pension as if I had worked 28.5 years. It was a good deal.

I then opted to take an employment deal at one of my accounts as an inside consultant and professor at Misericordia University. Part of my contract was a lot of time off for outside consulting. I created a consultancy with many of my former IBM customers as my clients. Former IBM Systems Engineers had little trouble finding work.

Ironically, one of my big challenges was convincing customers that IBM had actually withdrawn support. Many had such undying faith in IBM that they could not believe that nobody in IBM had told them how IBM changes would affect them. Their next surprise was when somebody from XYZ distributing called on them and said they were the customer's new IBM representative and showed an IBM business card with their name, IBM's Logo, and XYZ Distributing. IBM had taken a preposterously cowardly way out.

From the customer's perspective, it was as if one day they had a salesman and a technical representative and the next day, not only did they not have an account team, but the team was no longer employed by the IBM Company. They either had taken the retirement incentive or they were fired. If a field employee in systems or marketing had the misfortune of being ranked number "last," regardless of their appraisal rating, they were as good as gone.

Consequences of reneging on customer support

One might ask if it is coincidence that when the Company first unbundled in the late 1960s and early 1970s, IBM's sales took a turn for the worse. The question can be asked again when IBM again unbundled in the early 1990s, and IBM went through some of its worst years ever, losing $16 billion in three years; was it unbundling that created some of the business slump?

From 1991 through 1993, IBM lost money at a staggering rate. No company could endure such record losses. The three year record losses ended in the year in which Lou Gerstner took over as CEO of the Company, when Mr. Akers stepped down. In 1994, IBM began a rebound. Gerstner had reversed many of Akers' practices and IBM stopped its bleeding. The red ink days were over.

Definitely unbundling IBM support from the price of IBM hardware contributed to Akers' and IBM's demise. There was nobody left, who was trained by IBM to ask for a customer order. What company would fire competent sales people who worked on a commission basis when sales were down?

With a poor economy, the depletion of the rental base, and the demoralization and ultimate elimination of many key employees, and the purposeful irritation of the customer base, there was nothing and nobody left to help IBM recover... until Lou Gerstner showed up at the front door.

For his efforts in the major changes which rocked IBM at its very foundation, including the second unbundling, John Akers met a similar fate to that of Buck Rodgers. When Wall Street began to complain about IBM results, Akers was gone.

Ira Sager of Armonk, N.Y., a writer for Business Week, captured some of Lou Gerstner's thoughts on the IBM he inherited in 1993, shortly after Akers' quiet unbundling; his fire sale of IBM divisions, and long-awaited departure:

One of IBM's most glaring problems, Gerstner concluded, was not its various technology gaffes but that it had basically screwed up relations with its customers. Once famous for blanketing big corporations with legions of pin striped marketing and field engineering troops, Big Blue had become distant, arrogant, unresponsive...

... Meanwhile, the Company squandered what it had taken decades to build: a position of trust with customers and the ear of top decision makers in corporations... Gerstner saw firsthand how bad things had gotten shortly after joining. When he invited CEOs of major corporations for a technology briefing, [IBM] managers had to scramble to find enough chief executives to fill the 20 slots.

Chapter 46

IBM Invented RISC Technology in 1974

IBM Research has created many wonders

We have already introduced RISC technology in prior sections and chapters and noted a small amount of the history of the RS/6000 machine. IBM's first real minicomputer, The Series/1 was replaced by this second generation RISC machine that was designed to succeed.

Not many know the biggest secret of RISC technology. Well, we're going to tell you. An IBM computer research engineer named John Cocke, who worked in the IBM Research facility in Yorktown, New York, originated the RISC concept in 1974.

Yes, Virginia, along with many other new concepts in computing, IBM invented RISC technology. Yet, few to none of today's great RISC systems manufacturers, including Sun Microsystems (Oracle) and Scott McNealy are known to be pumping the press to deliver their thank yous to Big Blue for enabling their billionaire status. It might be helpful if they did.

Research Engineer Cocke and his team reduced the size of the machine's instruction set, eliminating certain instructions that were seldom used. "We knew we wanted a computer with a simple architecture and a set of simple instructions that could be executed in a single machine cycle—making the resulting machine significantly more efficient than possible with other, more complex computer designs," Cocke noted in 1987.

John Cocke proved that about 20% of the instructions in a computer did 80% of the work. The first modern RISC machine was the IBM 801 minicomputer built by IBM, in 1975 as a research project. It was so informal the number 801 was selected simply because it was the IBM campus building number in which the machine was conceived. This was long before any commercial vendor, including the yet to be born Sun Microelectronics (at the time) had built a RISC box.

In what one checking opportunities might call a management mental lapse, IBM never really marketed the 801 and for the longest time showed little visible interest in RISC technology. The Company did not even publish anything about its work with RISC until 1982. IBM always thought of itself as a mainframe company and so, for business managers in IBM, ignoring RISC had little risk.

As noted in this book and many other books, IBM's biggest blunder of all time was giving up its PC business to its partners and losing as much as $1 trillion. RISC technology is another of these big losses but not at such a grand scale. Sun Microsystems became a $billion dollar company because IBM again was not watching its assets. It was all happening at the time that IBM was preparing to introduce its infamous PC.

I am reminded of a movie that was out when I was a young kid in 1957. It was called *Will Success Spoil Rock Hunter?* It seems that the worst thing that circumstance could ever bring to the post Watson IBM was success. IBM could not handle success in its PC area. It could not handle success in RISC Systems or Relational Database or Networking, etc. etc. etc. Maybe one day another Watson or Gerstner will come along. I sure hope so. In the meantime, it may not help to wish IBM success in the future.

Chapter 47

Sun Microsystems Makes It Big With RISC

The path to billionaire status

Though IBM did not see RISC Technology as a major opportunity, perhaps because it was just another IBM invention, its competition saw it full of dollar signs. Scott McNealy of Sun Microsystems, for example, a hair short of being a billionaire today thanks to IBM's lack of due diligence, for example, saw RISC for what it was. He saw it much differently than IBM. In fact, one might say that he saw RISC as being risk free, and he envisioned a wide path to the billionaire success he enjoys today thanks to IBM.

Born on November 13, 1954, and still in his twenties at the time, McNealy dreamed up Sun Microsystems, a company that soon became IBM's biggest RISC competitor. McNealy owes IBM a big thank you, which he may never give, for ignoring its gold mine and permitting him to become the billionaire in RISC technology and for permitting his company Sun Microsystems to achieve unprecedented success.

McNealy, co-founded computer technology company Sun Microsystems along with Vinod Khosia, Bill Joy, and Andy

Bechtolsheim. All four Sun founders are today billionaires. They got their billions as IBM frittered away its big lead in RISC technology to Sun and other companies that played the RISC game for keeps.

Simply stated, Sun started out in 1982 selling RISC-based desktop workstations for engineers and other technical users. By the mid-1990s, Sun capitalized on the need for Internet Servers. The Company began to build more powerful systems that provided needed server functions. At this time, most of the Company's revenues came from this source. Sun's SPARC servers powered the fledgling World Wide Web—prompting the marketing slogan that Sun provides "the dot in dot.com."

Scott McNealy and Bill Joy are the historical figures from Sun

The early eighties were a time of real innovation and opportunity in the information technology industry. However, while most new hardware and software ventures of this era were related to the 1981 IBM PC announcement, Scott McNealy and Bill Joy, founders of Sun Microsystems, along with the two other founders, were planning a different tactic.

They were not interested in cloning PCs. They were interested in moving forward the notion of Unix based computing with RISC processing and open systems. That was why they founded Sun in February 1982, just five months after IBM introduced the PC.

Before being acquired by Oracle, the Company reported over $11 billion dollars in annual revenue and at one time Sun was growing revenue at such a nice clip, there were no signs that it would ever stop growing. Sun was recognized as the world's leading provider of powerful UNIX workstations, servers and related software and hardware technologies based on open, distributed, network computing... and of course Java and its derivatives.

Sun was a victim of itself of course as well as the 2008 Great Recession from which it never recovered. On January 27, 2010, Sun was acquired by Oracle Corporation for $7.4 billion, based on an agreement signed on April 20, 2009. The following month, Sun Microsystems, Inc. was merged with Oracle USA, Inc. to become Oracle America, Inc.

The real question perhaps for this book about people and companies needing to thank IBM is: "Why did IBM not buy Sun if Oracle found it so attractive?" First let's talk about why IBM should have bought Sun.

Had IBM been able to convince Sun to sell the Company to Big Blue instead of to Oracle, IBM would have immediately become the dominant supplier of high-priced Unix servers. Moreover, it would have gained the rights to a number of popular business software franchises, including the Java technology used on many Web sites and imbedded in many IBM products.

IBM was a major adopter of Java and had billions invested in Java software. Rather than risk that Sun would sell to somebody else, especially a major competitor such as Oracle, IBM needed to do a better job of protecting its options, and grabbing them when it had the chance.

The deal would have also helped IBM compete against the hardware breadth of its arch rival HP and would have given Big Blue some needed momentum to combat Oracle's ever-expanding business software empire. IBM was not known to take many chances and the Company certainly has too many lawyers.

IBM was very concerned about the likelihood of antitrust reviews tied to its stronger positions in Unix servers and mainframe storage that it would have gained under the deal. Microsoft, a company with a lot of guts and a far better sense of reality than IBM, would have seen market dominance as a plus, not a minus. IBM has been self-destructive in so many IT sub-industries that it no longer finds dominating any marketplace as a positive. Soon, its poor management under duress will perhaps achieve its goal. IBM will be a bit player in the markets in which it chooses to compete and perhaps nothing more...ever.

IBM made a weak play for Sun

After that set up, you may not believe it but IBM actually did try to buy Sun. It lost out on the deal by $60 million. That's million with an "M," in a multi-billion dollar overall deal. That's chump change. IBM was beaten to the acquisition by arch competitor Oracle. Sun's acquisition by Larry Ellison's gang will make life miserable in the trenches for IBM forever. With the acquisition, Oracle has been able to deftly use Sun's products to enhance its own software.

Sun's Java programming language is used by many to develop applications for websites, mobile phones and even DVD players. Most IT analysts and even most programmers know that IBM as a company has a love affair with Java though it makes nothing on it. IBM is in fact, the world's largest user of Java technology and, as a result, it has placed emphasis on giving DB2 and other software areas within IBM what the Company would call stellar Java support.

Earth to IBM: Java is owned by Sun which now is owned by Oracle, one of your biggest competitive nemeses. Why not concentrate on IBM I, instead of Java. IBM is the best OS in the world and it is built by IBM?

Sun's Solaris operating system is a leading platform for Oracle's database software. Oracle became a much stronger player in the database industry and the "ERP/CRM" marketplace. IBM did not need that for sure. It lost the Sun deal for peanuts. Why?

IBM had placed more money on the table than its last offer of $7 Billion. As often happens with IBM, its team of highly skilled lawyers found some "flaws" in the deal. IBM more than likely spent more than that $60 million by paying for a team of more than 100 lawyers to conduct research on potential problems in the purchase of Sun. They especially looked at antitrust concerns to Sun's contracts with employees and IBM competitors.

After the lawyers did their thing, IBM chose to nickel and dime Sun by reducing its offer to $9.40 a share. The original proposal that Big Blue placed on the table in a prior meeting was $9.55 a share. The difference was $60 million. When the offer was given to Sun, its board was irritated and balked about the new terms. They did not reject the offer outright, but wanted certain guarantees that IBM's legal team felt were too "onerous."

Sensing that Sun Management was not happy with the deal, a spiteful team of IBM negotiators burned their bridges by withdrawing the $9.40 offer completely. Oracle got the news and quickly snapped up Sun at just $40 million more than IBM's offer. Again, let me say that this was chump change for such a large, product rich company. Perhaps Oracle one day will tighten the screws on its control of Java. Then what IBM?

This, by the way brought to about $40 billion, Oracle's spending on acquisitions over the short term. IBM should be worried. Under the deal, Oracle paid $9.50 in cash for each Sun share. IBM lost the deal for $40 million but really because of poor negotiating and perhaps downright failed bullying. IBM should have known better. Oracle owes IBM another big thank you for being an inept negotiator.

Bill Joy, a computer science master mind

Just as Jobs and Wozniak at Apple used a mixture of skills to gain success, the somewhat hermit-like Bill Joy, who is looked upon today as being one of the greatest minds in computer science, joined forces with the strong business marketer, and industry innovator, Scott McNealy, to become one of the best teams in technology industry history.

After quickly getting contracts which made Sun a multi-million dollar company in its second year of operation, McNealy assumed the CEO spot, and Joy continued being the technical pioneer. In 1998, Joy was rewarded for his outstanding achievements at Sun by being promoted to the title of Chief Scientist, and member of the Executive Committee, where he continued to serve until 2003.

Bill Joy received his B.S.E.E. in Electrical Engineering from the University of Michigan in1975. Later, he attended graduate school at U.C. Berkeley where he immediately took to the myriad of sandbox opportunities. At Berkeley, for example, Joy is credited with being the principal designer of Berkeley UNIX (BSD) and, in addition to his M.S. in Electrical Engineering and Computer Science, he gained tremendous industry respect.

For his efforts in improving Unix, he was awarded the ACM Grace Murray Hopper Award for outstanding work in Computer Science for work done when he was under the age of thirty.

As we already examined in Section III, the Berkeley version of Unix (BSD) became the standard in education and research, garnering development support from the Defense Advanced Research Project Agency (DARPA). BSD Unix was noted for a number of innovations, including virtual memory and internetworking using TCP/IP as an integral part of UNIX.

BSD was widely distributed in source form as an educational tool, so that others could learn from it and improve it. Many of the popular BSD facilities have also been implemented in Linux and have been brought back to the original AT& T Unix.

Scott McNealy, CEO from 1984

Joy was joined in 1982 by a bright and brash Scott McNealy. It did not take long for Sun to become the leading global supplier of network computing solutions, with1999 revenues of more than $11.7 billion. After taking the reins as CEO in 1984, McNealy led Sun along a path of constant growth and profitability until the roof fell in during the Great Recession of 2008.

In many ways, a Steven Jobs type, McNealy has always been recognized for his vision and business acumen. These qualities plus his animated personality have made him one of the most influential and widely quoted leaders in the complex, fluid, and fast moving IT industry. In fact, "60 Minutes" called him "one of the most influential businessmen in America." Scott McNealy has something to say about everything.

He is a great speaker and makes the circuit quite regularly. Bill Gates is one of his favorite topics, as McNealy's desire for open computing conflicts with his perception of the self-serving Microsoft-first philosophy as espoused by the former Microsoft Chairman.

Sun's idea of computing, as promoted by McNealy in his time as CEO, is different than most. When he ran Sun, the Company believed in building software with publicly available, open specifications so the software, which one company uses, could interact with whatever software its customers and partners were running.

McNealy and Microsoft

McNealy singles out one company, Microsoft, who he thinks clearly does not like the "OPEN" strategy and, according to McNealy has used a variety of tactics to undermine cross platform compatibility. (Indeed, the courts have already backed up a number of McNealy's claims.) He always hoped that his messages would one day unseat the champion of me-first computing from Redmond Washington.

On the big front, vindication is sweet. In the early Sun days when Scott McNealy would suggest that "The Network Is *The Computer,*" he would get funny looks. Folks understood, but did not quite understand. That is, until after Lou Gerstner came to IBM in 1993. At the time, the IBM Company was a system oriented company, which had a networking philosophy called SNA (Systems Network Architecture).

The objective of SNA was to let IBM computers and terminals "talk" to each other in a rigid IBM-defined way. This is a far cry from McNealy's posture, and his mantra, "The Network Is *The Computer!*" a succinct statement of the Company's vision of seamless connectivity. In many ways the idea that the network is invisible predates the industry's acceptance of this viable notion.

McNealy and IBM

But this was bound to change. In 1995 at the Fall Comdex, when IBM's Lou Gerstner coined the terms "network-centric-computing," and "eBusiness", it all added up to "The Network Is *The Computer*". Of course Gerstner could not say that, because it had already been said. Gerstner was, in fact, rephrasing McNealy's message. Gerstner's mere utterance immediately gave "The Network Is *The Computer*," its place in the hall of brilliant notions.

Gerstner saw network-centric-computing as a means of transacting commerce between disparate systems, joined together on the Internet. In this speech, he clearly paid homage to Sun's notion, but no names were mentioned.

Homage may not have been Gerstner's intention. Regardless, Lou Gerstner took the Sun mantra, framed it, hung some meat on it, and made sure that IBM would have a major role in the process. In many ways, IBM's adoption of the Sun mantra has assured Scott McNealy his place in computer history.

One might even suggest that the internetwork is the computer. Starting with one person connecting to the Internet, this network of networks known as the Internet offers all of the functions that one could ever want with the same facility as if all of the functions were delivered by one machine. But they are not delivered by one machine. So much could never be housed on one system.

Yet, through the PC client tool, the browser, the function and facility is provided by millions of inter-connected systems working together as one. From the user's perspective, the network is the computer... the internetwork is the computer... the Internet is the computer.

Java

Java, one of Sun's most significant innovations, is both a programming language and an operational environment. As such, when applications are written in Java, if the operating system is 100% pure, any Java application can be run on any computer. It is a breakthrough concept, and it has many proponents, the biggest, of which, perhaps surprisingly, is and has been IBM almost from day one.

Industry sources suggest that IBM is so much behind Java that the Company has spent even more than Sun on its implementation and deployment. Of course, there is a Grinch lurking behind all of the Java goodies. Peering through his Windows, and trying to block the light of day from a portable Java. Bill Gates is afraid that a house built with Java will need no Windows.

Sun hardware and software

Sun Microsystems was a very important company in the history of computing. Though it was a microcomputer company, as Intel, the Company focused on the Unix environment. Like Microsoft, Sun also built an operating system. Their Unix-like Solaris operating system ran best on the Company's SPARC, and UltraSPARC RISC-based microprocessors (millions of Ultra-SPARC chips have been sold). In 1987 for example, Sun's SPARC and Solaris OS-driven computers took the lead in the powerful workstation market. By this time, IBM was very interested in RISC.

Where was IBM while Sun was rising?

Can it be that the IBM Company, which was sued by the government in 1952 for achieving a 70% market share in the computing industry did not notice Sun? They were an $11 billion + company! IBM surely recognized Oracle, who now owns Sun but the recognition admittedly came a bit late to make a difference.

While Sun was prospering with IBM-invented RISC technology, IBM was dabbling with a doomed-for-failure machine known as the RT PC. It used the old 801 processor IBM developed for inside experiments years earlier. It was RISC but old technology.

It was also very poorly named and at best a half-effort on the part of IBM. This machine gave IBM two claims to fame. First, just like Sun Solaris, it ran a derivative Unix, which IBM called the Advanced Interactive Executive (AIX). It was not as well formed as the Sun Solaris offering. Second, it used a RISC processor.

Sun had quickly become the leader in Unix scientific workstations, and the leader in RISC technology. Not surprisingly, IBM, the mainframe company, had invented and had rejected RISC years before. IBM had also rejected times sharing and Unix when it had the in at MIT. And so, MIT developed Unix for GE and DEC machines rather than for IBM's System/360. One might call IBM a two time loser with RISC and Unix. IBM left a lot of billions behind for others, with such poor corporate decisions.

After the RT PC marketing failure, it would take the IBM Company a number of years before it would collect its RISC knowledge within the organization; figure out how to do it right; and come back with a vengeance with the PowerPC chip architecture.

It helps to repeat in a book intended to show the Company's lack of diligence with its opportunities that Big Blue could have had it all. It had invented RISC and it was destined for major rights to Unix right from the start. But it the RISC opportunity and permitted Sun to win, and it fumbled the Unix opportunity with both MIT and AT&T. The cost for full Unix use for IBM could have been no more expensive than the cost of cooperation with MIT, AT&T, and others.

The IBM Company had already invented RISC. Despite IBM always beginning an adventure in the lead, companies such as Sun have consistently won the market. RISC and Unix are great examples. Scott McNealy thanks the Almighty for giving him such a docile, loving IBM with which to compete. Thank you, IBM

Oracle as the caretaker of Sun

One of the biggest reasons why Oracle bought Sun was to own Java. Sun also now owns MySQL, the industry leading open source relational database. Additionally, Oracle picked up a number of high-value customers with the acquisition.

Oracle did not inherit all crown princes but enough to make it a great deal. For example, analysts suggested right from the time of the acquisition that much low end hardware in Sun's portfolio was dog stuff and their suppositions proved correct. Hardware revenues immediately went down even though Oracle is now strategically positioned to better compete against IBM and others in today's markets.

Oracle executives stayed positive on hardware believing it would eventually grow. They were mostly right. Though the hardware resurgence was long in coming, it has now being realized. Yes, it did take five years or so to turn the corner, but the Oracle hardware business today is again profitable.

Oracle will also contend that it has turned out to be a critical differentiator at the high end, such as with Exadata and Sparc Supercluster technologies. Most analysts knew that Oracle's hardware business had to shrink before it could grow. Oracle recently refreshed its SPARC server lines and frequently cites potential growth from this business. Combined, these businesses are in fact growing nearly 50% year over year.

Storage is the hardware business within which Oracle desires to compete. Ironically, IBM exited the storage business, a business which Big Blue created in the 1950's with its groundbreaking RAMAC Disk Drive.

Big Blue unfortunately got little for its groundbreaking discoveries and inventions. IBM always was more concerned about mainframes than anything else. For Oracle, storage has a major upside because Sun's storage business was in the pits for quite a while and storage continues to be a large and constantly growing market.

IBM's limited marketing and lack of vision, helped enable Sun's success and now Oracle's success with the Sun portfolio. Of course the success of Sun and Oracle could have been prevented by IBM's paying attention to business and so, by letting others win the day, it likewise limited IBM's business fortunes and stockholder returns. Most stockholders are unaware of IBM's failings or perhaps there would be a revolution.

In 2010, when Larry Ellison became the big boss for Sun, McNealy was out of SUN. Two chiefs would not have done Oracle well. McNealy founded and continues to serve as the chief executive officer today of Wayin, a social technologies company based in Denver Colorado.

IBM has worn out the chair, in which it has been seated, while others have succeeded. You recall that IBM sat idly by in the RISC arena, an opportunity it had invented. Big Blue simply gave others the opportunity to lead the ventures into RISC technology, which today powers the technology industry's most powerful computers including IBM's Power technology. Thank You IBM!

IBM finally noticed the light

Though IBM had invented RISC in 1974, it sat on it. It was not until the Company introduced the IBM RT Personal Computer (RT/PC - RISC Technology) on January 21, 1986 that Big Blue finally chose to use its RISC research work for commercial purposes.

The aging 801 RISC CPU developed in the 1970's and used for internal testing but not much else was selected as the CPU for the RT/PC. The 801 had been selected by IBM to power some "non-computer" office products after it was spun off as an office engine known as the IBM ROMP (Research office products division microprocessor). These guys built WP systems such as the Office System/6 with ROMP back when IBM played well in the office game.

This technology was deployed under the covers of IBM's most sophisticated office products such as the best word processor in the industry—Office System/6. It was not seen as an idea in RISC processor technology whose time had come. Nobody knew what engine powered Office System/6 nor did anybody care. Later, as noted, the 801 ROMP processor formed the basis for the ill-fated IBM RT PC in 1986.

This time at least, IBM got its corporate head out of the clouds and it added the Unix Operating System to the deal and the Company marketed the RT/PC as a complete system. IBM's flavor of Unix, for its own reasons, was not called Unix. Instead, it was dubbed AIX for Advanced Interactive Executive, a Unix-like operating system that was true to the Unix standards. In other words, AIX was in fact Unix with an IBM brand.

Unlike the barebones Series/1 announcement previously highlighted in this book, the RT/PC had Unix and the Structured Query Language (SQL) data base management system, plus first class software development tools, and application programs. The aging ROMP processor was its only detraction.

IBM had built a nice system to sell to all comers. But at the time, it was not best of breed. IBM had given up its edge by using an old, almost prehistoric RISC processor. The only advantage was that the processor was already on the shelf and did not require a development cost.

This aging IBM RISC processor did give IBM a RISC-based product. However, IBM's mini-effort using its old technology was outclassed by the competing products of the day. The 801 may have been revolutionary in its conception years earlier, but later when it was finally deployed, it performed like a dog compared to the bloodhounds in the industry.

Because IBM took nothing 100% seriously other than mainframes, its competitors owe a big thank you to Big Blue in yet another high tech area for helping them amass their lead in RISC technology. The RT/PC was underpowered, and the PC nomenclature, with which it was saddled, gave the notion to potential customers that this was not a powerful minicomputer-level machine. They viewed it as a PC-class machine.

Once IBM showed its cards with the RT, however, the IBM Company was determined to out-RISC all other RISC vendors, and out-Unix, the Unix crowd. Their next cut (RS/6000) did a much better job of achieving both objectives. But the IBM battle in this foreign territory was always uphill.

Chapter 48

IBM RISC System 6000 (RS/6000) – A Great RISC/UNIX System

Just don't call me a PC

On February 15, 1990, IBM announced the Power Chip driven RISC System/6000 family of desktop, deskside, and rack mounted workstations and servers. IBM was careful not to brand these machines RSs as they had branded the RT/PC with the RT nomenclature, and it quickly denigrated into just another PC offering. The systems were to be known as The RISC System/6000s and that was that. However, the product line quickly became known as the RS/6000 family despite IBM's desires.

The RS/6000 was a best of breed RISC technology and Unix box. It was a fine system. Ten years later, after the RS/6000 had received acclamations of success, and after IBM had enhanced its CPU engine (Power Processor) to remain the fastest of fastest UNIX processors, IBM was no longer satisfied with its name.

Many of us in the business wish that IBM was not playing with system names as often as it did. By changing names so often, the IBM Company prevented its loyal customer set from keeping their IBM product perspective. University degrees could have been given so regular people could learn to understand IBM's naming notions.

As the IBM Company began to integrate its product lines, on October 3, 2000, IBM rebranded its RISC units, formerly known as RS/6000s—as the eServer pSeries. The "p", according to IBM at the time, stood for power. IBM was hunting and pecking for meaning for its names but IBM customers kept getting more and more confused with the changes.

IBM had brought forth the natural progression of its 801 RISC efforts and the market knowledge gained by the introduction of the RT/PC into a very nice and very powerful package. The first cut was RS/6000 but then the chip became the focus instead of the full systems, which regular companies and organizations purchased from IBM.

IBM aptly nicknamed the line the POWERstations and POWERservers, since they were based on IBM's newly introduced POWER architecture and a brand new RISC processor chip dubbed the Power chip. Industry observers believe that all of the renaming was more confusing than helpful. Having an Apple take on the name Cadillac would not help in marketing Apple's computers.

The RS/6000 (pSeries) family was designed to provide a broad range of various power level platforms for engineering/scientific, technical, and multi user applications. The processors were noted as being especially appropriate for numeric intensive use.

The RS/6000s were designed to deliver high performance and to provide IBM customers with a platform for development of industry leading applications. When the line was introduced, IBM cited several business areas as being particularly appropriate for this technology:

- CAD/CAM/CAE
- Computer Aided Software Engineering (CASE)
- Technical publishing
- Securities and trading systems
- Financial and economic analysis
- Statistical analysis
- Geological
- Multi user
- Other applications requiring high performance platforms.

As the IBM expert product "namers" joined the foray over time, the RS/6000 as noted above, became known as the pSeries. Later, it was rechristened as the System p, and finally it was called the IBM Power System using PowerPC technology within the Power Architecture. That is what the machine is known as today. It uses the AIX flavor of Unix as its OS. For me, this is too many changes and so, IBM's message loses clarity.

The RS/6000 heritage is fully used and enhanced when the 2015 Power Systems run Unix (AIX) or Linux. Incidentally, the AS/400 box which was discussed in Section II, was remanufactured to use the same hardware, though it would always use a different operating system such as i5/OS, later rebranded as iOS and then in recent years, rebranded again as IBM i.

The AS/400 technology heritage is fully used and enhanced when the IBM i operating system is deployed on the Power System box. The Power System box hosts both AIX (RS/6000 heritage) and IBM I (AS/400 heritage). It also hosts the best version of Linux. I am so sorry that IBM made this all so hard to fully understand if you do not use legacy RS/6000 or legacy AS/400 terminology. Despite that drawback, the IBM Power System is a phenomenal innovation and used by many companies worldwide that love high speed processing without down time. Too bad that IBM does not know how to make the world understand how good it is at making great systems.

Chapter 49

RISC Power Architecture Has Produced the World's Fastest Supercomputers

IBM leads the supercomputer race

IBM's research endeavors in RS/6000, AS/400 and the Power Architecture formed the basis for a very special machine (Deep Blue) which, in 1997 gained world recognition in a chess match with Garry Kasparov, the world's best human chess player of the day.

When IBM's Blue Gene supercomputer was introduced in 2004, it was both the most powerful supercomputer and the most efficient, consuming only a fraction of the energy and floor space of any other supercomputer. IBM originally built the Blue Gene system to help biologists observe the invisible processes of protein folding and gene development. Now, you know why the name Blue Gene was picked.

IBM is # 1 in supercomputing thanks to sticking with improvements in the Power chips and to IBM's incessant desire to be the best in the world in supercomputing. In many ways this is a tribute to my favorite IBMer of all time, Thomas J. Watson Jr.

And, so, from Blue Gene, after a few more technology leaps in Power chip technology and supercomputer research, in

2011, IBM aptly named its newest and fastest computer of all time, and the industry's finest, after TJ Watson Sr. & Jr., but mostly Jr. TJW Jr. could not stand any other company, such as Amdahl or Cray out-performing IBM and when they did, it annoyed him immensely. The new Watson Supercomputer is thus aptly named, and is IBM's best offering of today to save the world. Watson continues to be enhanced by IBM as IBM has been continually innovating in supercomputer technology. Too bad IBM can't make a good buck on this as it is clearly the leader in supercomputers.

To net it out (an IBM phrase from the 1960's), the Watson Supercomputer is an AI machine. AI means artificial intelligence. You may recall from prior work in this book the five defined generations of computing. They are Tubes (1) Transistors (2), Integrated Circuits (3), Microcomputers (4) and Artificial Intelligence (5). AI is the fifth and most advanced generation of computing and IBM's Watson is one of few units operating within this new generation. I know of no others.

From ENIAC, MARK I, EDVAC, EDSAC and other one of a kind computers at the beginning of the computer era, through commercial systems that enabled the same system to be built many, many times, supercomputing has brought us back to our roots. Computers are again being named as one-of-a-kind freaky units of sort that cannot be duplicated. Who knows what will come after Watson? Many of us who worked for IBM in the early 1990's sure hope the next supercomputer is not named Opel. Gerstner sounds like a nice name!

Watson is the product of a lot of fast technology hardware research as well as the best research in Artificial Intelligence, bar none. With its Artificial Intelligence, Watson was built to be able to answer questions posed in a natural query language, which was also developed by IBM.

Those TV nuts who like Jeopardy may remember that Watson got its debut on the quiz show Jeopardy in 2011. IBM had trained the machine for this encounter. Jeopardy lovers may recall that Watson was a contestant on Jeopardy and competed against former winners Brad Rutter and Ken Jennings. Watson had no way of spending its winnings but nonetheless the Robot took home first prize of $1 million.

IBM knows how to deploy technology to solve problems. My forte at IBM and since has been in problem solving. Using the best tools and the best information provides the best chance of success. IBM is not a slouch organization though its marketing management could have been sharper at times.

The Company's smartest scientists and engineers gave Watson access to 200 million pages of structured and unstructured content. This content and its structural arrangement consumed four TB (trillion bytes – aka trillion machine storage positions).

Wikipedia got to take some bows as the full text of Wikipedia was used for training but Watson was not connected to the Internet during the game. To help the audience know what Watson was *thinking*, for each clue, Watson's three most probable responses were displayed on the television screen.

Watson, the fastest computer in the world at the time, consistently outperformed its human opponents on the game's signaling device. Admittedly, there were a few categories that caused the machine trouble such as those questions with short clues containing only a few words.

IBM loved the success of Watson and so would TJ Watson Jr. In February 2013, IBM proudly announced that Watson software system's first commercial application would be helping with decisions regarding lung cancer at Sloan-Kettering Cancer Center.

As a testimony to IBM's work on this project, Watson's former business chief Manoj Saxena says that 90% of nurses in the field who use Watson now follow its guidance. Wow! I think computers will never out-fox human beings but if decisions can be programmed or inferred, watch out for Watson and its next generation.

IBM for years was the largest micro-chip manufacturer in the world but its supply was all consumed internally as parts for mainframes, minicomputers, and small business systems. Big Blue, however, was not the only company that engaged in micro-technology, though it may have been the best. IBM has been making chips in its own foundries for huge computers since the 1960's.

Supercomputers using IBM designed micro-chips sure are a tribute to the goodness and the greatness of the IBM Corporation when its power and muscle are applied to help the universe. If IBM could apply the same power to making money from its projects, the US Federal Reserve would have to create new vaults to store IBM's new cash hordes.

Chapter 50

IBM PC Introduced in Opel Years

I met Charley Chaplain the day the IBM PC was announced

In the introduction of this section, I lightly boasted about my involvement in the announcement of the IBM PC. John Opel was the IBM CEO but he did not expect me to be in the IBM Plant in Boca Raton, Florida the day that he and Charley Chaplain introduced the new IBM PC There were no MASH characters on this day as Charley Chaplain was the first hero of the PC and he was there in full regalia. We shook hands!

I do remember it well. I just happened to be in Boca Raton Florida, the original plant of manufacture for the IBM PC. I was there for an IBM System/38 banking class. Hoping to one-day be a writer, I had just purchased an $1800 memory typewriter using my employee discount. I write; therefore today your humble scribe is a writer. This is my 62nd book. At the time, I had just one baby child and so I thought I could afford IBM products to help my fledgling writing career.

The IBM PC was announced during my one week stay in Boca Raton. Using EasyWriter software, it could do everything the memory typewriter could do as well as things nobody had ever dreamed about. I had planned to begin my writing career imminently; but the IBM PC suggested that I might not want to do it on a typewriter, even if it did have five whole pages of memory. It surely had no permanent storage other than printing and filing sheets of paper in file cabinets.

The IBM Company assembled a multitude of press and interested technicians and marketers for its well anticipated announcement. I was probably the only person in Boca that day that did not have a clue about what was about to happen. I was in GSD and our product at the time was the System/38. IBM had chosen a GSD plant in Florida to manufacture its first PC.

It was August 12, 1981. IBM had a big, big show and a press conference at the Waldorf Astoria ballroom in New York City. At the conference, Don Estridge, the Project Coordinator for the IBM PC announced the IBM Personal Computer with an entry price tag of $1,565. That was the barebones price.

The biggest deal for the announcement of which I was aware at the time was conducted at the home plant of the IBM PC in Boca Raton Florida. I can't get over being on-site on the very day for other purposes. The banking sector in IBM GSD had borrowed some space at the plant for a class I was attending.

There was a very big buzz that day. I did not know the IBM PC was being announced. Yet, I was privileged to see a demo of the machine in the IBM cafeteria during lunch time and I met Charley Chaplain, the IBM PC mascot. The free lunch was also quite nice.

I fell in love with the machine's word processing capabilities with EasyWriter. After lunch and a demo, I went directly from the cafeteria to the closest pay phone. I called home and asked my wife if my memory typewriter had been delivered. Much to my heartache, she affirmed my worst fears. She said they were there and getting ready to install it.

For a typewriter, the installer was not much more than an IBM guy with a suit, most often a college intern, unpacking the machine from the box, and placing the unit on a desk and plugging it into a wall outlet. I said, "Tell them to take it back. I am going to buy a PC!" I bought the PC. It was $3200.00.

My IBM Branch Office took back the memory typewriter and nobody was any worse for the experience. This was one time it certainly was to my advantage to work for IBM. However, for delivery of my new PC, I had to get in line with everybody else. It took forever—more than a year for it to arrive even though I ordered it the first day.

While in Boca Raton, I learned that my PC would cost me about $3200 with a printer and green-screen monitor, which for me were definitely not optional.

The white box enclosed system unit was powered by an Intel 8088 microprocessor operating at speeds that were hyped to be measured in millionths of a second. The part that sat on the desk was no bigger than a portable typewriter and contained 40K of read-only memory and 16K of user memory, as well as a built-in speaker for generating music. Though the case was small, toting the cables, the keyboard, display, and printer along with the system from point A to point B presented some challenges.

The system unit had a "bus" which later was termed an industry standard bus with five expansion slots that could be used to connect such features as expanded memory, display and printing units and game "paddles." The unit also ran self-diagnostic checks so it could check on itself to be sure it was running right.

I loved the keyboard and its 83 keys. It connected via a six-foot coiled cable. It was long enough that the keyboard could be rested on one's lap or on the desktop without moving the rest of the system. The keyboard also included such advanced functions for the times as a numeric keypad and 10 special keys (F1 to F10) that enabled users to write and edit text, figure accounts and store data.

IBM Scranton's de facto PC expert arrives

When I came back to the IBM Branch Office after my one week in Florida, my peers thought I was there to learn about the PC. They knew I was there for the big announcement, and this sort of made me a celebrity within my IBM office. Management took credit for sending me even though no Branch office expenses were used as my class was funded by the IBM Banking Industry Group. The new PC was that big a deal. Though I was officially in a banking class in Boca Raton, I did come home with a lot of PC memorabilia (fun stuff) for my co-workers and I gave it all away.

My managers rewarded me by asking me to conduct a big PC announcement meeting for our customers in Northeastern PA. It went over quite well. IBM customers loved the new PC. Early on, details such as: "How do I get one of those PCs?" were not available. So, when I did the IBM announcement, there were no obvious negatives needing to be discussed about the PC.

With the Personal Computer, or PC, for the first time, IBM began to enter homes such as mine, small businesses, and schools. The PC machine had been designed, developed and assembled in little more than a year from mostly all readily available industry piece parts. P.D. Estridge, the *Father of the IBM PC* had formed a group of technology design and manufacturing experts In Boca Raton Fl. to get the job done.

IBM executives were not about to wait once they committed the funds. The project was unbudgeted but IBM found the money. Estridge's group got the job done for the Company. Nothing in IBM had ever had a design to manufacturing cycle of one year. The IBM PC was the exception. Bill Lowe, IBM Lab Director in Boca Raton promised he would deliver the forecast and he did.

Few IBM parts in the IBM PC

This new IBM machine had little IBM in it. This was an IBM first. The only really noticeable IBM part in the new "IBM" PC was the well-designed Raleigh keyboard. I love that keyboard and use one just like it today. In fact I bought my first IBM replacement keyboard more than twenty years ago and it just failed me last year. I bought a replacement just like it. This keyboard has audio and tactile feedback. You know when you hit a key. It does not have that spongy feeling of a $5.00 offshore keyboard.

When it broke and I could not find an old one just like it on EBay, I bought a new one from Unicomp for $85.00. The Unicomp keyboard even has the Microsoft Windows key, which my older IBM keyboard never had as it predated Windows. Unicomp's keyboard is as good as my old Raleigh keyboard. Thank you, Unicomp.

Anyway, the PC was a real computer... and it was an "IBM." Mine had 16 kilobytes of memory (expandable to 256 kilobytes), two floppy disk drives (available with just one), and a monochrome (green) monitor. You could also get an optional color monitor. There was no hard disk available on the PC. Hard disk was introduced with the IBM PCXT in 1983.

For a guy getting ready to use a memory typewriter, I figured, who needs a hard drive? I could not wait to get my PC, but it was about a year later (some time in 1982) that it arrived to replace the ghost memory typewriter. Fully configured an IBM PC would run close to $5,000.00.

My best friend, Dennis Grimes, a great IBM Systems Engineer with large systems experience partnered with me to produce a series of books highlighting the IBM PC and its competition. We wrote a book for Ballinger/ Harper Collins called the Personal Computer buyers Guide. Sorry, the poorly materialized graphic below is the only pic I have.

Shortly after the success of this project, our Author's agent Mike Connolly, the former President of Ballenger, hooked us up for a six-book deal with John Wiley & Sons. I had hoped for a writing career. I figured if you wrote something people wanted to read, the career was on. Grimes was not looking for a writing career but nonetheless he could write well and he was pressed into service for these ventures. Here is an equally poor graphic of one of the six Wiley books we produced. Yes, it does say Kelly/Grimes on the top. I convinced Dennis that sounded better than Grimes/Kelly. Don't you think it does? See cover below:

Built from piece parts

To get the piece parts for the IBM PC, the late Philip, D. (Don) Estridge had to go shopping or so he thought. Estridge was the point man for the IBM effort, along with a group of 12 dedicated top flight IBM engineers and technicians. They contracted the production of the PC's components to outside companies. The processor chip came from Intel, and the operating system, called DOS (Disk Operating System), came from a 32 person company called Microsoft, from the absolute other end of the United States of America.

Lots of PC billionaires need to thank IBM— starting with Intel

Let's begin the necessary thank-you's with Intel. Though IBM had a lot of its own small processors that it could have and should have deployed for its new IBM PC, Estridge believed that he would have run into negotiation problems with divisions within IBM wanting too high an internal price for their processors. That would delay the availability of the new PC and so this would not work well in the short timeframe. IBM did not have a good forecast in the first place to assure a big enough supply.

Chairman Opel could have resolved that problem but he really did not care from what company that IBM sourced any of the parts. He had no idea of the ultimate success of the PC. Moreover, it was not an essential product at the time. The PC was to be a sideshow necessary to prove a point.

It was never supposed to be an important IBM product. IBM was blinded by its success with mainframes and so it missed out on all the points of value that their PC could bring to the Company. Public Relations on the PC was what IBM cared most about; but the way the Company handled its rollout, it sure did not seem that way. IBM followers were more annoyed with IBM than thankful for the introduction.

IBM precursor to the PC

IBM had been toying with the idea of Personal Computers during the early 1970's. In fact, by 1973, the Company had developed a prototype machine called the SCAMP (Special Computer, APL Machine Portable). IBM's General Systems Division, created in 1969 as the Company's most unique division ever, brought out the SCAMP as the IBM 5100 Portable Computer in September 1975. Compared to the PC, its price tag was quite hefty.

IBM had supposedly not figured out how to create an inexpensive PC-like version yet. This unit weighed in at approximately 50 pounds, which is not too much considering the shipping weight of an IBM Selectric II Typewriter was about 25 pounds.

The IBM 5100 desktop computer was comparable in power to IBM's third generation1130 scientific computer system in storage capacity and performance but it was almost as small and as easy to use as an IBM Selectric Typewriter. IBM sold these units, depending on the configuration from $9,000 to $19,000. IBM needed some pricing lessons before it could release this unit as a PC.

Big Blue followed the IBM 5100 with similar small computers such as the IBM 5110 and 5120. The PC internally in IBM was known as the IBM 5150 and sold barebones for $1595 with hardly any IBM components.

In the late 1970's IBM had a number of other prototypes using IBM processor technology that were operational within the Boca Raton Lab. Unfortunately, Lab Director Bill Lowe could not convince IBM that there was a real market for IBM if it had released these for the PC at the right price. Think about what a mistake that was when you look at the PC market today worth in excess of a trillion dollars. It would drive heavy IBM stockholders into major lamentations.

Intel overall was a good choice

For the processor, if IBM had to go outside, Intel was a reasonably good choice. In this way, IBM assured a good price and it assured supply. They went to Intel, a company that was already pumping out computer chips from its founding of July 18, 1968. In fact, when IBM showed up at the door to buy Intel processors for the IBM PC, annual Intel revenue already was approaching $1 Billion. The full Intel story is given in Chapter 33.

The Company had been created by semiconductor pioneers Robert Noyce and Gordon Moore, both of whom had left Fairchild Semiconductor to start their own chip-works.

Of course IBM always had some of its own great processors ready to go in the research labs. IBM had in fact released one of these in its 5100 line. It was the processor that ran the APL Programming Language. This was a microcomputer version of the huge System/360 model 30 mainframe computer.

Without writing a new compiler / interpreter, IBM deployed this microprocessor so the 5100 would run the System/360 version of APL right on the 5100 system. This little micro could have been the PC's engine. IBM also had its first baby RISC processor built and functioning. Later it was used in the RT/PC.

IBM considered using the IBM 801 processor in the original PC but for its own reasons, it went to Intel anyway. The IBM 801 RISC processor and its operating system were developed at the Watson Research Center and they were both ready to go. The 801 was a full order of magnitude more powerful than the Intel 8088.

This was a big blunder seen in retrospect as Intel and Microsoft stole the whole industry from IBM. IBM would have been the first in RISC and could have saved both the RISC market and the PC market by making this choice instead of Intel and Microsoft. Second guessing can do nobody any good at this point. Intel got IBM's business and they, not IBM have been making a ton of money on this IBM decision for well over thirty years. Thank you, IBM!

The Grove effect at Intel

Andy Grove, the genius and great all around guy who many think founded Intel was not quite sitting on the sidelines waiting for the Company to become successful. In fact, he was a vital member of the young company's team. He joined Intel as its first hire soon after the Company founding.

Since Grove was not an original owner and not a scientist capable of inventing things, the patents of which would bring in a continual revenue stream, Grove is the only Intel guy of the four who did not make multibillionaire status.

In fact, his best mark was being a half billionaire plus. Not too shabby! After all, he was an employee, not an owner or inventor. Despite his failing in this one measurement (being a billionaire), which is the essence of this book, Grove is not a failure at all as a human being. He is one of my heroes. And, many of us in the tech field would trade our net worth for Grove's $half billion.

Grove's struggles help others who struggle

As I write this, Andy Grove has Parkinson's disease and he has prostate cancer and he has been fighting them for some time. Like John Huntsman Sr., a cancer survivor, who invested in hospitals and technology to eradicate cancer from the face of the earth in his lifetime, Andy Grove is very active in finding cures for diseases where the progress is not as rapid as the progress in the computer industry.

With Grove on board, Intel released its first product in 1969, the 3101 Schottky bipolar RAM and it also launched another important product, MOS static RAM. When IBM came along, Intel was already a huge financial success but not yet in the $ multi-billions in revenue.

In addition to these early innovations, the Company had developed the first commercially available dynamic RAM (i1103), the first EPROM (i1702), and the first commercially available microprocessor (i4004).

When P.D. Estridge's IBM team came to Intel in 1980 to buy lots of its 8088 microprocessors to power the yet to be developed IBM PC, Intel already was a big player in the chip market. Yet, none of the players were yet billionaires. Estridge knew Intel could supply all the microprocessors that IBM needed. Intel never slowed IBM down.

IBM internally was more difficult to deal with than outside companies. As noted above, Big Blue had created many small processors within its many research projects but it chose not to market any of them. And, so Intel is a company that needs to thank IBM for not being aggressive with its own technology stored in the IBM barn over the years, never to be used. Some liken the barn to the island of unwanted toys in that great Christmas classic.

Thus, Intel (not IBM) rightfully gets credit for creating the world's first commercial microprocessor chip in 1971. Despite this technical achievement, its founders still had to come to work every day. None were yet billionaires. It was not until the success of the personal computer (PC) that microprocessors became the Company's primary business. Now, my suggestion for Intel management and stockholders is to be nice. Say thank you to IBM!

It is commonly known through lawsuits and court records that during the 1990s, Intel invested heavily in new microprocessor designs fostering the rapid growth of the entire computer industry. During this period, the Company became the dominant supplier of microprocessors for PCs, and was known for its aggressive and what many saw as illegal tactics to defend its market position.

Intel v AMD and Microsoft

Intel was especially harsh when competing against AMD (Advanced Micro Devices), a fierce competitor that won a number of battles against the giant, if not in the marketplace, then in the courts. Additionally, Intel was also well known for duking it out with Bill Gates and company (Microsoft) for control over the direction of the PC industry.

IBM gave up lots of revenue

During this period, IBM, the originator of the IBM PC, and the Company that theoretically provided the blueprint for the IBM compatibles that followed—the same company that had created Intel's three multi-millionaires, forgot how to hold onto marketing opportunities. Great IBM sources for major revenue were thus never tapped.

In fact, IBM willingly gave $ billions of what would have been its own profits to both Intel and Microsoft. At the time, many in the IBM Company, such as my co-workers, would argue that the Company that gave us all our paychecks had ceased being able to market its way out of a paper bag. It seemed that accepting defeat in so many areas of the computer industry was a top management decision—not a default position.

Everybody from Microsoft and Intel who were associated with the founding, with the exception of Andy Grove, who became a half-billionaire, made it to billionaire status. I am talking about Gordon Moore, Robert Noyce, Arthur Rock, and almost Andy Grove. Robert Noyce passed away in 1990 at age 62 as a multi-billionaire and his ex-wife, who received

half his net worth at the time had enough funding to become
a major philanthropist for the best causes.

Talking about billionaires and millionaires, we have a whole
chapter on Microsoft coming up in this section. In this
coming chapter you will be surprised just how many at
Microsoft became multi-billionaires; multi-millionaires; and
millionaires. Let's say for now that it was enough employees
to make the IBM guys working with them quite jealous.

Before we discuss Microsoft on the software side, let's look
at IBM's movement in PC hardware technology. IBM does
not have to issue its own thank you to itself. This next part
of this chapter will help round out our knowledge of what
happened to IBM in the PC / Clone marketplace.

The PC Jr.

Over the years, IBM continued to enhance its 1981 PC line.
In 1983, for example, in addition to the PC XT, the
Company announced the "Peanut," a machine whose
formal name became the IBM PC JR. It's famous chicklet
and infrared capable keyboards live on in infamy in the
minds of many IBMers and industry watchers and high
school students of 1983. It was a favorite of high school
students who loved pointing their wireless infrared
keyboards at other students' units to disrupt their lab
sessions.

Yes, the young will try to have fun at all costs. I can still
recall students pointing their infrared keyboards at other
students' machines just for the sheer fun of it. Where did
that "S" come from on the unaware student's screen? ... You
can just imagine. The PC Jr was a nice new machine. It was
a junior sized version of the very successful Big PC which
had been launched just two years prior.

Some, like me, think that if it had been named the Peanut, instead of Jr., it would have been more successful. Few purchasers of technology like to buy the weaker model but they would sign up in droves as they have today for smaller models such as Apple iPads, iPhones, etc.

Peanut would have been a fun name but IBM at the time was not a fun company. Apple never chose to market an Apple PC Jr. and that is why it rules the small device marketplace today.

In 1983, IBM also announced the PC XT which added hard disk to the already familiar IBM PC unit. In 1984, IBM used the Intel 80286 chip to create the PC AT. In 1987, IBM introduced the PS/2 line with the Intel 80386 processor. By this time, many believe that IBM had lost all of its chances in the marketplace for PCs. The clones had already won. They simply out-marketed IBM. IBM was just not ready to admit defeat yet.

Here come the clones!

Since P.D. Estridge, the IBM PC project leader had subcontracted out just about the whole machine, it is well known that IBM did not invent anything that was inside the IBM PC, other than the keyboard and the little square thing that said IBM. Consequently, it did not take long for the engineers of the electronics world to reengineer the IBM PC and make it perform as well if not better than the IBM branded version.

IBM, worried about its mainframe sales and not being pulled apart by the Justice Department at the time, chose not to protect what would have been its major asset of all time. And, so, the IBM PC became the design point for many of today's PC industry billionaires.

I do not recall IBM ever taking on any clone manufacturer suggesting they had stolen IBM's secrets. IBM had opened its opportunities to others by building its PC from generally available industry piece parts. How could IBM dare to complain?

Look-alike clones began to appear as early as 1982 and IBM struggled trying to devise clever ways to fight this unwelcome invasion. Yet, IBM was still making its living on mainframes and so the Company's response could not be too forceful or the government would be back at the Company. IBM did not see the PC marketplace as bringing in $ billions in revenue ever so the fighting back that IBM seemed to produce was at best measured as a powder puff response.

IBM Announces Personal System/2 (PS/2)

The first real wave of defense from IBM came six years too late. In 1987, Big Blue funded and introduced the mostly closed architecture IBM Personal System/2, aka the PS/2. It was incompatible with the IBM PC and the clones. This was six years after IBM had already lost the marketplace on day one. IBM made one unfortunate mistake with this announcement. It believed its customers still loved the IBM Company. Those days had passed.

The PS/2 box was nicely built but nobody cared. It came with three major technical innovations for the times: 1. IBM invented super Microchannel bus, 2. Operating System/2 (OS/2), and (3.) the innovative 3.5" diskette. Too bad for IBM that nobody was looking for any of these.

The Clone vendors quickly came out with counterclaims that the PS/2's, no matter what they were called were no longer IBM compatible. The inference was that PC purchasers would have to seek out a clone vendor to maintain PC compatibility.

Over the years from 1981, IBM manufactured PCs had often been out-performed and out-priced by the clone crowd—especially a new startup called Compaq, created by Rod Canion. Canion is another billionaire with a need to thank IBM. Because nobody likes to buy underpowered units for more money, IBM suffered a drain in its customer set. Compaq units were much better in many ways than IBM's, and they cost substantially less.

Customers always preferred faster, less expensive machines. IBM's assurances of reliability, availability and good service were beaten by one factor—even though many clones were faster. That factor was that the clone PCs were more affordable to the masses and few could find differences between these duplicates and the real thing. Nobody was willing to spend an extra buck for IBM.

After PS/2 failed miserably, to answer the competitive charge, IBM introduced a number of new PC lines over the years, which were better and more price competitive than those completely assembled by IBM.

These include IBM's PC-bus ValuePoint line, IBM's own clone company Ambra; the IBM Aptiva and the NetVista PCs. These were always too little too late ventures into a marketplace that the clones controlled after they recognized that IBM was an impotent player in their market space.

IBM should have admitted defeat and like HP acquired a big clone company such as Compaq. IBM was too arrogant to consider this as an option. And so, as we all know IBM is not in the PC business in any way, today

As a death blow to IBM as a leader in PCs, the clone consortium was very tough on IBM. This group of successful entrepreneurs, clones companies, aka IBM compatible manufacturers announced that IBM was no longer compatible with its PS/2. The clones plus Microsoft and Intel began to call the shots in an industry that IBM had created. Poor IBM did nothing in response.

IBM did not know what hit them. There was no lingering industry respect for old Big Blue. IBM had become far too easy to take out. Maybe there is a secret IBM billionaire out there someplace that benefitted from the demise of the IBM PC dynasty. If so, I do not know their name. Regardless, the IBM PC dynasty is gone. It was little more than a flash in the pan and then; poof—gone! IBM blew it but then again in the beginning when plans were made, IBM seemed quite happy with just 250,000 units in five years.

The clone manufacturers, plus Intel, and Microsoft, and the many individuals within their companies who became millionaires, multi-millionaires, billionaires, and multi-billionaires need to give IBM a hearty "Thank You, IBM," as it is only fair. If IBM were astute in its marketing and if it protected itself in its product's early design plans, nobody would have had a chance. Nobody would need to thank IBM. IBM would be the most successful computer company of all time. Right now, IBM is struggling to compete and survive.

Clones redefined the PC marketplace

In August 1981 in Boca Raton Florida, IBM created the PC marketplace. After IBM created the marketplace, as a surprise to many, with its financial muscle, it chose not to dominate it. In 1987 with the introduction of microchannel PS/2 units, the Company tried to get back the momentum that it had given away but it could not. The clones already owned the marketplace. IBM was becoming more and more of a bit player in a marketplace that it once was predestined to dominate.

When the 80286 processor was announced, the clones soon began to be known as x86 boxes, rather than IBM compatibles. Eventually, IBM along with clone desktops and laptops formed their own subindustry and larger x86 units were packaged in more powerful frames with more cache and more power performance extensions. These became known as x86 servers. IBM had no believable response.

Clone originated x86 Desktops and laptops were in one subindustry, while x86 servers were in another. Somehow, though IBM had its RISC processor RT/PC, and its System/36 and Series/1 product lines in place early on, and it had an in-place marketing team to get IBM all the business, it chose to give it away by supporting Wintel machines instead of its own.

Chapter 50 Appendix

The PC Story Is a Story of IBM at Its Worst

PC should have been Big Blue's crowning achievement

The PC industry is worth well over $1 trillion and every dollar should be IBM's. IBM had it all. IBM created the industry. IBM had the product. IBM had the licensing power. IBM could have called all the shots. Unfortunately IBM saw its leadership in the PC marketplace as a burden.

Even when President Reagan ended antitrust action v IBM in 1982, the IBM Company still permitted itself to be taken for a ride. For six years from 1981, IBM did not even try to regain its leadership. I cannot think of any single mistake that any other company has ever made that is as significant as this huge IBM blunder.

System/360 was seen as Chairman Thomas Watson Jr.'s $5 billion gamble when he used $4billion in cash and borrowed another $billion to be able to launch the most successful venture in IBM history. If this went south IBM would have been out of business. IBM won big time because it chose to win by fighting for its rights.

In 1981, IBM was 100% unaware that its decisions about its PC launch and how it ran its PC business, would affect its ability to reach the $1 trillion threshold by 2015. The 2015 market value of PC endeavors is at least $1 trillion. IBM, when it announced its PC did not even view it as a money-maker. How could IBM have been so wrong?

Here's how: IBM haphazardly disregarded all PC opportunities and was so benevolent to its partners (competitors) that it took itself completely out of the future earnings picture.

I set this Chapter Appendix up to show the negative side of the IBM PC story because it is as much a part of the whole story as anything else. Yet, I wanted to tell the good part of the story first as we did in the main chapter. As a one-time loyal IBM employee, I sure wish I did not have to write the rest of this story.

The IBM PC story is emblematic of the Company's penchant to create billionaires from regular technology entrepreneurs, when Big Blue, instead, should have been bringing home the bacon for its stockholders. Now, for a while at least, I have chosen to take off the gloves. Forgive me IBM, and please continue to send the pension checks to all of us who did our jobs for the betterment of the company.

Don't get mad at me for calling it as I see it. I am about to say a few things about the outright disgust I feel—having been an IBM employee—and still being an IBM stockholder. It was really tough for me to watch my company fritter away so many different huge opportunities.

The PC was undoubtedly the biggest bungle for sure and the biggest loss for IBM stockholders. But, there were many others. All of these are noted in this book. The only one who ever paid the price for mismanagement is John Akers, and he in many ways was a victim, like the rest of us. John Opel messed up more of IBM than we will ever know.

The blind visionaries

In trying to understand how IBM's demise in the PC industry could ever happen, it helps to note that IBM's marketing visionaries had predicted that there would be a mere 275,000 PCs sold in the first five years of its PC's existence. All were expected to be IBM PCs as IBM had a hard-coded basic output input system (BIOS) that the engineers had attested could not be copied or emulated. IBM felt safe from its competition.

In other sections I have already noted that the forecast was really just 55,000 units per year. Unfortunately with such a paltry forecast, IBM was overwhelmed with the reality of the first-day orders.

The real customer response to the announcement was overwhelming. The IBM Archives offer this notion about the demand. Please note the last part of this in which the New York Times offers its thoughts on IBM's reaction:

> One dealer had 22 customers come in and put down $1,000 deposits on the machines for which he could not promise a delivery date. By the end of 1982, qualified retail outfits were signing on to sell the new machine at the rate of one-a-day as sales actually hit a system-a-minute every business day. Newsweek magazine called it "IBM's roaring success," and the New York Times said, "The speed and extent to which IBM has been successful has surprised many people, including IBM itself."

Hah! IBM was surprised! However, IBM was not doing its job if it was surprised. What did IBM do to come up with its poor forecast? IBM predicted 55,000 units per year. What were they thinking? Their first order was for 250,000 on the first day.

There are billions of PCs today. Would 55,000 a year have been your forecast? Would it have been the forecast of anybody who understood the notion of marketing to consumers and the marketing precepts of product, price, promotion, and place? If I told you that a PC could do everything that a word processor could do and word processors cost about $10,000.00, and a fully configured PC was half that and could do more, would that help in understanding the value of this industry? It gets worse trying to justify this forecast.

In 1981, right before the PC came out, there were more than one million 3270-type IBM terminals installed on customer premises. There were also at least 500,000 5250-type terminals used by System/34 and System/38 small business systems installed on customer premises. What if you knew that those companies with such terminals would be happy to trade them in for personal computers? Would you think 55,000 was a good forecast?

Finally, what if you knew that ComputerLand, one of the industry's largest PC retailers at the time were ready to order 250,000 PCs on the first day? Would you wonder if IBM had even asked ComputerLand what its order plans might be before IBM put its 55,000 forecast in stone?

IBM would not be doing reparations if only its forecasting were bad. IBM made bigger mistakes than the forecast along the way with its PC product. What company ever invented a product and a marketplace and permitted others to take control of the market and finally force the inventor out of the business? Other than IBM, I know of none. IBM was completely forced out of the PC business and made to look like the worst company from which to buy a PC. I saw it happen.

Regular human beings who have never worked for IBM or watched IBM in action would ask: "How could companies come from no place to beat IBM?" "With all of IBM's lawyers and industry watchers, why did IBM not see any of this coming?" "How could it take six years and a full five-year IBM product development cycle to mount a counterattack to the theft of innovation and product that had occurred?"

Could IBM management have made better decisions?

Is it possible that *unqualified management* is the only possible answer? No other answer other than ineptness or incompetence can explain all of IBM's decisions away. Nothing else makes good sense? If IBM corporate management cared about the PC marketplace, some executive in charge of such a huge bungling, would have been fired.

It was flagrant mismanagement regardless of IBM's situation with the Justice Department lawsuit or its lack of familiarity with consumer products. Who did IBM hire to save its neck in the first six months as it was losing the industry already? Answer: Nobody!

Big Blue first needed a CEO to spell out directives to protect company assets so that such a theft could never occur. Secondly, when it somehow got away from IBM, IBM needed a CEO to get rid of the bureaucracy in IBM and do whatever was necessary to take this marketplace back without having to develop new products over a five to six-year cycle.

IBM could have learned from Intel. The only time Intel ever lost ground in its history from my recollection was when it changed from x86 to Itanium. Intel admitted its mistake quickly and went back to x86 Xeons where the company kept making money. It permitted Itanium to fritter away by itself. When you are being held under water, it is an inappropriate action to hold onto a rock on the bottom for security.

Why could IBM, with all its money, not have reacted to protect itself? The answer: *Only the mainframe was on IBM managers' minds.* Even if that is so, it is incompetent to be in a marketplace and not fight for the business because you have other products to sell to your other customers.

Did the piece parts supply channel care what IBM thought?

As we all know, several hundred million PCs are sold each year, and in the early days, as clone companies came from nowhere to compete, IBM seemed to be the only company that could not ship a PC box within a reasonable period of time. Did the startup clone companies have better forecasting tools than IBM, a company that once sold meat scales? IBM's suppliers happened to be the same suppliers that sold to the clone manufacturers. Did IBM have no control of its channel? Why would IBM not contract its PC out to these available channels to protect its marketplace and intellectual property? IBM arrogance believed the company could not lose and never felt it would need any help.

As an IBM employee and an early IBM PC customer, it took me over a year to get my own first-day order machine from the IBM Company bureaucracy. I knew that IBM was compelled by government agreements to time stamp every order and ship each system in the sequence of the time stamp. Things were bad on deliveries and seemed never to get better.

Missing the forecast by a hundred-fold margin, did not help what then appeared to be a clueless IBM to ever gain the manufacturing / assembly facilities or outsourcing vendors necessary to bring deliveries to a reasonable level--ever.

Last words on the Justice v IBM lawsuit

For those who thought the Justice v IBM suit was all bull... and would never go against IBM, how would you have reacted to the big scare IBM got on January 8, 1982? Chilling news came forth for those watching the Reagan Administration's Justice Department. On this day, The American Telephone and Telegraph Company settled its Justice Department's antitrust lawsuit. Some still can't believe AT&T did this.

The Company agreed to give up the 22 Bell System companies that provided most of the nation's local telephone service at the time. In other words, The Department of Justice broke AT&T up into twenty-three little companies. That was exactly what kept Frank Cary up at night. What would the Justice Department do to IBM? Cary's fear was always a broken-up IBM.

Thankfully for IBM there was minimal time separating both decisions. IBM sweating was soon abated. The Company got word on this landmark antitrust day that the Justice Department had made a determination in the IBM case. Not much information was released other than that Justice had dropped its marathon case against Big Blue. The date was January 8, 1982—less than five months from August 12, 1981, when IBM announced its PC line.

One watching the events that day would have believed that IBM would break out the champagne and pull out all the stops to protect this new PC industry. By January 8, 1982, the Company knew or should have known that the PC industry had far greater long-term potential than the mainframe industry. True to form instead of protecting its interests and leading an all-fronts assault to capture whatever mindshare it had lost, IBM did nothing. Few analysts could understand why IBM chose to remain such an easy target for those preying on this major opportunity business.

The Justice Department had sought to break up the IBM Company because according to them, IBM dominated the computer industry. On January 8, 1982, The Reagan Justice Department said the suit was "without merit and should be dismissed."

This suit had cost IBM tons of money and it affected IBM's key planning and its ability to compete and maintain its strengths. It was a 13-year investigation that went no-place. IBM was exonerated.

The Company had retained 200 attorneys at one point. There was no need for the lawsuit when it was brought. The mere engagement in the lawsuit had already tamed "wild duck" IBM. The purpose of the lawsuit fizzled as the computing landscape shifted from mainframes to minicomputers and then to personal computers. The government abandoned its tainted effort entirely in 1982, as clones of the IBM PC were gearing up to erode Big Blue's dominance in its newest frontier. .

For those who like the facts, and facts alone, as you will see, this suit was a major burden on IBM. It is a major wonder that the Company IBM was able to pay expenses for this suit and maintain a healthy profit picture during these years. The Justice Department demanded attention from IBM and the stakes were high and they got the attention from everybody in the corporation.

The case against IBM -- U.S. v. IBM had been filed by the Justice Department way back on January 17, 1969. IBM's dominant market share in mainframes in the mid-1960s had first led to antitrust inquiries by Justice. This was followed by the formal complaint in the United States District Court for the Southern District of New York. The lawsuit charged that IBM monopolized the mainframe market for computers and noted this was a violation of Section 2 of the Sherman Act.

The suit made a number of allegations claiming that IBM eliminated new competitors offering services and peripherals by maintaining a single price policy for its machines, software and support services. In other words, everything was bundled together. The suit further alleged that IBM used such bundling to convince universities and other educational institutions to select IBM computers v competing brands. Though it hurt IBM's business, it is understandable that IBM unbundled on June 23, 1960, on my first day of work with the company.

The U.S. also alleged that IBM blocked competition in certain instances by prematurely announcing computers at unrealistically low prices and tight delivery deadlines, specifically noting the System/360, which IBM claimed could do more than competing models and would be introduced quickly, was not ready to ship and some models never shipped. Justice alleged that IBM took these "predatory" actions knowingly to block its competitors from the market when its own products were away years from completion.

After years of preparation, on May 19, 1975 the Federal Government's antitrust suit against IBM finally went to trial. Along with thousands of hours of testimony by 950 witnesses with 87 in court and the remainder via deposition and the submission of tens of thousands of exhibits, on

January 8, 1982 the anti-trust case was abruptly withdrawn on the grounds that the case was "without merit."

It is a good thing IBM was in the information processing industry as there were over 30,000,000 pages of documents generated in the course of this anti-trust case. It was a major burden for IBM for sure.

Despite being off the hook and with a pro-business Republican Administration getting the reins on the economy, IBM still was fearful of the watchful eye of the Justice Department. I joined IBM mid-1969 and IBM was very concerned about refraining from any action that would give the appearance that its marketing team was behaving in a monopolistic fashion. This was long after IBM had relinquished its hold on the market. IBM had lots of competition in 1970. In my time with IBM, it was a big company but there was competition galore and we had to treat the competition with far more respect than they gave us or else, IBM would come down on us.

Many who worked with me in the '80s and early '90s saw that the company would routinely fall victim to a "pricing death strategy"--a reluctance to lower prices below cost, even on products that weren't selling--to avoid what the government would call predatory pricing. IBM's PC prices were way too high and IBM never addressed this major fault. It was easy for Clones to compete against IBM as IBM did not protect its assets or its industry might, and its prices were often twice as much for half as fast.

As we have discussed in the Opel and Akers chapters, by the mid-'80s, the IBM Company was in bad shape. The antitrust troubles, combined with ill-timed product failures, selling the rental base, and quickly giving up on products that would have been successful, pinched revenues to the point of IBM wishing it could cry uncle. The Company in the Akers' years began a nearly decade-long financial slide. IBM was in no way a monopoly during this period. Until Lou Gerstner came in 1993, the sting of the Justice lawsuit had affected Big Blue for far too long after the suit had gone away.

IBM's PC venture upset its regular high value customers

IBM bungled the entire way it brought out its PC. It forgot, for example that it already had a lot of customers. These customers liked IBM products and they liked how IBM did business. None of this mattered to IBM when the PC supply was too tight to manage properly. IBM made the situation even worse than it was with gestapo-like rules for purchasing PCs.

The hundreds of thousands of existing large systems and mid-range systems customers were not permitted to buy PCs from their sales representative from the IBM Branch Office. They could buy coding pads and programming templates and other items costing a dollar or less locally from their personal sales person with simply a phone order and a follow-up letter; but mother IBM decided that if IBM's direct sales customers wanted a PC, they would have to walk into a computer store since the PC was not intended for businesses.

Eventually mainframe IBM, not wanting a police role during its leadership role in the PC industry, had a lot to lose by upsetting any of its largest customers. The favored mainframe part of IBM got the rules changed for its largest customers. They were permitted to buy directly from their assigned sales representatives.

Can you imagine how incensed IBM's local customers became at their representatives over this PC debacle? IBM overplayed its game. It lost. If there were another wrong thing the IBM from back then could do, it would think of it and do it.

Poor IBM response

I worked as a Systems Engineer in an IBM Branch Office during this time. At most, I had fifty good IBM GSD customers assigned to me for technical support and help with installing IBM systems to run their businesses. I worked with many IBM Marketing Representatives (AKA salesmen) but probably about three or four of these "owned" the particular IBM clients that I supported. Most were larger System/3 and then System/38 clients at the time. Their systems cost between $100,000 and $1,000,000.

Most of my clients were using IBM 3270 terminals or IBM 5250 terminals with their systems. These devices were dumb terminals. They received all of their intelligence from the system to which they were attached.

When the IBM PC was announced and terminal emulation (the PC software pretended to be a 3270 or 5250) was promised, many of my clients wanted to abandon their dumb terminals and place intelligent desktop units (PCs) in their organizations for their knowledge workers, customer service personnel, and order takers. With emulation, the PC could be both a productivity workstation and could also serve as a terminal to the IT system.

IBM dug in and informed us that we could not sell or deliver PCs to these clients even if they were to use the PC only as a terminal to their larger systems. Customers no longer wanted to buy terminals once they saw the PC.

IBM permitted us to ship terminals but not PCs to our customers. Only IBM could take a bad situation and make it worse. Big IBM expected and in fact wanted all of its customers to continue to buy terminals. Customers did not like IBM's rules and because of all the rules it was not long for customers to develop a distaste for IBM and all IBM products.

IBM was not ready to lose its terminal business to its PC business. Quite frankly, IBM in many cases at the time charged more for its terminals than it did for its PC units. IBM customers recognized this and began to think that they should not even give their system business to such a company.

IBM sold hundreds of thousands of terminals per year, yet it forecast just 55,000 PC units per year for what my customers saw as a more intelligent terminal. Clearly whoever was giving advice to top IBM managers did not understand the IBM GSD-heritage (small business computers) marketplace. I suspect they understood little about anything. IBM mainframe customers for a time were similarly frustrated by poor IBM PC customer policies.

Some very large IBM customers could buy PCs from IBM

Think about this for a while. My clients bought systems that approached a million dollars per system with all devices included. Across the hall in my office, the big systems guys operated. They sold traditional mainframes. Scranton PA was a small office but at one time its gross revenue was about $150 million per year.

The large system (mainframe) customer base for IBM in the US also wanted PCs as intelligent workstations. IBM wanted to continue to sell them terminals. The largest of IBM customers refused to go to computer stores for their intelligent workstations and so IBM conceded to them the opportunity to purchase PCs directly from IBM Branch Offices.

Too bad for our office's large systems marketing representatives. Their large systems customers in Scranton PA were not large enough. Just like my midrange customer set, the local mainframe folks got the same shabby treatment from IBM. They learned all about IBM PC clones at the computer stores since IBM would not ship a PC to any of them. They were not big enough customers. How would you feel?

Who would have ever set something up that not only prevented IBM from becoming the only PC vendor of all time but also encouraged its eternally loyal customers to jump ship to other systems?

I do not know Virginia, but, yes, it happened for sure. I saw it and could not believe it. And I was merely an IBM Systems Engineer listening to the banter and the chatter in an IBM Branch Office where I was employed. IBM's local managers were powerless. It was unbelievable then. It seems even more unbelievable now.

Customer loyalty works until the Company upsets the customer.

So, what happened? In frustration, IBM's loyal customers who never had bought any other computer or part from any other vendor but IBM went looking for a PC from whoever would sell them one. Not only did many companies only buy IBM, most of these loyal customers had never used anything other than IBM for their computing needs. They even bought small items such as coding pads from us. Think of the customer loyalty IBM gave away by chasing its customers to experience other computer vendors with clones.

Not understanding the tremendous irritation that it was causing its customers, IBM executives compounded the problem with more rules. IBM customers got sick of dealing with IBM. Even good marketing reps could not explain away this shoddy treatment.

IBM executives decreed that these loyal customers, trained by none other than Thomas Watson Sr. to buy from IBM Branch Offices, and only IBM Branch Offices would not be permitted to buy PCs directly from these IBM Branch Offices in the fashion in which they purchased all their other IBM gear, including typewriters. Watson would not have approved.

This IBM dictate was very disruptive and very annoying to customers. Unfortunately for IBM, its customers got accustomed to it. IBM trained its loyal customers to shop for products that IBM eventually could readily ship.

It not only hurt IBM PC sales, it made customers want to buy everything computer related from somebody other than IBM with a real passion. Because of the PC debacle and the trauma and irritation it caused loyal customers, from that point on, IBM's direct sales force had to work much harder for all of its sales. At the time, an arrogant IBM believed that no knowledgeable customer would want to buy any computer gear that was not IBM.

They learned quickly how wrong they were. IBM had a lot of employees, such as yours truly, who over the years gained a lot of IBM stock; but none of whom I was aware were on the list of US millionaires. We might have become millionaires and more stockholders might have become millionaires if the Company had played the game of business well. IBM was the greatest technology company ever. It simply forgot how to win and keep the business.

Computer stores sold the IBM logo for white box clone machines

The PC machine that IBM clients got, had very little IBM in it. IBM did nothing to stop this. IBM had nothing to ship. Sometimes the only part that was IBM on a customer PC was the small logo on the front that the clone builders could purchase from IBM as a piece part. The IBM PC logos were easier to get than IBM PCs. IBM lost billions through its carelessness with its customers and its sloppiness in dealing with its "independent" retail outlets.

The clone industry was an industry waiting to happen thanks to IBM's mishandling of every aspect of its PC business, as well as its vaunted word processing business. Can you believe that IBM was once the premiere word processing company in existence, but that opportunity too was frittered away by poor marketing decisions? IBM had even invented the term word processing. Now IBM sells no word processing products at all. Until 2013, Word Pro was included in the Lotus SmartSuite but SmartSuite was soon discontinued.

PCs kept getting bigger and more powerful

As time went by, IBM lost more and more sales. Compaq and the other clones began to rule the PC industry. IBM made some attempts to compete against the real PC server vendors of the day. No matter what it did, however, it could not come up with a good enough plan.

Though all x86 servers are very powerful, IBM felt it could create branded PC servers better than the clone makers. So, Big Blue decided that it would put some special stuff from its mainframe labs into the chassis of larger servers to give them some extra zip. Regardless of what IBM did, "IBM" was no longer the name that called for PC (X86) servers. HP, Dell, or Compaq (pre-merger) would be their best bet and they knew it. IBM went from the best to the worst in PCs almost overnight.

Chapter 51

Compaq Beats IBM BIOS to Become Top PC Company

Compaq had a better idea

In 1982, not too long after the August introduction of the PC, Rod Canion, Jim Harris & Bill Murto, who were senior managers at Texas Instruments, left the Company to found Compaq Computer. Their idea was to make a better PC than the IBM PC and cash in on the promise of the PC revolution. This is one of the things which future billionaires were inclined to do in the early 1980's.

Compaq designers proceeded to re-engineer IBM's basic input output system (BIOS) without copying it. Nobody wanted to go to jail just for being successful. By late 1982, they had reverse engineered the code functions and had written new BIOS programs without copyright infringement. Though it was not a code copy, the Compaq BIOS performed the same functions in the same way as the IBM PC. Compaq had built a perfect IBM clone.

BIOS in essence provides a gateway for machine setup to load the rest of the hardware functions of the system. In some ways it helps users set up the hardware personality of the machine. You could not run an original IBM PC without an accurate BIOS.

IBM's mistakes in protecting its PC rights through avenues other than copyright were about to come back to haunt them big time. Compaq did such a good job that IBM engineers did not challenge them. IBM had banked that nobody would have enough resources to accomplish a reengineering of BIOS, and the IBM Company was ready to prosecute copycats. Once Compaq perfected the machine BIOS, IBM's secrets no longer mattered.

BIOS goes big time in its own industry!

Compaq by necessity for its own clone PC line created a BIOS version better than IBM's and in so doing proved it could be done. After Compaq, BIOS became a big industry unto itself.

There was another young company during this time which was about to profit from Compaq's success and IBM's mistakes. Phoenix Technologies, founded in 1979 by Neil Colvin, developed the first commercial BIOS in 1983. Compaq did such a good job of reverse engineering IBM's BIOS, this little company decided that they could make a business out of BIOS.

After this, any company wishing to clone the IBM PC could simply purchase Phoenix BIOS. Prior to Phoenix, the BIOS had been the only part of the PC that was not already available off the shelf. Once Phoenix got in the act, BIOS also became a shelf item.

With an Intel 8088 processor, a bunch of readily available piece parts, and with MS-DOS readily available from Microsoft, anybody could have themselves an IBM look-alike. Phoenix became very successful in a very short time.

By 1989, BIOS for clone PCs had become a big business. Microid Research, Inc. (MR.BIOS), Award Software,

(Award BIOS), and American Megatrends (AMI BIOS) were all players in this new huge industry. Twenty years ago, American Megatrends boasted well over 100,000,000 PCs. My buddy Al Komorek decided to make PCs and he used American Megatrends first and then Award, and finally he came back to Phoenix Technologies with Award in its stable.

Phoenix and Award Software merged in 1989 and continue to operate under the Phoenix Technologies name. The combined company now rules the BIOS world. Phoenix products are incorporated into over 125 million computing devices every year, making them the worldwide market share leader.

Phoenix has over 1300 employees, with revenue eclipsing $500 million. None of these companies would have been possible without the graciousness of IBM in sharing its secrets, and not protecting its assets. IBM clearly gifted these startups with the tools necessary to compete against Big Blue itself. Even before IBM exited the PC business, Big Blue stopped making its own BIOS. Yes, even IBM was buying its BIOS, as the "IBM PC" had long escaped its proprietary control.

Compaq's meteoric rise

Compaq (a take-off on the words compact and portable) started their product set with the first IBM compatible portable computer. It was an immediate success. It did everything the IBM PC did, and it was faster and it was portable.

They shipped their first computer in January, 1983, just 16 months after IBM had introduced the original PC. By the end of 1983, in its first year of operation, Compaq sold over

$110 Million worth of PC clones, the greatest first year sales in the history of American business.

One year later, Compaq would clone the PC XT, IBM's latest and greatest at the time, again in its portable form. At the same time, IBM was also getting whacked by Phoenix Technologies as it successfully created PC XT BIOS for the other clone makers. For just three pounds more than the Compaq Portable, the Compaq Plus sported a hefty 10 MB Winchester style hard disk drive. (IBM invented the Winchester Drive in 1974.)

If Compaq did not perfectly emulate an IBM PC XT, it seemed that nobody could tell the difference. Many industry experts observed that Compaq was a better engineered system than IBM's, which it was emulating. This certainly did not help IBM sales, but with PC delivery being its biggest perceived problem, IBM still had not gotten the complete marketing message.

Compaq begins to lead the PC marketplace

Compaq was so successful, the Company decided to beat IBM at its own game. It was clear that when Intel offered a new chip, or Microsoft offered a new operating system version, that new products would be forthcoming from IBM.

In August, 1986, however, when Intel released its 80386 processor, this was not the case. Though it was expected that IBM would soon introduce a new line based on the 80386, IBM was busy developing its proprietary micro channel, PS/2 systems and Big Blue missed the boat for including this new microprocessor into its standard machine offerings. Compaq was at the dock and boarded the technology boat long before IBM arrived.

Compaq aimed right and beat IBM to market with the first Intel 386 machine in an IBM compatible PC. They took the lead in 1986 with the introduction of their new Deskpro 386. It was a bitter pill to swallow for IBM. IBM dominance in the market it had created just five years prior was over. COMPAQ beating IBM to market was the death knell. IBM dominance would never return.

By 1996, COMPAQ owned 83% of the personal computer marketplace. They had become so successful, that in 1998, they had become big enough, and powerful enough to buy another big company, IBM's old minicomputer nemesis, Digital Computer Company (DEC).

With this, Compaq became the third largest computer company in the world, behind IBM and Hewlett-Packard. For more on COMPAQ, check out Hewlett Packard in Chapter 20. HP bought COMPAQ in September 2001.

The Compaq approach before the HP takeover

Unlike IBM and many of the other clone manufacturers of the day, Rod Canion's COMPAQ saw the hazards of offering computers both directly from the Company as well as through dealers. He decided the path to success lay in selling only through dealers, thereby avoiding the headaches of competing with his own channel market.

During the Company's first year in business, Compaq shipped more than 53,000 PCs and set its first of many U.S. business records with revenue topping $111 million. Compaq was off and running-at a dead sprint.

Based on Canion's philosophy of advancing existing technology while offering more power and more features, Compaq continued to grow and prosper, becoming the youngest company ever to join the Fortune 500-just five years after it was founded.

Compaq killed IBM as incompatible

In 1987, then 42-year-old Rod Canion and Compaq faced a major potential roadblock when IBM introduced its new line of PS/2 computers. Big Blue finally announced its Intel 80386-based machine but that was not what the big hoopla was about. I

Canion made a big deal about IBM abandoning the industry standard MS-DOS. The new PCs were to run on IBM's newly created OS/2 operating system, which when released was buggy, slow, and did not work as well as IBM had promised.

Originally, the industry pundits claimed the PS/2 was a "clone crusher" that would run Compaq and all other clone makers out of business. But they were all wrong. Compaq emerged as the leader and IBM lost a lot of PR and a lot of business in that battle. Canion was masterful in protecting the compatibility of his units. He made IBM look like the piker.

Compaq had already established a reputation for providing superior quality, speed and features at competitive prices. Compaq actually became the industry's technological leader, surpassing IBM. It was the # 1 PC Company in the world.

Compaq pioneered every new class of personal computer, introducing the first 386 machine, the first 20MHz, 25MHz, and 386SX-based systems. After IBM missed its chance in 1986, COMPAQ was always there each time Intel came out with a new microprocessor.

In 2001, HP and Compaq merged into what became the # 1 computer company in the world beating out IBM for the # 1 spot.

I would suspect if IBM's John Opel had a chance to remake his decisions regarding Compaq and the clones, knowing that Compaq would one day, along with HP, eclipse Big Blue's top spot in the computer industry, they may have been a lot different.

Chapter 52

Gateway Computer Company – 2000

Cows and Computers

It seems that with all these PC / technology upstarts, there is a cool story behind their success. Gateway's is a story of cows. The Company was founded by two great-great-grandchildren of George Waitt. Their names were Norm Jr, after his dad, and Ted Waitt.

Figure 52-1 Cows on a Barge

As the story goes, way back in the 1800s, George Waitt had some success with cattle. By hanging around the Missouri River, watching the cattle barges go to the stockyards, George sometimes was favored with good fortune. The Waitt legend suggests that George built his first herd from cattle who chose not to complete the trip.

Seems like there were always a few cattle that jumped off
the barges right into the Missouri, rather than tempt the fate
which was sure to be theirs at their final destination.
George's fishing pole caught some big "fish."

Cattle roots

The Waitts were thus in the cattle business, and became a
lot more than just a little successful. George's cattle business
passed to the offspring in due course. Eventually, Norm Sr.,
who was Norm Jr., and Ted's dad, as well as George's
great-grandson took his turn with the cattle business. He
created one of the largest cattle farms in the Midwest.

So, Ted and Norm Jr. did not come from anything close to a
wanting family. Instead, they are descended from one of the
greatest successful scrappers of all time—George Waitt.
Can't you see George trying to coax those cows off the
barge from a distance?

Ted and Norm Jr. did not want to be cattlemen. Instead,
they took a liking to computers. In 1985, they paired up to
form the "Gateway 2000" company. The Company began in
their dad's office, with 22 year old Ted becoming the
engineer president, and Norm Jr. becoming the businessman
vice-president. The boys would joke with their dad about
how much easier computers were to ship than cattle... and
with no mess.

The younger generation: from cattle to computers

Ted Waitt had gotten his tremendous marketing insight after
his college days, during a 9 month stint at a retail computer
store in Des Moines. In many ways, he formed his vision
and marketing plan based on his observations of retail action
during this brief period. In a nutshell at age 22, Ted Waitt

dropped out of college, quit this retail job nine months later and returned home to launch a personal computer business, dragging jus brother Norm Jr. with him.

Ted and Norm Jr., together with their one employee, Mike Hammond, started by selling parts for the TI Professional computer, and with the help of grandma's $10,000 investment, they were soon able to build complete systems. By year-end, 1985, they had sold 50 systems, had earned of $100,000 in revenue, and they were off. By the end of 1986, they had made their first $ million, and by 1992, their annual sales were in the $billions.

Ted, the engineer president became the marketer for Gateway. Many may remember the early Gateway ads. The campaign was kicked off in 1988 by Ted, who put his own national exposure ads together. The two-page ads highlighted the family cattle farm, and offered "Computers from Iowa?"

Though this may not have been what was expected for a computer firm, it got attention, though at first in a comical way. Eventually the Company got some serious attention and sales went through the roof. You may recall seeing the Gateway Computer shipping boxes with the Company's famous cow spots logo.

In the early 1990s, Norm Wait Jr. stepped down as an officer of the Company to pursue other interests. Ted Wait became the CEO. Though Ted was the "engineer" part of the businessman / engineer combination of 1985, he really became the marketeer and his buddy Mike Hammond became the technical guy.

Ted Waitt's retail observations

In the retail business, as Waitt observed, sales clerks waited on customers in order to get sales. Occasionally, however, a prospect for a computer would call the store and speak with a sales technician in the back room. These conversations often resulted in sales of $3,000 units. Though the retail store considered these gravy and not a focus item, Ted Waitt did not see it this way.

In his own words: "I was fascinated to see that if you knew what you were doing, you could sell a $3,000 computer system over the phone... Everybody seemed to be looking at those sales as just gravy." He built his business on the notion that people will buy computers from their home or business without having to visit a retail store. He was right!

While at the retail store, Waitt also studied why people bought PCs in the first place. From this, he developed his guiding notion of the "value equation" Waitt explained his value equation in these words: "The PC business is not about price, it's about value, or what you can give the customer for his or her money." Waitt observed that PC sales clerks would often try to sell low-cost, bare bones PCs that could do little and with which nobody would be happy after the sale.

Or they would stuff every bell and whistle in a machine, which made it expensive, and less affordable and thus, less desirable. From these observations, Waitt believed he had the right solution - a middle ground approach, not too little, and not too much. He explained this as, "not to add technology for the sake of adding technology, but to go after it when it offers the best value for consumers."

Waitt also believed that keeping prices affordable was especially important. From his retail experience and observations, he was convinced that the direct model would be quite successful. Waitt dreamed of a major national business which could be launched with minimal effort. It would be a business in which the customer never saw the inventory of products. Therefore the business would not need much inventory.

The startup cost would be quite low. Moreover, there would be no showroom at all required, and the facility could be located anywhere, since nobody would see it. For example, it could even be in the family farmhouse. And so it was!

Gateway: honesty and good-naturedness

Good-old mid-western honesty and good-naturedness has helped Gateway along its bounteous ride to the top. The home-spun attitude from the start has been, and if the Waitts had their say, would always have been, about treating consumers the way you would like to be treated yourself.

And that includes everything from giving customers honest advice, great products and services, and the overall best value, all wrapped up in a package, which gives a sense of genuinely caring about a customer's happiness. Gateway always called this "humanizing the digital revolution." They followed the principle of: "keep it personal, make it simple,"

During Gateway's early years, Ted Waitt lived on $200 per week salary and reportedly was often broke by the time the bars closed on Saturday night. When Gateway finally went public in December 1993, just before Ted's 31st birthday, he and Norm became multimillionaires overnight. Norm Waitt, Jr. had remained a silent partner after he had stepped down as vice president of the Company in March 1991.

In these formative years, the natural next step was to take the Company public, which they did in December, 1993, just eight months after selling their one millionth computer. Gateway was pushing the $10 billion threshold in 1999, which at the time was somewhat less than half the size of Dell. They were shipping about 4 million systems per year.

Despite their huge success, there was always a little levity in the way the Company conducted its business. You may have noticed that when you buy a Gateway computer, it comes in a box painted to look like a dairy cow: white with black spots.

With 1300 employees, including 100 sales folks, and 200 technicians to handle the questions, by 1992, the Company was shipping 2000 computers per day. Unlike Michael Dell, who, at the time was a billionaire with about 15% of Dell's equity, The Waitt boys for the longest time owned the whole company. They became exceptionally rich almost overnight, however, when they went public, it was their day in the sun.

As part of their 1993 initial public offering, Ted Waitt kept 50 percent of the business, while Norm Waitt, Jr. had 35 percent. Ted sold the remaining 15 percent, or 10.9 million shares and raised more than $150 million. Not a bad night's work.

A lesson for IBM from Gateway!

Could IBM learn anything from Gateway? A few cows and a few friendly faces and some attempts to be interesting and lovable would help. It would also help if somehow IBM were able to understand Ted Waitt's original way of attracting and keeping customers.

Though there was no way that IBM could ever attract Ted Waitt into the fold, when there was time to win the PC war, once upon a time, there was a rumor. On the day before New Year's Eve, 1997, an "insider" at the IBM PC Company, who did not want to be identified, jested about rumors that Big Blue was considering acquiring the Gateway 2000 Company. It could have saved both organizations.

For IBM to not have made that happen, they missed a great opportunity for a rebound. It was not a product line that IBM lacked; it was motivation, innovation and marketing know-how. Gateway could have fit the bill.

All of a sudden, the IBM names would have become Gateway names. That would have been positive. Although IBM along the way, when it was big into disk drives, supplied Gateway's needs for disk drives, with Acer now in charge of Gateway, and IBM out of both the disk and PC businesses, there will be no marriage anytime soon—but it would have been nice—at least for IBM.

Every one of IBM's competitors in the PC arena seemed to be able to find success, even if they lost it, regained it and lost it again... Gateway was bringing in close to $10 billion which IBM had not ever seen from its PC business from when it built its first PC. IBM, the historical market bully, had become a milk-toast in a market where only bullies and extremely nice guys survived.

Ted & Norm Waitt Jr. & Mike Hammond create Gateway 2000 Computers

Gateway 2000 Computers, one of the most successful name brand "IBM PC Compatibles" vendors is still out there though now working under the Acer umbrella selling to large retail outlets and the general public. The absorbed part of Gateway still makes a lot of money, all of which could and should have been IBM's.

As discussed, Ted Waitt, was the push behind Gateway's founding. He still is a major stockholder. He was born and raised in Sioux City, Iowa, and attended the University of Iowa. Ted left without a degree but he left with a lot more. He never needed the degree. Waitt and Mike Hammond named their company Gateway 2000 on September 5, 1985. They co-founded the Company with a $10,000 loan secured by Waitt's grandmother. They then both graduated from the college of hard knocks.

To set up shop, Norm Waitt Sr., whose cattle business had fallen on hard times, offered Hammond and the two Waitt's space rent free in the family's two-story farmhouse. They set up their office in an area in which the cowhands once bunked.

In interviews Waitt said: "We could live upstairs and work downstairs; our biggest expense was filling up the fuel oil tank when it ran out. It was expensive." And, nothing in life comes easy so Waitt and Hammond were expected to help load cattle trucks that often arrived in the middle of the night. You do what you "gotta" do.

Ted Waitt's biggest regret was moving the business to California.as few of his small city dedicated workforce made the trek to the coast. The Company slid after that. Ted was right!

Ted Waitt dropped out of his own company in 2005. Mr. Waitt is listed as a billionaire on Forbes Richest Men in the World with a net worth of $900 million to $1.3 Billion after some poor real estate action and a divorce. Say thank you to IBM, Ted!

Hammond spent a lot of years as Gateway's Senior VP of Operations and he graduated Gateway University as a multi-millionaire. Norm Waitt Jr also is a billionaire. Hammond is a millionaire. Life at Gateway was sure good while it lasted.

In October 2007, Gateway was acquired by Taiwan-based Acer Inc. for $700 million. At the time of the acquisition, the combined entities comprised the third-largest PC Company in the world after HP and Dell. Gateway had acquired eMachines but in 2004, Acer shed that brand, concentrating instead on its Gateway and Packard Bell lines. Their new computing environment involves various different usage models and form factors.

Acer continues to invest in both Gateway and Packard Bell to sell "a variety of devices that would have been thought of as beyond the PC in the past." Companies do what they must do to survive.

Chapter 53

Dell Computer still on top

Michael Dell takes Dell private

Michael Dell from Texas, born in 1965, got another $500 million richer during talks of the founder taking the Company private. So, he has more net worth but it cost more to acquire the Company and make it private. Seemingly, Dell stock had always kept paying Michael Dell dividends. The stock was up 15% year in its last year as a publicly traded company.

Figure 53-1 Michael Dell CEO of DELL!

The net of the deal is that Dell has bowed out of the stock market in a $24.4 billion buyout; Microsoft participated in the deal with a $2 billion loan. Dell's stock stopped trading on the NASDAQ nearly 25 years after the Texas company raised $30 million in an initial public offering of stock. We'll see how things work out but Dell is still making $billions. IBM, the founder of the entire PC industry in 1981 makes nothing from its creation today.

One of Dell's interesting and unique "problems" under the buy-back is that as the sole owner, it does not have to create quarterly and annual financial reports. Dell is a private company again, and that means they don't need—or apparently want—to report their financial performance regularly.

Who knows how this will all work out overall but Michael Dell will still be a billionaire, regardless. From selling computers from his college dorm room in 1984, and then from taking Dell public in 1988, Michael Dell, checks in at # 10 on Forbes' Richest List with $19.2 Billion in net worth. There are no reports of Michael Dell thanking IBM for his great marketing savvy and financial success. Though as one of the clone manufacturers that made good, it would be a well-deserved thank-you.

For its last reported full fiscal year (2013), Dell revenue hit $14.3 billion in the fourth quarter, with a whopping $56.9 billion for the year. So, upstart Dell Computer, just one of the many by-products from the IBM PC introduction in August, 1981, made about $60 billion, all of which would have been IBM's revenue if it had paid attention to its business. IBM is now just one third greater in annual revenue size than Dell.

IBM wishes Michael Dell were on its team

Meanwhile, IBM is on a downward spiral that I sure hope stops soon. Its stock is down and its business is down. Its fourth-quarter net income from continuing operations was $5.5 billion in 2014 compared with $6.2 billion in the fourth-quarter of 2013, a decrease of 11 percent.

With Dell approaching $60 Billion and IBM heading in the other direction towards $90 billion, I suspect somebody in IBM is wondering how they let all that PC revenue just slip out of their hands. Can you imagine if IBM had just Dell's share? Soon, Dell will be bringing in more revenue per year than IBM. Maybe when Dell passes IBM, Michael Dell will be heard blasting out a hearty "Thank You, IBM."

IBM exits PC desktop and laptop marketplace.

In 2004, IBM seemingly was not going to take it anymore. It had enough of losing money and being bullied by the PC billionaires and their successful companies. And, so rather than help any of them, IBM instead sold off its entire PC Desktop / Laptop / ThinkPad division to the China-based Lenovo Group. In addition to $1.75 billion in cash, IBM took an undisclosed minority stake in Lenovo. By this act, it added a new, very viable competitor to the PC industry race. It was not IBM. It was Lenovo

The two companies formed a complex joint venture that at the time, made Lenovo the third-largest PC maker in the world, behind Dell and Hewlett-Packard. IBM's fingers have continued in the pie just a bit but they are not in control. Some say IBM still has a hand in its PC business but do not expect Lenovo to give any credit to anybody but Lenovo.

Insiders at the time knew that this move was for the consumer marketplace, which also provides such units for the desk tops and travelling needs of knowledge workers in corporate and institutional America. If your fingers were touching an IBM keyboard when the deal was struck, you were included.

Chapter 54

IBM Says Good-By to the PC Industry

IBM sells its x86 server business to Lenovo for $2.3 billion

It took ten more years from this first Lenovo sale for IBM to realize that the PC business that it had lost in 1982 / 1983 would never be regained no matter how hard it may choose to try. Even adding powerful server accoutrements to the X86 line using the IBM brand along with IBM unique mainframe attributes could not bring PC technology back to life for IBM.

And, so, in January, 2014, Big Blue gave up a major PC technology product line once again. This was also expected as from 1983, the Company never made its *proper* profit level on any PC products! And, so the expected deal to sell off its Intel-based servers happened without much fanfare.

Lenovo again emerged as the clear winner in the deal and it really gave the Lenovo Group a shot in the arm in terms of being able to compete against the regular players in the industry. This IBM move reflected the shifting realities of the market for powerful networked Intel processor powered machines.

Once IBM had given up the edge in 1982, it never got it back. Yet, the Company seemed content for years at stabbing at air. Then came this January 2014 announcement. IBM admitted that it did not really know how to compete in the Intel / Microsoft server marketplace, and made a less than graceful exit. In 1981, that which is now the Intel / Microsoft server marketplace was the IBM PC marketplace. IBM let the market erosion happen without much of a fight.

Big Blue threw in the towel after many years of not knowing what to do. It was always a fight for profits in a highly competitive part of the market for powerful networked x86 machines and desktops and laptops before that. IBM simply failed. There are no good excuses for IBM's poor performance.

Instead of thinking it could do all things, IBM finally saw its own handwriting on the wall and was forced to admit that it had done a very poor job of shepherding its opportunities in the PC arena. And, so, though very late in the PC game, the Company agreed to exit and sell its x86 server business (those units powered by Intel and AMD) to Lenovo for $2.3 billion.

Grading IBM for its PC efforts

As a Marketing professor at Misericordia University and as a professor of Business Information Technology at Marywood University, I would grade IBM's performance as a PC vendor in the consumer and server business as a barely passing D+. As a former IBM employee who still loves Watson's IBM, I wish I could round IBM's grade into the honors category, but I cannot. There was little honor in IBM's performance.

IBM surely could have done better as a competitor in the x86 and the PC business if it had engaged the competition early with a desire to win. Unknown competitors from this deal became billionaires thanks to IBM's lack of effort. They should all thank IBM for the sure gift of their success. IBM's not playing well helped many companies and many individuals make many $millions and a lot more than a handful made $billions.

Meanwhile, IBM still has not consistently eclipsed John Opel's prediction that by 1990, the Company would no longer be supply constrained and would therefore reach the $100 million revenue plateau from which it would dominate the entire computer industry.

Instead, IBM was lucky to have survived its mistakes of the Opel years. IBM stockholders should never thank the IBM Company for the poor performance of the stock while Big Blue gave up one opportunity after another to the technology billionaires of today. Yet, somehow IBM has never suffered a stockholders' revolt.

IBM's former x86 server line, which it sold to Lenovo, used both Intel and AMD microprocessors. IBM had done a very good technical job of beefing up the power supplies, frames and buses, cache, and other hardware to make the IBM units the beefed-up cousins to its industry competitor's machines, operating systems, and components that run the vast majority of personal computers.

IBM continues to be profitable

As noted, IBM in 2004 sold its consumer and corporate personal business to Lenovo, also. At the time it kept its PC x86 server lines – x86s. IBM's mainframes and those business systems that use its own Power Processors (IBM p—RS/6000 legacy and IBM I—AS/400 legacy) processors continued to make respectable profits, but its two big revenue generators are now system software and IT services.

The sale of the X86 business reflected the changing dynamics of the market for servers, which provide services for hosting Web sites, tracking inventory, and managing banking transactions. In bygone days servers were usually expensive, hulking machines, mostly manufactured by IBM.

However, over the last two decades, the market has shifted toward the relatively small, inexpensive models that are stacked by the dozens into racks of blade centers in data centers. Without a field marketing force and manufacturing executives determined to win, IBM lost the edge in hardware, especially small scale boxes.

To put it bluntly: "IBM blew it big time!" By not giving up after it had completely surrendered, the Company wasted billions of dollars by developing high-end x86 PC servers with some of the "big iron," aka mainframe power, reliability, flexibility of its proprietary servers.

On the way to complete failure, IBM met new competitors—companies such as Google and Amazon that did not play by computer industry rules. These relatively new behemoths in an adjunct industry charted a new course in which reliability was provided by software that could withstand the failure of a few dead systems in much the same way that an anthill isn't bothered when somebody steps on a couple of ants on the sidewalk. They were not willing to spend big bucks for IBM's almost 100% reliability and no down-time.

Even worse for traditional server makers, companies like Google and Amazon and Facebook now make their own hardware servers rather than buy them already manufactured. Times have changed and IBM has been forced to move out of sameness into the areas in which its hardware is unique.

Companies like Amazon, Facebook, and Twitter and others are not standing still. Amazon Web Services for example and rival offerings led many customers away from buying their own machines and instead renting services from Amazon and other providers, who are better able to provide a large-scale server infrastructure for Shopping Cart and other customers who one day may need much more power—even if that day is tomorrow!

So, not only is Amazon not an IBM customer, it is an IBM competitor. Companies such as Amazon have stolen IBM traditional customers away by providing the same type of services that IBM would provide. For several years, I was an Amazon customer because they offered an application solution for me.

At the time of moving on. IBM sunk to become an also ran in the server maker business behind Hewlett-Packard. Industry Analyst Gartner Group estimates of last quarter revenue show Dell, a company no longer publicly traded, happy to be in third place.

IBM's sales percentage in the x86 marketplace, which will be zero from now was 22.9 percent of a $12.6 billion market.

HP stood at 27.6 percent and Dell checked in at 16.4 percent. IBM's share was dropping and it had dropped 18.9 percentage points from the year-earlier quarter. Lenovo plays for keeps so HP and Dell will not be able to rest on any laurels. When IBM fails it bails. If the numbers are bad for just a little while, IBM calls U-Haul to get the remains of the company's failing industry sub segment off of IBM's hallowed grounds.

Who is Lenovo?

Lenovo is an up-and-comer in the world of Chinese electronics. Rightfully so, the Company patted itself on the back for the IBM x86 server purchase, which had been rumored for months. Yang Yuanqing, Lenovo's chairman and chief executive, sees a very positive future for the Company. Lenovo's executives are the new millionaires in an industry with many millionaires and billionaires who secretly say Thank You to IBM for helping them be so successful. IBM is the company that gives up, sells out, and let's others become rich on its great work.

Lenovo was nowhere in sight in August 1981 when IBM launched its PC business. Yet, this company made $14.1 billion in its last fiscal year, with two thirds or about $10 billion of that revenue coming from PC sales—the two businesses it got from IBM. IBM had not come close to that level of sales in its years with the products. Why?

Lenovo not only grossed $10 billion, it actually made a profit, something IBM somehow could never seem to do with PCs, no matter how big or small, how weak or powerful that it had created the units. I suspect quietly that the Lenovo Group is thanking IBM but we won't hear them do it publicly as they work too hard to not take credit for their own great business acumen and accomplishments.

Chapter 55

Microsoft Becomes Champion of PC / x86 Software

Many heroes become billionaires

Every war has many heroes. If we hypothesize for a moment that the Information Technology Industry from its inception has been a war unto itself, fraught with many battles for the innovative edge, technological superiority, and marketing leadership, we will find many heroes.

Some of these heroes are now legend in their own right, and pure and simple champions of the computer Industry. This book is filled with them: Their ranks include Bill Gates and Paul Allen to Steve Jobs and Steve Wozniak, from Ted Waitt to Michael Dell to Rod Canion, to Bill Joy, Larry Ellison, Ray Noorda, Robert Metcalfe Jack Kilby, Scott Piotroski, Paul Harkins, Jeff Bezos, Pierre Omidyar, Big Jim Macaleer, Hasso Plattner, and Gordon Moore. There are many others besides these who owe IBM a hearty thank you for their extreme riches. Thank you, IBM.

Most of these industry stalwarts were little more than kids when they began to move on their special idea. Most of these listed champions in their field of endeavor are multimillionaires or mega billionaires and most are relatively still young in age or at the very least, still alive. Some unfortunately have passed on and we honor them for their contributions to the computer age.

These unbelievable personas became the driving forces in the computer industry, despite IBM or because of IBM, depending on your perspective. Meanwhile, IBM, whose huge mainframes and supercomputers can still get a computer transaction finished more rapidly than any other computer manufacturer, continues to be a major industry force.

IBM has some thanking to do also. For example, the Company should thank whichever manager it was within Big Blue who first said, "Whoa!" to going after goals that were no longer achievable such as the John Opel $ 100 billion goal that was killing the company.

Ironically, Microsoft's Bill Gates, the richest man in the world—a man who actually asked John Opel if it would be OK that he become a billionaire—in his heart has been thanking IBM for granting him full permission to succeed for years. At least I figure he has been doing that because IBM is responsible for the bulk of his wealth.

Gates of course has not only succeeded; he has even superseded IBM since the early 1980's. Bill Gates is the recognized richest man in the world for sixteen of the last twenty-one years. Nobody who ever worked for IBM can ever make the same claim?

IBM Chairman John Opel and Mary Gates

Many do not know that John Opel and Mary Gates, the mother of Bill Gates, were board members together at the same Seattle United Way Organization. If John Opel, the guy in IBM who promised too much and could not deliver—If he had hindsight as a tool regarding that chance United Way meeting in Washington between him and Mary Gates about her son, Bill; he hopefully would have responded less affirmatively.

If Opel had given Mary Gates a definitive "no," all IBM stockholders today would be raking in huge dividends. Gates would be a millionaire for sure but he would be the 14,323,651st richest man in the world. Opel's decision to help a punk kid at his mother's request has had a profound effect on IBM's success and its profitability from the moment Gates met IBM. Gates rolled over IBM like an ingrate that felt that his benefactor was compelled to help him since he was he.

Either history or folklore will find IBM's OK to help Bill Gates was the first act in a "bad marriage." It ultimately resulted in IBM giving away custody of its financial children to the care of the Gates' family. History has already played this hand out for real. The Gates' are the billionaires in the deal; IBM came in second place. If IBM had the PC as its only product, Bill Gates would have made IBM a pauper. Gates would have taken IBM's last dime. I think Bill Gates not only needs to thank IBM but he needs to apologize to IBM for taking advantage of a trust. In a real marriage that works, both parties treat each other fairly.

In the folklore play, we would find Microsoft as the king of PC operating systems, never having written an operating system, and a company, for which most of its years, completely dominated IBM in the marketplace. IBM was always very nice to Bill Gates and the representatives of his company.

IBM was kind enough to have "adopted little Billy as a stepchild at his mother's request. John Opel demanded that Bill Gates be treated as an honorary IBM executive so he would report well to Mrs. Gates. Bill Gates' Microsoft forgot to be nice, despite how nice John Opel was to Bill Gates and to Mary Gates. Sometimes trust does not work in business.

Bill Gates for all accounts, was not quite the gentleman to IBM, as IBM was to him. As his success began to outclass IBM's success in its business, Gates was simply not a good guy and he was not inclined to help IBM even when the Company deferred to his supposed wisdom. IBM unfortunately for its stockholders continued to trust Bill Gates as he planned to finish IBM off in the PC industry.

Bill Gates true mentor was WC Fields

WC Fields once said: "Never give a sucker an even break, and never smarten up a chump! Bill Gates, who some suggest has yet to earn a college degree, may have studied under W.C. Fields. He conducted business with no heart at all.

Besides software, the one-time little Gates' Company from Redmond Washington has also made significant inroads in areas which are not PC-traditional and not always software oriented in nature. These include production computers, which are used to run whole businesses as well as some classy game consoles such as its Xbox line.

But when John Opel spoke with Mary Gates, at their chance meeting at the United Way in Seattle, Microsoft was just a small computer firm with perhaps a $million in annual sales. Microsoft at the time operated out of Bellevue, Washington. Opel agreed to help Mary Gates' son in an innocent endeavor between a really small company and a mega-giant. Which company was the fool?

From the start the only real deal on the table was for Bill Gates and Paul Allen's BASIC, written by Allen to be emblazoned into the ROM on the IBM PC. In this way, every IBM PC user would be able to use BASIC at a primitive level for their own needs—even if they had no diskette drive on their units to store their programs or data.

Other than Microsoft BASIC being burned into ROM, Gates was to get no other favors from IBM. But, he carried the United Way chance meeting further in his expectations than the ticket it actually gave him. IBMers in Boca Raton, home of PC development did not know what to make of him but they did know that if they crossed the Chairman, their careers would be short.

John Opel kept his word about helping Mary Gates' son Bill. Opel told the IBM guys in Boca Raton, who were putting together their historic PC to help the young Mr. Gates as much as they could. They did! They were unaware that they should stop helping when IBM's own business opportunities were threatened by the relationship. The Chairman of IBM carries a major weight.

Gates eventually asked IBM if it were OK for him to compete with Big Blue. IBM was more concerned about what the Chairman would say and nobody wanted to ask. So, Gates got permission to nail IBM in the marketplace right from IBM itself. Additionally, IBM was still more worried about the anti-trust actions from the government than protecting its PC market opportunities.

IBMers were very worried about appearing unkind to Mr. Gates, than competing for business. Therefore, as many see it, the IBM Company basically gave Bill Gates all the keys to the Boca Raton plant where the PC people lived, and IBM promised not to look at his nefarious adventures as he stole more than he was given.

Additionally, Big Blue gave this "favorite insider" the full OK to compete against IBM in the PC Operating System space; even though IBM had invested tons of money cleaning up the OS Gates had purchased from Seattle

Computer Products. The OS was not clean and as appropriate as purported and in fact it had been obtained illegitimately. Ironically, IBM, even Opel, had never agreed that Microsoft was to be a PC OS supplier. BASIC was the Gates and Allen ticket. Nothing more!

IBM trained Bill Gates to ask for the moon

Many of us believe that Bill Gates, thankful at the time for John Opel's help, would have been happy just being IBM's largest software supplier. IBM in essence said to Bill Gates: "The PC OS marketing space is all yours. Do what you need to do; we will market PC-DOS; MS-DOS is whatever you want it to be". Of course this is the same IBM that expected no more than 55,000 PCs to be shipped each year. IBM miscalculated what a pimply faced millionaire part brat, part geek might do to IBM if left unchecked in the IBM treasury.

MS-DOS, the Bill Gates' solo product, and not PC-DOS, the product for which IBM paid Bill Gates for the rights to market with the IBM PC became the most successful PC operating system of the day. Gates knew what he was doing but IBM simply trusted this guy to whom the Chairman had given a blue ticket.

Though embarrassed that this rogue OS was beating the endorsed PC DOS, IBM never claimed its bounty. IBM stuck by its version, PC-DOS, an identical yet unsuccessful product because of its association with IBM-only PCs. Bill Gates screwed IBM at every turn.

As we look back, it only seems natural that Microsoft was the chosen company to make the default operating system for the PC. What is not obvious however, is that at the time, IBM was really looking for a number of operating system partners.

The part of this nasty deal for IBM that guys like me, who worked for IBM cannot understand, is that the IBM Company was the premier operating system development company in the universe. IBM at the time needed help from nobody to scrounge up a simple operating system. IBM could have built a simple operating system for the PC in less than a week.

IBM did not need any of its three candidate operating systems—two of which were UCSD-p, and Gary Kildall's CPM/86. IBM surely did not need Q-DOS, from which Gates' MS-DOS sprung. The notion of buying from outside IBM to expedite the process and minimize the expense had to come from somebody way up in IBM. Regardless, it was not good for the IBM Company.

IBM's misguided position with its PC was that it actually feared controlling the marketplace because it feared the anti-trust division of the Federal Government more than it felt it needed to increase profits and opportunities for stockholders from a unique product offering. Bill Gates took advantage of every piece of insider information that was fed to him. He was and perhaps still is an unscrupulous and very greedy man.

What was best for IBM was thus well-compromised by the Mary and Bill Gates combo and then, again, by the federal government.

IBM invented operating systems

Nobody could build a better OS than IBM. So, in reality, IBM could have done the job better alone. IBM did not need Bill Gates or QDOS or anything! Even if the IBM Company did not do it alone at first, they could have built a better

DOS than Q-DOS—even for a later model, such as the PC XT or AT!

IBM instead chose not to build an operating system for six more years (OS/2). And, when they chose to engage, their specs were way too advanced for what was needed. Worse than that, IBM had yet to learn its trust lesson about Microsoft. They contracted with Bill Gates to write their newly IBM designed OS. Hard as it is to believe, IBM went back to be burned again. It picked Microsoft instead of a reliable IBM Lab to build their new OS.

Microsoft of course at the time had everything to lose and nothing to gain by being successful in delivering the best OS in the world for the PC to IBM. By this time, Microsoft had designs on being top gun in OS land for the IBM PC. If Microsoft would not gain the most from the venture, why would it build an OS better than a Microsoft flavor? Why would Microsoft want to give IBM exclusive rights to an OS built by Microsoft even though they had signed the contract? MS was merely a subcontractor.

IBM had held back parts of the coding for IBM labs to assure it was done right; but ultimately IBM relented and gave MS the whole deal. Microsoft figured out how to make the deal work for Microsoft and not IBM, or so it surely seems. Check out the history of OS/2 on your browser and you will find how gullible and business stupid IBM was and how greedy and business nasty Microsoft was.

Is it not amazing that Microsoft, a company that today would claim to be the foremost vendor of high quality operating systems, never was able to bring a viable OS/2 operating system to the table for IBM... even though IBM paid them to do just that! I am sure many of us have ideas about why OS/2, as written by Microsoft, never met anybody's expectations.

At that time in 1987, history tells us that it was already too late for IBM anyway in the PC arena. IBM had lost the whole marketplace to the clones. I often wondered how it could be that I knew that at the time, and I was just an IBM midrange technology guru, not a PC aficionado. More importantly, why did IBM not know that? Why did Microsoft not tell IBM the truth?

Much of the PC story is unbelievable because IBM at the time really did not seem to care if its star product, the PC, was a success or not. IBM either did not know or chose not to know that Bill Gates had been undermining the IBM Company's market opportunities every chance he got. Big Blue kept coming back to Bill Gates for additional doses of Microsoft's habitually bad medicine.

So, it was no surprise to industry observers that in the mid 1980's when IBM finally chose to build a beat all operating system and call it Operating System/2 (OS/2), Big Blue went back to the master perpetrator again for some more big disappointments. IBM subcontracted the writing of OS/2 to Microsoft rather than doing it itself.

I heard first-hand Bill Gates speak at a conference about OS/2 and IBM's PC opportunities. He had no love for IBM. I bought him a beer as he sat at my table simply so that I could say I did. There were about fourteen IBMers who I knew and Bill Gates sitting around one small cocktail table where all the beers had a tough time fitting at once. Gates was just 31 years old at the time. He never plugged OS/2 at the table but he plugged Windows, which had yet to be released -- his own OS and he liked the Mac, believe it or not!

IBM at the time had not OK'd Windows for Microsoft. Gates downplayed OS/2 at the IBM conference where I

heard him speak, and deferred to Windows, which also was
not available. He was planning to make Windows great
while being paid by IBM to make OS/2 the greatest. I have
little respect for Bill Gates. I did not know what he was up
to at the conference but I have paid attention since.

Burn me once!

Knowing that Bill Gates did not give a darn about IBM's
success, and having seen that he had already minimized
IBM's PC efforts to that point, it was amazing that IBM
would go back to get burned again. It was laughable or
something even more indicting of IBM's abject failure in the
marketplace, and its failure to differentiate business friends
from enemies. I still wonder if malfeasance may have been
part of the deal.

The idea of IBM earnestly working with Microsoft brings up
a lot of survival questions: Why not ask the wolf to make
the locks for your home or for the home where the sheep are
living comfortably? Why not give the Fox the full layout /
blueprint of the henhouse and then give the Fox the key?
Why not treat the Fox and the Wolf as partners if they have
agreed to be partners and they say they will behave?

IBM's attitude with Bill Gates, still in his late twenties at the
time, (even before the conference where we spoke together)
was to take his advice in all matters and let him make as
much money as he possibly could make. IBM suffered
continually from misplaced blind trust because John Opel
and Bill Gates had become buddies, or at least those
working for Chairman Opel felt that was the case.

IBM needed real operating Systems before OS/2

When Bill Gates showed up in Florida at the Boca Plant as
IBM was preparing to introduce its PC, he came with the

threatening words to all IBMers: "John Opel sent me." IBM gladly opened whatever kimonos it had and Bill Gates became a defacto IBM partner from that day forward.

Bill Gates and Paul Allen had written a BASIC Language Interpreter for the MITS Altair hobbyist computer. That was their claim to fame. They had a major product to sell IBM. They hoped to port BASIC to the to-be announced IBM PC. IBM eventually agreed to burn it into the PC's ROM.

Nobody at IBM could say anything bad about a Bill Gates product because the Chairman had already interceded. What a bad mistake for IBM to simply satisfy a United Way relationship between the Chair and a UW board member. Mary Gates had as much a role in the PC history as her greedy billionaire son.

Inside information helped Gates understand IBM's needs

From that meeting on, IBM had more than a de-facto contract relationship with Microsoft for the development of languages, which the IBM Corporation took very seriously. Bill Gates became a frequent visitor with the IBM PC development team.

Along the way, as IBM discussed its plans with Gates, and he offered his opinions as to the direction in which IBM should take the machine, Gates became aware that IBM was looking for an industry standard operating system for its new unit.

In 1979, before Mary G. and John O. had met, trying to make a buck in a new industry, Microsoft had licensed a Unix derivative from AT&T, which the Company called Xenix. Their version was based on Seventh Edition Unix.

Right after moving to Bellevue, they found the time to develop Xenix from AT&T source code. Back then, AT&T wasn't licensing the Unix brand itself, only the source code, so Microsoft named their new OS Xenix. It was the Company's first true operating system, but it was in fact, Unix. It had the familiar "icks" sound.

IBM had already ruled Unix derivatives out for the PC. IBM was not ever at that point at least, a Unix fan. Too bad as Bill Gates and Paul Allen had nothing else in their OS tool kit at the time.

Gates, whose only initial goal was to sell his BASIC interpreter to IBM, nonetheless saw dollar signs when he heard about the need for an OS for the PC. H never let the idea rest. Though he had no OS at the time, he nonetheless dwelled on the notion of having an OS to sell to IBM for its PC as a tremendous personal financial opportunity.

Since IBM could license Unix directly from AT&T and did not need Microsoft in this scenario, Xenix was not a good choice anyway if Microsoft was to make any real money on the deal.

Quick and Dirty DOS (QDOS)

Gates knew IBM was hurting for an industry standard type OS for the 16-bit 8088 and 8086 Intel microprocessors. Not willing to let any low-lying fruit on the vine, Gates discovered a small company named Seattle Computer Products (SCP). SCP had a product that seemed to fit the IBM requirements. Gates chose not to give IBM the author's name or help the IBM Company negotiate with him so Microsoft could reap the full rewards from its inside information. So, Microsoft decided to become the de-facto author of his OS work—a work they had not written.

SCP's principal, Tim Patterson, had written his own operating system in April, 1980. After two man months, Patterson had completed his task. (Think of how long a team of IBMers would have taken for something that took a guy two months part-time, to write). Patterson had modeled his OS after Dr. Gary Kildall's CP/M, and he called the resulting Operating System, Quick and Dirty DOS (Q-DOS). It sure was dirty. It ran on Intel's 8088 microprocessor—the same chip used for the August 1981 announced IBM PC. It actually seemed to work. How fortuitous for Microsoft!

Patterson had written the OS mostly in frustration waiting for Dr. Gary Kildall of Digital Research to port his CPM/80 OS to the Intel 8086/8088. He figured it would all be put to rest when
Kildall's 16-bit OS hit the streets. Patterson had great respect for Kildall. Then Bill Gates came along with some quick and dirty cash.

Gates and his best buddy and partner Paul Allen made a deal with Tim Patterson for his 86-DOS system. Patterson never expected Q-DOS to be a commercial venture. So, Tim Patterson let it all go for just $50,000. Bill Gates did not quibble. Patterson probably invited everybody he knew to a barbecue that night. I know I would have!

The buyer was identified by Microsoft as an unnamed client. It was IBM. Patterson had never taken the project seriously but he got it working with a "few" bugs for his own use, Mr. Patterson was preparing to defer to Kildall's CPM/86 when it came out. His effort was as full of bugs as a humid summer night with no bug spray.

But, Bill Gates and Paul Allen were willing to buy Patterson's almost OS as it was a grand deal and it offered great promise for Microsoft to have an OS for IBM to procure and pay huge royalties to Microsoft. Microsoft knew IBM needed a viable 16-bit OS for its new PC, and John Opel had said for IBM to pay attention to these Microsoft guys, especially Mary's son Bill.

Soon, because of the helping hand from the Chairman of IBM, Gates and company knew they had the upper hand, no matter how bad the 16-bit OS code might be. IBM was a sucker that did not need an even break, and Microsoft was not about to smarten up this chump.

When inspected, the entire OS was little more than 4000 lines of assembler code. Considering the tens of millions of lines of code in Windows NT when I first wrote this line in this book twenty some years ago, we might call this a modest beginning in PC operating systems.

Why would Microsoft buy Q-DOS from Patterson?

First of all Microsoft was not an operating system vendor. They should have hired Tim Patterson but instead they decided to keep him from reaping any rewards. Patterson later sued Microsoft and got some of what he was due.

Regardless of Microsoft's ultimate treatment of Patterson, in September, 1980, Tim got the opportunity of a lifetime to show Microsoft his new operating system. At this time, he was referring to it as 86-DOS. It was Paul Allen, Bill Gates' partner from the start, who got the assignment to get this operating system in-house for Microsoft.

For something between $5,000 as reported in folklore to something less than $100,000 (most say $50,000), Patterson took the money and ran. He felt he would get nothing when Kildall's CPM-86 hit the streets so he was tickled to get any money for his test case work.

IBM could have had CP/M, best of the day

By the way, IBM did want Kildall's port of 8-bit CP/M, the most popular OS at the time, to the 16-bit 8088/8086 Intel chip for its PC before Gates even approached them.

Kildall, an independent man, made the mistake of snubbing IBM and he was o-u-t. IBM set up an appointment and sent a team to negotiate a fair price for Kildall to sell rights to his OS for the IBM PC. Kildall did not particularly like IBM and left his wife home to talk to IBM while he want on a fishing trip the very day IBM came.

She reportedly asked for too much compensation and IBM did not want to negotiate with her. The IBM team was very upset for what they saw as the Kildall snub. Bill Gates was a real opportunist. He seemed to know everything that was happening and he was in there every day as a buddy helping IBM decide that he was all the IBM Company needed in all software areas.

Right after this poor experience with Kildall. Gates made sure that he was ready to take advantage of it. Kildall, the premier OS vendor of home and hobby computerists for years snubbed IBM and IBM as a company has never taken well to snubbings.

The entrepreneur in Bill Gates was working overtime as he made sure that Microsoft benefitted from the IBM snubbing. If you are an entrepreneur such as Bill Gates, and you know CP/M would bring in no revenue to your company, then something like 86-DOS, Q-DOS or MS-DOS or PC-DOS would definitely be the better answer.

It happened to be fortuitous for both IBM and Microsoft. Patterson's Q-DOS looked a lot like CP/M and that was enough for IBM to want to repay the snub from Kildall and leave him without any of his potential IBM $millions. Gates as the broker of the deal with a fiduciary interest to say the least, was ready to snag all of Kildall's potential $millions. There would be none left for Dr. Gary if Bill Gates got his way...and he did.

Kildall knew what was up

Gary Kildall was no dummy. He simply was not a suck-up to IBM like Bill Gates and he wanted to assure his company a proper size piece of the pie. Going fishing was part of his negotiating style. He had no idea that he was being outclassed however by Bill Gates with a knock-off OS that behaved somewhat like his CP/M.

After learning about the deal, Kildall knew that it would cost him a lot of money to not be included in the biggest PC deal to date. So, Digital Research founder, Dr. Gary Kildall threatened to sue IBM for infringing DRI's intellectual property. To settle the claim, IBM agreed to offer CP/M-86 as an alternative operating system on the PC. CP/M-86 was made available about six months after PC-DOS on IBM's PCs. It was much more expensive than DOS and quite frankly it never caught on. Gates had won a big one. Kildall knew the fix was in because he did not charge IBM per copy anything close to what IBM chose to charge its customers for CPM/86. IBM loved Bill Gates and hated DR. Gary Kildall. That's it!

Bill Gates: right place; right time!

It helps to recall that because of his connection with the IBM Chairman Opel, Bill Gates was like an IBM partner and sometimes even a consultant on the IBM PC project. IBM trusted him implicitly but their trust as we see over time was never really earned by the Microsoft CEO. From day one, Gates was for Gates and IBM paid the price a hundred thousand or more times over.

Though the reported amounts, which Bill Gates paid for the rights to sell MS-DOS to its "one" customer vary, one thing is for sure: Considering the number of multi-billionaires and multi-millionaires, which this operating system spawned, a price twenty times twenty times twenty times in retrospect would have been a steal.

By February, 1981, IBM had Gates' Q-DOS running on its prototype machines and it looked like a go. Recognizing the problems which Microsoft would have down the road as DOS became successful, the MS Company bought all rights to SCP-DOS (Q-DOS), and the product quickly became MS-DOS.

When IBM announced the PC on August 12, 1981, it called the operating system PC-DOS. MS-DOS was not announced but soon, with IBM's blessing, Microsoft would be independently offering the PC-DOS code under this Microsoft name.

A few (300) bugs and an IBM rewrite

From the beginning DOS was copyrighted by both Microsoft and IBM. Yes, IBM has always been the equivalent of a co-owner of MS-DOS, but the Company chose never to collect on Microsoft's private revenue stream. IBM even had the rights to Windows. IBM never profited from Gates but Gates' company now has more annual revenue than IBM.

Though IBM liked the notion of a nice little operating system for the PC, they did not like the structure of how it was written. Moreover, IBM did not like the 300 bugs that they discovered through closer inspection of the code. It helps to remember Patterson wrote this quick and dirty OS in two months.

IBM was great at operating systems and could have done it all itself. Considering the work IBM put into Q-DOS to make it work, one might say that IBM did write DOS. In fact it took Microsoft's "purchased" DOS, and rewrote it so both the OS and IBM would succeed with the new IBM PC. Both companies retained the product rights. However, as noted, it is not believed that IBM ever sold its version of the operating system to be pre-installed on clone PCs.

Yes—IBM had the rights to MS-DOS

Bill Gates invited IBM to have exclusive rights for the DOS operating system, since Gates wanted to have a good relationship with his new personal gold mine named IBM. He was about to make a ton of money because of the relationship and he knew it. Unfortunately for IBM and its stockholders, at the time, IBM was more concerned about mainframe computing and its lawyers were more concerned about the government's anti-trust action against IBM. Nobody was observing IBM getting shylocked by a nice "kid" from Seattle.

The Company sweated bullets over just how IBM would look if it began to dominate this new industry segment (PC) in a way which the Justice Department might consider as an abuse of IBM's monopoly power. IBM therefore did not want the rights to DOS, and thus it rejected Gates' offer of exclusivity. IBM did not view PC operating systems or PC software as a marketplace. It saw the PC as a complete product in in its own marketplace. Today, thanks to IBM's small thinking, Microsoft is now a company bigger than IBM itself. Thank you, IBM!

Microsoft revenues now stand at $93.58 billion annually, compared to $92.79 billion for IBM. The Company inched ahead of IBM for the first time in 2015. When we consider Microsoft makes just about all of its money on software, and IBM did not view PC software as a marketplace worth keeping, it shows the extent of the IBM shortchanging of its stockholders over the years.

With its annual revenue at $56 billion and growing, it will be just ten years and perhaps less before Intel surpasses IBM. Wintel is just two companies in the $trillion dollar PC and small computer marketplace. Meanwhile with 3Q 2015 results of about $50 billion, Apple is now a $200 billion dollar per year company.

IBM gave it all away

When we consider the collective net worth of all of the companies which IBM "created" by its laissez-faire policy towards its own proprietary work, this was the greatest blunder of all time in all industries. It was IBM's greatest gift to its competition in the PC arena.

Where would companies like Phoenix technologies, Compaq, Microsoft, Dell, Gateway, Intel, Microsoft, and others have been if IBM had introduced a proprietary system, or at least protected its options for license royalties? The net worth of the PC industry outside of IBM is many, many times the net worth of the entire IBM company today. Decisions such as not using its own chips and protecting the rights to DOS, have relegated IBM to the role of a smaller and smaller bit-player in a market which it had created and which it should have owned and dominated.

OK for the clones!

With IBM being too timid from the Justice Department pressure to lock in Microsoft's Operating System, Bill Gates knew the whole show was his. At the time, he was being pressured by the upstart clone manufacturers to negotiate distribution rights to the Microsoft DOS operating system. Gates likewise applied pressure to IBM for a decision as to whether such actions by Microsoft would be OK by IBM.

Under pressure from Gates to decide one way or another, IBM chose to allow Microsoft to distribute its operating system constraint-free to whomever they wished. IBM took no royalties.

This move surely hurt IBM more than any action the Justice Department may have eventually taken. The Justice Department dropped its 10-year long case early in 1982. It was just under five months from the time the PC was introduced. IBM still had complete control of the entire PC market. It could have done anything and gotten away with it but IBM chose to do nothing and gain nothing. The bomb had been lit and it would go off in stages until there was no piece of the IBM PC company left to keep making Microsoft rich. So, Microsoft went on its own.

Despite no threat from Justice, IBM never went back to Microsoft and Intel to discuss a more restrictive posture regarding the distribution of processors and operating systems for the soon to be IBM PC clones. Perhaps they should have? Perhaps if they had fought for their own business, IBM today would be wondering if it would be a $trillion dollar company by 2020?

When Microsoft was able to out-muscle IBM, it had little regard for any other competitor it might face. The team from Redmond knew that it had the power to blow all competition away. In fact, when IBM came back looking for stuff from Microsoft that Big Blue had long given away, Bill Gates' little company had no problem blowing IBM out of its marketing space. By this time, Mary Gates did not have to intervene. Microsoft was the dog with the tail up and IBM's tail was down. IBM's tail stayed down until IBM withdrew from the PC business entirely.

Microsoft knew that it would enjoy lots of revenue from being the OS vendor for IBM and "IBM-Compatible" PCs. But, it could easily have lots more and so it planned to be more than it was intended to be.

Microsoft was a nasty, ruthless, competitor

Besides writing OS/2 for IBM and "secretly" launching Windows at the same time, Microsoft snookered a lot of its OS software vendors into believing it had their backs. The list of failures in the industry caused by Microsoft's not so nice business practices is replete with famous names. As an example, if Lotus was not assumed by IBM, it would have been out of business. Microsoft would have destroyed it.

In 1986 WordPerfect and WordStar were the two leading word processors, with moderately larger market shares than several other programs (DisplayWrite, Word, MultiMate, and Samna Word). In the next few years, however, WordPerfect broke away from the pack, and by 1990 it clearly dominated the market.

As Microsoft came out with new OS releases there was always some reason why the applications from WordPerfect did not run as cleanly as when they were tested on the newer MS Operating system version. By 1992, Microsoft Word mysteriously became the # 1 Word Processing package and by 1997, it had over 90% of the business. It was not nice to fool with Mother Microsoft.

I watched as great companies disappeared. By the early 1990's, I had left IBM and had become the Internal Consultant for MIS at Misericordia University. I also managed the Administrative PC Department. So, as one of my responsibilities, my department supported all PCs used by non-Faculty. Faculty were handled by the Student Lab Coordinator. Misericordia had a love affair with Word Perfect that pre-dated my arrival so I witnessed the software package's Microsoft-caused demise first-hand. It was not pretty.

I noticed that rather than support the software companies (its customers) offering word processing, spreadsheet and graphics presentation software, Microsoft launched competing products such as MS-Word, Excel, and PowerPoint. Additionally, it came out with Access to dispose of dBase, and all other PC database software packages. As the prime OS vendor, this gave Microsoft a decided advantage, which was unfair to all other competitors. Bill Gates as expected did not care much about the complaints.

Afraid of Microsoft?...everybody even IBM!

Every now and then Gates would authorize the purchase of a company like Fox Pro, when Microsoft needed the expertise or a top-shelf product or it wanted to do away with some potential competition.

Most of the time, however, it would simply cheat. The Company would choose to keep some salient OS features a secret and make all competing vendors say *Uncle* in order to make their stuff work without crashing on the next Microsoft OS version. Some say it wasn't fair. It was not fair—but nobody at the time was challenging Microsoft on anything. They feared it could get worse. It always did!

Microsoft had sharp teeth while IBM was toothless and smiling.

Even IBM did not try to fight Microsoft, which always bothered me as a former employee and as a stockholder. Microsoft played to win, while IBM played to survive by not upsetting Microsoft.

Just so that we do not slander IBM for its impotence against the latter day Microsoft, most companies got the same deal from Bill Gates and company. IBM, could have fought but did not. Some other companies such as Novell, who at one time owned Word Perfect and the best LAN package in the industry, chose to take on Bill Gates and what was seen as his "monopolistic" company. IBM instead chose to do handstands to show that it was not monopolistic while many think the Gates' regime took pleasure in knowing that it controlled all markets. Gates surely was not afraid of the government or IBM.

It was not until in 2004 that Novell finally cried foul but everybody thought that Microsoft had all of its game covered. Novell, however said that their WordPerfect product never got a fair shot on Windows 95 since Microsoft shut it out of the development process, ostensibly in favor of Word.

Novell did not pull any punches. It named Gates himself as a major perpetrator, claiming the Microsoft Mahoff ordered the Company's engineers to reject WordPerfect as a Windows 95 application because it was too good and it would make Word look inferior.

In the trial that ensued, Bill Gates himself took the stand to give his side of the story. While questioned by Microsoft lawyer Steven Holley, Gates said he denied the central premise of Novell's suit—that the software giant withheld elements of Windows 95 that undermined WordPerfect.

Gates also offered that that the notion of Little Red Riding Hood was also overstated as the wolf that he knew from the story had already registered with authorities as a wonderfully good guy with a penchant for providing for charities.

Microsoft lorded over IBM in negotiations

Over the time that IBM had met Bill Gates, he understood IBM more than IBM managers understood IBM. Gates was becoming a billionaire plus. Meanwhile, IBM executives were still trying to figure out how an industry ally could be making more dollars in the industry than the Company that created the industry and sponsored the ally.

Microsoft kicked the pants off IBM. It was polite at first, not knowing how much business IBM would permit the upstart from taking before Big Blue got the scent of a misdeed. By 1990, IBM, with Opel long gone, finally realized that Bill Gates was not its bosom buddy, though IBM had already made Gates a billionaire.

IBM learned that it was not good to have Bill Gates as an ally because a real ally he could never be. It was not in his nature. I would only have recommended Gates as an ally to IBM in the 1980's if its management wanted to be eaten up in the middle of the night and be fully digested by morning.

Bill Gates and his company beat IBM plain and simple. Eventually, nobody in IBM had the resources of a Bill Gates and the resources he could call upon to keep Microsoft ahead of everybody including IBM.

How many billionaires came from Microsoft?

Let's make a premise that Bill Gates, who had a startup company when IBM launched its PC August 12, 1981, made a ton of money from his involvement in the IBM PC project. It would be an accurate premise. Let's say he is now the richest man in the world with a net worth of $84 billion. This too is an accurate premise.

For a system that IBM pioneered and Gates provided only OS software, how could such a man become the richest person on earth? You can imagine the big mistake IBM made when you look at just Bill Gates as a multi-billionaire. But there were lots more Bill Gates' and there were lots more Microsoft's that all become rich at IBM's expense. Yet, as noted in this book, stockholders were very merciful and called only for one head: John Akers' and it was given to. For the most part IBM stockholders were asleep and still are.

In the Forbes' list in 2015, Gates again beat Mexican businessman Carlos Slim to the top spot. It is like a game in that Mr. Gates' net worth rose by just over $8 billion to $84 billion.

The fun in figuring out how poor one is, is to see how rich some are. There were a record 1,826 billionaires in the world in 2015. Steve Forbes, a guy who would make a good US President said that there was an increase of 181 billionaires in the past 12 months. Despite the new additions, nobody can deny that Bill Gates has now been on top of the list for 16 of the last 21 years. Forbes, the publisher of the list could not help adding the tidbit of how often Bill Gates was # 1.

Legendary US investor Warren Buffett, a great friend of Bill Gates and a philanthropist like no other, found himself again in third place in the list with a net worth of $72.7 billion. Amancio Ortega, the founder of Spanish fashion chain Zara would like to beat out all of the 2015 billionaires. Oracle's Larry Ellison of course is getting close at $54 billion in fifth place.

What about Bill Gates? Let it not be said that Mr. Gates does not like being filthy rich. At more than $79 billion in net worth in Forbes' list and at $84 billion in recent accounts, Bill Gates is the richest man in the world, though it is an honor, he says he would prefer not to have. He claims he'd rather be a good guy.

IBM earnings as noted in its last fiscal year report were just over $92 billion. If Bill Gates does not start giving money away, soon, he will have higher net worth than IBM's gross revenue per annum. Microsoft itself has already eclipsed IBM in annual revenue.

Fox and the lamb

I watched Bill Gates outfox IBM, a lamb compared to Gates' cunning, when I was with IBM and afterwards as a consultant, Microsoft was making its mark. IBM did not know any company would or could play so dirty. IBM did not know what hit it.

When Microsoft put an X on your chest, your company was destined to be annihilated even if the team from Redmond had to be nasty. Many companies who thought they could compete, such as Ashton Tate with dBase, and WordPerfect in its many incarnations, were thrown curves by Microsoft's OS developers that inhibited their ability to compete on the same fair plain that they would have expected. But, Microsoft had not placed an X on their chests.

Microsoft destroyed any competitive company that might have threatened its empire. To hear that Bill Gates is not happy being the richest man in the world falls a bit short of how he played as a competitor. He played for keeps, and as I observed, when he was a player on the field, he played dirty, and winning was the only objective.

So, as he ages, he wishes he may wish he was a better man as what do we have in life other than our dignity, and the goodness we bestow on others; and of course, fair play. There is no question that Bill Gates is quite a philanthropist. Together with his wife, Linda, the Gates' have given away $30 billion since 2000, according to Forbes. To those wondering, a $30 billion fortune would make you the 16th richest person in America.

The question has been asked recently: How did Bill Gates became such a good guy in the people's eye, loved by Internet aficionados after he had been viewed by most as the incarnation of corporate evil in the '90s / early '00s? I would speculate that the billionaire looked in the mirror and did not like what he saw.

Though he won his fortune by shortchanging other good companies with good employees on the business scale, when he realized that the win was not worth the loss, perhaps he began to want to be a better man. But, in his day, when he was in charge, Bill Gates was absolutely ruthless in business, and was pretty open about it too. Gates' ought to consider starring in a Microsoft film about Microsoft in the role of Ebenezer Scrooge.

Paul Allen, Gates' co-founder; a gentle man.

Paul Allen, co-founder of Microsoft decided he would rather live his life as a fortunate man than be involved in

Microsoft's day to day activities. He left that to Bill Gates and his people so the business would continue to bring in big opportunities to guys like Bill Gates and eventually, Allen was happy to get a smaller share of the proceeds.

Paul Allen is a lot younger than I and I think I have a lot of years left. That part is up to God. He knew Bill Gates for a long time and in fact, went to the same private Seattle high school. Allen later dropped out of Washington State to work at Honeywell in Boston, then cofounded Microsoft with his high school buddy in 1975.

When he had had enough, he left. It was eight years later after being diagnosed with Hodgkin's disease. How about that for personal life acumen. A long life outside of Microsoft was better than death trapped within. Thank God Allen beat the disease and as reported briefly in all the synopses of Allen's life, he started living large, buying mega-yachts known to land at places like Cannes and the Sochi Olympics. Not bad, Paul!

As one whose life has been threatened by disease, Allen was much more appreciative for his ability to continue living than for being part of Microsoft. As noted, he has been living large ever since, and enjoying time on the planet Earth. Despite loving earth, Allen has been trying to get us all to other planets as quickly as his new company can take us.

Paul Allen owns a bunch of Sports Teams—the Seattle Seahawks of the National Football League (NFL), and the Portland Trail Blazers of the National Basketball Association (NBA) and he plays guitar in a rock band called the *Underthinkers*. He also owns an aircraft company aiming to put people into space—which I think he will one day.

The new (post Microsoft) Paul Allen likes to have fun and he likes to play or even watch games even though he often literally owns the ball. He never takes the ball and goes home. He wants no pucks—just balls. Allen is also a happy part-owner of the Seattle Sounders FC, which joined Major League Soccer (MLS) in 2009.

Paul Allen has a serious side and he uses his net worth of $18 billion—lots less than the persevering Bill Gates—for some great causes. For example, Allen is the founder of the Allen Institute for Brain Science, the Allen Institute for Artificial Intelligence, the Allen Institute for Cell Science, and Stratolaunch, the Company that one day may put people in space.

I am glad Paul Allen is well. Best wishes to Paul Allen, one of the good guys who beat IBM big time to become a multi-billionaire. I bet Allen every now and then issues a hearty thank you to IBM for its impact on his life.

Steve Ballmer took it on the chin and other places to help Bill Gates

Though not a founder per se, Steve Ballmer, Microsoft's 30th employee, is treated as one. He too is one of the world's richest men with net worth over $22.7 billion—even more than MS-co-founder Paul Allen. Ballmer had a reputation while on the Microsoft playing field with an opponent named IBM for doing whatever it took to make sure IBM loved Microsoft and that IBM knew that Microsoft had IBM's back (ahem!). There are a lot of other books that tell us all whether Steve Ballmer was actually truthful and sincere.

In these books and interviews with many of Microsoft's millionaires, it was clear that the Company would do whatever it took to win the day for Microsoft, and to heck with anybody else; and to heck with honesty!

Steven Anthony Ballmer's most fortuitous meeting in his life came when he met Microsoft co-founder Bill Gates. Both were sophomores at Harvard. Ballmer went on to finish his degree, rather than dropping out of undergraduate school as Gates did. Mr. Ballmer then spent two years at Procter & Gamble honing his Harvard business degree. He then decided to better himself and so he attended Stanford University's business school. But, Ballmer dropped out in 1980 to join Microsoft. Who can blame him?

Jennifer Edstrom and Martin Eller pumped out a great book in 1998 about insiders at Microsoft titled: <u>Barbarians Led by Bill Gates-Microsoft from the Inside</u>. This book confirmed my suspicions that Microsoft's aggressive play did not come by accident. It was all planned from the top down.

The tales about the early days of Microsoft are humorous but also are very telling about the lack of character the Microsoft players had when they became forces in the business world. They laughed at how they "screwed IBM." Internally, they used the acronym BOGU to describe their strategy for making deals with IBM.

Bend Over, Grease Up was the strategy. Outsiders trying to figure out what they meant in the book thought it meant that Microsoft was willing to bend over backwards for IBM. Hah! Funny! Microsoft wanted to win and that was the whole intent of the schmoozing.

Each meeting with IBM, the Microsoft team knew IBM would make demands that they would never meet but they had to grease themselves up so that IBM believed all the action occurred in a fair game.

Steve Ballmer was the guy who did most of the negotiating with IBM. When he was at the table, the rogues at Microsoft saw his negotiation victories in a not so positive light. They saw it as BOGU (bend over grease up – not too complimentary)

But, when Ballmer was directly involved in negotiations, they changed the acronym to BOGUS: "Bend Over, Grease Up, Steve." Pretty nasty but 100% true.

These rogues at Microsoft kept the Company technologically in the lead, by hook or by crook, and they had little regard for executives other than Gates himself. Historians note that Microsoft would basically bend over backwards to get IBM's business, even if it meant stretching the truth and promising things that would never happen.

Steven Ballmer was worth his weight in gold to Microsoft— both in BOGUS negotiations and in his business acumen as his dedication to Microsoft was second only to Bill Gates himself. When he retired from Microsoft in 2014, Mr. Ballmer had only nice things to say. He called Microsoft his "life's work."

He also expressed confidence in the Company's future by complimenting its strategic direction and management. He was ready to leave after 34 years and he noted that his new life precluded continued service on the board.

Nobody of whom I am aware has ever recorded Steve Ballmer thanking IBM for its assistance in bringing him his $billions. I would suggest that Steve Ballmer and all the Microsoft billionaires and millionaires need to say thank you to IBM one day.

They did not get to where they are without a little snookering of IBM and they got a lot of real help from Big Blue. Would anybody at Microsoft have been a billionaire or millionaire without IBM? What's a thank you fellas when it is the truth?

The records indicate that there are at least three multi-billionaires and; at least one billionaire from Microsoft and over 12,000 millionaires, many of whom are multi-millionaires. I wonder how many millionaires IBM created in all industries? Maybe this book is my ticket to the millionaire club if fifty-nine is the charm? Hah!

IBM employees worked with future Microsoft millionaires

As an aside, IBM employees during the Gates years worked hand in glove with Microsoft engineers. The folks who worked for Microsoft became very rich during the process. IBM would not permit its employees to invest in Microsoft and IBM was not growing. www.employee.com, an IBM "union" organization has this to say about that:

"We developed a lot of software that is still shipped in Windows, yet we were prohibited from investing in Microsoft as individuals because MS was a "competitor". IBM receives license income from this code, but there is no benefit to the IBM employees to be compensated appropriately. Our peers - those who worked jointly with us on the "New Technology" in the 1980's and 1990's at MS are many times over, multi-millionaires because of the tactics of Bill Gates and IBM's neglect of its own skilled developers."

In 1992, The New York Times wrote a piece about Microsoft's Unlikely Millionaires," that told a story much like IBM investors in the 1950's and 1960's.

While Microsoft was helping its employees become millionaires by permitting them to work for stock options and free coffee while grinding out 60 hour weeks to make the Company successful, obviously modern day IBM employees did not experience such wealth by working for IBM. I know IBM employees put in the hours but after the Watson's loyalty and respect were simply words at IBM.

"Microsoft's Unlikely Millionaires," it can be argued conclusively stands in unhappy contrast to the IBM employee story from the IBM Union web site. "An IBM employee, for example, who happened to own $10,000 worth of stock purchased in about 1974, would have seen it grow to about $19,000 at the 1992 market price of $98 a share. They would have enjoyed $12,500 in dividends also."

A good look at the IBM stock value from 1974 to 1992 shows that not many people in recent years have become millionaires with IBM stock...and this includes employees such as yours truly. I was able to sell enough shares of IBM in 1987 to put a down payment on a house but that was about it. Analysts would conclude that a tax-free bond might have been a better investment. Meanwhile IBM was creating millionaires right and left in other companies.

Looking at stock prices as Bill Gates was amassing his fortune, a lot of other "Softies" were making their own personal fortunes. They got in on the early stock options. From the 1986 to 1996, Microsoft's stock soared more than a hundredfold as the Company's Windows operating system and Office applications dominated the PC industry.

This is a fitting ending to a chapter on IBM's most illustrious and most successful direct competitor, Microsoft. Apple is now the big guy in town, but IBM never treated Apple as a competitor.

IBM's bungling with Microsoft and a host of other companies that it made successful, not only messed up its stockholders' opportunities and fortunes, Big Blue also messed up a few employees lives unnecessarily also. It would have been nice to become a millionaire, and IBM had what it took but did not know it.

Meanwhile tens of thousands of employees in Microsoft, a company which IBM helped prosper, became multimillionaires or at least millionaires. Then again, nobody said that life as a whole was fair.

Section V

Application Software: From Watson to Rometty

In the first edition of the book, I did not include anything about application software. The book told the story that I wanted it to tell about the many entrepreneurs who benefitted from IBM being asleep at the switch while they were becoming billionaires. I was very pleased with my work. Then, I got some feedback.

One of the early purchasers of the first edition asked me why I skipped at least five billionaires who had held the same position (Systems Engineer) as he and I at IBM. He referred of course to the founders of SAP, the # 1 ERP application software company in the world. That's why the second edition has come out so fast.

All of my tech life I was a player in the use of application software. At IBM, I helped my customers install it and use it and I even wrote it. It was so close to me that I did not include it in the book. When I woke from my fog, I found a number of very recent billionaires besides the SAP 5, who made most if not all of their billions on computer applications. And so, very quickly I began to research the application development companies to determine which companies needed to be in this book.

I learned that there are literally tons of application software millionaires and I knew I could not include them all or nobody would be able to take this book on vacations in their carry-on luggage. So, I did my best with the billionaires and I picked four specific millionaires who have done quite well for themselves in the application software / service bureau applications area of Information Technology. I also went back and reread the whole first edition and reedited it to be even more coherent than the first version.

The result is that I created this new section for application software and a partial litany of the technology stars who made their fortunes in the applications area.

Since I had not included application software in the first edition, I never really explained it. And, so, in the first part of this section, I discuss the notion of software and I discuss the types of software.

Then, I go into IBM's role in application software over the years. To maintain the theme of the book, I highlight all of the application software opportunities that IBM could have had if it had stuck with its original thought of providing application software for its customers.

From there in this section, I move the theme to some specific companies and some specific billionaires and millionaires about which I hope you enjoy reading. And after I finished with all that work, I redid the net worth table, adding enough new entries to take the table to 3 digits. I then replaced the older table in Chapter 1 with the new larger sized, more inclusive net worth table.

So, let's move on to Chapter 56 and start the lecture on application software.

Chapter 56

What is Application Software?

IBM SEs wrote all software for IBM customers

When I was a cub with IBM, IBM Systems Engineers (SEs) wrote application software for everybody and later on, when IBM said we could not do that anymore; in order to sell any new systems, we had to magically produce applications out of thin air for the customers. We had so many new accounts per SE that we could not cold code each account's software from scratch. So, we kept our last coding results and next to last and as many as we needed in our desk drawers in the office on disk packs, tapes, or diskettes.

When a new account system order came in, we brought out the drawer code. Everybody in IBM knew that was how we installed new accounts and everybody knew that if they stuck to the unbundling mantra, IBM would sell no more systems and we would all be fired. At the time, IBM sold systems for a living, not application software.

Application software has always been the reason why companies would buy computers. Today it is why people buy computers. Application software is why people buy phones and any other gadgets that are controlled electronically and not 100% circuit simple. If there is any logic in a circuit needed for your microwave to function, for example, and nobody wrote application software to test each of the buttons and the sequences, you could press any button and it would be unresponsive. It would not even beep. Application software buried on the chip makes the buttons come alive.

Application software is the king. System software of course enables application software to do its thing. And, so this chapter on Application Software, the king of software, now begins but we will explain system software first so we all know that not all problems are the fault of the guy who writes the applications.

Whereas it is easy to understand the term hardware as it is something physical such as a computer system, a display screen, a disk drive or a printer, the overall notion of software is a bit more difficult to define and to understand.

Software v hardware?

Software is simply a collection of programs. *Hardware* is physical while software is instructions that get loaded into hardware. *Programs* consist of a series of computer instructions that tell the computer what to do. Programs thus tell the machine to perform arithmetic operations such as add, subtract, multiply, divide, as well as logic operations such as compare and branch. The "branch" operation takes the machine to an instruction anywhere in the program based on the results of the "compare." When a bunch of programs perform a specific function such as payroll, the set of programs is called software.

It is the comparing and branching instructions that give a computer its logic capability. With arithmetic and logic, computer programs called software can be written. You have heard of Windows 10, Excel, Microsoft Word and you have probably heard of programs that perform accounting operations as well as those programs that can guide a spaceship to Mars.

Systems software and application software

Software itself can be divided into two general classes. One is called systems software and the other is called applications software. Systems software is software that helps the computer be smarter. Systems software thus includes programs such as the Windows 10 Operating System; the Mac OS; and the iPhone's IOS. It also includes programming languages such as FORTRAN, Assembly Language, COBOL, BASIC, and RPG.

Application Software is a series of end-user programs written in many different languages and subsequently translated into machine language. Each different computer type has its own machine language and it understands only those instructions that are in its own particular "machine language."

The programs are designed to work together to provide specific functions for a computer user. The term "application" signifies that the computer, through this type of software, *applies* the power of the computer to a particular problem, such as payroll or accounts payable or inventory control or to answering a cell phone. Application software also includes generic software such as word processors, web browsers and spreadsheets.

Nobody buys a computer to possess its hardware, and nobody buys a computer for system software. Those who acquire a computer of any kind, buy it so that it will do specific things for them. Those things desired by computer users are provided by application software.

Application software therefore is the reason why computers are purchased. Businesses want to be able to take orders and send out bills and private users want to work with Facebook or email or get highway directions from their computers. Application software provides these things.

How long has this been going on?

Back in the 1950's when the first commercial computers were brought to market, there was no software per se. There was no system software nor application software. Companies would purchase a huge machine and then train their best people how to program the unit. While the people were being trained, IBM Systems Engineers would be writing the applications for free. If the unit had an operating system and some high level languages, then their programming work was not as difficult.

Computers of course were and continue to be very versatile and so when a computer is programmed for payroll, it immediately becomes a payroll machine. When it is programmed for billing, it is a billing machine. In the 1950's the computers were all mainframe sized and there was no such thing as word processing or spreadsheet programs. Nonetheless application programs provided the value of the system.

The persons who programmed computer systems were known as programmers. Companies that could afford the early models using expensive tube-oriented behemoths could afford a team of highly paid programmers to get the job done. Their job was to create the business software for the company. There were no packages of software that could be purchased off the shelf in the 1950's when computer hardware was in its infancy.

Programs were not reusable

Each early machine had its own machine language and thus its own instructions. There were no specific sophisticated operating systems to mask any complexity. Therefore, when a company, for example, traded in its IBM 701 for an IBM 650 or it traded its IBM 7010 for a 7030, it was not a matter of simply replacing the hardware and firing the new system up on Monday. What about the programs that were running the business?

All of the programs needed to be recoded (reprogrammed) into the enhanced machine language of the new machine. The only two parts of the old software that typically had any value were the system design and the individual program design. Programmers would spend several years sometimes rewriting all of the programs for the newer systems so that the company could use faster and better technology to run its business.

IBM led the industry in everything from the 1950's through the 1970's, including hardware and system software. For example in 1957, after three years of work, IBM's Jim Backus and a small IBM programming team built a programing system that would enable a computer to produce its own machine language programs.

Through this effort, IBM was able to introduce the FORTRAN Programming Language. The name FORTRAN is an acronym for FORmula TRANslation, because it was designed to allow easy translation of math formulas into computer code. It was the first high level language and though it was built for scientific work. Despite its intended use for science, business users saw its potential. IBM then developed a set of FORTRAN commercial subroutines, which many business programmers would use to write applications for business.

This was a major breakthrough in making programs easier to write. Additionally, FORTRAN could be ported from one system to a newer one and then to an even newer one. Therefore it reduced the cost of transitioning from old hardware systems to new hardware systems.

FORTRAN is not an operating system. It is a programming language. When Programmers use it, their programs are written almost in English, When the FORTRAN compiler translates the programmer code, it creates machine code for the type of hardware being used.

When IBM introduced its first operating systems, it gave them away. With an operating system, a hardware model became much more intelligent and was more desirable to purchase. An operating system therefore is the software that supports a computer's basic functions, such as scheduling tasks, executing applications, and controlling peripherals such as card readers and printers.

An operating system is the most important program that runs on any computer. It manages all other programs on the machine. Every computer from a PC to a mainframe today has to have one to run other applications or programs. It's the first thing "loaded." Windows 10, for example, is an Operating System. The following schematic shows the four functions of an operating system permitting users to run programs which talk to the operating system and then to the hardware.

Figure 56-1 Four Components of an Operating System

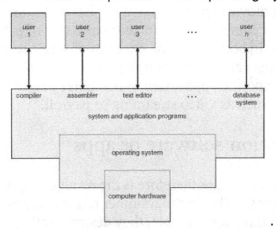

IBM programmers in the early years wrote all of the tough systems programs, such as operating systems, system utilities, such as COPY FILE, DELETE FILE, etc., as well as language compilers such as FORTRAN. The early compilers were actually called *assemblers* because they were not very sophisticated like FORTRAN and could produce just one machine language instruction for each assembly language instruction. These programs are regularly known as low-level languages.

FORTRAN is a high level language because one statement in FORTRAN, such as a WRITE operation would produce hundreds of machine instructions, thereby saving programmers such detailed coding.

Application programming

Today's application programmers use high level languages (more English-like than machine-like) such as FORTRAN, COBOL, BASIC, RPG, or others to build computer applications (known as apps on Smart Phone computers).

Applications or apps can be as sophisticated as providing streaming movie capabilities to a phone or as mundane as providing a company with an automatic way of processing its payroll. In both cases, the application software created through application programming provides instructions to perform a specific application of computer power to solve a problem—such as video streaming or payroll.

Application software or apps

Application software therefore is the result of application programming. When a programmer sets out to provide video streaming for example, they design a software system and the individual programs to provide the function they desire. Then they go about coding their work using high level application programming languages ----again such as BASIC or COBOL or C++. When it is coded, the result is translated (compiled) into a machine language program or set of programs. This set of programs is known as application software or Apps.

Programmers are needed not only to create operating systems and high level programming language compilers but also to create computer applications or apps. You can therefore imagine that there are a ton of programmers making their living in the Information Technology Industry as well as other industries—such as the automotive industry—in which computer technology is always deployed.

Just how many programmers are there?

International Data Corporation (IDC) recently published its Worldwide Software Developer and ICT-Skilled Worker Estimates. They looked at the number of professional software developers, hobbyist developers and Information and Communications Technology (ICT)-skilled workers in the world in countries that contributed to 97% of the world's

GDP. The bottom line is that there are about 12 million professional programmers and another 30 million including ICT workers and Hobbyists engaged in the computer technology business.

As difficult as it may be to believe today, in the 1950s and 1960s, computer operating software and compilers such as FORTRAN were delivered as a part of hardware purchases without separate fees. There were no such things as application software packages, such as order entry, billing, payroll etc. Each company wrote its own or IBM SEs wrote it for them.

The Watsons, who ran IBM during this period were smart businessmen. They recognized that customers were most willing to spend millions of dollars on new and better computer technology. They reasoned that if they did not have to spend millions of dollars on outside software services and additional staff to migrate their software to newer and faster machines, there would be more dollars left to pay for even bigger IBM mainframes. IBM's long term goal thus became the ability to move from small to large computers without any conversion with minimal to no expense. With the IBM System/360, explored in Section III of this book, IBM achieved this goal.

With the System/360, IBM introduced two specific advanced operating systems. One was called OS and the smaller of the two was called DOS—not to be confused with Microsoft's DOS. Two others were also made available – Tape Operating System (TOS) and Basic Operating System (BOS).

The revolutionary innovations in the System/360 family quickly became computer industry de facto standards that reshaped the computer industry and facilitated its sustained rapid growth. As the inventor of all of this innovation,

IBM's bottom line was burgeoning and its stockholders were reaping huge rewards.

There was only one piece of the full software game in which IBM was not really invested, though it was a player. IBM had no real application software business. It helps to remember that software was a throw-away item in that IBM gave it all away to customers who rented IBM equipment.

IBM AWOL from application software

IBM in these early years did not have what I would call a real application software business. IBM had software that it would ship for free as-is but it did not sell software that a business could readily deploy. Instead, to use IBM equipment, the business would have to hire a staff of programmers along with a Data Processing Manager, and this team would write the programs for the business.

Payroll was often the first application followed by order entry and billing, inventory control, accounts receivable, and sales analysis. In all cases, if there were any issues in the implementation, the local IBM office would dispatch one or several Systems Engineers to write the code and make the installation a success.

IBM wired TAB boards for rental customers

During the 1950's and the 1960's, the custom writing of customer of user applications, such as payroll and Invoicing, for each computer installation was normally done by the FREE IBM Systems Engineers (SEs). IBM systems were rental based and some IBM investment early on in the customer's applications earned IBM the right to be the vendor of choice for a long time to come.

It was a great model for keeping customers. IBM had been doing this for many years before computers were the norm.

IBM SEs for example in the 1930's, 1940's, and 1950's, and 1960's would even wire the unit Record Tabulating machine control panels for each unique customer and application, as long as the customer was willing to pay the monthly rental.

SEs, like me, would wire the control panels for the IBM Tab installations. With various boards, the Tab equipment could perform many of the same applications as computers, such as payroll. Each wired board was in essence a new computer program.

My first account in IBM was D'Arcangelo and Clark, a CPA firm in Utica NY. I wired their new rental TAB system and even wired an aged trial balance board which rolled totals at the end of each month and produced new balance records on 80-column punch cards.

Paul Harkins, another IBM SE, personally designed and wired the payroll control panels for a Unit record (Tab) customer, then he duplicated the same payroll system, including documentation, for at least 8 other new IBM customers, including the same 80 column card layouts and a payroll check with the same layout. In essence, using this approach, Paul had effectively implemented an application software package using TAB equipment before any applications were ever available for IBM computers.

This was the same approach IBM SEs used with computers. One SE would build a package of some software that was theirs only and they would give it to other SEs and use it to install many systems. When IBM unbundled in 1969, this activity was verboten but it was still done as IBM had no idea how else to survive.

In my case, I wired just one unit record shop. After that, in 1969, the IBM System/3 Model 10 Card system was

introduced and IBM moved me into that area of endeavor
and out of unit record gear.

Chapter 57

Business Application Software, Service Bureaus, & Clouds

Pre-built packages

As noted previously, **Business software** or business applications can be said to consist of any software or set of computer programs that are used by business users to perform various business functions. These business applications are used to increase productivity, to measure productivity and to perform business functions accurately.

In the early days and still today for the largest of corporations, business software is likely to be programmed specifically for a particular business and therefore it is not readily transferable to a different company. Few businesses even within the same industry sub segment operate exactly the same and so it is unlikely that Company A's software would run perfectly on Company B's machine.

Just about every company has a set of unique requirements that off-the-shelf software in unlikely to address at a 100% level. However, where a shelf-solution is available, even if the fit is not exact, some level of customization is lots easier than a full design and scratch software write. Thorough research of course is always required.

Even though IBM did not sell application software per se until the late 1960's. Big Blue knew that no business would use computer hardware without application software to solve the problems of the business.

And, so, hoping to create as many good systems designers and programmers as possible, IBM wrote a lot of how-to books and manuals about how to design and program generic business applications. Additionally, IBM coded and documented some basic application packages and made them available in a library for its customers to take and use free of charge. Besides this, as noted previously, IBM's local Systems Engineers often found or wrote specific code for new IBM hardware customers.

Since academics were the first users of computers, initially there were far more free scientific and university administrative application programs available than commercial. The development of standard business application programs lagged the scientific and technical advances as academics were not inclined to write billing or accounting programs. By 1964, however, when IBM introduced the System/360, the company and other vendors had built or collected huge libraries of business application programs for accounting, manufacturing, and retailing.

As one might expect, these pre-built programs rarely satisfied the full requirements of individual customers. However, with some great books that IBM engineers wrote, and with IBM systems engineering assistance, and a good in-house team, this software was used in many ways as a guideline or check list to simplify the development of custom application programs.

Designing systems and writing code from scratch was a particularly arduous task and fraught with many more errors than using a guideline set of programs. IBM was in the free application game for sure as were the rest of the BUNCH

(Burroughs, Univac, NCR, Control Data, and Honeywell). There was no question that the availability of these "model" programs helped all computer vendors sell computers to first time companies since it showed that working applications could be built.

In the pre-computer, pre hardware and software days, from 1932 onward, IBM provided a service for its customers so that they could use the power of data processing without the need for their own professional staff or even their own equipment. IBM ran what was known in the industry as a service bureau. Big Blue permitted its smaller customers, many whom rented typewriters from the company, to rent time on IBM tabulating equipment, and in the 1950's and later, computing equipment.

Using the service bureau approach companies therefore solved their business problems even though they could not financially justify a full-time equipment lease or a programming staff.

IBM's company was eventually known as the Service Bureau Corporation (SBC) IBM customers rented computer time—typically hourly—but had to have their own custom applications wired or programmed before using the SBC. So, IBM again solved the problem. IBM SEs would do this work for the customer while the customer was awaiting its own inexpensive computer to be delivered by IBM. It often took a year or more to get delivery. The William B Kessler Company of Hammonton NJ is a case in point.

In 1956, after years of the government pressing on IBM that it was a monopoly, the company signed a consent decree with Uncle Sam to behave as our dear uncle then dictated. As a result of this US DOJ pressure, IBM agreed and in fact did spin off its service bureaus. The government forced IBM to begin to operate these ventures at "arms-length" from the parent company.

And, so with no other choice, in 1957, IBM created a wholly owned subsidiary known as the *Service Bureau Corporation (SBC)*. It was designed to operate IBM's former service bureau business as an independent company. Because mother IBM was no longer permitted by the government to share its secrets with its subsidiary (SBC) according to the decree, the separation was as effective for the government as a selloff.

IBM killed cloud computing in 1957

Who knows where IBM's service and / or cloud business would be today if it had not acquiesced to the Justice Department's demands that it exit the service bureau space way back in 1957. Analysts with a penchant for history are going back and checking to see if the government really did its best to kill cloud computing way back in 1957?

FYI, *cloud computing* is the practice of using a network of remote servers hosted on the Internet to store, manage, and process data, rather than a local server or a personal computer.

Back in 1957, as noted above, technology was quite primitive. There were no clouds. The state-of-the-art data processing equipment included punch cards, sorters, and tabulators. Businesses and government agencies had to make a substantial investment in order to buy (or lease) their own dedicated equipment. Moreover, they had to hire a cadre of experts to run it.

Some companies did form "IT shops" in their companies, but many had just one or two accounting problems that they had to solve occasionally, such as once per month. Economically it made much more sense for such companies to rent tabulating time at IBM, run their card jobs (such as payroll or billing), then pack up and come back a month later.

IBM viewed this as an enormous revenue opportunity and the Company opened up so-called service bureaus around the United States. It was a good deal for IBM and for its customers. When a company became big enough or sophisticated enough to afford its own equipment, having had a positive IBM service bureau relationship most often prompted the customer to stay with IBM for its computer purchase. IBM competitors considered this a monopolistic practice.

In every way that's relevant, IBM's service bureaus from way back in the 1930s provided exactly what cloud computing providers such as IBM and Amazon do today. Back then, there were no clouds. There were no networks. And, so service bureaus were all local.

IBM service bureau application software customers accessed their local service bureau via the US road system. Some keypunched their own data into cards and others brought their source documents to the shop for an IBM employee to key the data to be processed. Despite the "sneaker-net" physical network model, the business model was exactly the same. It was cloud computing without the cloud.

So what happened to this great idea over 50 years ago? Why is it now that IBM is making a comeback in a business segment that it had once pioneered? Why are other companies who once were in other industries trying to compete with IBM in the cloud? Companies besides IBM, such as Microsoft and Amazon, are now trying to reinvent what IBM's SBC, National CSS, and other service bureaus were delivering many decades ago?

Telling the whole story; it was adding insult to injury for
IBM. Somebody was always trying to hack off a bit of IBM
for its own reward. IBM had so much business that it hardly
noticed the loss and mostly took the easy way out of
everything. This part of the answer is after the 1956 consent
decree but also goes back to the early 1970s.

CDC claims harm from IBM

In the 1970's, Control Data Corporation (CDC) competed
against IBM as one of the BUNCH. It was the C in BUNCH
and the number 5 computer manufacturing vendor at the
time. CDC sued IBM looking for a piece of IBM's huge
retained earnings. It claimed that Big Blue exhibited
monopolistic behavior. Having worked for Big Blue in those
days, I know that IBM played strictly by the rules of the
1956 decree in our Branch Office and we all knew what it
meant to work for IBM.

IBM chose not to fight the CDC lawsuit and eventually the
Company agreed to an out-of-court settlement. As part of
the deal, IBM sold SBC to CDC for $16 million. That is all.
It is a pittance now and it was a pittance then. IBM also
agreed to not compete against SBC for even more years.

It made the deal because IBM agreed that it had stretched
the rules with its System/360 Model 92. By 1973, as a direct
result of this particular lawsuit, IBM was completely out of
the service bureau business. Again, the cause was not the
service bureau industry. This suit had lingered on for some
time after IBM had announced a System/360 model known
as the "92," but had never delivered even one system.

Observers refer to this as the *"fear, uncertainty and doubt"*
(FUD) tactic. The FUD was created by IBM's pre-
announcement of the model 92, which never became a
product. However, companies planning to buy a powerful

CDC model were dissuaded by the mere mention of IBM having a model in the line that would outclass CDC offerings. Was IBM playing games? The company settled the lawsuit quietly!

I remember the day when it was announced in the Branch Office, even though it was not memorable. Although the model 92 never ever existed other than on paper in IBM someplace, sales of CDC's competing model 6600 dropped drastically as CDC potential customers waited for the release of the mythical IBM Model 92. Many IBMers, such as I saw IBM's disposition of SBC personnel as pulling the rug out from them. Through no fault of their own, they no longer worked for IBM.

CDC was not doing too well in any area at the time, suffering huge business problems. Even the acquisition of SBC could not help CDC turn its company around. SBC was simply not enough to save CDC. Ironically after CDC melted away, SBC was doing so well that it was able to survive the CDC implosion.

SBC was taken over by Ceridian, an existing service bureau company that provided human resources-related services, such as payroll processing. It used a Software as a Service (SaaS) model as well as cloud technologies (before cloud) to attract its customer base.

As we have discussed, IBM had operated service bureaus in major cities since 1932. The government was always pressuring IBM to give parts of its business opportunities to its competitors. Other than the Model 92 fiasco. IBM behaved notoriously too well for there to be a logical rationale for government intervention. IBM feared the government and so it did more than comply. IBM also was

making tons of money and it had lots of cash. It did not see
SBC at the time, as integral to success.

Microsoft was tougher than IBM

Years later in the 1990's, Microsoft, a software-only vendor
for years, when sued by Justice, chose to snub its nose at the
government regulators. IBM's response was weak. Big Blue
fought for a while, then gave in and lost a lot. Microsoft
won by holding its ground and in some ways the Bill Gates
company even taunted the government.

Bill Gates got away with ignoring the Justice Department
while IBM took it on the chin from both Microsoft and from
Justice for way to long without a whimper. IBM would
already own the cloud computing industry sub segment
today if it had not so readily given up its service bureau
business.

When IBM was finally ready to reenter the service business
after 28 or more years, there were a number of newly
renamed notions that smelled a lot like the service bureau
operations of old. In 2005, IBM's buzzword was On
Demand Computing and this in essence closed the full
circle. IBM was back with its own service bureau band.
When Big Blue began offering application hosting for its
customers, it was fully back in the time-sharing (service
bureau) business. But, why would IBM wait so long?

You may ask why service bureaus are germane in this book
and in this section on application software. The fact is that
with IBM back in the hosting business, regular companies
were able to use IBM's finest hardware and finest operating
systems and system programs such as its industry leading
database software to their advantage. Additionally,
companies were able to take advantage of IBM's finest
Systems Engineers merely by signing on the dotted line and
paying the monthly bill.

Small and large IBM customers were again able to have their business problems solved by computers run by the IBM Corporation in its huge datacenters. IBM would set up the network connections; install the customers' chosen application software; make sure it did the job, and then make necessary changes to the code or the environment if it did not initially measure up.

IBM's customers were almost guaranteed a successful venture. IBM spends lots more on its clients than any other company of which I am aware. IBM obsessed on making its customers happy. I saw this in every one of the twenty-three years that I worked for Big Blue.

Today IBM is back to making substantial amounts of dollars from services. Some analysts are beginning to project that hardware—even mainframes—are inconsequential to IBM's future. The new IBM future reeks in many ways of the IBM past. The old precepts and the remnants of the Service Bureau Corporation are back in the form of cloud computing guiding Big Blue's gingerly steps as it plans to make a killing using puff practices.

In the 1990's Lou Gerstner transformed IBM to a service company. Cloud computing using service bureau precepts is the new IBM. The Company is a service business. Though it still sells hardware, IBM is no longer a hardware company. Gerstner saved IBM with this "new notion."

Will the cloud give IBM back its industry preeminence? Just like Obi-Wan Kenobi might have been Luke Skywalker's only hope, cloud computing may be the only hope to reverse IBM's slide and move on to prosperity. But, IBM cannot make it a puff attempt.

To reflect on this topic; instead of service bureau or time sharing operations, as noted above, the newest IT business type that supplies application software and hardware to clients is called *cloud computing*. IBM CEO Ginny Rometty says this is IBM's focus for the future.

Computing functions are to be provided as services over the Internet. We discuss IBM's detailed plans for cloud computing in Section VI of this book. It is a principle, upon which IBM plans to bank its future. The notion may often be referred to as simply "the cloud." However, for IBM, its future is clear with clouds a plenty.

Cloud computing is the delivery of on-demand computing resources—everything from applications to data centers— over the Internet on a pay-for-use basis. It is also software as a service revisited. It is the new millennium version of the old notion of renting hardware and applications software from IBM. It is the modern service bureau.

These rented cloud-based applications—or software as a service—run on distant computers "in the cloud." The cloud and the applications are owned and operated by others, such as IBM. The cloud connects to users' computers via the Internet and, the user tool is typically a standard web browser.

Like the old service bureau model, users get to run their own applications without having to staff up with IT people. Better yet, all the IT headaches are borne by the cloud service providers. IBM is very pleased to be back in this business.

Chapter 58

IBM Was Once the Application Software Leader

IBM once half-heartedly sold computer application software.

If you are an old time computer company, but not in the business of selling service bureau computing; on demand computing; time sharing, or cloud computing, and you want to sell applications, then your choices are limited. Your mission would be to sell hardware and applications software and provide a support team of Systems Engineers (SEs). The SEs would help customers install systems and software and applications.

For those customers that decide to build their own applications, you would make sure your SEs are very smart, talented, versatile, and that they know how to lead customers to victory by using IBM equipment. For those customers who want to buy a software package in various forms of install-ability, with IBM, they would be able to use the same skilled SE team to assure their satisfaction with their unique IBM experience.

As an afterthought to its 1964 System/360 announcement, IBM introduced a machine that was upward compatible to the rest of the line but not downward compatible. It was called the IBM System/360 Model 20. For new accounts, IBM's sales personnel would sell this system model with no disk or tape drives. It worked with just 80-column punch cards. All programs and data would be processed on punch cards.

The System/360 Model 20 was successful, but it did not reach the bulk of small businesses as it required a lot of skill to deploy and its rental charge was not really inexpensive.

Near the end of 1969, IBM recognized the problem and it introduced a machine that was in many ways a clone of the smallest System/360 model 20. It had the same type of double card reader and it had no disk or tape drives. As a plus, it had a better version of the Report Program Generator (RPG) programming language than the System/360. IBM called the new unit, the System/3 Model 10 and the new language, RPG II.

Eventually, just as the System/360 family, the System/3 (S/3) model 10 turned out to be the first model of a six-model family of small computers with varying storage and processing capabilities. All models used the same processor, but through other mechanisms, such as memory and disk and operating system choices, some models could perform substantially better than others.

A System/3 card was not 80-column. It was about 1/3 the physical size of an 80-column punch card. However, each card contained 96 columns worth of information. See Figure 13-1.

System/3 was a huge success for IBM and for its 100,000 + customers. Few small businesses with 100 or more employees could resist signing up with IBM for one of these innovative systems. We tell the story of the System/3 line of computers in Chapter 13 of this book.

Just like all other computers, IBM's System/3 needed application software to provide the business function desired by its purchasers. IBM had no means in the early 1970's of selling applications. One thing IBM Systems Engineers did to help its salesmen sell "iron," was to help the prospect companies hire good people to create what we called a DP staff.

Additionally, IBM SEs would partner with systems analysts and programmers, who had become local experts. The companies would work out deals with these "experts" and they would either do all the work or they would work with the customer's IT staff and guide them to their ultimate success. IBM SEs would do what was necessary for the customer to be successful. '

Eventually Systems Engineers were so involved in so many successful implementations in the same industry that they developed top level expertise in designing customer solutions and in programming them. IBM began to recognize this phenomenon. Each subsequent installation in the same industry by a trained IBM SE took less time as the IBM team kept getting better and better at knocking down installation issues before they even had occurred.

IBM Field Developed Programs

IBM knew that its Systems Engineers (SEs) spent a lot of time in the office with order matters and miscellaneous administrative functions. The company decided to implement a program in which it would sell as-is software developed by its Systems Engineers and even those in the IBM plants that solved specific business issues for IBM potential clients. If an IBM SE had time while in the office or wanted to work late, he or she would receive additional compensation percentages for the number of field developed packages that were sold across the world. The packages were called Field Developed Programs (FDPs) by IBM.

This distinguished them from program products and other innovations that might be formally released by the IBM laboratories. The latter for example in the System.3 arena would be the Operating System and the Compilers and select applications for a few industries such as Hospitals.

Operating Systems were free at the time but clients paid for Compilers and for any of the few application programs that were available from IBM. The Field Developed Program idea was a huge success and it helped IBM SEs want to learn more about applications.

I can recall as a Systems Engineer thinking about what type of programs I might write to take advantage of this IBM opportunity. It was tough to perform all of IBM's preliminaries so I opted out. As I look at some of the FDPs that were introduced that I can either find or recall, many were in the systems programs category, but there were some such as the IBM System/3 Query FDP that was squarely in the application software bucket.

IBM Installed User Programs

IBM Systems Engineers found that a number of their customer account programming teams were very adept at solving problems with software developed for their specific industries. Often this software was designed and or programmed by an IBM Systems Engineer for the customer on the QT. IBM SEs after 1969 could theoretically get in trouble for providing billable services for free but IBM managers that wanted to sell hardware most often chose to ignore this rule.

Rather than develop the wheel again, SES suggested to IBM and IBM accepted the suggestion that Systems Engineers sponsor packages available from their customer accounts designed for specific application areas. Some to-be packages were built for specific industries by SE's specific clients, often with extensive help from the IBM Account Systems Engineer. These packages were sold world-wide and supported by the sponsoring Systems Engineer.

IBM's SEs indeed wrote many of the packages secretly to make the customer happy, but received no remuneration for this effort. For the nomination process, SEs would work with the customer team to get the package in a more generic form and then they would load it in an acceptable format to a library and a media for shipping. This innovative IBM program was known as the Installed Users Program (IUP). Its rules were similar to FDPs in that the sponsoring Systems Engineer was rewarded with a small percentage of the sales.

As IBM learned more and more from its new account teams that its customers liked having software to use to solve business problems rather than having to staff up to install a new IBM small System/3 or later a System/32, 36, 38, or AS/400, the company began to expand its application software offerings. IBM could have been the biggest application software supplier in existence if it had not given up on yet another innovation.

Big Blue was always there first with the hardware and every IBM client wanted IBM to guide its success by providing them with the solutions. Yet, IBM decided to give this whole industry away. I will get back to this after a short history of a lawsuit that changed IBM's application posture for a full decade. Then, we will look at the machines that

IBM was selling successfully to small businesses in the 1970's, 80's, and 90's.

Chapter 59

Impact of Catamore Lawsuit on IBM Application Software Strategy

IBM should have walked away

My good friend and Consulting IBM Systems Engineer Paul Harkins helped me in understanding the IBM Installed Users Program that IBM put together for its System/3 line. Its objective was so that IBM's new System/3 customers could have drop-in software when they purchased an IBM small business system.

The IUP program came about quickly after the Catamore lawsuit against IBM, The suit was originally filed in 1972, and it had a profound influence on IBM's application software strategy. In fact Big Blue change the way it supported its customers from that time onward. The institution of the IUP program was one such change.

The full facts are detailed in the lawsuit. Here is a brief synopsis:

In the IBM v. Catamore Enterprises lawsuit, an IBM salesman sold Catamore an $800 per month rental system to be used for production control. Catamore claimed that the IBM salesman orally agreed to furnish the system on a "turnkey" basis. This meant that all software programming

and installation assistance would be provided free of charge.
When the system failed to work, Catamore withheld
payment as the system in fact did not work as promised.

IBM filed a complaint to collect $68,000 from Catamore for
rental of equipment and payment for "agreed upon services."
Catamore counterclaimed, asserting breach of express and
implied warranties, breach of contract, and false
representations.

After trial, the jury returned a verdict in favor of IBM in the
amount of $68,000 and also a verdict for Catamore on its
counterclaims in the amount of $11 million. IBM felt
aggrieved and would not let it go. Big Blue appealed the
verdict.

The First Circuit Court found that the clause in the contract
providing that an action for breach of contract could not be
brought more than one year after a cause of action arose.
This theoretically precluded Catamore from prevailing on its
counterclaims for breach of warranty and breach of contract.
As a result, the First Circuit vacated the judgment and
remanded the action for a new trial. IBM was prepared to go
to trial again as Catamore appealed the decision. The news
ends at this point as the two parties reached an undisclosed
settlement.

IBMers close to the case are of the opinion that IBM settled
the Catamore case because its huge team of lawyers saw the
folly in IBM's installation strategy. This same group of
lawyers initially wanted their pound of flesh from Catamore
but after the verdict was vacated and a new trial was in the
offing, they re-examined IBM's posture in the case and how
Big Blue overall conducted new account business.

They concluded that the IBM way of helping new system
accounts become successful was seriously flawed. They

anticipated there would be thousands more Catamore-like lawsuits if the IBM Company did not rectify its procedures.

The lawyers then turned their guns on the IBM corporate management team to stop what they believed to be a messed-up, unworkable, one-on-one custom application installation methodology.

IBM simply did not have the resources to be successful when one or several Systems Engineers could be tied up for a year or more for a system that most often cost less than the SE's salary.

And, so, When IBM examined its one-on-one custom implementation application writing approach, the faults were obvious. As part of the correction, IBM announced Field Developed Programs and Installed User Programs, which totally changed the game. IUPs especially were very successful in assisting IBM customers with new system installations.

Paul Harkins is the IBM SE author of seven Apparel Business Systems (ABS) IUPs for various IBM systems. Paul shared his experiences with me. I learned more about the IUP program than I knew as a field SE. The ABS IUP's were based on the groundbreaking work Harkins performed for Goodimade Manufacturing, an apparel company in Philadelphia.

For his defined personal efforts in a number of installations across the world, Harkins received cash royalties from the 24 months of license fees. He also received peer recognition and the Systems Engineering Symposium, an annual honor for IBM's top SEs. Paul supported his packages across the world.

These new software programs were very good for IBM; for its SE force; and for IBM's sponsoring customers and receiving customers. The analysis of the litigation persuaded IBM to take necessary action to announce and actively support the highly successful customer Installed User Program (IUP) initiative in 1973. The FDP program was also successful but did not have the impact of the IUP program.

What it meant was that IBM further developed, marketed, licensed, and supported proven successful industry applications worldwide. It was a simple and powerful concept that was very successful. IBM, as a mainframe organization had never cared about application software as a revenue source. Its larger customers had huge staffs that built all the application software they needed.

However, a new account IBM System/3 Representative in 1970 had no such team of experts ready to program at a whisper's notice. And so, failures such as Catamore resulted and IBM's lawyers believed that without a major change, the failures would become the norm.

The coup de grâce for the success of the IBM Installed User Program (IUP) was that the local IBM marketing representative (salesperson) who sold the IUP to a customer received a nice additional commission that served as a motivation to sell such a package. Success breeds success as IBM found.

Moreover, another secret ingredient to success for IBM was that IBM insisted that the local IBM Systems Engineer, who in many cases had actually written the code, would need to agree to nominate the customer's application for the IUP program.

From its own one-on-one installation ineptness, IBM changed its policies in 1973 based on the Catamore outcome. IBM sold Application Software from that point on, and the change helped its new account business substantially.

IBM soon forgets.

In 1982, for its own reasons, IBM again decided to stop selling application software under this program. The Company did create other programs but their purpose did not eclipse the purpose of the IUP.

It was simply another sign of an inattentive corporate management team. Rather than solve customer problems and be the best it could be, IBM decided that it would become the industry's low-cost producer. IUPs and FDPs were no longer important. IBM never adequately explained why?

IBM never told its customers that excellence was no longer its strong suit. By 1993, the company was dying and Lou Gerstner came in to save the IBM Corporation from itself. Over 60,000 IBM employees lost their jobs. It was a catastrophic failure of IBM management.

In the other sections of this book, we discuss many other failures of IBM. Abandoning service bureaus and simple programs that provided application software solutions for new clients were two big mistakes. Today, as it tries to make it in the cloud business and the services business and the software business, IBM must have a few regrets.

Chapter 60

IBM's Post S/3 Systems -- Formal Application Software Packages

Lower cost systems for new accounts

After System/3, which had enough models to suit the smallest and the largest of small businesses, IBM decided to take the cost factor even lower to attract an additional set of customers to new IBM technology.

IBM introduced the System/32 in 1975. Taking the notion of FDP's and IUP's to the next level, IBM brought experienced, highly capable SEs into the labs to work with internal program developers.

My good SE friends Bonnie Becker and George Mohanco were SEs from Scranton who were part of the Industry Application Program (IAP) team in Atlanta GA. They created a number of top-flight application packages that would have stood the test of time if IBM chose to continue selling application software after 1993.

IBM customers always loved IBM packages and the fact that IBM assured that the packages would work. The IBM System/32 was supported by this even newer type of software product that had an affordable price. It was called the Industry Application Program or IAP for short.

In my role as an IBM Systems Engineer, I had the pleasure of dining on a Girtin Beef Sandwich at the Millville Town Restaurant and working with Al Harding, the CFO of Girtin Manufacturing. Together, we installed my first IAP, MMAS, at Girton.

The company bought a System/32 with IBM's Manufacturing Management Accounting System (MMAS) package, the predecessor of MAPICS. My job as an SE was to learn the package before they did and then to help them install it and use it successfully. My wife and I got to like Girtin Manufacturing so much that we went to Millville for years while off duty and while our kids were very small.

We would buy a recently cut Christmas tree from a friendly Millville neighbor's yard. This family had a snowmobile and right before Christmas, they brought trees from their lot several miles away to their front yard for sale to all of Millville. I had found a great decorated tree in the lobby at Girton and asked where they got it. After picking up the tree in Millville, we went to Bloomsburg with our tree inside the van and we feasted on Dick Benefield's Groaning Board at the Hotel Magee.

Similar IAP software package to the one which Girtin deployed were built for a number of other industries besides manufacturing. There were IAPS for construction, wholesale paper and office products, wholesale food, hospital, and membership organizations and association industries. They were all very well done. They were clean, and they were well received by IBM customers. IBM sold a ton of systems because of them. Big Blue priced these application software packages so that they were affordable and so it could make a bundle on them.

Between the IBM System/32 in 1975 and the IBM AS/400 in 1988, IBM's Rochester Laboratory in Minnesota created a number of new hardware systems, each of which supported the ever-expanding library of application programs marketed for profit by IBM. Systems known as the IBM System/34, and the IBM System/36, and the IBM System/38 were well known as being IBM's finest offerings for small businesses.

Moving from one system to another, just like within the IBM System/360 family, was a task but not formidable. Most IBM clients that needed more system power moved readily from one of these models to the next.

They all used similar control language and they all supported the RPG II or greater programming languages. The languages were designed for business use. All RPG and RPG II programs migrated well from system to system. IBM introduced RPGIII for the System/38 and RPGIV for the AS/400 and both of these new compilers could handle older RPG programs. Applications software moved readily from one IBM small system to another.

The reason I know this for sure is that I shepherded many migrations between and among IBM System/3X systems and I also helped my clients move from mainframe to S/3X and S/3X to mainframes.

IBM merges System/36 and System/38 with more applications

On June 21, 1988, IBM introduced the Application System/400 (AS/400). In today's world in which applications or apps run on phones, the box might have been called the *system for all apps*

The remarkable thing about the Application System/400 besides its power and ease-of-implementation was its name. IBM named this powerful set of machines to emblazon its purpose for this new family right on the units themselves so nobody could forget.

It was the IBM machine built to create and host and provide computer applications. It was built for the 1000 fully-developed and proven software solutions that were shipping with the AS/400 box on that particular June 21 in 1988.

And, if that were not enough, just like its predecessor System/38, it shipped from the IBM plant with a built-in database and an operating system designed with an E-Z button for creating brand new applications. All of this was on top of a powerhouse family of computer models that were built to avoid down-time. Avoidance of down time made the AS/400 the darling machine of Casino IT shops across the world.

Before the AS/400, IBM had kept a governor on its "smaller" systems so that none could be more powerful than the IBM vaunted mainframe line. The predecessor IBM System/38 had many of the same architectural characteristics of the AS/400 but IBM never gave it the processor juice to fully compete.

With AS/400, IBM took away most of the governors so that this new family had at least the power of a small mainframe and some say lots more was available waiting for IBM's RISC processors. IBM systems built in Rochester, Minnesota had never been known for power. They were known for ease of development and ease of use.

In my job as Senior Systems Engineer for the local Scranton IBM Branch Office. I got to understand the AS/400 before most Branch Systems Engineers. I attended pre-announcement sessions and with this background, I had the pleasure of presenting the IBM customer announcement materials for the AS/400 to IBM Northeastern PA customers at Marywood University in Scranton PA.

The 1988-introduced IBM AS/400 was an unprecedented new family of easy-to-use computers and it was fun to present. The meeting participants were very pleased with IBM for this most-anticipated offering. The Application System/400 (AS/400) showed IBM at least in 1988 knew that applications were very important for new system sales.

Like the predecessor S/36 and S/38 lines, this new system was designed for small and intermediate-sized companies. As part of IBM's worldwide introduction, Big Blue as well as its formal business partners worldwide rolled out more than 1,000 software packages in the biggest simultaneous applications announcement in computer history. IBM was positioned to kill the software industry with its AS/400 success machine.

It was not long after 1988 that the AS/400 quickly became one of the world's most popular business computing systems. By 1997, IBM had shipped nearly a half-million AS/400s. The 400,000th AS/400 was presented on October 9, 1996, in Rochester, Minnesota to Greg LeMond, the three-time winner of the Tour de France bicycle race and a small business entrepreneur.

The AS/400 family itself was unbelievably successful. IBM feared DEC so much, it unleased the AS/400 as its Vax Killer. DEC did not last too long after that. Unfortunately IBM, a mainframe-oriented organization by corporate design, would not continue to capitalize on the AS/400's uniqueness or its ease of programmability.

What happened to the AS/400 application machine?

Corporate IBM had always kept all non-mainframe products in a minimized status so that the mainframe operation would have its way. And so besides exiting the software business completely in 1993, IBM also buried its AS/400— ostensibly its finest application system by simply eliminating its name. The AS/400 was not built in New York, where all the fine mainframe IBM hardware units from the 1950's and onward had hatched.

IBM initially kept the AS/400 hardware and the operating system alive but it completely changed its identity. It confused even the hundreds of thousands of loyal customers who used these systems. The IBM AS/400 was force fit into the IBM eServer iSeries line. This was a brand that IBM had launched touting it as high-performance, integrated business server for mid-market companies.

IBM apparently forgot that the AS/400 already had a large customer base that believed that they were already using an AS/400 and not an eServer iSeries box. Since there was an existing IBM eServer pSeries (Unix RISC), and an IBM eServer x series (PC), and an IBM eServer z Series (mainframe), IBM AS/400 clients worldwide wondered what happened to the best system in the world—their IBM AS/400.

Alex Woodie of IT Jungle offered a great summary of the IBM AS/400 heritage machines in their new incarnation when IBM chose to reduce them further to the term IBM i. Here it is:

"What is so fascinating about the IBM i phenomenon at the end of the day is that it is a business computer. It runs boring accounting systems, but in a freakishly efficient sort of way...The IBM i server is an odd duck flying against the winds of standardization and homogenization, and that's one of the reasons that the IBM i community stands out from the pack.

"To the administrators, developers, analysts, users, and business partners who have worked with it, the IBM i server represents how practical and elegant solutions to business problems can be attained. Yes, it's a little weird sometimes, and IBM keeps changing the name of it, to the great exasperation of the users (do not confuse allegiance to IBM i as loyalty to the company that bears its name). But for those who have come to see how the IBM i platform delivers simplicity where others revel in complexity, it's a lesson they will never forget."

IBM could have done much better!

Chapter 61

IBM Failed in the Application Software Industry

IBM gave up its future success to ISVs

Nobody buys a new computer system without application software to use. Knowing this, IBM chose to exit the application software business in 1992. Industry analysts asked themselves if IBM was kidding just three years earlier when it had announced the Application System/400 (AS/400) with 1000 applications ready to go.

Additionally, AS/400 professionals saw the AS/400, with its integrated database as the machine for which applications are built. The conundrum was how could it have taken IBM just three years to know that it could not sustain a viable application software business? The answer still is unknown but each year without application software, IBM has floundered.

IBM signaled its application software retreat in 1982 when it removed FDPs and IUPs from marketing. At that time, it engaged in a very unholy alliance with independent software vendors. ISV pressure is what seemed to hasten IBM's retreat from applications but that does not make the decision a smart one.

IBM's top hardware, data base, and operating system competitors were doing just the opposite. HP, Oracle, and Microsoft were getting into application software big time while IBM was exiting. They are successful, and IBM's revenues are falling. There is an easily identifiable cause and effect here?

For those of us in the application software game, we were mostly surprised that IBM would sell off its great packages. We were even more surprised that Big Blue would sell or perhaps even give away its vaunted premiere applications— MAPICS and DMAS—to companies that knew they could be successful with IBM's rejected products. Too bad for IBM that it thought so little of its own accomplishments and its ability to sell products in the growing IT world.

IBM in the 1950's and during most of the 1960's gave as much free application software to its customers as they wanted. IBM paid the processing fees, storage fees, media fees and shipping fees. It was part of IBM's bundled services. With unbundling in 1969, IBM got out of the *free* business. Everything had a charge. The Company saved even more money by disposing of its application software inventory, while keeping and perfecting and selling copies of its system software, such as operating systems.

With Tom Watson and T. Vincent Learson (a Watson style manager) still as the CEOs at the time. IBM recognized that customers bought computers so they could run application software. IBM saw value in this and with its FDP and IUP programs began to amass a more formal array of offerings to provide solutions mostly to new IBM customers.

In the late 1970's IBM brought out the Industry Application Programs (IAPS), formally developed by funded labs and offered as "*bug-free*." They were built for the System/32. 34, 36, 38, and the AS/400. Until 1982, several years before the IBM System/3 was discontinued, FDPs and IUPs such as the Model 6 ABS package were available for the System/3 models.

Using IAPS as a smart tool, IBM redoubled its efforts to provide quality software in the new account marketplace. IBM was successful and profitable with application software if we take the price of the IAP and the price of the hardware into consideration.

IBM was struggling for its identity as a company for some strange reason while it suffered through very poor management at the top. The Company tried to get cash for any part of the company that somebody was willing to buy. So, Big Blue disbanded its formal application labs and sold those that it could.

Marcom, from Newton Massachusetts, for example, bought IBM's popular MAPICS software which subsequently switched hands a few times and today is owned by Infor. MAPICS is a competitor of SAP, which today is the leader in the ERP application space. IBM could have owned this distinction if it had played its application cards properly.

IBM also kept its DMAS software alive by transferring the rights to I/O International, Inc, a full-service supplier of e-business management solutions and a long time IBM business partner / ISV. The most recent version of DMAS is available exclusively from I/O International, Inc. and is referred to as I/O DMAS Plus. It consists of the original family of IBM's DMAS applications. It also has a number of attractive improvements from enhancements developed by I/O International.

When IBM decided to get out of the application software business, it got rid of its many formal packages for business management as well as software solutions for various industries such as public sector, construction, distribution, and manufacturing. These packages in one way or another could be tailored for just about any company's need. IBM had done it right and then, it just quit.

IBM had a major marketing edge as companies could use Systems Engineers or Independent local contractors to install, set up, and help businesses use the IBM software effectively. More importantly IBM controlled the game. But, nonetheless, Big Blue chose to get out of the game completely. This was a self-defeating move and today IBM is paying the price for trusting its independent software vendors to a fault.

Rather than continue with its application software success, the IBM Company chose to hitch its prospects for future success on the availability of Independent Software Vendors (ISVs) such as Marcom of Newton, MA, and many others. These companies supplied unique solutions to IBM's customers. Sometimes their code was very, very similar to what was once IBM proprietary code.

IBM could not say no to future failure

Unfortunately for IBM stockholders, the IBM Company could not deal with the grief that it was receiving from ISVs who felt IBM the hardware company was competing against them as application software suppliers for IBM hardware. So, IBM as was typical in most of its squandering, took the easy road out and sacrificed its own future to do so.

Big Blue decided to stop competing with ISV's by dismantling its entire successful application software business. IBM got rid of packages with names such as DMAS. PSAS, CMAS, BMAS, and of course the big-seller, MAPICS. Some packages, such as MAPICS were sold to other companies, and others simply were dumped off into the bit bucket of mismanaged IBM opportunities.

IBM had a great deal riding on the success of the AS/400, it's "midrange" application engine for the future. From the local office, I observed much of IBM's marketing actions. I knew immediately that abandoning application software was a bad decision. I could not figure out how IBM would trust its future hardware success to software companies, which it could not control.

Eventually these theoretically loyal IBM "partners" betrayed Big Blue and they built their software applications for other hardware systems, mostly Windows. As IBM reduced its System Engineering force, customers that bought IBM hardware and ISV application software had far greater loyalty to the ISV who supported their installation than the hardware company (IBM) that sold the box. Good will goes only so far when profit is the motivator.

Eventually most of the ISVs chose to compete against IBM's AS/400 heritage machines for their software business. Their Windows packages were always a better deal than their packages written for AS/400. IBM killed its future new account business opportunities when it trusted others to sell IBM systems. One would have thought that after the PC debacle, IBM would never trust its fate to another vendor.

Since IBM was always more expensive than Intel hardware, IBM ISVs jumped ship from IBM to sell the least expansive box. They made it up on Windows support services which were always required. At one point, in the late 1990s and early 2000s, IBM boasted about the AS/400 having over 20,000 applications and 8,000 ISVs. From my point of view that was a lot of potential IBM competitors.

Today, just fifteen years later, there are less than one thousand software vendors with any professed loyalty to

IBM. IBM could not stop them from leaving the IBM goodies stable, especially when Microsoft and Oracle began to put them on more lucrative feed bags. The IBM number kept getting smaller and less than a 1000 is surely not a great number, considering, as previously noted that there were about 8,000 ISVs at the turn of the century and about 2,500 just ten years ago.

The IBM ISV numbers continue to shrink. Selling IBM is not a good deal for ISVs any more. But, IBM disposed of its own sales force so it has nobody spearheading its system sales efforts.

While IBM was getting out of the software business to please its ISV "partners," HP, Microsoft and Oracle, three very astute business corporations, were upsetting their ISVs regularly by introducing or acquiring more software solutions. HP, Oracle and Microsoft knew something IBM did not know: Your own company comes first! At the same time, HP, Oracle and Microsoft were collecting former IBM ISVs into their stable, while IBM top management continued in its deep sleep.

Though IBM had no problem turning its million dollar system opportunities over to ISV's, which ultimately betrayed the company, IBM management kept an IBM direct sales team to sell mainframes. Now, IBM sales in midrange and small systems only happen when an existing customer wants to upgrade. IBM basically gets no new accounts from its ISV channel.

IBM has always been ambivalent about application software because some IBM top executives have less logic in their craniums than just one of IBM's old vacuum tubes of yesteryear.

When Big Blue stopped giving software away in 1969, there was not much software value in its stable. It was still the wrong move. Getting rid of FDPs and IUPs was a bad move in 1982. Removing all application software from the sales manual in 1992 was the dumbest move of all. IBM intentionally or unintentionally exited the software business that new accounts cared about. Today, nobody seems to care what IBM does. IBM rarely sells a new account today. It blew its big opportunity in application software.

Despite making mistake after mistake in strategic planning and in operations, IBM continued to make tons of money selling mainframes and mainframe system software. Nobody within the company was permitted to complain about the opportunities IBM left on the table.

Stockholders were not given the information that IBM management was selling them out for instant mainframe profits. Perhaps some at the top did not know that the company by its decisions had begun to remove the eye beams from the corporation even before the ship ran into icy water. Stockholders kept looking at earnings and despite poor operating performance, their dividends and the high stock price kept them on management's side.

Working through how bad a situation IBM's exit from the application software marketplace now called Enterprise Application Systems caused the Corporation, we simply have to look at the lost revenue. Companies, such as IBM, that withdraw from an industry too soon rarely have reaped any of the industry profits. Consider that in the next few years, Enterprise Application Systems (application software) will account for over $200 billion in software industry revenue. IBM still cannot get its revenue back up to the $100 billion level. Are you asking yet: *How much did IBM give up in yet another area of mismanagement?*

IBM gave away too much too soon by exiting the solutions software business. Nobody buys a system for the hardware or software products that IBM sells today. Companies buy solutions. IBM sells no solutions. IBM sells solution enablers for sure but its solution vault is empty. $200 Billion per year is a lot to leave on the table. IBM at one time owned the table, but the corporation chose not to play its cards to win.

For over twenty years, IBM has been the only hardware or system software company that believes that selling the application solutions that help a business choose which hardware or operating system to use, is a bad thing? IBM is on a solo flight here for sure. Nobody is flying with IBM in its decision to abandon application software solutions.

As we have said it many times in this section: Nobody buys hardware today and looks for a solution. They buy solutions and look for the hardware. If IBM has no solutions, then IBM must not be selling much hardware. Results show that IBM is losing hardware revenue each year and the company is unloading major hardware products each year. IBM is completely out of the PC Client, PC Server, and the Power Chip Manufacturing business. How's that been helping the bottom line?

Looking at reality. IBM's major competitors such as Microsoft, HP, SAP, and Oracle have taken an opposite path. They all sell application software or in some cases, they give it away. Since these companies are growing wildly while IBM continues to lose ground; upon which ship should we prefer to sail?

IBM management has a real issue looking at things objectively. Despite how IBM sees it; the results are in. Application software is another area in which IBM has failed miserably. What good is a cloud with no plug-in applications? Why would IBM have trusted its independent software developers who were paid by Microsoft and Oracle to develop for their platforms, rather than choose to sell front-line software solutions from IBM to its new accounts? It is called poor top management by anybody who takes a good look.

Let's now take a look at s a few companies that either used IBM's give-away code for their success or they were formed by some frustrated IBM SEs who knew that if IBM could not do it in application software, they could do it with or without IBM!

Chapter 62

Shared Medical Systems

A software company turned service bureau

The more I recall my past exploits as a Systems Engineer
with IBM, I realize all the challenges I had and how adept
this helped me become in the system design area. I could
program at a reasonable level, but in retrospect, I became
very good at systems design and I got to employ my trade in
many different industries. I loved the challenge of a new
industry and as an IBM Systems Engineer, the design
opportunities came frequently.

As an IBMer, I was assigned for many years to the higher
education industry—as well as banking, hospitals and
medical practices, government, and the product distribution
industry. As a Higher Education Specialist, for example, I
had the pleasure of leading the online student registration
software design efforts at Marywood University in Scranton
and Luzerne County Community College LCCC) in
Nanticoke, PA.

At the time, there was no such thing as online student
registration, and the design we put together stood the test of
time. In fact, Marywood sold its software twice—one time
to College Misericordia and a second time to Keystone
Junior College. Marywood could have made a killing on its
software nationally, but the University chose to concentrate

on its internal needs. At LCCC, I used my experience from Marywood to help this institution in their migration and online design efforts.

IBM PBAR in Ogdensburg, NY

My first industry design and programming experience was at the A. Barton Hepburn Hospital in Ogdensburg, New York. IBM Salesman Bill Campola had sold them a new 96-card-only System/3 along with IBM's own software package called Patient Billing, Accounts Receivable and Revenue Accounting.

This IBM program product software was not quite ready for prime time so in order to make it work, I had to learn its design by reading source code, making changes to the design to solve the necessary business problems, and then making the programming changes necessary for the hospital to productively use the software. After all the work that we put in making the package fit, the Hospital enjoyed its benefits for some time thereafter.

I had requested a transfer from IBM to get me closer to home when the hospital activity was finished. IBM agreed and when I began my 21 years in Scranton in 1971, I found myself under the tutelage of a talented Senior Systems Engineer, Fred Pencek. Fred handled all hospitals in Northeastern, PA. He welcomed me on his team.

A marketing Representative, John Kaltenthaler, Fred and I worked the medical territory (hospitals, labs, and medical groups) in Northeastern PA. Two Mercy Hospitals and St. Joes' Hospital used IBM systems with home developed software. The rest of the hospitals used SMS. SMS was a big player in our area. They could either run the software at their location as a service bureau or they could install a hardware system right at the hospital site.

SMS was not competing in 1969 and 1970 in Utica or Ogdensburg where I worked for IBM, but this Malvern PA Company was very successful in Pennsylvania at the time. Once I hit Scranton, I learned that they were our biggest competition in the medical industry. Before IBM had built the Patient Billing Software that I used in Utica, NY, it had built a mainframe software package that it called SHAS for Shared Hospital Administrative System. Its hope was to load software on a big mainframe at IBM and have multiple hospitals share it.

IBM eventually abandoned these lofty plans that would have almost definitely been successful. Big Blue most often did not realize when it had a good thing going. So, instead of capitalizing on SHAS, a nice package for hospitals built for the lower tiered entrants, it chose to give away its software code to a number of different companies.

SMS—Shared Medical Systems was one of the many companies along with dozens of Blue Cross plans and hospital associations around the country that acquired IBM's SHAS software. They sold this package to well over a thousand hospitals nationwide.

Using strange logic, IBM felt it was better to have others sell its software and IBM would not take a share of the software business revenue. As nice as it was for IBM to have given this software to SMS, it created a burden for offices such as Scranton and many others local offices across the country.

We had a difficult time competing for the hospital business against a company, SMS that had such great software. So, IBM's foolhardy decision not only excluded it from revenue opportunity on software sales, it hurt the sale of IBM hardware across all fifty states. Eventually SMS chose to run its software on competitive equipment and it was not known to favor IBM hardware.

Big Jim Macaleer was the top guy in SMS. He and Dr. Clyde Hyde and Harvey Wilson were the three founders of SMS, in 1970, SMS renamed their version of SHAS to "The Financial Management System" (FMS). They had vastly improved the original IBM SHAS code with many enhancements.

The apparently logical explanation for why IBM bowed out of SHAS goes like this. IBM dominated the hardware market in the 1960s with its 360 line of mainframes. The 360 sold so well to large hospitals that the IBM Company had almost 100% of the large hospital business in the country and the smaller hospitals out there were hard pressed to afford million-dollar IBM mainframe behemoths.

There were no large hospitals left that did not have an IBM mainframe or equivalent machine. That's when IBM got the idea to write the SHAS software package for small and mid-size hospitals who could then share a System/360. Thus, they called their software the "Shared Hospital Accounting System" (SHAS):

Just like the System/3 Patient Billing A/R system that I implemented in Ogdensburg, NY, SHAS was a complete suite of financial systems including census, inpatient and outpatient billing, accounts receivable, bad debt and general ledger.

IBM struck a goldmine with this package. SHAS became a runaway success, with hundreds of hospitals and many Blue Cross plans using it around the country. The price? Free! IBM gave SHAS away to "stimulate" System/360 sales. So, IBM never collected any gold for its application software work. But, SMS and others surely did. IBM did sell hardware nationally because of SHAS, and that was all it cared about.

SMS founders saw the software goldmine. The three amazingly talented individuals had the vision that SHAS could power a national network of hospitals. As a Systems Engineer myself at the time, I can see how these guys knew they could have immediate success. It was a gift horse for a trio at the right place, right time.

Jim Macaleer, a.k.a. "Big Jim," who is recognized as the founder and president of SMS started with IBM as a systems engineer. Harvey Wilson, a co-founder became senior vice president. He was a salesman's salesman. His technique sold more systems to more hospitals than anyone else in history or so goes the folklore. Clyde Hyde was a Medical Doctor with deep inside information for what was important and what was not. He had an amazing vision that shared computer processing could be applied to patient care, starting in his field: EKGs.

Nothing worth having is easy. The SMS team in 1969, while I was being deployed to Ogdensburg by the Utica Branch Office, Jim, Harvey and Clyde convinced a venture capital firm on Wall Street to lend them $5 million to buy an IBM System/360 so they could run SHAS. Additionally, they had enough to hire a team of specialists to sell, install and support SHAS under the moniker of SMS.

They had nothing but the $5 million and it was going fast. They rented office space outside of Conshohocken, Pa in a strip mall next to a dry cleaner. Things were tough in those early days. Big Jim, who was famous for pinching pennies and finding more barely turned the company from red ink to black, just as the $5M in venture capital was about to run out.

Their company went public in the mid-1970s, and from then it grew and it split its stock as it grew giving the early investors a handsome reward. Employees and the founders of course, also shared in the bounty. SMS was everything it could be and it grew to be the number one vendor on Healthcare Informatics "Top 100" list for more than 20 years. In 2000, the company was sold for $2 billion! All three founders made their multi-millions from the company and in the end walked away each with over $100 million.

This book of course is written not to tell great stories about successful companies. The job of this book is to prove beyond a shadow of a doubt that in each industry in which IBM had the lead, and a big lead in almost all cases, IBM management got lost and did not know how to monetize the opportunity.

We have shown so far in this section that the greater application software marketplace is about $200 billion and it could have all been IBM's for the taking. Few industry watchers can believe that IBM, which owned both SHAS and the System/3 PBAR package would give them away.

When SMS sold itself to Siemans, the value of the company was over $2 billion and SMS was just one of the many companies that were selling derivatives of SHAS. What was IBM thinking? The only plausible answer to the question is that IBM simply was not thinking about software as an opportunity at all. It eliminated itself from many other opportunities as we show in this book. If IBM ever dies, its death will be ruled a suicide.

Chapter 63

A Quick Look at IBM's MAPICS Application and SAP

MAPICS was IBM's key application software product

MAPICS was once an IBM manufacturing application software product for discrete manufacturers. IBM sold it to run on its S/36, S/38 and AS/400 product lines. IBM's MAPICS was a fine product and highly saleable. In 1980 when launched to replace MMAS, it became an extremely popular product. It was the finest package in IBM's early application software stable. It was always a great performer and a superior provider of solutions for businesses—even some not in manufacturing.

It continues to be a first-class total ERP software solution. In 1992, but it is no longer an IBM product. IBM bailed out of application software in 1992. MAPICS was acquired by Marcom of Newton, MA. In 1997, Marcom spun off MAPICS as a separate product.

In its last year as a stand-alone product, MAPICS had 4,500 customers in about 10,000 sites worldwide, and had sales of $172.8M. In January of 2005, Infor announced a definitive agreement to acquire MAPICS for $12.75/share. At the time, MAPICS had 27.2 million shares outstanding. And, so the one-time IBM # 1 ERP package known as—MAPICS— is now contained in the Infor stable of ERP applications.

The expected marketplace for software in 2016 for all ERP software is $32 Billion. What if IBM, instead of Marcom or Infor still owned MAPICS in the ERP software space? MAPICS is expected to continue to succeed with Infor.

SAP founders worked for IBM

SAP came about because IBM did not pay attention to its own software engineering talents. Theoretically, IBM could have built SAP, the top ERP company in the world, since all five of SAP's founders worked for IBM right before they left to form SAP.

SAP became a software leader in ERP perhaps for many reasons, among them is that the SAP Company cares about its customers. IBM unexpectedly withdrew from application software in the early 1990's, thinking it was a smart move. It was not. IBM is gone but others will make about $200 billion next year. In fact, others are proving that there is a lot of money to be made in application software, an area that IBM owned in the 1950's and 1960's, and of course if IBM were in the business wholeheartedly from the 1960's, it would be raking in at least half of the $32 billion in ERP industry take and probably half of the overall $200 billion for all industries.

The total application software marketplace in 2015 was $175 billion. Best estimates place the market at well over $200 billion in just several years. It is tough to get up to the minute results for any application software industry leaders or losers. One thing for sure is that SAP has retained its ERP market leadership position from 2013, where industry results are available. Sap sold $6.1B in ERP software. Oracle, the database magnate came in second with $3.117B in sales in 2013, Sage came in third with $1.5B in sales in 2013. Infor, the company that consumed MAPICS is fourth with $1.5B in sales.

Microsoft, a company that never says never is fifth with $1.169B in sales in 2013. Neither SAP nor Microsoft even existed when application software was all IBM's to keep. But, like many other areas of opportunity that IBM has had over the years, Big Blue simply gave up and exited the application software industry.

This book is about how IBM squandered many opportunities while making many entrepreneurs exceedingly rich. Application software is another big IBM loss area. The whole industry in the early days of computing was owned by IBM as only IBM could do. Unfortunately for IBM stockholders and employees, like many other profitable industries which IBM shed IBM's management team did not want to be in the application software business.

Comparing MAPICS to SAP

The below synopsis of an essay written recently by a SAP expert business analyst gives some great insights into the relationship of SAP v IBM's MAPICS. This technician participated in the implementation of SAP in a large company. In particular, he handled four separate locations. He moved from the company as time passed and was hired in a similar position at another company which used MAPICS. The second company was much smaller and for this reason had selected MAPICS over SAP.

Ii is not my purpose to give a blow by blow on SAP v MAPICS especially since MAPICS is now part of Infor. But, this little story shows IBM had real software (MAPICS) in its stable that could have passed the test of time and taken

IBM application software far past the millennium. Additionally, it helps to remember that all of SAP's founders once worked for Big Blue. They were not really looking to start SAP when IBM gave them some bad signals.

This particular manufacturing software analyst noted that SAP was a very complex package to support even for business analysts. Its integration was very good and there was a lot of facility available for the discerning. However, a big drawback was that the product was very expensive and from his perspective, it is lots tougher to navigate than MAPICS.

The analyst noted that end users would try to move from function to function in SAP to their best abilities; but for many it was overwhelming. SAP's Query facility (Report Writer) could not be used by most users so they were stuck with standard package results reporting. The analyst summed it up by saying that because of SAP's difficulty for regular nonprofessional use, it was very tough and remains tough to find anybody in the user community who understands all of SAP—even in the SAP world

He summarized that SAP is great for large environments with tens of thousands of users, but it is a big overkill for most businesses with just a few business units and about 100 users. He liked MAPICS very much and he enjoyed his new job in a less complex world supporting MAPICS users for Infor. My take is that MAPICS is easy to use and SAP is tough but larger companies may need the toughness of a SAP program to lead them to success.

Chapter 64

SAP—The Best in ERP Software

IBM Could have owned SAP

I was a Systems Engineer with IBM in 1972 when SAP was formed and I surely would have loved to have been part of their team. SAP is an acronym for Systems, Applications and Products in Data Processing. Today about nine out of ten Fortune 500 companies make use of SAP. SAP brings in about $22 billion per year in software revenue.

Before the rough cut version of this book was tuned like a quality instrument and Section V was added and the former Section V was bumped to become Section VI, Lets Go Publish!, my company, had chosen not to include the IT products of *foreign* billionaires and multimillionaires. In this chapter, I decided to break this rule. Why? The German company, SAP, truly is a major US player. It is undeniable.

Additionally, its five founders all had similar roles to my own as engineers with IBM before they felt they needed to leave IBM to form their company. SAP of course is more successful today than any of its founders, and even IBM, could have ever imagined.

SAP embarked on this major venture in the Manufacturing Application Software arena in 1972. Their idea was to create a corporate software company at level that was unheard-of at the time. SAP's five founders refused to let the improbability of success stop them. They set out on a path that would transform the world of information technology and forever alter the way that companies do business. They were immensely successful.

The Company is based in Walldorf, Germany, and it now boasts of being one of the world's largest software companies. SAP continues to espouse the same entrepreneurial spirit that drove them to be successful. From the top executives to the newest SAP employees, everyone comes to believe in the power of a good idea.

Like many Systems Engineers or Lab Engineers who worked for IBM across the world, SAP's five founders spent most of their time in the data centers of their first customers. For SAP, this included the German branch of Imperial Chemical Industries in Östringen.

Many of my cohorts at IBM would spend days sleeping while getting their testing done on expensive computers in the middle of the night and on weekends. Scotch Whiskey and bread or pretzels always appeared to be a fine nourishing accompaniment for elongated test sessions. SAP's five, likewise, had to be night owls as the development of their first programs needed to take place when others were not using the big data center machines.

SAP took off immediately. With just one year in business, the Company was able to hire nine employees and it generated DM 620,000 in revenue. As they say in long-term success stories—the rest is history.

The five IBM engineers who formed SAP include Dietmar Hopp, Klaus Tschira, Hans-Werner Hector, Hasso Plattner, and Claus Wellenreuther. All five were from Mannheim, Baden-Württemberg. They were all working in an enterprise-wide system based on this software. As IBM often does prematurely, it was ready to throw in the towel on what would have surely been a successful venture. None of the five engineers were looking to leave IBM in the near future.

Despite it being almost completed, the SAP five were told the project was no longer necessary for IBM. Rather than abandon what they knew would be a phenomenally successful venture, they said good-by to IBM and started their own company. Their first released version of the code could be operated in test mode and thus could be developed specifically for their first client. It included universal options so that it could be offered to other interested parties as well.

SAP's goals once were IBM's goals—the desire to help companies run their businesses better, faster and more efficiently with standard software solutions. The founders' vision holds true and the potential of their product vision continues to unfold. And they do get very tired carrying the many carriages of Deutsch Marks to the Bundesbank.

As in all enterprises that become extremely successful, the founders most often become successful. Other than IBM's Ted Codd, the inventor of Relational Database who escaped IBM to become a millionaire himself, these five IBMers are just a few of those coming from IBM's ranks who struck it rich.

IBM for example has always had lots of smart folks working for the company. Few made a killing financially while working for Big Blue. In Germany at the time, the SAP team who departed IBM included Dietmar Hopp, whose net worth is now $7.2 Billion; Klaus Tschira; whose net worth at his recent passing was also $7.2 billion; Hans-Werner Hector, whose net worth is $1.8 billion; Hasso Plattner whose net worth is $10.5 billion; and Claus Wellenreuther, whose net worth is $1.6 Billion.

In most of its recent days, IBM has had over 400,000 employees, many of whom are among the brightest in their fields. Other than executives who are on a different payroll, few IBMers make the big time in earnings and net worth. Few are written up for their unique accomplishments such as the many players in this book. None of the SAP insiders who formed the company would ever have been able to extol their success and reap their rewards if they continued to work for IBM. After all, IBM killed their project and they were all fighting for survival.

The SAP software package is made up of modules. Each module represents a business process. At the time of this writing SAP was discussing 19 such modules. The reason why SAP is so popular today is because of its open architecture. Just like SAP's second customer, organizations can use it without major modifications. They can tailor it without code modification to create any options required to meet their business requirements. As of today, SAP is the leading provider of business software, in the world. SAP customers are universally successful.

It helps to remember that the project that brought forth SAP was an IBM project. IBM always had a few diversions going on in the application software industry. Since it was always the first to understand the nuances of its hardware and the nuances of its operating systems, IBM clearly had the same advantages in the application software industry as Microsoft which leveraged system software to make its applications better than the rest of the pack.

IBM could have been phenomenally successful in systems or applications software, just like Microsoft. Big Blue chose not to be successful in either area. Until the 1990's whenever IBM peeked into the application software business, its purpose was to sell hardware, not to make money from software. In many of its ventures it gave the software end product away so it could sell more hardware. Even its service bureau ventures were all about selling hardware to its service bureau company. It was not to make money from being a service bureau providing software solutions. IBM needed a good pair of glasses to see opportunities more clearly but it would not ask for help.

Now that IBM wants to win the Cloud battle surely it must wish that it had paid more attention to application software, one of the linchpins to making cloud computing fully successful. Despite it being so obvious, I doubt that any executive from IBM will ever suggest the company could have done better with its opportunities. That's why IBM continues to make big mistakes. Executives like John Akers must first present a plan to destroy the company, then and only then may they be replaced.

As tough a company as Microsoft is, one thing is for sure. It works all angles and all products for the good of Microsoft. When it controls the game it plays hard so that Microsoft takes all the marbles. IBM simply does not play hard. How could it have permitted five engineers with such talents to leave the company with an IBM idea that today pays off about $22 billion each year? Tell me how?

Microsoft leaves no dust behind. It always uses its operating system control to leverage its application software business. Companies such as WordPerfect often wondered about the unique facilities in MSWord that were dependent on Windows operating system functions of which they were completely unaware.

For its reasons, IBM chose never to cheapen its goodness but it also never defended its honor when competing with scoundrels. Microsoft now has a substantially larger piece of the application software business today than IBM. IBM brags that it is in the Cloud Computing business hut without application software. Successful Cloud vendors eventually rely on application software to leverage their offerings. IBM therefore has a lot of work to do to catch up for all the times it said "no" to the possibility of success in the application software industry. One notable time that IBM said yes—at least temporarily—was with its MAPICS package, which lasted until the early 1990's.

MAPICS was a fine performer when it was included in IBM's one time large application software stable. The MAPICS software package has changed hands a number of times over the years since the 1990's—first to Marcom and eventually to Infor. IBM simply gave it up. Like most products that IBM scraps prematurely, somebody picks it up and makes a lot of money. MAPICS continues to do well for Infor as one of its leading ERP applications.

Chapter 65

Small Companies -- Application Software Millionaires

Millionaires who were not always millionaires

Not all software millionaires come from huge companies like SAP and SAS and Infor and SMS. Some capture their share of an industry and grow slowly. In this chapter, we look at four different entrepreneurs whose small application software / service bureau companies have brought their employees and themselves a nice living.

Paul Harkins

Paul Harkins is the IBM Systems Engineer who authored and sponsored the Goodimade Apparel Manufacturing IUP (Installed User Program) across seven different environments. The package was sold in most continents and was supported by Harkins across the world. Harkins is also the owner of Harkins Audit Software and the author/developer of the patented Real Time Program Audit, RTPA,

When I first began to work in the Scranton IBM Branch Office in 1971, among other accounts, I was assigned to Sturdi-Wear Clothes in Taylor, PA. They were a newly acquired Division of US Industries. In the first week, I learned that I was to design an Accounts Payable system for the company. It took me a month and it took two months for them to program it. The IT Manager did not believe it would work so he brought in his cousin, a full IBM Systems Engineer to examine the design. I was an Assistant SE looking for a promotion to Associate at the time. The design won his blessing.

Apparel Business System
System/3 Model 6

Installed At: Goodimade Manufacturing Company
Philadelphia, Pennsylvania

I did such a good job that I got full control over the account and our next mission was to create a full apparel software system including order entry billing, inventory control as well as the infamous cut and sold system. This was before Paul Harkins' ABS system was available. Each apparel product had multiple dimensions such as a valid size spread from say 28 to 42 and colors from red to black to plaid. It was a real challenge.

To get a real perspective of their business, I got to take a plane ride to New York City from Scranton. It was a half hour plane ride. We spent the day talking to folks about the colors and sizes and how we might solve the problem. Sturdi-Wear made suits.

We did not know all the executives of their company who guided us about how they do business. However, when we got home, we realized how tough this business really was. We had interviewed the executive and the team from the Pants Division. In other words, only the fact that a suit had a pair of pants did any of our design work really matter.

Overall it helped our perspective but we still were no further ahead in the design of the suit system with the cut and sold reporting than before we had taken the NY trip. It would take months to complete. Only people in IBM such as Paul Harkins and Robert D. White, an expert from NY, knew the difficulties we all faced in this difficult design.

Meanwhile, IBM had experts in application areas. Field SEs such as myself who were in tough situations could call upon these apparel experts for consulting. Robert D. White from New York, for example, an IBM worldwide Apparel Industry Consultant was very knowledgeable and he helped the IBM Scranton team get our arms around what appeared to be a real monster of a design.

As we were closing in on a way to get this design done, I found a Systems Engineer in Philadelphia named Paul Harkins, who was as good as it gets as a Systems Engineer, and as good as it gets in his knowledge of the apparel industry. Paul was very happy to talk to me and he helped our team through some sticky questions with real answers.

As a fellow System Engineer, Paul Harkins told me that he was working on the very software that we were beginning to build on the one-on-one program.

IBM was about to release an Installed User Program which Paul was shepherding for the corporation. It would be called the Apparel Business System. Paul shared documentation and concepts with me and he was a godsend as I was never quite sure that our unique design at Sturdi-Wear could be programmed and if programmed, if it would ever work.

From that day on, Paul Harkins for me was what IBM Systems Engineers were all about and I did my best to be as good as he was at his job.

In the last twenty years, I had the pleasure of working with Paul Harkins on a few of his other projects such as his *Real Time Program Audit*. Paul is a great designer and a crackerjack programmer. RTPA is Paul's Application Software Package that he sells through the Harkins Audit Software organization. RTPA uses groundbreaking products to determine exactly what a program is doing with data as it changes. It is a phenomenal aid to companies who must comply with extremely strict audits.

RTPA and ABS are both application software products, which are the essence of this section of this book.

Mr. Harkins has been working with IBM systems for 40 years including 21 years at IBM, where he was actively involved in hundreds of customer accounts worldwide. He created the original IBM Apparel Business System, the first on-line software package ever designed for the apparel industry. After leaving IBM, Mr. Harkins was a principal in Apparel Business Systems, Inc., a software development firm. He then founded his own software consulting and development firm, Harkins & Associates, Inc. in 1990.

Mr. Harkins has written articles for Midrange Computing and New York Citylife magazines and has published books including: "How to Be a Highly Paid Corporate Programmer" and "The Future of Corporate Computing".

There is no public data about Paul Harkins' Net worth but I would estimate it at over $one million. Paul proves every single day that being the best there is in IT can provide a more than comfortable living.

Gene Bonett

Gene Bonett got it all started in 1984 with one very strong idea -- software that integrates the complex information needs of the apparel & footwear industry, makes it accessible, and backs it up with the best training and support. We have already discussed the intricacies of apparel software with its multiple parts and dimensions, and it was Gene Bonett's idea to tackle the whole notion and create a solution to make his customers successful.

The company began as Online Data Systems and morphed into Xperia, an organization with software for the apparel Industry as well as for discrete manufacturing. Apparel is so complicated that it needed an Xperia touch. The company was one of very few application software development organizations with an expert comprehension of the myriad of details related to apparel and footwear manufacturing. In the beginning, Gene realized that practical use of technology would maximize productivity and optimize operations. He saw this as enabling apparel and footwear companies to compete more effectively against others in the industry.

In 2002 Gene and his team saw that a shift was occurring in the way users needed to see and access their data. Users were becoming savvier and required more modernization than ever. The Xperia answer was Xpressiv™, which was born to be the most intuitive and sophisticated version of any apparel solution. Work has continued with Xpressiv™ to the point that it now is a full-fledged business intelligence solution.

It is designed to address the information needs of the entire organization when a standard report is not quite enough. This advanced software addition is based on over 30 years of ERP solutions experience. Gene makes a point of telling the world that it not only is the best there is but it is priced to provide the lowest total cost of ownership in the ERP arena for a true, fully-integrated solution.

In a nut shell Gene Bonett and company in the form of their advanced apparel software provide an innate simplicity of design, ease-of-use, and complete access to the full power and functionality of the underlying software. A comprehensive package and a great Business Intelligence Tool together form the cornerstone of Xperia developmental efforts and Gene's many clients are happy that Xperia has the solution.

Over the years, Gene and his team, operating from their Bethlehem location, have maintained a rapid pace to continually update Xperia software and add new functionality as industry demands evolve. The solutions provide an unmatched level of powerful and practical functionality, combined with superior services and a business philosophy that produces exceptional results.

From start-ups to billion-dollar corporations, Xperia has been an ERP apparel software provider of choice for efficiency-minded apparel & footwear manufacturers and importers for 30 years running. For his great work in providing a great solution in a tough market, Gene Bonett has the satisfaction of knowing his customers run on the best software possible and Gene is listed in this book with a net worth of over one million dollars.

Garry Reinhard

APPCON was founded in 1991 by Garry Reinhard. His company has been an IBM Solution provider since 1992 along with being an IBM Independent software provider (ISV). In 1999, APPCON became an IBM partner in development and an IBM premier partner in 2000. Garry is proud to have web enabled his package early in the game using IBM's top Web package known as WebSphere. Reinhard calls his web enabled software version, AppSphere.

The senior staff members of the company had been providing apparel software and support to distributors, importers and manufacturers for more than twenty years before the 1991 founding. Garry Reinhard is a hands-on president. He is a former IBM Systems Engineer such as myself and Paul Harkins. Reinhard showed his versatility as an SE as he learned the apparel industry and he also supported a number of IBM's apparel customers.

Reinhard's apparel work goes back to the System/3 model 6 software originally put together by Paul Harkins. Reinhard worked with the first customer with the inception of IBM's first apparel offering for the System/3. In the early 1980's Garry was the key member of the IBM Apparel Competency Center in Philadelphia, PA where he helped support IBM's apparel customers on a worldwide basis.

Since then he and other key members of the APPCON staff have been providing information systems and technical support to the manufacturing, importing, and distribution industries, and have in fact, helped develop other software packages that are currently offered in the marketplace. Collectively, the APPCON staff has over 150 man-years of experience and it has installed numerous application software installations within the IBM system communities.

APPCON was formed for the sole purpose of developing a truly state-of-the-art and totally integrated package written to take advantage of the advanced database architecture of the IBM I with Power Architecture. APPCON developed its EIS/400 package with features and functions that were unavailable with other offerings.

In early 2000, IBM approached APPCON with an offer to be one of the first sites to use its WebSphere product. As the partnership evolved and the capabilities of the WebSphere environment were proven, APPCON developed a product specifically for the new online Web interface environment. With support from IBM, APPCON released a product to replace its EIS400 offering. As noted, above, the new offering has been given the name AppSphere. Garry uses the following chart to visually describe his offerings:

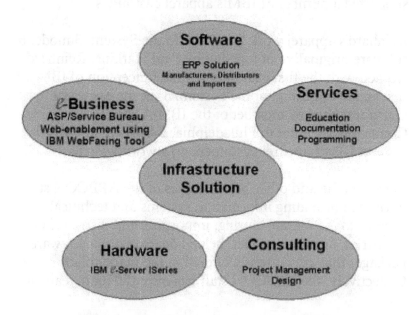

APPCON has installed the EIS system at a variety of clients ranging in size from approximately $5 million to just about a $billion in annual revenue. Some customers have installed Garry's entire set of business applications, while others have installed only the customer-service applications and they choose to interface them to their own manufacturing and financial applications.

In terms of hardware platforms, the Company has experience in migrating customers to the IBM I with Power Architecture from multiple platforms. If you have a need, APPCON has a solution. Garry Reinhard is pleased with his company's performance and his own entrepreneurship has gained him a spot as an application software millionaire in terms of his personal net worth.

G. Scott Piotroski

As a writer who pushes the truth more than fiction, I suspect that Scott Piotroski, the top executive at Webclients LLC would like to say that he created the company from scratch and that he brought it to life and everybody lived happily ever after. His penchant for the truth, however, keeps him a lot more humble than that.

Webclients today is an industry leading online marketing company located in Harrisburg, Pennsylvania. The Company designs and implements successful custom online lead generation solutions for top tier clients. It offers innovative marketing strategies through its extensive suite of premium online marketing services, and its top level online consumer reach, along with major industry expertise in online media planning.

Webclients is the best in the industry. It uses the best industry technology capabilities to satisfy its customers most pressing needs. The proprietary technology allows the company to effectively target and validate users within an advertiser's core demographic.

Webclients examines and evaluates each advertiser's specific marketing objectives and develops a custom online marketing plan to achieve the defined objectives. An industry-best dedicated customer service team closely monitors each advertiser's campaign and works with individual clients to ensure that the marketing program is achieving their ROI goals.

Webclients' owns and operates proprietary websites in the US, CA, UK and AU markets. The Company also owns and operates an affiliate network, Websponsors.com. Through its owned and operated websites and its affiliate network, the Company provides high quality traffic utilizing registration pathways, standard IAB banners, as well as stand-alone email placements and text links.

Scott Piotroski is especially pleased that the Company also deploys an advanced ad servicing and optimization engine to provide advertisers a unique opportunity to get their ads in front of the right audience at the right time. His customers love the pay for performance pricing model responsible for the success of many advertising campaigns. The Company also licenses the use of its email databases as appropriate.

History of Webclients, LLC:

The Company was incorporated in 1998 and by 2000, it was generating $2 million in revenue, EBITDA $500K.

In May, 2004 the company was sold to Apax Partners and Thoma Cressey Equity Partners for $84 million. The management team maintained a 30% equity stake in Webclients. Annual billing was approximately $35 million, EBITDA $8 million.

In June, 2005, the company again was sold. This time it was to the publicly traded company ValueClick for $141 million. The WebClients management team took half of the proceeds in cash and half in stock. Annual billing was about $59 million, EBITDA $14.5 million.

In February, 2010, the management team bought back Webclients, LLC from ValueClick for $45 million and stabilized the business by transitioning into mobile marketing by expanding its core technologies and concentrating on new advertisers and publishers.

Scott Piotroski is the current CEO of WebClients. He is also the majority owner of Webclients, LLC. Scott oversees the day to day operations for the lead generation business. His duties include oversight and management of all lines of business. In addition, he is responsible for new lines of business and client prospecting. All key personnel report to Piotroski. He is ultimately responsible for all revenue goals and profitability.

Scott was not on the roller coaster from the very beginning but once he joined, he drove a lead car like a professional. He joined Webclients in 2000 and has served as both Controller and then Chief Financial Officer. In 2003 he was promoted to Chief Operating Officer, taking on additional operational roles within the Company.

As COO, Scott Piotroski was responsible for the implementation of new marketing mechanisms and optimization of the Company's current lines of business. He led the Company's effort to critically analyze and improve the operations of each department. Prior to joining Webclients.net, he served as a Certified Public Accountant for KPMG, a leading national accounting firm. His areas of expertise included audit, financial forecasting and corporate/individual taxation.

His accounting and management background have given him the tools he has needed to be an effective leader. A humble man, Scott has not publicly released his net worth and so we credit him with a net worth north of $1 million. He takes pleasure in being another application software / service bureau success story.

Chapter 66

Large Software Companies—Many Rich Entrepreneurs

A lot of money belongs to these names

When we finished the first printing of this book in late 2015, I listed the net worth of the IT leaders that were included in the first edition. Of course, their net worth is bound to change as the value of their investments change over time. I wrote this section #5 so that I could add the application software industry as another area in which IBM failed and in so doing helped create additional millionaires and billionaires.

In addition to adding Section V to the book in this edition, and bumping Section V to become Section VI to close the book, I also went back to Chapter 1 and I changed a number of the dollar figures for billionaires whose net worth went down or up over the last four months. For example, Bill Gates is still the richest man in the world but his net worth is now $84 billion v $79 billion four months ago.

Being an Applications Entrepreneur

Application software is the easiest area for a determined entrepreneur to make her or his mark within the IT industry. For the most part all you need is a few customers who need things done. As long as those things can be done via programming, there is opportunity for anybody to become a millionaire by taking their programming work, packaging it, and then multiplying it.

In the rest of this chapter, we look at a number of billionaires and multi-millionaires who made it big in application software. There are too many millionaires in application software to begin to list them all. Besides those already shown in Chapter 65, I have a fairly nice sampling with some very big players included—especially the gang of five from SAP.

I also found a few small application software entrepreneurs who have been in the business for a number of years and whose skills are specialized. These folks are not big enough to want their net worth divulged but each is within the millionaire category. I think you will like reading about them. Check out Chapter 65. Now, let's take a random look at some of the big shots in the application software industry. Here we go:

Carol Bartz

Carol Bartz has a net worth of $100 Million. She rose to the top of **Autodesk, Inc.** an American multinational software corporation that makes software for the architecture, engineering, construction, manufacturing, media, and entertainment industries. She later became the CEO of the famous search engine company, Yahoo.

When she became CEO of Autodesk in 1992, Bartz changed Autodesk from what some would call an "aimless maker of PC software," into a leader of computer-aided design application software. Autodesk revenues increased five-fold from $300 million to $1.5 billion during her tenure. She moved on after 2006 and became the executive chairman of the board.

On January 13, 2009, Bartz was named CEO of Yahoo!, the Internet services company which at the time operated the fourth most-visited Web domain site in the world. In 2011, she was abruptly and unexpectedly fired from Yahoo. She has offered her unabridged thoughts about the Yahoo management team in no uncertain terms. They appear similar to what Carly Fiorina's full disclosure on Management would be after her ouster from HP.

Judy Faulkner

Judy Faulkner is another of the rich tech women charting in at #256 on the Forbes 400 at $2.4 billion. She started as a computer programmer. Faulkner is the founder and chief executive of Epic Systems. Their 2014 revenues checked in at $1.8 billion. Epic is a privately-held company that sells healthcare software. Epic has very prestigious clients including the Cleveland Clinic, the Mayo Clinic and Johns Hopkins. I

Mark Zuckerberg

The Internet has surely created its share of billionaires, and Mark Zuckerberg is one of the most famous. He can be called an original American computer programmer and Internet entrepreneur. , Mark has an estimated net worth of $46.1 billion as of December 2015, according to Bloomberg. Mark Zuckerberg is the creator of Facebook and that is why we need to tell you no more. Who has not heard of Facebook? His site is the second-most-visited worldwide, after Google. Like Bill Gates, this Harvard dropout has proven that Harvard does not make the man.

Dustin Moskovitz

Still yet another American entrepreneur is the co-founder of
Mark Zuckerberg's company, which as we know is a huge
social networking website. We also know that it is called
Facebook. Bloomberg estimates the net worth of Dustin
Moskovitz, at $10.3 billion. He is the world's youngest
billionaire. He was Mark Zuckerberg's Harvard roommate
and when Zuckerberg was hiring, he became Facebook's
third employee. Both dropped out of Harvard and moved to
California to bring their dream to us all.

Eight more Facebook billionaires

There are eight more Facebook billionaires besides
Zuckerberg and Moskovitz. I looked at all the faces of those
listed below and other than the older Russian investor, who
looks good also; they all look like kids. None look like they
have hit 40 years of age. I saw a lot of dark hair. Clearly, by
backing Zuckerberg, it did not take them long to become
billionaires.

I must admit that when I noted in the original book printing
that Microsoft created more millionaires than any other
company ever. I was not looking for any company with a
ton of billionaires. Microsoft has three billionaires. That's it.
Microsoft does have the most millionaires. Facebook has
ten billionaires and over time, I can see it having even more.
All of these eight billionaires below were on the original
Facebook IPO. Some already were billionaires in other
industries but most became billionaires because of their
particular role in the founding or in the operations of
Facebook. Here they are:

Chris Hughes, cofounder of Facebook, officially worth $935
million—soon to make the billionaire's club. Chris is a
cofounder of Facebook and a college classmate of Mark
Zuckerberg's.

Sheryl Sandberg is Facebook's COO. She's worth $1 billion.

Yuri Milner is the founder of DST, which made a big investment in Facebook. He owns 12.5% of DST's Facebook shares, which gives him a net worth of $1.1 billion

Mark Pincus had a lot of patents around social networking which secured him a good chunk of Facebook shares. He is also the founder of Zynga and his net worth is noted at $1.3 billion

Peter Thiel doubled his net worth via his Facebook investment. He was the first outside investor in Facebook. He invested a half a million in 2004. He's now worth $2.7 billion. He manages Founders Fund,

Eduardo Saverin, is the cofounder who infamously sued Facebook. He is now worth $2.7 billion. There is more to the Savarin story but we told enough for our purposes. The industry research analyst that checked Saverin's numbers for publication was not sure what happened to another .2 billion (point two billion) that had been attributed to Saverin. It may have gone to taxes as Saverin has citizenship both to the US and Singapore, where he is now a permanent resident.

Sean Parker is Facebook's first president. He's now worth $2.8 billion.

Alisher Usmanov is a Russian billionaire investor who put down some rubles for Facebook shares. He is now worth $13.6 billion and is reportedly the richest man in Russia.

This completes the Facebook Eight Billionaires!

Facebook millionaires

Microsoft created about 12,000 millionaires from the ranks of employees and other stockholders. Google created 1000, and Facebook has also created 1000 millionaires. Facebook's smaller level rich folks have not surfaced yet so we do not know who they are as the IPO was not so long ago.

Sergey Mikhailovich Brin

Sergey Mikhailovich Brin is a Russian-born American computer scientist and internet entrepreneur. Together with his buddy, Larry Page, he co-founded Google. Google of course is one of the world's most profitable Internet companies. Bloomberg has Mikhailovich Brin's net worth at $39.1 billion as of December 2015. Let me say it again. He is the co-founder of Google. Enough said!

Lawrence "Larry" Page

Another American computer scientist and internet entrepreneur, Larry Page checks in with a Bloomberg-reported net worth of $40 billion as of December 2015. Page is co-founder of Google along with Sergey Mikhailovich Brin; and he is the CEO.

Eric Schmidt

Schmidt has had a very exciting IT career and is also in the original pages of this book. He has an estimated net worth of $10.9 billion. He is Google's chairman and he likes to enjoy technology as a leader and he enjoys life as a guy who can certainly afford a splurge or two.

Schmidt may be included elsewhere in the book because he is clearly a member of the IT Hall of Fame. He was joint author (with Mike Lesk) during his summers at Bell Labs as the two produced a notion called Lex, a program that generated a lexical-analyzer program.

Schmidt held technical positions with Byzromotti Design, Bell Labs, Zilog, and Xerox's PARC. Schmidt was a Sun Guy and he eventually became president of Sun Technology Enterprises.

During his technical life which continues, in 1997, Eric became the CEO and chairman of the board of Novell. Google interviewed Schmidt to run Google in 2001 under the guidance of venture capitalists John Doerr and Michael Moritz. Schmidt probably never cared about a dime as much as his work. Yet, he checks into the billionaire's column at 10.9 billion. It is good to see that exceptional talent as possessed by Schmidt can result in exceptional net worth.

Other Google Millionaires

Techcrunch.com does a great job of netting this out quickly.

"In the 1990s, we loved to tally up the number of Microsoft millionaires. Now, it's Google's turn. The New York Times cites estimates that there are 1,000 Google employees whose stock grants and options are worth more than $5 million. So there are more than 1,000 Google millionaires, including Google's former masseuse, Bonnie Brown."

"And anyone who joined a year ago is worth, on average, $276,000. According to the story, the average options grant to an employee who started a year ago was for 685 shares, plus an additional 230 shares in outright stock. At the current price of $662, that comes to $276,000 (assuming full vesting of the shares). Google currently has 16,000 employees, of which roughly 6,500 were added in the past year alone. So 9,500 are worth at least $276,000. Plus, as it is rumored, they still get free massages."

Bob Parsons

American entrepreneur, Robert "Bob" Parsons has a net worth of $2.2 billion. This is the wild man who runs GoDaddy, a huge Internet Service Provider and Internet Registrar. In many ways Parsons runs a service bureau, the business which IBM gave up years ago. Parsons runs his service bureau lots better than IBM would. I am a Bob Parsons customer.

David Duffield

David Duffield, who is now 74, clocks in with a net worth of 6.8 billion. Duffield definitely has a magic touch. He founded two very successful enterprise software companies: *PeopleSoft*, when he was 47, and *Workday*, when he was 65.

Duffield mortgaged his home to bootstrap PeopleSoft, which was eventually sold to Oracle for $10.7 billion in 2005. He currently serves as chairman of Workday, which went public in 2012. Duffield says he plans to leave his fortune to his animal charity, Maddie's Fund--named after his beloved schnauzer--not his 10 children.

Charles B. Wang

Charles B. Wang is a businessman and philanthropist who was a co-founder of Computer Associate along with Russel Artzt. He was also the former CEO of the company when it was renamed to CA Technologies. Wang's net worth is a cool $1.2 billion. To prove that rich people who *earned* their money in tech, unlike Bill Gates, can find some pleasure in other ventures, Wang begins a new mold. He is currently the owner of the NHL's New York Islanders ice hockey team and their AHL affiliate. He is an investor in numerous businesses, and a continual benefactor to charities including an interesting notion called SmileTrain.

In 1976, at age 31, Wang got the company going by cheating his way to success. He launched Computer Associates, using his credit cards for funding. There is a man who wanted to succeed. We cannot find American Express or Master Charge for comment. He grew the company into one of the country's largest software vendors. It still is. He is a genius.

Computer associates and Charles B. Wang are both still humming despite being prey for Oracle and others who want to win in Application Software. Perhaps IBM should buy in and give itself the start it needs.

Russel M. Artzt

Russell M. Artzt, 68, co-founded the CA Company in June 1976. His net worth is just over $100 million. He has been Vice Chairman and Founder of the Company since April 2007. He played an instrumental role in the evolution of the CA vision.

Artzt also provided counsel in the areas of strategic partnerships, product development leadership, and corporate strategy. He was the Company's Executive Vice President of Products from January 2004 to April 2007 and was Executive Vice President, eTrust Solutions from April 2002 to January 2004.

James Henry Clark

James Henry Clark was born March 23, 1944. Over time he became an American entrepreneur. He started as a computer scientist. He had a business sense and a technology sense. He founded several notable Silicon Valley technology companies, including Silicon Graphics, Inc., Netscape Communications Corporation, myCFO and Healtheon.

His research work in computer graphics led to the development of systems for the fast rendering of three-dimensional computer images. His net worth from technology projects is 1.51 billion. Yes, my dear readers, I would settle for half of that but in his area of specialty, I would have to claim that I earned none of it.

Jeff Bezos

When he was at 58.2 billion net worth, Jeff Bezos was # 2 on Forbes' list just below Bill Gates and a bit above Larry Ellison from Oracle. Things change and he lost a few points recently. Bezos nonetheless is very rich. He is the founder and chief executive officer of Amazon.com. Amazon began as a company selling books cheap and then found it could warehouse products and sell everything cheaper than anybody could get it anywhere else. The company is in the distribution business.

In the last ten years it has moved to the Cloud Business. My own company BookHawkers.Com once used Amazon's shopping cart software to process orders. Many use Amazon author services and other services which use technology to enable business. Instead of Amazon choosing to use IBM's huge mainframes to support its businesses, it has chosen to compete against IBM in the cloud business.

I will be watching this battel closely as I am not sure that IBM has any executives in their stable who know how to do anything other than how to milk a mainframe dry. Amazon's revenue increases while IBM's is definitely going down. The best thing for IBM would be if Jeff Bezos, who surely knows how to logistically prepare for sales and then sell everything in sight would sign up as CEO of IBM. After all, his net worth was once 58.2 billion, a figure at least 52 times the number any IBM CEO has ever achieved in Net worth.

The Watsons were very private so we cannot include their numbers right here.

Pierre Omidyar

EBay Chairman Pierre Omidyar saw the company he founded spin off payments arm PayPal and now he sits on both corporations' boards. He's the largest individual shareholder in eBay with an 8% stake, but he is not involved with day-to-day operations. He launched a new company *First Look Media* in late 2013 with the aim of presenting new forms of independent journalism. With a promised $250 million from Omidyar, First Look launched its first digital magazine, *The Intercept*. We can expect more from Pierre for sure as his net worth is $ 9 billion. There is a lot one can do with a lot less.

James Goodnight

SAS and IBM's SPSS were competitors from way back. James Goodnight founded the business analytics software firm SAS in 1976 with fellow billionaire John Sall, whom he met at North Carolina State University while working on his PhD. Goodnight has been at the helm since its inception, when its software was developed to analyze agricultural data, He has steered the private company to continuous growth. With its analytics software in use in over 75,000 companies around the world, SAS revenue for 2014 was $3.09 billion. It is heading through the sky.

When it comes to analytics software, SAS pretty much reigns supreme. Its software is used by about 79% of Fortune 500 companies and the man at the helm of the company is still active in building software for it. James Goodnight has no reason to say goodnight as he checks in with a whopping $11.6 billion and it is all credited to the SAS institute.

John Sall

The only thing one can do alone in life is fail. And, so, as a part of the founding team behind software behemoth SAS, Sall was particularly close to Jim Goodnight, his mentor at the university. Sall did his share of the work as he designed, developed, and documented many of the earliest procedures of the SAS language. He also led the development of JMP, designed to perform simple and complex statistical analyses. Despite his immense wealth, Sall is still working, doing programming, and leading a team of developers. His net worth from the highly successful SAS Institute is a cool $5.8-billion. Nice for sure!

Norman H. Nie

Norman H. Nie was an American social scientist, university professor, inventor, and pioneering technology entrepreneur, known for being one of the developers of the Statistical Package for the Social Sciences (SPSS). Born in St. Louis, Missouri in 1943, Nie was educated at the University of the Americas in Mexico City, Washington University in St. Louis and Stanford University, where he received a Ph.D. in political science in 1971. The world lost a great man when he died on April 2nd, 2015.

He had a savvy and innovative spirit that was evident even when Nie was a graduate student in political science at Stanford in the 1960s. He and two colleagues, fellow Stanford graduate student Dale Bent and Stanford alumnus C. Hadlai "Tex" Hull, developed a software package to perform the complex statistical analyses often required for social science research.

Their software, Statistical Package for the Social Sciences, or SPSS, automated, standardized and streamlined the often cumbersome data analysis process for researchers. In 2009, after Nie retired, IBM purchased SPSS from Nie and the others for $1.2 billion. Norman Nie became a multibillionaire. I would estimate his net worth at about $1 billion at the time of his passing last year.

Meg Whitman

Both William Hewlett and David Packard were billionaires when they left their final mark on the Hewlett Packard Corporation. Carly Fiorina became a multimillionaire there while positioning the company to be the largest IT manufacturer in the world. Meg Whitman is now in Carly Fiorina's spot.

As CEO, Whitman is currently digesting the result of the $111 billion Corporation's historic split of HP into two publicly traded companies on November 1. Preparing for the separation was a lot of work for the IT folks. Now there is a PC and printer-focused HP Inc. and there is also a business-oriented Hewlett Packard Enterprise. To do this Whitman ordered that the company build 4,000 servers, and generate 400,000 email boxes and manage 500 projects across 170 countries. It was quite a task as was Fiorina's, when she managed the assimilation of Compaq into HP.

Whitman now leads the new HP Enterprise, which will handle business hardware, software and services, while Dion Weisler, who had been an executive vice president, will head HP Inc., the PC and printer business. Good luck to both HPs. For all her work in both major enterprises and elsewhere, Meg Whitman has amassed a net worth of $2.2 Billion

SAP Billionaires

We described the great founding and the great run of SAP in Chapter 64. To close this chapter on the net worth of Application Software billionaires, we will highlight each of the five IBM SAP engineers very briefly. They started SAP and made it a household word in manufacturing software.

IBM has always had lots of smart folks working for the company. Few made a killing financially while working for Big Blue. But, when IBM told these German Engineers, it was over for their project, they told IBM it was over for IBM but not for their project, and they built SAP, a world renowned package for ERP.

Dietmar Hopp: Net worth is $7.2 Billion

Klaus Tschira: Net worth at his recent passing was $7.2 billion

Hans-Werner Hector: Net worth is $1.8 billion

Hasso Plattner: The leader whose net worth is $10.5 billion

Claus Wellenreuther: Net worth is $1.6 Billion..

Section VI

Lou Gerstner, Sam Palmisano, & Ginni Rometty—IBM's Latest CEOs

The fitting way to end a book about IBM that is mostly chronicled by CEO tenure is to finish it with the last three to hold the top spot.

Lou Gerstner in many ways was like having a Watson back at the Company. He first protected IBM from dissipation and then he moved IBM in a positive direction with the force of a caring warrior, to regain a place of prominence in the IT Industry.

Sam Palmisano has little written about him but he has a legacy like most inbred IBM executives. He is not an IBM hero like Gerstner or Cary or Watson. He is a guy who got by after Gerstner, and he figured out some shortcuts that shortchanged IBM's future.

Rometty of course made the cardinal mistake of a CEO. She respected her predecessor as John Akers did long before her. She has a good resume as did Akers but so far, she has nothing but poor results. Industry analysts suggest her poor results have to do with signing on too early for the new book that I would be privileged to write called, "The Worst of Sam Palmisano." I wonder if I could get Lou Gerstner to co-author it with me.

Chapter 67

Lou Gerstner, The First CEO Not Bred in IBM's Culture

IBM was at its lowest point ever

In many ways, the first sixty-six chapters of this book have served as the backdrop for this chapter about Lou Gerstner. Rather than start abruptly by going through Gerstner's first day of work coming from the airport with Thomas J. Watson, Jr., I have instead put forth the overall notion and the feeling of John Akers' IBM. This points out the employee, stockholder and industry sentiments of IBM before Gerstner. IBM was already a shipwreck, partially submerged when Gerstner walked in.

In this way, right before we look at Gerstner in some level of detail, we can be reminded of the poor circumstance and poor IBM employee morale that Mr. Gerstner faced when he came to work on his first day. Everybody in the Company and those of us recently retired, and all IBM stockholders for sure, wanted Gerstner to succeed. Here we go!

Gerstner did not sign up for IBM chicanery

In 1991 John Akers announced an early retirement incentive plan called the Individual Transition Option (ITO). Akers

needed cash and the payments to transitioning employees
would be coming from the retirement fund, not current
earnings. Once somebody left Akers' IBM, IBM's treasury
no longer had to pay them from sales revenue. That was
why Akers' liked the retirement deals so much. It had
nothing to do with his respect for IBM employees.

The ITO included a monetary bonus and an improved
retirement pay calculation. For those who knew that IBM
had often promised employees lifetime benefits, they found
that if they did not take the deal, they might not get medical
coverage for life as "promised." However, anybody taking
the offer, along with their spouse, would "definitely" be
covered under the IBM medical plan for life. Wow! No
Watson would have ever approved.

At this time medical care was 100% free to employees and
retirees under the unwritten bond between IBM and its
employees. Then, Akers decided to write things down that
never were. IBM had no caps on medical. Akers changed
the IBM benefit package to save himself. The benefit fund
had more than enough to pay the benefits for all employees
but Akers was hoping some leftovers might be driven to
current earnings.

Over my years with IBM I can recall many IBMers looking
forward to the year in which they turned 55 or the year in
which they marked their thirtieth service year. This meant
that if they were ready, they could begin IBM retirement
and / or go get another job in whatever field they chose to
pursue.

I was in my early forties and I needed about eight years to
get thirty years of service. The original ITO was not built for
me so I did not apply. I did not realize potential retirees at
the time were being bullied to accept it. My best friend,
Dennis Grimes took this particular ITO because he had a

position waiting for him that offered more promise than
IBM.

I did retire from IBM on June 30, 1992 under a second and
better plan called the ITO II. In addition to IBM benefits for
life, I received five years extra service and was able to take a
pre-retirement leave of absence during which time, I
received the company's full benefits package as if I were an
active employee. I had to make it without a retirement check
for seven years. It was actually a great deal.

I got two week's pay for each year with the Company,
rounded to the next half year. In my case, I received lump
sum payment for 47 weeks' pay—the same amount as if
IBM had fired me. Plus, I was paid for about twenty weeks
of accrued vacation, which I had not been able to take over
the years at managers' requests. I had already received my
pay for the time worked so far in 1992.

After I retired, IBM started forcing employees to take their
accrued vacation instead of paying them for it when they left
the Company. Ironically, I knew no IBM employee who
actually did not want to take their vacation over the years in
the year in which they had earned it under the IBM plan.

Unfortunately, IBM would not let us take our vacation if
they needed us for any reason in those years. However, they
did permit us to accrue the time and for years, they paid
employees for such time at the end of our careers. It was
something everybody expected. It was another broken bond.

During this period as John Akers seemed to be dismantling
the Company, one promise at a time, IBM was also
beginning to secretly lay people off for the first time ever.
Consequently, many IBMers simply let IBM take their
accrued vacation rather than risk having their manager think

they were not a dedicated IBM employee. Many got fired regardless.

This was a big change for IBM. It was a big broken promise to employees. IBM was never the same after that. There is a book called Broken Promises, which tells this part of IBM's story without pulling any punches. In this book, my purpose is to show what it cost IBM to permit incompetent managers to run the whole show, but I too experienced the broken promises.

John Opel's build plan and the hiring of 100,000 new employees during his tenure, put John Akers in a quandary that he was unprepared to face. What would he do with the buildings and the people? Things had always been good at IBM and so contingency plans never had to deal with the possibility of the Company going under. Akers was all alone with no prior CEOs experience to reference. He seemed to bungle everything as if there was nobody at all for him to talk with.

John Akers took prisoners but no blame

While bungling everything at IBM, Mr. Akers chided IBM managers and his sales force for not making IBM successful. He knew how to cast blame, and blaming others for his failure assured the IBM Board that Mr. Akers was not worth saving.

In 1991, right before the IBM Annual Meeting Akers commented that there were "too many people standing around the water cooler waiting to be told what to do." I can say this, when the note came to every sales employee's PROFS in basket, you could count the number of Akers' supporters on one closed fist.

John Akers resorted to the blame game to excuse himself in his worst hour. My best imitation without getting to the meat of Akers' comments does show how it sounded to IBM employees at the time that the Chairman delivered his most famous rant. Think of hearing this instead:

"It wasn't me! I had pork and beans for dinner! That's one from soup!" Think about it for a while and then smile. Soup John? Really!

Mr. Akers was looking for employee excuses that would be unforgiven as he placed the blame across the corporation. None of that sticky blame would find itself into the Chairman's office.

"The tension level is not high enough in the business -- everyone is too damn comfortable at a time when the business is in crisis." Akers was very wrong. He had created more tension than I had ever seen in IBM. Everybody was wondering about the stability of their jobs.

IBM spokespersons were all over the place trying to put a hero look on Akers after his eruption. There was an extensive internal IBM discussion carried out on the corporate office Email conferencing system (PROFS). The question was "who is to blame for IBM's woes?"

A lot of brave IBMers responded to the re-written Akers' speech in memorandum email form. We could not believe this was from the top dog in IBM. To a one, the authors blamed Mr. Akers for the Company's problems. Akers unfortunately had forgotten to take any of the blame.

Not too long after the infamous Akers' memo, in April, 1991, at the annual meeting, the Company reported its operating earnings. It had plunged 48.7 percent while revenue fell 4.5 percent during the first quarter.

IBM forgot to send in any good plays

I knew I was not to blame. So, I looked around our local
IBM office and wondered which IBMer in Scranton PA was
responsible for that dismal showing that the report
highlighted? Nobody of course. It was a top management
issue that was not about to be fixed anytime soon by the top
blaming the bottom for the problem. After the memo, it was
vice versa.

The Company's stock plunged $12.75. Nobody in Scranton
knew how to fix the problem. We were already doing what
we thought was the best we could.

The chairman called for some real 'street fighting' to get the
business. He said: "Market share loss in any sector of the
business would not be tolerated." Regular Joe's like me
asked ourselves: "So John, what does this mean that I am
supposed to do to help matters—that I am not doing now?

Akers called the performance of the Company's United
States business unsatisfactory and said that although the
Company had shed 5,000 people; there had been no
evidence in terms of financial return. Nobody of whom I am
aware suggested to the Chairman that perhaps the people
who had left IBM were the Company's top 5000
salespersons from 1990?

"Where's the beef?" Akers asked: "What the hell are you
doing for 'me'?" This was the ranting of a mad man or so it
seemed!

Yes, I do have a summary for this bad day in the life of a
soon-to be former chairman

Akers sat back; simply wanted it all to work

IBM Chairman John Akers clearly had forgotten to take enough valium on this day in 1991—the day he chose to excoriate his sales managers. The managers dutifully took copious notes that are credited as being very exact. None of the words I read that were discussed in this "sales meeting," were instructive. There were no exhortations about how to attack the marketplace. What should these sales managers be doing that they were not doing? That information did not make it into the notes.

Everybody who worked for IBM at the time, remembers Akers' outburst and if we were all given our turn, the outburst would have come back as Akers' fault several hundred thousand times over. Some had called him the IBM emperor and as such, he made no mistakes and needed no input. Worse than that; he took no input!

Mr. Akers bluntly criticized the Company's performance and in many ways, individual employees' performance at this meeting of IBM senior sales management in Armonk, N.Y. It was held April 25, 1991. I suspect Mr. Akers was so vain he wanted everybody to take notes on his meeting speech and rip it down the IBM chain of command so that even the guy who cleans the floors in the smallest office in which IBM does business would know that Chairman Akers was upset, and that he blamed that guy for IBM's problems!

The great notes that circulated across the corporation were said to have been originated by a sales branch manager in IBM's Calgary office. He sent his notes on Akers' rant out as a PROFS (email) note to his distribution list. Most IBMers saw him as almost a suck-up kind of guy who believed that if the Chairman said this, he must have wanted all employees to know he was not happy with our performance.

The Calgary IBM Branch Manager Executive may not have been a suck-up but when a corporate Chairman goes wild, and potentially postal, and is focused on solutions that are undefined, a better explanation than Mr. Calgary being a suck-up might be that even the Calgary guy wanted IBM to take out this jerk.

Maybe he figured Akers *had to go* before the Company had to suffer more embarrassments and more catastrophic revenue and profit losses. Too bad the IBM Board of Directors were not earning their keep in those days as paid watch-dogs. They surely did not ever protect IBM stockholders from what I have observed. But, they collected their huge stipends for sure.

There was little to be gained by any low-level IBMer taking this all the way and showing up at the annual meeting. I never saved my exact copy of the PROFS note and I sure wish I had.

Everybody was talking about it at the time. Nobody was happy with Akers! As a Senior Systems Engineer, with no intimate knowledge of the Company's books, I had no idea that Akers was actually destroying IBM. I just thought it was good banter, and it made sense.

As expected, somebody, who could have been anybody, even a Branch Manager, leaked the PROFS note to the press almost immediately after the rant. Not all of the quotes below are verified to be Akers' verbatim. They are taken from a version that I have right in front of me now that are purported to have come from the Calgary Executive's notes.

They show how deeply troubled John Akers was by IBM's continuing loss of business to competitors. As a member of IBM's sales force, IBM's mantra during the Akers years was cut, cut, cut, and then when nothing else can be cut; cut some more. I do not recall any Akers initiative that offered a solution to any problem.

At one time IBM Executives would say, *Sell; Sell; Sell,* without telling us how. This would have been better than what we got from Akers—simple chastisement for apparent failure. Even before the nasty blame-thrower memo, the IBM sales team in our office and all those of which I was aware from my national contacts, believed that Akers was IBM problem # 1.

Akers as a leader: blame but no solutions

Among the highlights from the notes on Akers' comments to IBM Sales Executives in 1991 are the following specifics:

> *- On keeping IBM's leading position in the computer industry:* ``*If any one of you is not keeping pace with the industry, then that is unsatisfactory performance.*''

> *- On customer complaints:* ``*I'm sick and tired of visiting (IBM) plants to hear nothing but great things about quality and cycle times, - and then to visit customers who tell me of problems. If the people in labs and plants miss deadlines, tell them their job is on the line too.*''

> *- On IBM overstaffing: After receiving a letter from an IBM account executive stating that the head count on a project had dropped from 22 to 16 and that revenue from that account had dropped from $35 million to $25 million, Akers exploded:* ``*For Christ's sake, you don't need 16 people to drive $25 million!*''

> *- On the performance of IBM's operations in the USA:* ``*Unsatisfactory.*''

> *- On the performance of IBM's operations in Japan:* ``*Japan has been losing share for a couple of years. First quarter 1991 results are disastrous. STEM THE TIDE!*''

- On the performance of IBM's European operations: Akers says Europe has a ``better economy than the USA, with indigenous competitors flat on their face." IBM is ``being seen more and more as a European company - the business benefits should therefore accrue... WHERE ARE THEY?"

- On changing IBM's corporate culture: ``We get A's for being a company with an ability to change, but with our current structure, A is not good enough."

- On IBM's stock performance: ``There's no fun in having the stock at a 25% discount. There's no fun in being a no-growth business. It's not the shareholders' fault. The problem belongs to those people who manage the business."

- On working hard enough at IBM: Too much time, money, and resources are spent talking instead of working at assigned tasks in an excellent manner. And there are ``too many reps popping out for coffee with their customer ... and calling it a CALL."

- On doing your job: ``If you are in sales, sell; - if you are in manufacturing, build. We do not have time to waste."

- On steering clear of IBM's massive bureaucracy: The Company ``can't afford the time to make sure that everything is `consistent with IBM.' "

- On the computer industry and competition: its ``growing 10% worldwide and someone will get the business."

The General was clueless

Maybe Akers was right in almost all of these statements. Maybe! But, he was the general. What would have happened to any of the lieutenants in the room with him if they had the guts to speak up? That was the problem with Akers' IBM. Lots of blame came for sure but nobody was looking for a solution. Those who could suck up the most to Mr. Akers were rewarded. Those who told the truth were lucky to be able to go to work the next day.

To deal with what IBM believed to be the excess employees, somebody suggested that Akers fatten the sales force and sell more products for cash. I love the altruistic idea behind this suggestion.

Unfortunately, many of the folks that had been hired for plant jobs and became sales personnel did not have the sales skills to become field marketing representatives for IBM, so they really did not help us generate more business. They made our jobs easier for sure but they offered little else.

IBMers were all waiting to be fired

IBM's idea of a layoff was being fired and *don't call us since we won't call you*. IBM could have instituted real layoffs in which good employees were able to come back. There would have been more hope.

Additionally, as Akers phased out IBM's Office Products Division (word processing and typewriters), a number of former typewriter salesman were sent to a two week computer sales school and were expected to begin selling computers almost overnight. Few could meet the muster and so most wound up being disposed of by future Akers' plans.

Akers really did not know what to do. Because IBM had a "no-layoff" practice, nobody in IBM was ever fired without real cause. Bad business results had never been a good enough reason to fire anybody in the past. Akers OK'd some underhanded practices in the sales offices to get rid of what management called "the dead wood." Employees were ranked for the first time that I was with IBM. The lowest ranked employee, regardless of appraisal grade was put on a performance improvement program.

Until Akers instituted his version of the performance improvement program, it had been a real gift to employees for six months of real improvement schooling with every effort being made by IBM to reclaim the employee. The program was only successful when an employee came back and became successful.

That was not the purpose of the Akers' plan. It was pure chicanery. IBM began to lie to its employees, and we knew the Company was already lying to our customers so their words to us were simply unbelievable. The improvement program was successful under Akers when the employee agreed to leave IBM and not sue the Company for a dime more than promised.

The Akers' plan was two months and out. The word success was not part of the deal. It was a purge process. Management was supposed to lean hard on the employee to get them to quit, since IBM theoretically fired nobody. These were low points in the life of IBM and one-time loyal IBM employees. Morale hit the toilet. Akers' IBM at the top and at the bottom of the hierarchy could do nothing right.

Rather than risk more of the same by hiring a replacement CEO from within, IBM looked outside IBM for the first time to find a CEO with enough chutzpah to get the job done. Lou Gerstner interviewed for the job. Thankfully for the soul of IBM, he was their man. I know of no IBM employee who wept when the late John Akers got the axe. Of course, at the time, I had been out of IBM for just ten months when Akers was replaced.

IBM looks to survive!

Akers' IBM was answering its business challenges internally by reducing expenses, primarily by cutting its workforce. The Company decided that it could not afford a direct sales force any longer and turned its business over to distributors, who for years had been making their numbers by claiming sales from the direct sales force with local management's approval.

Since the local support team was eliminated, these "third parties now had to perform." The Company also reduced expenses by no longer offering free customer support for its long-term customers. Akers' IBM had gotten rid of the local support team.

By 1993, before Lou Gerstner walked in for his first day of work, the IBM Company was looking at survival as its major issue. With annual net losses reaching a record $8 billion in that one year, cost management and streamlining continued as a business necessity. During this period, IBM was examining itself as a large company and had some misgivings about its ability to compete in all areas of the information technology industry.

John Akers began to restructure even more of IBM's major divisions, such as printers and storage. Akers intention it seemed was to sell off as many divisions as need be to raise the cash necessary to survive. The large printer division, for example, was spun off into a separate unit, and IBM appeared ready to further split the Company into separate business units that could be readily sold.

Akers' IBM did not want to be in all of the businesses in which IBM was engaged. The report card for Akers was in. Many aspects of IBM's businesses were not holding their own. Akers and company were preparing to bring in some well-needed cash by selling these parts of what had once been the Company's core businesses.

In other words, if the IBM body's heart had to be sold to get a few more years before IBM's probable collapse, the heart would be harvested and sold. A small pump would replace it for sure. That's how bad it was. We felt it when I was with IBM and IBMers felt it until Akers was eliminated from IBM.

John Akers never did recover from the debt left him by his predecessor. In 1985, when Akers, who was 50 years-old at the time, succeeded John Opel as the Chairman and CEO, most IBMers believed that he represented long-term stability for the next ten years until he reached retirement age at sixty years old.

However, by 1993, it was obvious to the world, the industry press, and the IBM Board of Directors that the old methods in IBM would not keep the Company in business. Akers stepped down from his responsibilities before it was his natural time. He was in effect fired for incompetence. I suspect normal Joes at IBM got him fired as well as the press and those IBM managers who did not owe him a modicum of allegiance.

Mr. Akers had placed the IBM Company in such a precarious position that, for the first time in its over 80-year history, the Watson Company was forced to look outside the corporation for a person with the smarts and the fortitude to bail IBM out from the quicksand in which it seemed to be buried.

That sets the stage for Lou Gerstner sure. The stage setting began in Section IV, when first we recounted the travails of Mr. Akers. I will say this even before I tell the Lou Gerstner story. I fear that IBM's new Board of Directors post Gerstner, with Palmisano and Rometty as their Chairs, have decided that as long as life on the Board is good, they won't tell any bad tales about Sam or Ginni—just like the pre-Gerstner board would not take on Opel and Akers.

Lou Gerstner takes over

On April 1, 1993, after a few misfires, IBM's Board hired a born leader in Louis V. Gerstner Jr. He became IBM's Chairman and CEO on that day. Gerstner's executive experience included eleven years as a top executive at American Express and four years as the CEO of RJR Nabisco during its major restructuring efforts.

Gerstner seemed like an ideal candidate from a business perspective, though some felt his lack of experience in the computer field would limit his ability to take charge and become effective. This proved not to be the case, however.

As a consumer products executive, he already had a customer oriented sensitivity and he had strong executive and strategic thinking strengths, which he had built and sharpened even before his American Express days as a management consultant for McKinsey and Co.

The fact that John Akers was burdened by a John Opel run Company in which only a super human being such as Lou Gerstner could manage, did not hold water with run of the mill IBMers who saw Akers destroy the IBM they admired.

Despite what we all thought, in a normal IBM, Akers would probably have done fine. How fruitful for IBM that Thomas Watson Jr. picked up Louis V. Gerstner Jr. at the airport on his trip to IBM for his first day of work. Watson's message to Gerstner was quite simple: "Save IBM!" "Period!"

IBM stockholders around the world watched closely. It was not long after he arrived that Gerstner began to take dramatic, unprecedented action to stabilize the Company. These steps included rebuilding IBM's product line, while continuing to shrink the workforce and making significant cost reductions.

For IBM to survive and thrive, because things had gotten so bad, Gerstner believed he had to break the unwritten job security contract and long-standing full-employment practice with his employees, and IBM executed massive layoffs for the first time in its history.

No IBM employee was singled out in the Gerstner initiated purge as being an incompetent or an old-timer. Even when the Gerstner necessary axe came to the IBM employees that Akers left working for the Company, it was far less unpleasant. Everybody remembered that in the Akers' years it was always the employee's fault that they were fired for being bad for IBM.

I was glad to be out of IBM at the time, but I understood Gerstner's role in saving the Company. Every IBMer who had ever worked for the Company had a load of IBM stock certificates. They would all have zero value in a bankrupt IBM. Thank you Lou Gerstner for saving IBM.

Unlike John Akers who had some problems managing the success of divergent units within IBM, and who was preparing a major break-up of the Company one piece at a time for quick cash, Gerstner had a much different idea.

Though there was mounting pressure, due to IBM's poor record, to split Big Blue into separate, independent companies as Akers had intended, Gerstner decided to keep IBM intact.

He believed that one of IBM's biggest strengths was its ability to create and deliver integrated solutions for customers, rather than what could be called the piece-parts solutions du jour as served by necessity by IBM's competitors. He decided to keep IBM's unique advantage and move the full company in a direction to suit the times.

When Gerstner came to IBM in early 1993, the business he came to, in many ways was dying. It had been sapped of its financial strength. It was on its last legs. It was not the tradition-rich IBM, which every other Chairman had inherited. It was not the old IBM. It was a beaten, broken company when Tom Watson Jr. accompanied Lou Gerstner to work on his first day.

Neither Gerstner, nor any other magician, could have created the old IBM from what Akers left behind. IBM was not Gerstner's heritage. If there were still an old IBM at the time that Gerstner came aboard, he would probably not have been the right pick for CEO. The IBM which Gerstner got, did not have the luxury of a recession-proof rental business. It did not have a crackerjack sales force. It did not have a leading Office Division. It did not have a thriving disk-drive (storage) business or a leading networking business, or a front-line application software business or even a printer business.

They had all been sold off or disposed of. IBM still had a great mainframe division, a powerful set of midrange systems, and it received a great CEO who knew how to sell,

The IBM that Lou Gerstner inherited had already been prepared by John Akers to be sectioned off, with parts being dissolved or sold. In a desperate attempt at survival, his predecessor had already begun selling the Company's assets for cash.

Gerstner inherited an IBM with a death wish marketing strategy on its way to the bone yard. He was the right guy to rescue IBM. He came with no constraints. Though cuts continued, even the IBMers did not have the same disdain for Gerstner's cuts as they did for Akers. They were not haphazard. They were logical.

Akers had once been one of the IBM team himself and he did not protect the Company nor its employees. Lou Gerstner was an outsider, brought in to breathe life into a dying company. Employees expected that Lou Gerstner would continue to cut costs, His mission was to save IBM. IBM employees wanted IBM to be saved.

Gerstner saved IBM from bankruptcy

When the cuts were mostly done and IBM began to return to some sense of normalcy, Lou Gerstner had actually saved the Company. As much as the prior chairman was determined to split the Company into a bunch of tiny and weak IBM's, which could be sold to raise cash, Gerstner was determined to join it back together to form a strong, formidable IBM.

After the cuts began to mend the Company; it was joined back together, and the wounds began to disappear. IBM became successful again. But, even so, the old tradition-rich IBM would never return because it could never return or IBM would simply fail again.

EBusiness was Gerstner's theme song

Indisputably, Lou Gerstner's battle cry was eBusiness, and he led IBM well in this regard. He coined the term. When he arrived in 1993, amidst all of the Company's other problems, IBM was not positioned to do well in much of anything, including the Internet.

Through sheer neglect, and a touch of arrogance, neither the mainframe nor the AS/400 product lines were capable of providing even a basic Internet service without major costs and a big hassle. With at least a basic Internet service being a prerequisite for eBusiness, Gerstner very quickly recognized the problem and effected the solution.

He decreed that all of IBM's server computers would fully support Internet protocols and be prepared for eBusiness. He set up a dedicated Internet organization in IBM until things were rolling on track. It was a tall order, but the new IBM was able to comply. For years IBM had fought the Internet's major protocol, TCP/IP with all its might. IBM meant SNA. Non-IBM meant TCP/IP. Gerstner saw IBM losing big time without adopting an integrated and powerful Internet program.

In the fall 1999, the Internet mission was completed, and Irving Wladawsky Berger, the head of the Internet unit, had his success acknowledged, and was given another challenging assignment, Linux.

With IBM's commitment, and Lou Gerstner's tenacity, eBusiness is not expected to ever arrive at the IBM graveyard of coined terms. For example, it is not expected to join the likes of PC, word processing, teleprocessing, and other long-gone IBM buzzwords, representing once key technologies. These were terms coined by IBM, and made famous and profitable by other companies.

As it stood in his day, Gerstner had all of IBM's divisions holding at attention ready to serve any of the needs of eBusiness. Clearly, IBM's renewed commitment to the Internet permitted the Company to survive the client/server era and begin to prosper in the server-centric world of eBusiness and the Internet.

Let me say it again. Lou Gerstner saved IBM!

Gerstner and Watson Jr.

Lou Gerstner, and the late Thomas Watson Jr. seem to share a number of common attributes. Watson Jr. knew that IBM was successful because of its customers, even more than its products. Gerstner Jr took on the task of rebuilding IBM's relationships with its largest customers, many of which had turned from IBM during the years of IBM trying to be the low cost producer and finding themselves the *cow* in the IBM cash-cow mentality.

Watson Jr. was always very concerned that IBM maintain its leadership in the power and performance of supercomputers. Unfortunately, when either Watsons was in charge of IBM, their own marketing organization added *general purpose* and *affordable* to the development constraints for supercomputers.

To Watson's dismay, especially Watson Jr., Seymour Cray, a former IBM exceptional employee, because of *general* and *affordable* being added to IBM's constraints for supercomputers, was then able to build faster computers than IBM. But Gerstner would not add constraints and would not be put off, as Watson to achieve the same goal.

Lou Gerstner removed the constraints. It did not matter to Gerstner if the machine was not general purpose or affordable, as long as it was F-A-S-T, and of course, fastest! And, so, he took IBM's vast R&D budget and like Watson decreed that they design and fabricate the fastest computers imaginable. Unlike Watson, Gerstner's IBM was able to pull it off constraint-free!

Even more recently, just a few years after Kasparov, IBM moved on a new project called "Blue Gene," dealing with genetics. This project lifted the performance bar 1000 times more than the Deep Blue machine which beat Kasparov.

Watson would be proud. Now the Supercomputer to beat is named *Watson.*

The Chessmaster/6000

IBM became a tough competitor in all facets of computing under Gerstner, including what some might consider trivial. Gerstner believed that IBM should be the best in the markets in which it chose to compete. In one of the most famous computer events of all time, in May 1997, as the world looked on in suspense, IBM dramatically demonstrated its computing potential with a machine called Deep Blue.

IBM's fastest computer at the time, this 32 node IBM RS/6000 SP computer entered a chess game as an underdog for the last time. IBM had not been known for building the fastest computers. As of May, 1997 this no longer is the case.

IBM programmed this computer to play chess on a world class expert level. To test its work, IBM invited World Chess Champion Garry Kasparov to a six game match in New York. Deep Blue, running on a machine capable of assessing the ramifications of 200 million chess moves per second, defeated Kasparov. This sent shockwaves around the world with public debate on how close computers really come to human intelligence. It also sent the Russian away hoping for a rematch... hopefully during a power storm?

The Internet as the Information Superhighway

In the early 1990s, the Internet was re-christened by VP Al Gore as *The Information Superhighway.* In many ways, it was this act which set the stage for the commercializing of the Internet and the beginning of the dot com craze. Instead of a haven for academics, tax-free organizations, hackers, and the government, The Internet became an avenue for commercial ventures. The term dot com, a period and the phrase *com* became the symbol for those businesses that took up the challenge of conducting commerce (.com) on the Internet.

No Virginia, Al Gore did not invent the Internet, but he did give it a nice push into commercial ventures. Gerstner was quick to recognize the potential of this new medium and the unique role, which IBM could play in this new environment.

Neither Frank Cary, John Opel, nor John Akers had prepared IBM for having the proper technology to deploy behind Gerstner's plan to save the Company through networking. In fact, all three resisted the temptation to engage IBM in such helpful technology because it was against the precepts of IBM's corporate networking architecture, called SNA.

IBM's CEOs lost a lot of revenue by sticking with SNA and thankfully as an IBM stockholder, I saw Mr. Gerstner end those days. I could have suggested a few other areas if the new chairman was listening for more. IBM was replete with areas ignored by top management.

The Internet and the rise of network computing represented a major paradigm shift within the IT industry. Unlike the PC and client/server revolutions, however, this time, IBM was a little better prepared but it needed some command and control decisions from the top of the Company to get it moving.

IBM retracting lots and refocusing lots

Gerstner quickly charged all IBM divisions with making sure that all of IBM's products were Internet ready. The PC and RS/6000 divisions were already there. Developers for the AS/400 and the mainframe product lines had a much bigger task in bringing Internet standard TCP/IP functionality to their platforms.

In May 1994, IBM finally brought its AS/400 up to Internet speed with the introduction of high quality, integrated TCP/IP stacks and well known applications' support. Shortly thereafter, IBM upgraded its Internet-ware for the mainframe product line.

In both instances, this involved major rewrites by IBM Labs with major performance enhancements. Internet facilities got stronger and stronger with each release of these respective systems. In fact, by 2000, under Gerstner's mandate, IBM had used this strong TCP/IP support as a basis for becoming the unquestioned leader in eBusiness.

The next wave: from client server to the Internet

They say, what goes around, comes around! Though IBM did eventually catch up to become an effective also-ran in the client/server arena, this form of computing accentuated the positive aspects of the client v. the server. The desktop (client) PC was the king of client/server in its day.

This was never where mainframe oriented IBM's traditional strengths existed. IBM's strengths were on the server side. Internet computing, unlike client / server computing does not rely on strong clients, but on thin, universal clients or that part of a PC or a handheld device or phone that is driven by nothing more than the modern equivalent of a browser on the desktop or on a handheld device.

IBM provided power from the server outward

Substantial power ... the more the better... is required in the back-room to support the work being done on the client device. The back room is IBM's traditional haven, where its key strengths had always been.

In many ways, Gerstner's eBusiness initiative saved IBM from its potential demise from the hands of client oriented client/server. Gerstner's IBM boasted a granular server product line (eServers), newly enriched with Internet protocols, and the power to serve non-trivial business applications over the Web.

Again playing to IBM's strong suit, it just happens that to be good on the Internet, and in eBusiness, it takes much more than a hit and miss piece-parts philosophy. IBM's strengths had always been in business integration and this was again the focus area for Lou Gerstner's IBM customers wanting to extend their storefronts to the electronic highway.

In this new world, nobody was better prepared to be successful than IBM. Lou Gerstner knew this and he played his hand to IBM's strengths. Lou Gerstner saved IBM using its recognized strengths.

The need Gerstner realized was integrated business solutions. This prescription could only be filled by IBM. Gerstner soon realized that The IBM Company was the only specialist in town. As the only company that could bring the total answer to the table   the combination of expertise in solutions, services, products and technologies, Gerstner's IBM had already begun a major turnover.

If it weren't for the Zoomers on NASDAQ, one might offer that IBM's unique strengths and exceptional performance had again made the Company one of Wall Street's darlings. But IBM CEOs after Gerstner were not so astute.

Though Gerstner is long gone at IBM, his plan mostly continues to work when it takes precedence over nuances preferred by the later IBM CEOs. Keeping the Company together permitted IBM to capitalize on a new technology wave. And into the new millennium, Wall Street acknowledged that IBM was again on the right track, as the street brought the Company's stock right back through the roof.

According to Gerstner's plan

This was all part of Gerstner's plan, which he revealed shortly after his arrival. In fall of 1995. Mr. Gerstner delivered the keynote address at the COMDEX computer industry trade show in Las Vegas. Here he presented his new vision   that network computing would drive the next phase of industry growth and would be the IBM Company's overarching strategy. All the while he held the helm, he was certainly right, and his blueprints for success live on.

If you don't have it, buy it!

You may recall that in 1995, IBM quietly stopped development of its own groupware product known as IBM Workgroup. That year, IBM made big industry news by acquiring Lotus Development Corp., for $3.5 billion. Lotus already had the complete suite of office integration functions, which the IBM Workgroup effort was attempting to achieve, and so this costly development was no longer necessary.

In 1996, IBM also acquired Tivoli Systems Inc. This acquisition gave the Company a first-class product in the growing systems management area. Cloud computing was right around the corner and a Tivoli driven IBM would help assure its success.

IBM services are not an afterthought

A total solutions company must bridge the function gaps of software with high quality services to create complete solutions. Gerstner was high on bringing the total resources of IBM to its customers to solve business problems. He believed that a strong services business was necessary to round out IBM's total picture.

Under Gerstner, services soon became the fastest growing segment of the Company, with growth at more than 20 percent per year. All of this success had a dramatic effect on investors' perceptions, as the market value of the Company increased by more than $50 billion in the short span from 1993 to 1996. Clearly, Mr. Gerstner had won public and stockholder approval. He and the Watsons brought IBM the same thing: SUCCESS!

Here is some nice, succinct and pithy information about Lou Gerstner brought to us by the IBM Corporation:

> *In 1991 Louis V. Gerstner, Jr. was chairman of the board of IBM Corporation from April 1993 until his retirement in December 2002. He served as chief executive officer of IBM from 1993 until March 2002. In January 2003 he assumed the position of chairman of The Carlyle Group, a global private equity firm located in Washington, DC.*

> *Prior to joining IBM, Mr. Gerstner served for four years as chairman and chief executive officer of RJR Nabisco, Inc. This was preceded by an 11-year career at American Express Company, where he was president of the parent company and chairman and CEO of its largest subsidiary, American Express Travel Related*

Services Company. Prior to that, Mr. Gerstner was a director of the management consulting firm of McKinsey & Co., Inc., which he joined in 1965.

A native of Mineola, New York, Mr. Gerstner received a bachelor's degree in engineering from Dartmouth College in 1963 and an MBA from Harvard Business School in 1965. He is a member of the National Academy of Engineering, a Fellow of the American Academy of Arts and Sciences and has been awarded honorary doctorates from a number of U.S. universities.

Mr. Gerstner is a director of Bristol-Myers Squibb Co. and a member of the advisory boards of DaimlerChrysler and Sony Corporation. He is vice chairman of the board of Memorial Sloan-Kettering Cancer Center, a member of the board of the Council on Foreign Relations, a member of The Business Council, and a fellow of the America-China Forum. In past years he served on the Boards of The New York Times Company, American Express Company, AT&T, Caterpillar, Inc., Jewel Companies, Melville Corporation, and RJR Nabisco Holdings Co.

A lifetime advocate of the importance of quality education, Mr. Gerstner recently created a Commission on Teaching to develop specific policy recommendations to deal with the teaching crisis America is facing. From 1996 to 2002 he co-chaired Achieve, an organization created by U.S. Governors and business leaders to drive high academic standards for public schools in the United States.

At IBM he established Reinventing Education as a strategic partnership with 21 states and school districts which utilize IBM technology and technical assistance to eliminate key barriers to school reform and improve student performance. He is co-author of the book Reinventing Education: Entrepreneurship in America's Public Schools (Dutton 1994).

He has received numerous awards for his work in education, among them the Cleveland E. Dodge Medal for Distinguished Service to Education - Teachers College, Columbia University, and

*the Distinguished Service to Science and Education award from
the American Museum of Natural History.*

*In recognition of his efforts on behalf of public education, as well as
his business accomplishments, Mr. Gerstner was awarded the
designation of honorary Knight of the British Empire by Queen
Elizabeth II in June 2001.*

As an ex-IBMer and a continuous stockholder, I am very
that Lou Gerstner came along when he did to save a
faltering IBM. I am just as glad that Tom Watson Jr. gave
the future IBM CEO a pep talk on his way from the airport
on his first day of work. Few CEOS have the work ethic of
Lou Gerstner or Tom Watson, Jr, or Sr.

If I could have either a Watson or a Gerstner back running
IBM, and I were consulted, I would give my OK in an
instant. I have developed a distrust for inbred IBM
Executives who are missing an entrepreneurial flare for
business.

Chapter 68

The END: IBM's Sam Palmisano and Ginni Rometty

Are Opel and Akers giving an encore presentation?

Is this the End?

When I wrote this book for the first time twenty years ago and I chose to let it rest for a long time, Lou Gerstner was at the beginning of his new IBM career and there was no Sam Palmisano in the front lawn of IBM technology and stock price manipulation. Ginni Rometty at the time, was an unknown to the regulars who had to make their living with or without IBM.

Lou Gerstner had just about already saved IBM. I had left IBM even before the big Gerstner save. I had assumed the role of chief technology officer at College Misericordia in Dallas PA, now Misericordia University. My title at the time more fit the times.

Sam Palmisano, a lifetime IBMer, was Gerstner's pick for CEO of IBM when "Lou" chose to retire in 2002. I was not an IBM follower at this time as I was working hard to keep my new consulting practice moving in the right direction.

Consequently, I was not a big fan and not a little fan of Sam Palmisano. I was, however, concerned about IBM ever going back to IBM bred and sponsored CEOs.

I did not pay much attention to IBM per se through the Palmisano years since I was fully engaged as an IBM product consultant and independent consultant in my own accounts. Palmisano just happened to be the guy running IBM from the top. As you might expect, he never gave me a call for help or advice. Yes, I had some thoughts that he could have used.

Rometty becomes new IBM CEO in 2012

IBM CEO Sam Palmisano kept the IBM stock price moving during his time as CEO. I was happy about that and I benefitted. Mr. Palmisano stepped down from the IBM top spot after ten years in 2012 and was succeeded by Virginia (Ginni) Rometty.

She had most recently served as the Company's sales chief. For a while at least, Palmisano remained Chairman of the Board. IBM and Sam Palmisano have always been high on Ginni Rometty. That's why after three successive years of depressed earnings, she still gets to call reveille in the morning for IBM.

She successfully led several of IBM's most important businesses over the past decade. Palmisano noted when he turned over the reins to her, that Rometty helped form IBM Global Business Services to the build-out of IBM's Growth Markets Unit. He then added that "She is more than a superb operational executive - with every leadership role, she has strengthened our ability to integrate IBM's capabilities for our clients."

Does Rometty mean good things from IBM?

Sam Palmisano did not mention that Rometty also worshipped his questionable "roadmap" plans and having her in place would be like as if he had never left IBM's top slot regarding his famed roadmap to success.

Palmisano was very high on Rometty for the CEO position because he felt she brought to the role of CEO a unique combination of vision, client focus, unrelenting drive, and passion for IBMers and the Company's future.

Palmisano is quoted as saying: "I know the board agrees with me that Ginni is the ideal CEO to lead IBM into its second century." Not many reasons but a really positive endorsement of a long time co-worker. John Akers himself would have asked, "Where is the Beef?"

Industry analysts credit Palmisano, who led Big Blue since 2002, when Lou Gerstner stepped down, for successfully guiding tech giant IBM through the economic downturn. Sam Palmisano also helped "architect" IBM's push towards high-margin areas such as software and services—the areas that Lou Gerstner had triumphed.

Palmisano has been quoted since his retirement, such as in the June 2014 issue of the Harvard Business Review (HBR), about how he was not necessarily managing high margin technology areas but had triumphantly "managed" investors and had induced IBM's share price to soar. Gerstner seemed at least to be more concerned about success in IBM's core businesses rather than its stockholder opinions.

Business Week and Sam Palmisano

Others in the industry besides Ginni Rometty suggest that Palmisano was not as successful at this as he touts to have been. Business week, for example, came out with a take-down article on Sam Palmisano, conjuring up thoughts like the Opel to Akers turnover.

"Palmisano is reported to have handed over to his unfortunate successor CEO, Ginni Rometty, a firm with a toxic mix of unsustainable policies". That surely sounds like an Opel/Akers mix.

Unfortunately, the supposed key to Palmisano's success in "managing" investors at IBM was—and is–"RoadMap 2015." Like Opel's $100 billion promise, the Palmisano plan promises a doubling of the earnings per share by 2015. Lots of people who are much smarter than I have gotten sucked in.

For example, Warren Buffett invested more than $10 billion in IBM in 2011, along with many other investors, who were impressed with the methodical way in which Palmisano's IBM was able to make money.

Facts do not always assure the future will sustain them. Under Palmisano, earnings per share doubled, and were "on track" to continue under Rometty, who like Sam Palmisano is another long-time IBMer.

Rometty as CEO

Rometty became IBM CEO in 2012. She is prohibited from calling Palmisano bad things as she embraced his "Roadmap" with as much gusto as the former Chairman himself.

Business week thinks that Sam Palmisano's roadmap is the biggest force in the universe that is *killing IBM*. According to BW, "IBM's soaring earnings per share and its share price are built on a foundation of declining revenues, capability-crippling offshoring, fading technical competence, sagging staff morale, debt-financed share buybacks, non-standard accounting practices, tax-reduction gadgets, a debt-equity ratio of around 174 percent, a broken business model and a flawed forward strategy."

As a stockholder, I sure hope BW and all the analysts are wrong as America could use a strong IBM. As a former employee, I know that to save its skin, IBM is willing to lie and do whatever it needs to do to survive.

Since Rometty took over IBM, things have gotten worse not better with revenue falling year after year from one time lofty heights above $107 billion to just above $92 billion. Keep your roadmap, Ginni. Instead, please just bring in results without selling off the divisions that produce the results, such as the recently foregone chip division and the x86 server division before that. Why should investors believe in your ideas when in execution, you have an Akers plan in place to get rid of IBM's most obvious assets?

Here is the most damaging statement that I can make on IBM and I wish it was not coming from me:

This book is about all of the millionaires (12,000 at Microsoft alone and 2500 at Cisco) and the multimillionaires and billionaires that IBM's failure to execute in its core business has created in many side industries to the major league computer industries. I suspect there are a few more billionaires and millionaires in this industry since Lou Gerstner took over IBM in 1993. But, not many!

This next notion is filled with pain. IBM to the best of my knowledge has not been a leader in any areas in which such wealth has been created for entrepreneurs for about twenty years.

IBM is no longer doing well enough that anybody finds what it creates to be worthy of emulating or stealing. I am getting a little sick reading about Palmisano and Rometty in the same way that I got sick reading about Opel and Akers. Not being an insider for sure anymore, I deeply hope that I am wrong about IBM. I would vote as an IBM Board Member to bring in another Gerstner and ease IBM's current pain from two in-bred CEOs in a row. But, IBM's board of Directors again appears to be asleep.

IBM is hurting today. The press articles are not positive. Each quarter that passes appears to bring no relief to a beleaguered earnings picture. Forbes Magazine recently interviewed some IBMers on the inside of the software group and other areas within the Company and nobody but the CEO right now seems high on IBM. Forbes had the bravado to write an unabashed, truthful, un-mollified version of a number of aspects of IBM today that are not as positive as what the CEO says.

For example, IBM has been using some marketing tricks to make it look like things are getting better. For example, in software, where the Company says it has been doing well for years, it has begun to make its annual numbers by increasing prices and by auditing customers for licensing compliance.

Some quick-sales have been registered for sure and in total, the amounts are lucrative. IBM's software team is helping its customers get back to 100% licensing compliance but that surely is not a strategy for sustained growth. In fact, I would suspect that those companies caught in the licensing web, who now have unbudgeted expenses, blame IBM for that.

While its revenues have been decreasing, IBM has continued to cut, cut, and cut expenses again – mostly employees. Recently Forbes Magazine noted that the employee cuts are so close to the bone that simply getting price quotes from Big Blue's administrative staff has become a very slow and painful process inside IBM.

Forbes calls this IBM's cause/effect, action/reaction phase. When a company cuts too far, after it has already cut deep enough, instead of feeling the results in a year or perhaps more, it feels operational difficulties immediately or in the next quarter. The consensus says IBM has made too many cuts. They are too deep and they have been done haphazardly without regard to their effect on ongoing operations. Cuts today may result in decreased sales tomorrow.

Forbes is also worried about IBM's Global Services. Since Gerstner, this too had been one of IBM's bright lights. But it is now so poorly run that its customers are shying away from making new IBM IT investments. Customers are seeing the internal IBM problems and are balking. That is never good for customer confidence and continual sales.

IBM has lost $15 billion in revenue in just three years and good business principles suggest that cost cutting cannot make up for lack of sales beyond the pain level. IBM is in trouble and there are few divisions left that Big Blue can package up and sell at fire sale prices. That is bad news for CEO Rometty who would like the cash. Perhaps in the spirit of this book, it is also bad news to any engaging entrepreneurs out there hoping that by craftily doing business with IBM they can become the next Bill Gates.

Speaking of Mr. Gates and his successful relationship with IBM in the 1980's, one would think that the IBM Board and IBM executive management including CEO Rometty today must have a bad taste about the overall Microsoft experience. After all, they know that their IBM Company is solely responsible for creating the richest man in the world. And, Bill Gates never worked a day for the IBM Company.

It would be nice for me to be wrong about this. When companies don't get it right for an awful long time, they eventually fail. I fear that is the future for IBM? Yet, I still own stock. Perhaps I am a dedicated fool who if cut would bleed blue—not Palmisano blue or Rometty blue. It would be Watson blue.

Gerstner was in fact, a lot like the Watsons—full of prospects for success. However, Palmisano and Rometty are more like Opel and Akers, ready to take advantage of the works of others, and blame them when results are poor.

So, will IBM be successful in the future or will it fail sometime soon? Will anybody be calling me anytime soon to see if I can help? Not willing to wait for IBM, I think I will write another book,

Thank you for being such kind readers. I hope you enjoyed all the tales in this book. I wish they did not need to be told.

Calling upon the spirits for help

I think we can ask Charles Dickens for some guidance here as we ponder the future of IBM. Any company—especially IBM—can change for the better. Here are Dickens and Scrooge's words to encourage us all. Good luck, IBM!

The Ghost of Christmas Yet to Come conveyed him to a dismal, wretched, ruinous churchyard.

The Spirit stood among the graves, and pointed down to one.

"Before I draw nearer to that stone to which you point," said Scrooge, "answer me one question. Are these the shadows of the things that Will be, or are they shadows of things that May be, only?

Still the Ghost pointed downward to the grave by which it stood.

"Men's courses will foreshadow certain ends, to which, if persevered in, they must lead," said Scrooge. "But if the courses be departed from, the ends will change. Say it is thus with what you show me!"

This is the end of the book. Now you know why many of today's tech billionaires and multi-millionaires owe IBM a big thank you.

Please tell your friends to read this book. Additional copies can be gained by shopping at techbooksisus.com. Other books by Brian Kelly are available at www.bookhawkers.com .

God bless you all!

LETS GO PUBLISH! Books by Brian W. Kelly

www.letsgopublish.com; Sold at www.bookhawkers.com
Email info@ letsgopublish.com for specific ordering info. Our titles include the following:

Great Moments in Notre Dame Football Check out the particulars of this great book at bookhawkers.com or www.notredamebooks.com

WineDiets.Com PresentsThe Wine Diet Learn how to lose weight while having fun. Four specific diets and some great anecdotes fill this book with fun.

Wilkes-Barre, PA; Return to Glory Wilkes-Barre City's return to glory begins with dreams and ideas. Along with plans and actions, this equals leadership.

The Lifetime Guest Plan. This is a plan which if deployed today would immediately solve the problem of 60 million illegal aliens in the United States.

Geoffrey Parsons' Epoch... The Land of Fair Play Better than the original. The greatest re-mastering of the greatest book ever written on American Civics. It was built for all Americans as the best govt. design in the history of the world.

The Bill of Rights 4 Dummmies This is the best book to learn about your rights. Be the first, to have a "Rights Fest" on your block. You will win for sure!

Sol Bloom's Epoch ...Story of the Constitution This work by Sol Bloom was written to commemorate the Sesquicentennial celebration of the Constitution. It has been remastered by Lets Go Publish! – an excellent read!

The Constitution 4 Dummmies This is the best book to learn about the Constitution. Learn all about the fundamental laws of America.

America for Dummmies!
All Americans should read to learn about this great country.

Just Say No to Chris Christie for President!
Discusses the reasons why Chris Christie is a poor choice for US President

The Federalist Papers by Hamilton, Jay, Madison w/ intro by Brian Kelly
Complete unabridged, easier to read version of the original Federalist Papers

Kill the Republican Party!
Demonstrates why the Republican Party must be abandoned by conservatives

Bring On the American Party!
Demonstrates how conservatives can be free from the party of wimps by starting its own national party called the American Party.

No Amnesty! No Way!
In addition to describing the issue in detail, this book also offers a real solution.

Saving America
This how-to book is about saving our country using strong mercantilist principles. These same principles that helped the country from its founding.

RRR:
A unique plan for economic recovery and job creation

Kill the EPA
The EPA seems to hate mankind and love nature. They are also making it tough for asthmatics to breathe and for those with malaria to live. It's time they go.

Obama's Seven Deadly Sins.
In the Obama Presidency, there are many concerns about the long-term prospects and sustainability of the country. We examine each of the President's seven deadliest sins in detail, offering warnings and a number of solutions. Be careful. Book may nudge you to move to Canada or Europe.

Taxation Without Representation Second Edition
At the time of the Boston Tea Party, there was no representation. Now, there is no representation again but there are "representatives."

Healthcare Accountability
Who should pay for your healthcare? Whose healthcare should you pay for? Is it a lifetime free ride on others or should those once in need of help have to pay it back when their lives improve?

Jobs! Jobs! Jobs!
Where have all the American Jobs gone and how can we get them back?

IBM I Technical Books

The All Everything Operating System:
Story about IBM's finest operating system, its facilities; how it came to be.

The All-Everything Machine
Story about IBM's finest computer server.

Chip Wars
The story of ongoing wars between Intel and AMD and upcoming wars between Intel and IBM. Book may cause you to buy / sell somebody's stock.

Can the AS/400 Survive IBM?
Exciting book about the AS/400 in an System i5 World.

The IBM i Pocket SQL Guide.
Complete Pocket Guide to SQL as implemented on System i5. A must have for SQL developers new to System i5. It is very compact yet very comprehensive and it is example driven. Written in a part tutorial and part reference style, Tons of SQL coding samples, from the simple to the sublime.

The IBM i Pocket Query Guide.
If you have been spending money for years educating your Query users, and you find you are still spending, or you've given up, this book is right for you. This one QuikCourse covers all Query options.

The IBM I Pocket RPG & RPG IV Guide.
Comprehensive RPG & RPGIV Textbook -- Over 900 pages. This is the one RPG book to have if you are not having more than one. All areas of the language covered smartly in a convenient sized book Annotated PowerPoint's available for self study (extra fee for self study package)

The IBM I RPG Tutorial and Lab Guide – Recently Revised.
Your guide to a hands-on Lab experience. Contains CD with Lab exercises and PowerPoint's. Great companion to the above textbook or can be used as a standalone for student Labs or tutorial purposes
The IBM i Pocket Developers' Guide.
Comprehensive Pocket Guide to all of the AS/400 and System i5 development tools - DFU, SDA, etc. You'll also get a big bonus with chapters on Architecture, Work Management, and Subfile Coding.
The IBM i Pocket Database Guide.
Complete Pocket Guide to System i5 integrated relational database (DB2/400) – physical and logical files and DB operations - Union, Projection, Join, etc. Written in a part tutorial and part reference style. Tons of DDS coding samples.

Getting Started With The WebSphere Development Studio Client for System i5 (WDSc) Focus on client server and the Web. Includes CODE/400, VisualAge RPG, CGI, WebFacing, and WebSphere Studio. Case study continues from the Interactive Book.
The System i5 Pocket WebFacing Primer.
This book gets you started immediately with WebFacing. A sample case study is used as the basis for a conversion to WebFacing. Interactive 5250 application is WebFaced in a case study form before your eyes.

Getting Started with WebSphere Express Server for IBM i Step-by-Step Guide for Setting Up Express Servers
A comprehensive guide to setting up and using WebSphere Express. It is filled with examples, and structured in a tutorial fashion for easy learning.

The WebFacing Application Design & Development Guide:
Step by Step Guide to designing green screen IBM i apps for the Web. Both a systems design guide and a developers guide. Book helps you understand how to design and develop Web applications using regular RPG or COBOL programs.

The System i5 Express Web Implementor's Guide. Your one stop guide to ordering, installing, fixing, configuring, and using WebSphere Express, Apache, WebFacing, System i5 Access for Web, and HATS/LE.

Joomla! Technical Books

Best Damn Joomla Tutorial Ever
Learn Joomla! by example.
Best Damn Joomla Intranet Tutorial Ever
This book is the only book that shows you how to use Joomla on a corporate intranet.
Best Damn Joomla Template Tutorial Ever
This book teaches you step-by step how to work with templates in Joomla!
Best Damn Joomla Installation Guide Ever
Teaches you how to install Joomla! On all major platforms besides IBM i.
Best Damn Blueprint for Building Your Own Corporate Intranet.
This excellent timeless book helps you design a corporate intranet for any platform while using Joomla as its basis.
IBM i PHP & MySQL Installation & Operations Guide
How to install and operate Joomla! on the IBM i Platform
IBM i PHP & MySQL Programmers Guide
How to write PHP and MySQL programs for IBM i

www.letsgopublish.com

www.techbooksisus.com

www.bookhawkers.com

www.conservativebookshop.com

www.brianwkelly.com

Thank you all for enjoying this book!

www.ingramcontent.com/pod-product-compliance
Lightning Source LLC
Chambersburg PA
CBHW071353050326
40689CB00010B/1626